T0271463

BEST-WORST SCALING

Best-Worst Scaling (BWS) is an extension of the method of paired comparison to multiple choices that asks participants to choose both the most and the least attractive options or features from a set of choices. It is an increasingly popular way for academics and practitioners in social science, business, and other disciplines to study and model choice. This book provides an authoritative and systematic treatment of best-worst scaling, introducing readers to the theory and methods for three broad classes of applications. It uses a variety of case studies to illustrate simple but reliable ways to design, implement, apply, and analyze choice data in specific contexts, and showcases the wide range of potential applications across many different disciplines. Best-worst scaling avoids many rating scale problems and will appeal to those wanting to measure subjective quantities with known measurement properties that can be easily interpreted and applied.

JORDAN J. LOUVIERE is Research Professor, School of Marketing, UniSA Business School, University of South Australia. He is particularly known for pioneering work in the design and application of discrete choice experiments (also called "choice-based conjoint") and he also pioneered best-worst scaling (also known as "Max-Diff Scaling"). He is co-author of *Stated Choice Methods: Analysis and Application* (Cambridge University Press, 2000).

TERRY N. FLYNN PhD is the Director of TF Choices Ltd (UK) and Adjunct Fellow at the University of Western Sydney (Australia). He is globally renowned in the use of discrete choice experiments and best-worst scaling in health and allied fields. He is also a world expert in the scoring of quality of life and end-of-life instruments, particularly using BWS, and is a founding member of the International Academy of Health Preference Research.

A. A. J. MARLEY is Adjunct Professor in the Department of Psychology, University of Victoria and Research Professor at The Institute for Choice, University of South Australia. He is particularly known for his work in probabilistic models of choice, perception, and voting. He is a co-author of *Behavioral Social Choice: Probabilistic Models, Statistical Inference, and Applications* (Cambridge University Press, 2006).

BEST-WORST SCALING

Theory, Methods and Applications

JORDAN J. LOUVIERE, TERRY N. FLYNN AND A. A. J. MARLEY

(With Invited Chapters on Applications)

CAMBRIDGE
UNIVERSITY PRESS

University Printing House, Cambridge CB2 8BS, United Kingdom

One Liberty Plaza, 20th Floor, New York, NY 10006, USA

477 Williamstown Road, Port Melbourne, VIC 3207, Australia

314-321, 3rd Floor, Plot 3, Splendor Forum, Jasola District Centre, New Delhi - 110025, India

79 Anson Road, #06-04/06, Singapore 079906

Cambridge University Press is part of the University of Cambridge.

It furthers the University's mission by disseminating knowledge in the pursuit of
education, learning and research at the highest international levels of excellence.

www.cambridge.org
Information on this title: www.cambridge.org/9781107043152

First published 2015

A catalogue record for this publication is available from the British Library

Library of Congress Cataloging in Publication data
Louviere, Jordan J.
Best-worst scaling : theory, methods and applications / Jordan J. Louviere,
Terry N. Flynn, and A.A.J. Marley.
pages   cm
Includes bibliographical references and index.
ISBN 978-1-107-04315-2 (hardback)
1. Scaling (Social sciences)   2. Scaling (Social sciences) – Mathematical models.
Louviere, Jordan, J.   I. Flynn, Terry N.   II. Marley, A. A. J.   III. Title.
H61.27.L68   2015
300.72–dc23
2014044866

ISBN 978-1-107-04315-2 Hardback

Contents

Figures

Tables

Contributors to application chapters

Richard T. Carson: Professor, Department of Economics, University of California, San Diego

Eli Cohen: Associate Professor, Department of Management, Gilford Glazer Faculty of Management, Ben Gurion University of the Negev, Israel, and Ehrenberg Bass Institute for Marketing Science, University of South Australia

Charles Corke: Intensive Care Specialist, Barwon Health, Australia

Terry N. Flynn: Director of TF Choices Ltd (UK) and Adjunct Fellow, University of Western Sydney

Bart D. Frischknecht: VP Research and Customer Success, Vennli, South Bend, Indiana

Elisabeth Huynh: Postdoctoral Fellow, Institute for Choice, University of South Australia

Towhidul Islam: University Research Chair, Professor and Graduate Coordinator of the Department of Marketing and Consumer Studies, College of Business and Economics, University of Guelph, Canada

Larry Lockshin: Professor, Ehrenberg Bass Institute for Marketing Science, University of South Australia

Jordan J. Louviere: Professor, School of Marketing, University of South Australia

Janet R. McColl-Kennedy: Professor of Marketing, UQ Business School, University of Queensland

Emma McIntosh: Reader in Health Economics of Public Health, Institute of Health and Wellbeing, University of Glasgow

Geoffrey N. Soutar: Winthrop Professor of Marketing and Head of Discipline, University of Western Australia Business School

Jillian C. Sweeney: Winthrop Professor of Marketing, University of Western Australia Business School

Preface

Jordan J. Louviere first proposed best-worst scaling (BWS) in the late 1980s as a way to capitalize on humans' tendency to be more reliable and accurate at identifying extreme options. Louviere first called the method maximum difference scaling, to describe what he hypothesized as the underlying process, namely choosing the pair of stimuli in a set of stimuli that exhibited the largest subjective difference on the underlying continuum of interest. Since that time BWS has been adopted by academics and practitioners in many fields globally. However, marketing researchers continue to refer to it as maximum difference scaling (or "maxdiff"), while academics have overwhelmingly now begun to call it best-worst scaling. Louviere and colleagues changed the name to reflect the fact that years of academic research had made it clear that no one actually used a maximum difference choice process, so a much better general term for the method was BWS.

So, BWS now is almost 25 years old. The current authors began receiving numerous requests for assistance and explanations about how to do BWS around 2005; such requests have continued unabated since then. It became clear from the requests, comments and interactions in BWS and more conventional choice modelling short courses that there was a need for a book that brought BWS theory and methods together in such a way that as many people as possible could learn the basic theory and ways to design, implement and analyze BWS experiments in as simple a pedagogical manner as possible. Therefore, this book began with many discussions between Louviere, Flynn and Marley about the need for such a book, leading to them spending time together in the Seattle, Washington, area in 2009 to begin the writing process. That led to discussions about the need for application chapters, which in turn led to invitations to various researchers, principally academics, who were early adopters of BWS, to contribute such chapters.

So, our key reason for writing the book was to introduce as many people as possible to choice-based measurement methods (of which BWS is one type) with the hope of eventually eliminating the many atheoretical and ad hoc measurement methods that are applied in the social and business disciplines. BWS provides a theoretical framework to measure latent, subjective quantities that can produce measurement values with known properties. The theory can be tested and falsified; hence, if the theory is a good first approximation to the underlying choice process(es) being studied, one can have confidence in the measurement properties of the derived values. Unfortunately, one cannot falsify ad hoc measurement methods such as category rating scales. Indeed, it is surprising how uncritical their use is by so many academics and practitioners, especially in light of the fact that, despite some past attempts, it is unlikely that there will ever be a theory from first principles that represents the process by which humans produce category ratings values in response to various stimuli and/or experimental manipulations of interest. More importantly, BWS can replace category rating scales in most commercial and academic applications, and our hope is that we will eventually see many ad hoc measurement methods replaced by BWS.

We hope that those who read this book will be inspired that it is possible to develop and apply theory-based measurement methods in the social and business sciences. We think that the book is important because it finally puts forth a theoretically sound measurement method that can be used in virtually all academic and commercial research applications in which category rating scales currently are used. Better yet, BWS measurement tasks are simple, reliable and accurate, and at the worst require a few more evaluations than category rating scales in almost all cases. As we also note in the book, BWS has been compared with and tested against category rating scales, and virtually every comparison of which we are aware has strongly favored BWS, with the exception that it typically takes humans longer to do BWS tasks. While there are some who see the extra time BWS takes to be a problem, we see this, instead, as a serious opportunity, because it suggests that in many instances the humans involved in the tasks are taking them seriously. Therefore, it is not at all obvious that the fact that BWS tasks take longer for humans to do is a bad thing.

We also hope that the book will inspire some to see the many research opportunities that remain, and take on the task of filling in the research gaps that we note in Chapter 6. It is also our hope that many with backgrounds in psychometrics will see clear opportunities to use BWS tasks where they currently use rating scales and matching tasks. Likewise, and without further comment, we would like to suggest that it may well be in the interest of psychometricians and scale developers to consider whether one can use BWS to replace the current process of selecting items using various factor-analytic and related methods. We also note in passing that "structural choice models" provide statistical theory that integrates structural equation modeling with choice modeling and choice tasks (Rungie, Coote and Louviere, 2011; 2012). BWS is a natural fit to these types of models. So, theory and methods currently are in place to take advantage of the BWS choice-based measurement approach.

Acknowledgments

Writing a book such as this one necessarily involves many people besides the authors.

We would like to acknowledge the considerable contributions made by Edward Wei, who was the head of the online survey programming team in the Institute for Choice (also known as I4C) until recently. During his tenure with the Institute for Choice team, Edward developed many innovative new ways to greatly enhance online surveys and consequently the ability to be at the forefront of online survey work for discrete choice experiments and BWS globally.

We also would like to acknowledge similar contributions made by Karen Cong, who assisted Edward Wei, and now is the team leader in the Institute for Choice for online survey development and implementation. Like Edward, Karen developed a number of new and innovative ways of creating online surveys. Karen also worked tirelessly to prepare, organize and correct figures and tables for a number of the chapters, and to compile the full list of references.

We received extensive encouragement and assistance from Cambridge University Press. Chris Harrison (publishing development director, social sciences) visited us in Sydney and encouraged us to send the outline and sample chapters to the Press; Claire Wood (editor, economics and management) provided major assistance and support in getting the document into production; and Mike Richardson (copy-editor) and David Mackenzie (production editor, academic books) expertly guided us through the final stages of production.

Likewise, our thanks go to the authors of the contributed chapters. They have waited patiently for this book to come out, and it has been a long journey.

Over the past 10 years we have received outstanding support for our research on BWS from various universities and granting agencies. These are: the University of South Australia (Institute for Choice); the University of Technology, Sydney (Centre for the Study of Choice); the University of Victoria, Canada; the Australian Research Council (ARC); the National Health and Medical Research Council (NHMRC) of Australia; the Natural Sciences and Engineering Research Council (NSERC) of Canada; the Social Sciences and Humanities Research Council (SSHRC) of Canada; the Medical Research

Council (MRC) of the United Kingdom; and many other grants and contracts from funding bodies and private and public sector organizations.

We must thank our families, who put up with us during this long process.

Thanks also go to Bart Frischknecht and Fedor Ishakov, who commented on early versions of many of the chapters. Thanks, too, to the anonymous reviewers of the first sample chapters. We did our best to take account of their comments and suggestions; of course, any remaining limitations are our responsibility.

There are many others who gave support and encouragement along the way, as listed below; if we have omitted anyone, it is entirely unintentional:

Adam Finn, for his early support and encouragement;

editors and reviewers in marketing, health economics, environmental and resource economics, personality and social psychology and other fields, for accepting the original papers;

commercial marketing and survey research firms, for jumping on the best-worst bandwagon as early adopters (special thanks to Sawtooth Software!);

many colleagues and co-authors (you all know who you are!).

Ultimately, the responsibility for the book and its contents rests with us. We welcome feedback and suggestions for improving potential future editions. The primary goal of this first edition is to communicate in the simplest way we know how, so as to allow the widest possible audience to be able to understand and apply the theory and methods. We hope we have achieved this goal, but we also know that we will hear from you if we have not.

Theory and Methods

Chapter 1

Introduction and overview of the book

This book is written for researchers and practitioners who have minimal prior knowledge of best-worst scaling (BWS). Many readers will have experience with discrete choice experiments (DCEs), and to avoid making this a two-volume book we take some knowledge of that field as a given. However, the purpose is explicitly *not* to build a subdiscipline that is accessible only to a small number of practitioners who are already experts in a highly technical field. On the contrary, we wish to show that BWS is accessible to the average applied practitioner and that in many cases it can be successfully implemented using spreadsheets rather than statistical programs. However, to do this we will refer to ongoing methodological and cutting-edge theoretical work and will draw on methods and techniques used across several disciplines. Thus, while the book should enable any moderately quantitative practitioner to run a BWS study, academics interested in any non-routine application should have (considerable) cross-disciplinary experience with the methods: many important insights are gained only by experience, and the days of the generalist health/environmental/transport economist doing a DCE or BWS study are (or should be) numbered. Nevertheless, we hope to encourage practitioners with knowledge about discrete choice methods to apply BWS, as many of the design and analysis techniques are simple, though not part of the typical analytical "toolbox" taught to academics and practitioners.

1.1 A brief history of BWS

Best-worst scaling was developed by one of the authors (Louviere) in 1987 at the University of Alberta. Louviere was curious about what could be done with data that resulted from asking people not only to report the "top" choice in each choice set but the "bottom" choice as well. He constructed a small design and made a choice task to go with it, and asked Tulin Erdem, a PhD student at Alberta, to "do" the task. Tulin "did" the task, and brought it back asking what it was for and how it worked. Louviere told her that he had no idea how it worked, but thought that it could be a useful addition to choice experiments because it provided extra choice information. Crucially, it provided information about less attractive choice options and much more information about the respondent's value (utility) function. Louviere spent the next several years working on how to conceptualize such a task, and how to interpret and use the resulting data.

These efforts resulted in a paper with Adam Finn in the *Journal of Public Policy and Marketing* (Finn and Louviere, 1992), in which they showed how to apply BWS to typical public polling problems, illustrating the approach by quantifying public concern over food safety. Not only did they show that food safety was of little concern to their sample, but they also helped to avoid spending a significant amount of public funds on an advertising campaign to "convince" the public represented by the sample that their food supply was "safe." Louviere next wrote a section on another type of BWS in a chapter in Richard Bagozzi's *Advanced Methods of Marketing Research* (Louviere, 1994). This was followed by several working papers on BWS with Joffre Swait in the early 1990s. BWS languished during the 1990s despite attempts by combinations of Louviere, Swait and Donald Anderson to publish papers on the subject (all papers were rejected by academic marketing reviewers – a lesson in perseverance for young scholars).

Louviere was contacted by Emma McIntosh (Oxford University), who was interested in discrete choice experiments and thought that BWS was a promising way to approach several problems in health economics. This resulted in a talk by McIntosh and Louviere (2002) at a conference on applications of discrete choice experiments in health economics (a dental care application) and a chapter in McIntosh's PhD thesis.

Meanwhile, Louviere was motivated to persuade Tony Marley that BWS tasks were interesting and important. Much earlier Marley (1968) had proposed a complex probabilistic choice model that included judgments of "the superior alternative" and "the inferior alternative" in a choice set. However, Marley did not originally see the potential of those ideas for what became BWS. In time Marley signed on to provide formal theory linking the task to various cognitive processes that humans could use to "do" the task. Each such process potentially has different implications for how it can be formally represented (that is, "modeled"), as well as different implications for the mathematical properties of the resulting measures that one derives by applying the theory. This culminated in a paper on the theory of BWS and associated statistical properties in the *Journal of Mathematical Psychology* (Marley and Louviere, 2005).

Eventually, a number of marketing research practitioners were attracted to BWS because of its potential to avoid some of the problems associated with category rating scales, such as differences in the way individuals use them. One particular advocate, Steve Cohen, presented several papers on BWS at ESOMAR (originally the European Society for Opinion and Market Research) conferences (Cohen, 2003; Cohen and Neira, 2003), winning "best paper" awards for his efforts, which led to considerable interest in BWS by practitioners. Shortly afterwards Bryan Orme of Sawtooth Software teamed with Cohen to present a paper on the approach (Cohen and Orme, 2004); Sawtooth also produced commercial applications software to implement BWS in surveys. This led to more interest in BWS, which resulted in its widespread adoption and use by marketing researchers in many countries.

McIntosh's work led several other health economists, including Terry Flynn at Bristol (then in Sydney), to approach Louviere to collaborate on projects. These collaborations produced several conference talks in health economics and papers, most notably a "how to do BWS" paper in the *Journal of Health Economics* (Flynn *et al.*, 2007). Many other applications have followed in health economics, particularly since the National Institute of Health Research (NIHR) funding body in the United Kingdom publicly stipulated its use in research related to valuing social-care-related quality of life (Potoglou *et al.*, 2011; NIHR, 2006).

Another parallel stream of interest and application arose in personality and values measurement. Julie Lee and Geoff Soutar of the University of Western Australia contacted Louviere for assistance and collaboration in applying BWS to Schwartz' list of values, resulting in invitations to speak at Schwartz' annual values conference in 2006, and two recent papers (Lee, Soutar and Louviere, 2007; 2008). The Australian Research Council has since funded a Discovery grant application by Lee, Soutar, Schwartz and Louviere to compare Schwartz' new refinements to the values categories and test them using BWS.

Interest in BWS also arose in food and wine research, with researchers from the Wine Marketing Institute at the University of South Australia collaborating with Louviere on several projects to measure the importance of various wine attributes, using BWS in sensory measurement. These collaborations culminated in a large grant from the Australian Grape, Wine and Brandy Research and Development Corporation to the University of South Australia to use choice experiments and BWS to model and predict demand for new wine styles in developing markets (Casini, Corsi and Goodman, 2009; Cohen, 2009; Goodman, 2009; Mueller and Rungie, 2009). Additionally, several researchers in Australia and elsewhere have begun studying ways to use BWS to obtain sensory measurements in food science and related areas. These collaborations and applications are only a few of many currently under way on BWS, and include only those currently known to us.

As a result of these collaborations and applications it became clear to us that there was a need for a book on BWS that brought together the theory and methods and illustrated their application in various case studies in one handy reference guide. Thus, the idea of this volume was born out of experience working with others on a diverse array of applications, seeing a clear need to bring together as much material on BWS as possible to help people get started in their learning of BWS theory and methods.

1.2 The plan of the book

The book is organized around three areas of BWS theory that we call (1) the object case (Case 1), (2) the profile case (Case 2) and (3) the multi-profile case (Case 3). Each case is presented in a separate chapter that includes basic theoretical results and discusses their meaning and implications. Formal statements of these theoretical results are given in Chapter 5, which also summarizes recent extensions of BWS that include measures of the time to make responses (viz, response time). Each case discusses the design of the relevant statistical experiments, before going on to describe the various methods of analysis, using case studies. For Cases 1 and 2 there is also a discussion of how the theory can be implemented and applied, focusing on different processes that individuals can follow to provide best-worst data. (These processes are equally relevant to Case 3 but are omitted to avoid repetition.) Each theory and methods chapter is linked to three applications chapters written by collaborators or the authors, and used to illustrate the major ideas and themes in the theory and methods chapters. The "looking forward" Chapter 6 discusses limitations, theoretical and empirical research gaps and important problems that we would like to see resolved.

1.3 A non-technical introduction to BWS

Best-worst scaling is based on the idea that a person faces choices among collections ("sets") of three or more items or options, and can identify the best and the worst options in the collection. Here "best" and "worst" simply constitute a metaphor for any appropriate terms that define the extremes of a latent, subjective continuum. For example, one can think of a set of three or more people, with the extremes being "tallest" and "shortest," or a set of three or more weights, with the extremes being "heaviest" and "lightest," or a set of three or more brief biographical sketches of individuals, with the extremes being "most like to meet" and "least like to meet." Many more such examples could be provided. At this point, it is important merely to recognize that these simple principles defining the extremes of a collection (continuum) are common to all types of BWS. The three cases that will be described merely differ in terms of how complex the items or options under consideration are. Moreover, a best option and a worst option in a set of available items are not, in general, the same as an *acceptable* (as in "would purchase") option and an *unacceptable* (as in "would not purchase") option in a set of available items; we discuss this important distinction in Chapter 6.

1.3.1 The object case (Case 1)

This is the "classic" case of BWS that was developed by Louviere in the late 1980s (Finn and Louviere, 1992). In this case a researcher is interested in measuring a set of objects, items, statements, people, pictures, product features, brands, towns, countries, environmental settings, health equity and efficiency issues in priority setting, public policy issues, etc. on an underlying, latent, subjective scale. For example, one may want to measure individuals' perceptions of: product feature importance, brand quality, public issue priorities, the attractiveness of persons, degrees of agreement with statements, the scenic beauty of towns or environmental settings, or the priority that certain types of people, such as smokers, should be given in setting health policies for treatments.

Thus, the object case requires one to have a "list" of items, objects, people, brands, etc. that one wants to measure. This list is exogenous to BWS projects, but integral to them. In any event, if one has a list of objects (we now refer to "objects" in this section, but it should

I think that this is the best Airline (☑ one)	Airline	I think that this is the worst Airline (☑ one)
☐	American	☐
☐	United	☑
☑	Qantas	☐
☐	Delta	☐

Figure 1.1 Example choice set containing four airlines

be clear that "objects" refers to any list), the objective is to measure each object on one or more underlying, latent subjective scales. To do this one must complete a series of steps consistent with the theory discussed in Chapter 2.

The objects, items, people, statements, etc. are systematically organized into subsets of three or more, and a sample of people evaluate each of the subsets and make best and worst (most and least, etc.) choices in each subset. Figure 1.1 presents a hypothetical choice set containing four airlines that one may consider for a trans-pacific flight.

The principles underlying the analysis of the best-worst choice data are similar to those in a discrete choice experiment, and the theoretical framework common to both is random utility theory (RUT). RUT assumes that people make errors, but when choosing repeatedly their choice frequencies give an indication of how much they value the items under consideration (Thurstone, 1927). Thus, how often item A is picked over item B gives an indication of how much item A is preferred to item B. So, how often a respondent picks Qantas over United on the trans-pacific airline route provides an estimate of how much he/ she prefers Qantas to United; in particular, with best-worst choice, this information is obtained from how often the respondent selects Qantas (respectively, United) as best and/or United as worst in the presented choice sets.

A key issue for DCEs and BWS concerns the composition of the choice sets: what subsets of items (in this case airlines) should be presented to respondents? Chapter 2 will detail the principles of experimental design used to achieve this in the object case of BWS; at this point it is important merely to understand why asking for least preferred as well as most preferred is useful. Using the airline example, the researcher may notice that for the "most preferred" choices (for example) a particular respondent picks one of the Star Alliance airlines only when there are no airlines available from the OneWorld airline partnership. However, those data will provide little information as to *which* Star Alliance airline is *least preferred* by a respondent. Presenting additional choice sets containing different combinations of Star Alliance members is an inefficient way of inferring the least preferred airline when a researcher can obtain that information from asking additional "least preferred" choices in choice sets that a respondent *has already considered*.

Asking for two pieces of information per choice set raises the question of how and if one should combine them into a single outcome variable. Chapters 2 to 4 will explain this issue, but at this point it is sufficient to note that, under very mild assumptions about how a person makes choices, there are a variety of mathematically acceptable ways that the best and worst data can be combined; a single outcome variable can draw on the strength of the best data to make inferences at the "top" of the utility function and the worst data to make inferences at the "bottom" of the utility function. Chapter 5 presents further formal material on the aggregation of best and worst data, and Chapter 6 discusses when such aggregation makes sense.

1.3.2 The profile case (Case 2)

Here "best" and "worst" choices refer to attribute levels described/displayed as "profiles." "Profile" is a commonly used term in the conjoint analysis literature (Louviere, 1988b) that refers to a combination of attribute levels. Specifically, a profile is a single treatment combination from an experimental design. In other words, a product, a person, a holiday place, a transport mode, a job, etc. can be described by an underlying, basic set of attributes (features, factors, characteristics, dimensions, etc.) that pertain to and describe all specific members of a generic class of products, persons, holiday places, etc. Each attribute is represented by two or more values called "levels" that typically are chosen to span the entire domain of the class. For example, if the price is an attribute of a certain type of product, the levels used to represent and vary the price should span the range of recent prices or a range of prices expected to occur in a future period of interest. Some attributes are quantitative or numerical and are (more or less) continuous; other attributes, such as a person's gender, are discrete types of attributes (they have mutually exclusive, discrete values). Each attribute has its own unique type and suitable number of levels.

The levels of three or more attributes (features) are systematically combined into a *profile* (namely a description of a product, person, place, etc.). Each profile (combination of attribute levels) can be viewed as a subset of choice options, with a choice option in this case being one of the presented attribute levels. As in the object case, a sample of people evaluate each of the profiles (subsets) and make best and worst (most and least, etc.) choices of the attribute levels that describe each profile.

We illustrate Case 2 with a more complex version of the airline example given earlier. In fact, this example is based on a real online choice experiment that was administered by the Institute for Choice at the University of South Australia. The experiment focuses on profiles of airline tickets for long-haul flights (such as Boston to Seattle, Sydney to Perth, Haikou to Burgin, Moscow to Vladivostok, Montreal to Vancouver, etc.). Each ticket profile is described by six attributes and associated levels (in parentheses): the round-trip airfare ($350, $450, $550, $650), the total flying time (3hrs, 4hrs, 5hrs, 6hrs), the airline name (American, Delta, Northwest, United), frequent flyer points (no, yes), the number of stops en route (0, 1) and whether there are free drinks en route (no, yes). Figure 1.2 presents a hypothetical Case 2 choice set containing a particular ticket (profile) described by the six attributes.

Again, respondents are asked to respond to a number of such profiles (choice sets of airline ticket attribute levels). All possible combinations of these attributes and levels

I think that this feature is the most attractive (☑ one)	Ticket option features	Specific details of Ticket Option	I think that this feature is the least attractive (☑ one)
☐	Airfare	$650	☐
☐	Travel time	6 hours	☑
☑	Airline	United Airlines	☐
☐	Freq flyer pts	Yes	☐
☐	No. of stops	None (direct)	☐
☐	Free drinks	No	☐

Figure 1.2 Hypothetical choice set for a Case 2 study

(tickets) can be represented as a $2 \times 2 \times 2 \times 4 \times 4 \times 4$ (or $2^3 \times 4^3$) factorial (512 combinations or profiles). Chapter 3 will describe how to select a suitable experimental design, as in many cases the researcher may be unable to administer all 512 profiles (and certainly not all 512 to each respondent).

Once each respondent has answered the choice sets the researcher must analyze the choice data. As for Case 1, analysis is usually conducted within a random utility theory framework. How often a feature (attribute level) is picked as best provides an indication of how much it is liked, and how often a feature is picked as worst provides an indication of how much it is disliked. Again, the worst data provide much better estimates (in terms of statistical precision) of the unattractive features of an airline ticket. For example, the best choice data from a respondent who never picked $650 airfare or six-hour flying time as best tell us nothing about which of those two features is less attractive, whereas the worst data almost certainly do. As for Case 1, the best and worst data are usually pooled to draw strengths from each, and Chapter 3 describes how this pooling is achieved.

Much more detail is provided in Chapter 3 for the following topics: (1) different ways to design profile experiments, statistical properties of these ways to design experiments, and the pros and cons of each; (2) how to translate designs into profiles, how to block profiles into versions to obtain more statistical information, and the pros and cons of each; (3) how to lay out and administer best-worst choice experiments for profiles, how to ask best-worst questions (including repeated best-worst questions), and the pros and cons of each; and (4) how to do basic and more sophisticated analyses of best-worst choice data, how to derive measurement scales for attribute levels, and test if the implied assumptions/properties underlying the models hold for empirical best-worst choice data, and the pros and cons of each.

1.3.3 The multi-profile case (Case 3)

The third case is associated with classical discrete choice experiments – that is, a person is offered a sequence of choice sets, with each choice set having three or more profiles (Louviere, Hensher and Swait, 2000; Hensher, Rose and Greene, 2005). The person's

Ticket option features	Ticket 1	Ticket 2	Ticket 3
Airfare	$650	$450	$550
Travel time	3 hours	5 hours	4 hours
Airline	United Airlines	Delta Airlines	American Airlines
Freq flyer pts	Yes	No	Yes
No. of stops	None (direct)	1	None (direct)
Free drinks	No	Yes	No
I'm most likely to choose (☑ one)	☑	☐	☐
I'm least likely to choose (☑ one)	☐	☐	☑

Figure 1.3 Example Case 3 choice set for airlines

task is to choose two profiles that are, respectively, the best and the worst (most, least preferred; most, least attractive; most, least like them; etc.).

As in the BWS object and profile cases, we have to identify a relevant "list" of things to be measured. In the multi-profile case, the list consists of attributes or features of options to be offered to people. Returning to the airline example, these might be the same six attributes used in the profile case: round-trip airfare, total flying time, airline name, frequent flyer points, number of stops en route, and free drinks en route. In the case of mobile (cell) phones, the features might be price, brand, camera/megapixels, Bluetooth capability, international roaming capability, GPS, etc.; in the case of delivered pizza products, the features might be brand, price, type of crust, number of toppings, delivery time, etc.; in the case of holiday destinations, the features might be type of environmental setting, flying or driving time, typical daytime high temperatures, range of activities, total cost, etc.

Once a list of features is determined, one must assign values or levels to each feature to represent a range of relevant possible variations, as in the profile case. Thus, for the airline example, if the same levels for each of the six attributes are considered, then the full factorial of airline tickets is still 512 profiles. The difference between this case and the profile case is that, instead of experimental participants evaluating one profile at a time, they evaluate three or more at a time. Instead of making choices *within* a profile (which feature of this single ticket is most/least attractive), they make choices *between* whole profiles (which ticket is most/least attractive), as they would do in a traditional DCE. We now return to the airline example to illustrate this case with an example choice set, as shown in Figure 1.3. Note, again, that the best-worst choices are conditional on the presented set of profiles (options) and some, all, or none, of those options may be acceptable (say, in the sense of possible purchase); we discuss this fact in Chapter 6.

As before, one must select or construct an experimental design to create the choice sets. This is more complex than Case 2: as well as deciding if one wants to use only a subset of the full factorial, one must decide how (in this case) to construct the sets of three tickets. We discuss the design of multi-profile choice experiments, or discrete choice experiments, in Chapter 4.

When analyzing the choice data, again one typically works within a random utility framework: how often a respondent picks a ticket as most (least) preferred provides an estimate for how much he/she likes (dislikes) it. However, it is not the tickets themselves that are of primary interest; it is the features (attribute levels) describing each ticket that are of interest. This is because we ultimately wish to "construct" any ticket (based on any combination of features) and estimate its utility (value to the respondent) using the values associated with each of the features that describe it.

1.4 A note on naming conventions and processes

BWS is sometimes called maximum difference scaling (or, simply, maxdiff), particularly in the United States. We find it curious that the inventor of the approach (Louviere) apparently is not allowed to choose its name and/or that others who did not invent or contribute to the approach have decided to give it a new name. This new name refers to the fact that one can conceive of a BWS task as asking an individual to simultaneously or sequentially report two options in a set of three or more options that are the farthest apart on an underlying latent, subjective continuum of interest, with the "largest" ("smallest") reported as "best" ("worst"). Thus, the two chosen options can be viewed as the two that are maximally different on the latent, subjective scale. We adhere to the name BWS in this book, as this nomenclature is widespread both inside and outside the field of marketing research. It also is a more inclusive term, in so far as choosing the two objects or options in a set that are the farthest apart on the underlying continuum is only one of several possible ways in which humans might choose the two options named "best" and "worst," respectively (as we discuss in some detail later in the book). In other words, there are a number of different psychological *processes* by which a person can provide best-worst data.

For instance, in a given Case 1 choice set, which did the respondent do?

(1) Pick Qantas as best, then United (from the remaining three airlines) as worst?
(2) Pick United as worst, then Qantas (from the remaining three airlines) as best?
(3) Simultaneously consider all possible pairs of airlines (there are in fact 12 unique best-worst pairs) and choose the one (Qantas = best, United = worst) that maximized the (positive) difference in utility between the two airlines in a pair?

Only strategy (3) is the (well-established) psychological *maxdiff* model; this model is an example of BWS, but BWS encompasses much more than just the maxdiff model (Marley and Louviere, 2005). This may seem like an esoteric issue, and we go on to show that if a researcher is interested in making inferences about large numbers of people then it is largely irrelevant. However, there are situations in which the process *is* important, so we urge readers not to use the term *maxdiff scaling* (unless they are actually estimating a *maxdiff model*, which most practitioners are not).

To summarize, BWS is useful not just in obtaining additional choice information, with its possible use in data aggregation, but in providing a better understanding of the process by which the person makes best and worst choices. We return to both uses in greater detail in later chapters, but for now we simply note that the *same* task can be used to achieve both ends in most cases. Recent work using responses times in BWS contributes significantly to the understanding of process (Chapters 5 and 6).

1.5 General topics and issues in BWS

We now turn our attention to some general topics and issues that will recur in many, if not all, of the chapters to follow. The purpose of discussing these topics and issues in this chapter is to alert the reader to the fact that they apply widely. Thus, it would be useful to recognize and understand them prior to reading the later chapters. Additionally, there are several useful definitions and distinctions that are noted and discussed in advance of the remaining chapters.

All BWS models are probabilistic discrete choice models. Many readers familiar with the well-established literature on probabilistic discrete choice models also will be familiar with the random utility theory basis of these models (see, for example, Thurstone, 1927; McFadden, 1974). Random utility theory is an interesting, but unnecessary, basis for deriving probabilistic choice models. Choice models also can be derived from what is known as *fixed utility theory*. The distinction between the two approaches to deriving probabilistic choice models is as follows. (1) Random utility theory assumes that the decision process underlying the choices is deterministic, but the utilities have a random component. (2) Fixed utility theory (also called *constant utility theory*) assumes that the utilities are deterministic but that, regardless, the choices are probabilistic for some reason, such as the decision process not being deterministic. In each case, the probabilistic nature of the choices can be interpreted as due to researcher inability to understand or know all the factors that impact choices and/or as due to mistakes and/or inconsistencies in an individual's choices. As a general statement, economists take the former view (researchers' lack of knowledge) and psychologists the latter view (variability in a person's choices).

The two theoretical perspectives can lead to choice models that are mathematically equivalent, even though they may imply potentially different economic or psychological processes (see Chapter 5). Fixed or random utility versions of BWS models may be discussed and/or applied or illustrated, depending on which more easily demonstrates the point being made. For example, it may often be easier to identify and estimate variance components associated with BWS models when the models are specified as random utility models.

The perspective that we take in this book is an individual-level one – that is, the BWS models that we derive and discuss are models for single persons. If one wants to summarize some sample or population of people, one must make various strong assumptions that may or may not be true in order to aggregate the choices of these individuals. For now we simply note that any aggregation of individuals necessarily requires assumptions that may pose an array of empirical issues. For example, (1) Arrow's impossibility theorem (Arrow, 1963) tells us that, under a particular set of reasonable assumptions, there is no satisfactory way to aggregate individual utilities or preferences, and (2) many choice models estimate utilities for individuals in such a way that the origin and/or scale unit of the utility scale for each person is different and incommensurable, in turn suggesting that it is unclear how to interpret any aggregation of individual utility estimates.

As a result, we focus on individual-level choice processes and models of these processes. From time to time in various chapters we aggregate individuals for different purposes, but when we do so it is important to note that this requires assumptions that should be tested. We also describe and discuss various ways to design BWS experiments that allow one to test some of the assumptions, as well as to show that particular BWS models are incompatible with the observed choices.

Chapter 2

The BWS object case

Society in every state is a blessing, but Government, even in its best state,
is but a necessary evil; in its worst state, an intolerable one.

Thomas Paine (1737–1809) *(1776: ch. 1)*

2.1 Introduction

As noted in Chapter 1, the BWS object case (henceforth, Case 1) deals with a list of objects, or things, that one wants to measure. Generally speaking, Case 1 can be used to measure things typically measured with rating scales and/or with variants of the method of paired comparisons (Thurstone, 1928; David, 1988). The types of things that Case 1 can be used to measure include the following indicative, but by no means exhaustive, list:

- batteries of "agree/disagree" statements;
- traits or characteristics that apply to brands, people, even animals, etc.;
- pictures or graphical images, such as landscapes;
- politically relevant issues;
- electoral candidates;
- food products, wines, drinks, etc., tasted blind/non-blind;
- potential job candidates;
- academic journals; and
- product features.

One first develops a list for measurement purposes; then the process of using Case 1 to measure the things on the list is straightforward, which is part of its appeal.

We are agnostic about the various ways researchers using Case 1 can compile lists of things to be measured. Therefore, we assume for the purpose of this discussion that a list of things is generated exogenous to the Case 1 process. It is the researcher's job to validate and justify the list and the things contained in it. However, we note that Case 1 can be applied equally to poorly justified and well-justified lists. Hence, poorly constituted and ill-justified lists of things to be measured have nothing whatsoever to do with the validity of BWS theory and measurement methods. Instead, the onus of doing this properly falls fully on researchers.

Table 2.1 *Nine public policy issues (objects)*

Object code	Object
1	Streets and roads
2	K–12 education
3	Tertiary education
4	Parks and recreation
5	Sports facilities
6	Housing developments
7	Job creation
8	Broadband access and speeds
9	Tourism facilities

Note: "K–12" = "kindergarten to grade 12", and is a commonly used term for the sum of primary and secondary education in countries such as the United States, Canada and Australia, where grade 12, for 17- to 19-year-olds, is the final year of secondary education.

Accordingly, we assume that a properly validated and justified list of things to be measured has been compiled, and we want to measure each thing on one or more underlying, latent subjective scales (one scale at a time); in the remainder of this chapter, we use the term *objects*, a general term by which we mean any list of things that can be measured on an underlying, latent subjective scale. We illustrate how to apply Case 1 to different types of lists, but note that the process always is the same regardless of subject matter or content of lists. Assume a list of J objects (J = number of objects to be measured), and denote individual objects on the list by j=1,2,...,J.

We illustrate this and future steps in designing and implementing a "study" with a simple example. As noted, one must first develop a list. Table 2.1 lists nine major public issues for which the latent scale is "public sector spending priority."

2.2 Design

The next step is to obtain a suitable experimental design to construct the choice sets. In other words, a design tells us which objects (or, more accurately, which object code numbers) to put in each choice set (question, "scenario" or "comparison set"). We first give an account of methods used in the early development of discrete choice experiments, as understanding their limitations is useful to understand the newer designs now used.

2.2.1 Choice set construction: old ways now rarely used

A method proposed in the early literature was that of paired comparisons (David, 1988). In this case, each of the J total objects (for example, public policy issues) is paired with every other object. Participants in the "study" are asked to pick which one should receive higher priority in every pair. Unfortunately, for J objects there are J(J–1) /2 pairs, which in the present example gives 36 pairs. Most participants can "do" 36 pairs, but many researchers may be reluctant to ask that many questions, particularly if the BWS questions are part of a larger survey. However, in general, as the number of objects increases, the burden on respondents to make comparisons is increasing.

Louviere and Woodworth (1983) proposed designs that no longer restrict sets to size two (pairs). In particular, their method is a multiple-choice version of the classical method of paired comparisons that relies only on "best" choices. They used Monte Carlo simulations to show that multiple comparisons based on what are known as orthogonal main effects designs (or "orthogonal main effects plans": OMEPs) constructed from 2^J factorial designs were nearly optimally efficient for estimating McFadden's (1974) conditional logit model. The latter was later formally proven by Street and Burgess (2007). The 2^J design merely means that each object, j, can appear or not appear, and the total number of possible choice sets is given by a 2^J factorial. Thus, for our example with nine objects, there are 512 sets; one set contains all nine objects, nine sets contain eight of the objects (that is, one object is missing in each set), etc., to nine sets containing only one object, and the null (empty) set. This is clearly a large design; and such factorial designs grow exponentially in size with the number of objects, which is why Louviere and Woodworth (1983) proposed using fractional factorial designs as a way to select an intelligent sample from the complete factorial. A potential problem with this design approach is related to the psychology of the task. In other words, generally speaking, such fractional designs produce comparison sets of varying sizes: some sets are relatively large (containing most or all objects) while some sets are small. Unequal set sizes may unintentionally signal to respondents that the choice questions in the survey pertain to something unintended by a researcher and/or that they are supposed to choose differently in sets of different sizes, etc. (that is, set size differences in a survey may lead to "demand artifacts").

2.2.2 Choice set construction: balanced incomplete block designs (BIBDs)

The problems noted with fractional factorial designs means that they now are rarely used. Indeed, most Case 1 BWS studies use a balanced incomplete block design or related design (for example, covering design or latin square) to assign each of the J objects to various subsets of a fixed size, k; each such subset is called a "block" and can be viewed as a "comparison set," in so far as the objects in a block are what are presented to a person or sample of people to evaluate and compare. Those familiar with discrete choice models will recognize that comparison sets are "choice sets"; indeed, a block or comparison set *is* a choice set. At the time of writing, Wikipedia provides this on BIBDs (http://en.wikipedia. org/wiki/Block_design):

In combinatorial mathematics, a **block design** (more fully, a **balanced incomplete block design**) is a particular kind of set system, which has long-standing applications to experimental design (an area of statistics) as well as purely combinatorial aspects.

Given a finite set X (of elements called points) and integers $k, r, \lambda \geq 1$, we define a **2-design** B to be a set of k-element subsets of X, called **blocks**, such that the number r of blocks containing x in X is independent of x, and the number λ of blocks containing given distinct points x and y in X is also independent of the choices.

Here v (the number of elements of X, called points), b (the number of blocks), k, r, and λ are the **parameters** of the design. (Also, B may not consist of all k-element subsets of X; that is the meaning of *incomplete*.) The design is called a (v, k, λ)-**design** or a (v, b, r, k, λ)-**design**. The parameters are not all independent; v, k, and λ determine b and r, and not all combinations of v, k, and λ are possible. The two basic equations connecting these parameters are $bk=vr$, and $\lambda(v-1)=r(k-1)$.

As Wikipedia notes, BIBDs do not exist for all J. One often can use available designs by adding/deleting items and/or combining BIBDs.

The next step is to assign items to "places" in a BIBD by numbering each item from 1 to J (v in Wikipedia). A BIBD is a table with b subsets of k items. Each item occurs r times and co-occurs with each other item λ times. BIBDs have a fixed size (in the case of BWS) of $k \geq$ 3 items. Typically (but not always), BIBDs have more subsets than 2^J designs; therefore, BIBDs create b subsets (or scenarios) from which people make best and worst choices. The total number of comparison or choice sets is the parameter b. Each of the J (v) things occur r times, and co-occur with the other J-1 things λ times. The first four columns of Table 2.2 show a BIBD that gives 12 subsets of nine objects with three objects per set.

One then uses a "find and replace" procedure to replace the object code numbers in columns 2 to 4 of Table 2.2 with the object names (here, public policy issues) to make comparison sets, as shown in columns 5 to 7. Table 2.2 shows that the BIBD ("Design no. 9," Table 2.3) used in the public policy task has the property that each issue occurs four times and each pair of issues co-occurs once across the 12 sets.

BIBDs can be found in various sources (see, for example, Street and Street 1987). A list of some BIBDs is given in Table 2.3.

Table 2.2 *A BIBD for nine objects*

Subset	Objects in each subset			Issues in each subset		
1	2	4	8	K-12 education	Parks and recreation	Broadband access/speed
2	1	4	5	Streets and roads	Parks and recreation	Sports facilities
3	4	7	9	Parks and recreation	Job creation	Tourism facilities
4	3	4	6	Tertiary education	Parks and recreation	Housing developments
5	1	2	3	Streets and roads	K-12 education	Tertiary education
6	2	5	7	K-12 education	Sports facilities	Job creation
7	2	6	9	K-12 education	Housing developments	Tourism facilities
8	1	8	9	Streets and roads	Broadband access/speed	Tourism facilities
9	5	6	8	Sports facilities	Housing developments	Broadband access/speed
10	3	7	8	Tertiary education	Job creation	Broadband access/speed
11	1	6	7	Streets and roads	Housing developments	Job creation
12	3	5	9	Tertiary education	Sports facilities	Tourism facilities

The BWS object case

Table 2.3 *Illustrative list of potential BIBDs*

Design no.	Objects (v)	No. sets (b)	Occurs (r)	Set size (k)	Co-occurs (λ)
1	4	4	3	3	2
2	5	5	4	4	3
3	5	10	6	3	3
4	6	10	5	3	2
5	7	7	3	3	1
6	7	7	4	4	2
7	7	21	15	5	10
8	8	14	7	4	3
9	9	12	4	3	1
10	9	18	8	4	3
11	9	12	8	6	5
12	9	18	10	5	5
13	10	15	6	4	2
14	10	30	9	3	2
15	10	18	9	5	4
16	10	15	9	6	5
17	11	11	5	5	2
18	11	11	6	6	3
19	11	55	15	3	3
20	12	44	11	3	2
21	12	33	11	4	3
22	12	22	11	6	5
23	13	13	4	4	1
24	13	26	6	3	1
25	13	26	12	6	5
26	13	39	15	5	5
27	14	26	13	7	6
28	15	35	7	3	1
29	15	35	14	6	5
30	16	20	5	4	1
31	16	16	6	6	2
32	16	24	9	6	3
33	16	80	15	3	2
34	16	48	15	5	4
35	19	57	9	3	1
36	19	57	12	4	2
37	21	21	5	5	1
38	21	70	10	3	1
39	21	42	12	6	3
40	25	30	6	5	1
41	25	50	8	4	1
42	25	100	12	3	1

Table 2.3 (*cont.*)

Design no.	Objects (v)	No. sets (b)	Occurs (r)	Set size (k)	Co-occurs (λ)
43	26	65	15	6	3
44	28	63	9	4	1
45	31	31	6	6	1
46	31	93	15	5	2
47	37	37	9	9	2
48	41	82	10	5	1
49	49	56	8	7	1
50	57	57	8	8	1
51	64	72	9	8	1
52	73	73	9	9	1
53	81	90	10	9	1
54	91	91	10	10	1

Table 2.4 *Example survey BWS task based on Table 2.2*

I think we should spend the most on (☑ one)	Issues in set 10	I think we should spend the least on (☑ one)
☐	Tertiary education	☐
☑	Job creation	☐
☐	Broadband access/speed	☑

One also can mix and match BIBD designs to make designs not in the table (NB: smaller BIBDs may exist). For example, design 17 (J=11) has 11 comparison sets; each of the 11 objects occurs five times in sets of size 5, and co-occurs with the other 10 objects twice. If one wants a smaller comparison set size (for example, four) one can combine design 17 with design 2 to get 55 sets of size 4. This is accomplished by taking the five objects in each of the design 17 sets, and expanding them into five sets of four objects using design 2. Thus, each of the 11 original sets (design 17) is expanded into five additional sets using design 2. Each of the 11 things occurs 20 times and co-occurs with the other 10 things six times. The combined design has the same number of sets as all pairs, but gives more information for measurement purposes.

The next step is to embed the comparison sets in a survey. One way to ask BWS questions is shown in the format in Table 2.4.

This table merely separates the sets into a respondent-friendly format. A respondent chooses the "highest-priority" and "lowest-priority" issue in each of the 12 sets.

The BWS object case

Table 2.5 *Hypothetical person's best and worst choices*

Set	Issues shown in each subset			Spend most	Spend least
1	K-12 education	Parks and recreation	Broadband access/speed	K-12 education	Parks and recreation
2	Streets and roads	Parks and recreation	Sports facilities	Streets and roads	Sports facilities
3	Parks and recreation	Job creation	Tourism facilities	Job creation	Tourism facilities
4	Tertiary education	Parks and recreation	Housing developments	Tertiary education	Housing developments
5	Streets and roads	K-12 education	Tertiary education	Tertiary education	Streets and roads
6	K-12 education	Sports facilities	Job creation	Job creation	Sports facilities
7	K-12 education	Housing developments	Tourism facilities	K-12 education	Tourism facilities
8	Streets and roads	Broadband access/speed	Tourism facilities	Streets and roads	Tourism facilities
9	Sports facilities	Housing developments	Broadband access/speed	Broadband access/speed	Sports facilities
10	Tertiary education	Job creation	Broadband access/speed	Tertiary education	Broadband access/speed
11	Streets and roads	Housing developments	Job creation	Job creation	Housing developments
12	Tertiary education	Sports facilities	Tourism facilities	Tertiary education	Sports facilities

Case 1 surveys usually start with an introductory set of questions that concern the primary topic(s) constituting the focus of the project; the BWS questions then follow. A final section contains questions about individual or household characteristics, opinions, attitudes, etc. not available from the online panel provider's information set about each panelist. Many variations can exist; we simply note that question types, question sequences, etc. are problem-specific, and do not lend themselves to generalization.

2.3 Analysis

A conventional BWS task requires respondents to choose a best and a worst object in each comparison set. For example, columns 3 and 4 of Table 2.6 show one hypothetical person's best and worst choices.

2.3.1 Analyzing one respondent's data in a spreadsheet

A simple way to summarize the best and worst choice data is to count the best and worst choices for each choice object, as shown in Table 2.6. A simple scale and weak order of the objects can be obtained by subtracting the worst count for each object from the best count for that object, and ordering the objects by those scores. We show this in the last column of Table 2.6. The extra information given by the worst choices is clear for the lower-ranked objects: best choices cannot distinguish objects 4, 5, 6 and 9.

The final column of Table 2.6 shows that the person in the BWS task supports spending more money on tertiary education, but does not support spending more money on sports facilities. Job creation is a close second for spending, whereas tourism facilities come next to last, with other issues somewhere in between. Marley and Louviere (2005) show that, if the maxdiff model holds, best-minus-worst scores are a sufficient statistic[1] for a conditional (multinomial) logistic (MNL) regression model. This implies that all the information needed for more sophisticated conditional (multinomial) logistic regression models is available from these scores, so researchers need not use logistic regression analysis to estimate model parameters (scale positions, or "scale values," of each object). Nonetheless, it is worth noting that there does not yet exist a formal proof of the unbiasedness of the scores.

Researchers should be cautious about making inferences for individual respondents (Flynn, 2010a); in this case, the 12 subset questions give a complete (rank) ordering of the issues for a person – that is, there are no "ties." In other applications, two or more objects will have the same "score," and so cannot be differentiated by their values on the subjective scale of interest. Such indeterminance tends to be associated with small BIBD designs and/or larger set sizes relative to the number of objects studied. That said, our experience suggests that one has to aggregate choices across only a few people for the average scores of

Table 2.6 *Summary choices of public policy issues*

Issue no.	Issues (spend more on)	Best	Worst	B minus W
1	Streets and roads	2	1	1
2	K-12 education	2	0	2
3	Tertiary education	4	0	4
4	Parks and recreation	0	1	−1
5	Sports facilities	0	4	−4
6	Housing developments	0	2	−2
7	Job creation	3	0	3
8	Broadband access/speed	1	1	0
9	Tourism facilities	0	3	−3

[1] When respondents are using the maxdiff model to make best-worst choices, sufficiency means that the estimated scale values will be a function of the best-minus-worst scores, but not necessarily a linear function. Chapters 5 and 6 discuss cases in which the maxdiff model does not hold.

a subgroup of choosers of interest to perform well and correlate highly with more sophisticated estimates.

2.3.2 *Analyzing a complete data set in a spreadsheet*

Best-minus-worst scores can be calculated at different levels of aggregation; and, as noted earlier, experience with many data sets suggests they are highly (linearly) correlated with the conditional logit estimates at a sample level and in most cases at subgroup levels. Thus, one does not have to use statistical software to estimate models but, instead, can use the scores directly in clustering (or similar algorithms, such as latent class) to identify market segments or other types of groups. However, as noted, formal proof of the unbiasedness of the scores is lacking, so we rely on empirical experience. It also should be noted that, when one has an individual-level estimate of the value of each object, one can graph the empirical distribution of the value (utility, or some other subjective scale) for any object in a sample population. No assumptions (frequentist or Bayesian) about distributions need be made. Examples below illustrate clustering (segmentation) analyses conducted using the BWS scores.

We now discuss two Case 1 applications using a sample of approximately 500 Australians over age 18 who voted in a recent federal election. Participants were recruited from an online web panel in Australia (Pureprofile). Each completed two Case 1 tasks: (1) best and worst choices from subsets of nine ways that one could save money in the federal budget; and (2) best and worst choices from subsets of nine ways that one could spend money in the federal budget. Basically, each task asked participants to prioritize various ways to spend or save money. The two sets of nine ways to save and spend federal money are shown in Table 2.7. The BWS Case 1 task is designed using a BIBD for nine objects (ways to spend or save money) that is Table 2.8.

We begin by displaying the sample aggregate best and worst choice counts (Table 2.9) and other measures that can be calculated directly from them for the saving and spending choices. In particular, we show the best (most) frequency counts minus worst (least) counts (hereafter, "BWS scores"), the square root of the ratio of most-to-least counts and the natural log of the ratio of most-to-least counts. The square root ratios follow directly from assuming that most counts = 1/(least counts). The log of the square root ratio is centered about zero, like most-minus-least counts. We begin by testing whether most and least counts are inversely related. Figures 2.1 and 2.2 graph most and 1/(least); the figures are consistent with most being approximately = 1/(worst). Most-minus-least frequency counts should be directly proportional to the log of the square root ratio. Figures 2.1 and 2.2 show that the expected relationship holds for both tasks.

Naturally, one does not expect voters to have homogeneous priorities about ways to save or spend money; hence, we now try to identify groups whose priorities differ by applying cluster analysis to each person's BWS scores. We used SPSS two-step cluster analysis to identify two clusters for saving money and four clusters for spending money (a discussion of the SPSS two-step approach can be found at this link: www.spss.ch/upload/ 1122644952_The%20SPSS%20TwoStep%20Cluster%20Component.pdf). The two-step

Table 2.7 *Ways to save/spend money in the federal budget*

No.	Ways to *save* money in the federal budget
1	Not proceeding with Company Tax cuts
2	Reprioritizing tax reform
3	Improving fairness in the tax system
4	Improving compliance measures to prevent fraud and tax evasion
5	Deferring defense spending and acquisitions
6	Deferring foreign aid increases
7	Introducing caps and eligibility changes for certain benefits
8	Increasing road user charges for heavy vehicles
9	Increasing Departure Tax for travelers

No.	Ways to *spend* money in the federal budget
1	Spreading the boom benefits and supporting families
2	Helping the most vulnerable in society
3	Building an aged care system for the future
4	Helping businesses adjust to structural changes
5	Improving national infrastructure
6	Building a more productive workforce
7	Continuing development of personal control e-health records
8	Maintaining current levels of biosecurity
9	Maintaining presence in Afghanistan/Middle East; helping stability in East Timor/South China Sea

Table 2.8 *BIBD for nine objects*

Set	Objects (ways to save/spend)		
1	2	4	8
2	1	4	5
3	4	7	9
4	3	4	6
5	1	2	3
6	2	5	7
7	2	6	9
8	1	8	9
9	5	6	8
10	3	7	8
11	1	6	7
12	3	5	9

Table 2.9 *Most and least choice counts for nine ways to save and spend money*

Saving	Most	Least	M–L	SQRT (M/L)	Ln (SQRT)
Not proceeding with Company Tax cuts	779	799	−20	0.99	−0.013
Reprioritizing tax reform	1056	381	675	1.66	0.510
Improving fairness in the tax system	1589	195	1394	2.85	1.049
Improving compliance measures to prevent fraud and tax evasion	867	373	494	1.52	0.422
Deferring defense spending and acquisitions	525	801	−276	0.81	−0.211
Deferring foreign aid increases	609	877	−268	0.83	−0.182
Introducing caps and eligibility changes for certain benefits	867	442	425	1.40	0.337
Increasing road user charges for heavy vehicles	301	1278	−977	0.49	−0.723
Increasing Departure Tax for travelers	139	1586	−1447	0.30	−1.217

Spending	Most	Least	M–L	SQRT (M/L)	Ln (SQRT)
Spreading the boom benefits and supporting families	985	685	300	1.20	0.182
Helping the most vulnerable in society	1094	360	734	1.74	0.556
Building an aged care system for the future	1427	235	1192	2.46	0.902
Helping businesses adjust to structural changes	542	1013	−471	0.73	−0.313
Improving national infrastructure	953	365	588	1.62	0.480
Building a more productive workforce	797	447	350	1.34	0.289
Continuing development of personal control e-health records	373	1161	−788	0.57	−0.568
Maintaining current levels of biosecurity	348	965	−617	0.60	−0.510
Maintaining presence in Afghanistan/Middle East; helping stability in East Timor/South China Sea	213	1501	−1288	0.38	−0.976

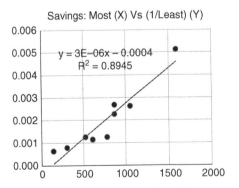

Figure 2.1 Most versus 1/(least) saving

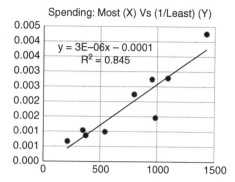

Figure 2.2 Most versus 1/(least) spending

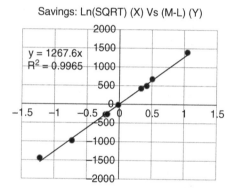

Figure 2.3 Ln(SQRT) versus (M–L) saving

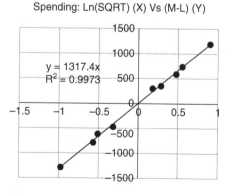

Figure 2.4 Ln(SQRT) versus (M–L) spending

Table 2.10 *Two-step cluster analysis results for ways to save and spend money*

Savings measures	Mean	Clusters		Clusters	
		1	2	1	2
		Mean cluster results for saving		**Clusters minus mean**	
Not proceeding with tax cuts	−0.03	−0.12	0.01	−0.09	0.04
Reprioritizing tax reform	1.21	−0.19	1.92	−1.40	0.71
Improving tax system fairness	2.49	1.06	3.22	−1.43	0.73
Improving compliance measures to prevent fraud and tax evasion	0.87	0.74	0.94	−0.13	0.07
Deferring defense spending and acquisitions	−0.50	0.22	−0.86	0.72	−0.37
Deferring foreign aid increases	−0.48	0.64	−1.05	1.12	−0.57
Introducing caps and eligibility changes for certain benefits	0.76	0.42	0.94	−0.34	0.17
Increasing road user charges for heavy vehicles	−1.74	−1.12	−2.06	0.62	−0.32
Increasing Departure Tax for travelers	−2.58	−1.65	−3.05	0.93	−0.47

Spending measures	Mean	Clusters				Clusters			
		1	2	3	4	1	2	3	4
		Mean cluster results for spending				**Clusters minus mean**			
Spread boom benefits and support families	0.53	−1.01	0.05	2.11	0.34	−1.54	−0.48	1.58	−0.19
Help vulnerable	1.30	−0.11	1.42	2.54	0.15	−1.41	0.12	1.24	−1.15
Aged care	2.14	1.66	3.02	2.32	0.02	−0.48	0.88	0.18	−2.12
Help business adjust to changes	−0.85	1.11	−1.90	−1.56	−0.21	1.95	−1.05	−0.71	0.64
Improve infrastructure	1.05	2.42	0.70	0.57	0.21	1.37	−0.35	−0.48	−0.84
More productive workforce	0.62	1.79	−0.81	0.98	0.55	1.17	−1.43	0.36	−0.07
Health e-records	−1.39	−1.92	−1.03	−1.60	−0.36	−0.52	0.36	−0.21	1.04
Biosecurity	−1.10	−1.08	−0.38	−1.96	−0.21	0.02	0.72	−0.86	0.89
Afghanistan, Middle East, South China Sea	−2.30	−2.85	−1.07	−3.41	−0.49	−0.56	1.22	−1.11	1.81

clustering approach automatically determines the optimal number of clusters and provides an index of how "good" the solution is. The cited SPSS link states: "The first step calculates BIC [Bayes' information criterion] for each number of clusters within a specified range and uses it to find the initial estimate for the number of clusters. The second step refines the initial estimate by finding the greatest change in distance between the two closest clusters in each hierarchical clustering stage." We now profile and describe each cluster in Table 2.10.

A brief description of each cluster follows.

BWS saving choices

Cluster 1: more priority to deferring defense spending, deferring foreign aid spending, having a road user charge for heavy vehicles and having visitor Departure Tax; less priority to tax reform and fairer taxes.

Cluster 2: more priority to tax reform and fairer taxes; less priority to deferring foreign aid spending and visitor Departure Tax.

BWS spending choices

Cluster 1: more priority to helping business adjust to structural changes, improving infrastructure and increasing workforce productivity; less priority to spreading the benefits of the boom, helping the vulnerable, investing in aged care, continuing personally controllable e-health records or continuing overseas military involvement in Afghanistan or elsewhere.

Cluster 2: more priority to overseas military involvement in Afghanistan and elsewhere, aged care and biosecurity; less priority to increasing workforce productivity or helping business adjust to structural changes.

Cluster 3: more priority to spreading the benefits of the boom and helping the vulnerable in society; less priority to helping business adjust to structural changes, biosecurity, overseas military involvement or improving infrastructure.

Cluster 4: more priority to overseas military involvement, e-health records, biosecurity and helping business adjust to structural changes; less priority to aged care, helping the vulnerable or improving infrastructure.

We now show how one can use BWS scores as individual-level measures. If the BWS scores are linearly related to each person's conditional logit estimates, one should be able to use them in a conditional logit model to predict the choices. We test this using the savings choices. Specifically, we create a single variable that associates each person's BWS score for each of the nine ways to save and include that as a predictor in a data set that has each person's 12 choice sets times nine choice options (ways to save), or 36 "rows" of data per person. In each row we insert the BWS score associated with the choice option (way to save) associated with that row of data; then we use only this variable to predict the observed choices. The estimation results produce a starting log-likelihood of -14791.7 and a log-likelihood at convergence of -4314.3. This compares with a log-likelihood at convergence for an aggregate sample conditional logit with parameter estimates for eight of the nine ways to save of -11930.1. Clearly, the individual-level measures explain massively more of the data. The model with BWS scores as a single predictor gives an estimate of 1.42 (Wald=2301.2). Now we compare these sample mean BWS scores with the estimated conditional logit parameters for most and fewest choices. This yields a relationship that is almost perfectly proportional, as shown in Figures 2.5 and 2.6. Both graphs have approximately the same proportionality constant, which suggests that the primary difference in BWS scores and logit estimates is differences in error variances (scales).

The preceding results suggest that there is value in examining the distribution and associated statistics of the BWS scores. Table 2.11 provides summary statistics for each

28

The BWS object case

Table 2.11 *Summary statistics for the BWS scores for ways to save money*

Ways to save	Min	Max	Mean	S.E.	S.D.	Skew	S.E.	Kurt	S.E.
Company Tax cut	−4	4	−0.04	0.086	2.025	0.142	0.103	−0.540	0.206
Tax reform	−4	4	1.20	0.072	1.702	−0.498	0.103	−0.183	0.206
Fairer taxes	−4	4	2.48	0.073	1.732	−1.317	0.103	1.388	0.206
Better compliance	−4	4	0.88	0.079	1.881	−0.376	0.103	−0.458	0.206
Defer defense	−4	4	−0.49	0.084	1.982	0.253	0.103	−0.357	0.206
Defer foreign aid	−4	4	−0.48	0.089	2.109	0.527	0.103	−0.474	0.206
Cap eligibility	−4	4	0.76	0.081	1.928	−0.146	0.103	−0.736	0.206
Road user charges	−4	3	−1.74	0.072	1.713	0.695	0.103	−0.150	0.206
Visitor Departure Tax	−4	4	−2.58	0.068	1.621	1.397	0.103	2.159	0.206

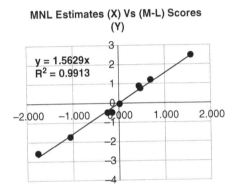

Figure 2.5 MNL(most) vs (M-L)

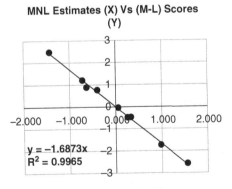

Figure 2.6 MNL(least) vs (M-L)

way to save money. One can clearly "see" that "Fairer taxes" has the highest mean, followed by "Tax reform," whereas "Departure Tax" and "Road User Charge" have the lowest means. Most of the ways to save have means that differ significantly from zero, but one must take into account the fact that BWS tasks involve repeated measures within individuals. Hence, as Louviere and Woodworth (1983) noted, standard errors can be corrected by dividing each by the square root of the number of sets, or SQRT(12) = 3.464. All then differ from zero.

The summary statistical results also suggest that the distributions of several of the ways to save money are significantly skewed and kurtotic. Thus, we investigate the histograms associated with each measure. We also include a measure of the variance in each person's choices. This measure is particularly simple to calculate for BWS scores: one simply squares each BWS score and sums the squares. The distribution of individual-level variance, or "choice consistency," is depicted in Figure 2.7a, which clearly shows a highly skewed distribution consistent with a log-normal or gamma distribution, which is typical of distributions we have obtained from BWS tasks. Higher values on the variance scale mean more consistency, with lower values meaning less consistency; hence, most people were quite consistent.

As expected, Figures 2.7b to 2.7j indicate several highly skewed distributions of BWS scores, such as "Fairer taxes" and "Visitor Departure Tax." Most of the remaining distributions are somewhat lumpy, suggesting that they are non-normal, and confirming the need to cluster the individuals into subgroups (segments). We now test how well the ways to save and spend discriminate between the clusters by treating the cluster membership indicator (1 to 2 for saving; 1 to 4 for spending) as a dependent variable in an unconditional multinomial logistic regression analysis. The nine saving or spending ways are the predictors; however, it is important to note that the BWS scores sum to zero, so they are linearly dependent if all are used as predictors.

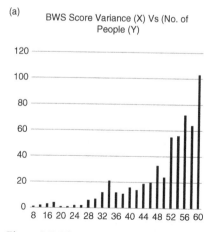

(a) BWS Score Variance (X) Vs (No. of People (Y))

Figure 2.7 Histograms of individual error variances and BWS scores. (a) Histogram of individual error variance estimated from BWS scores

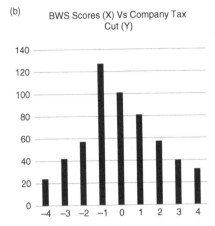

Figure 2.7b Histogram of individual BWS scores for Company Tax cut

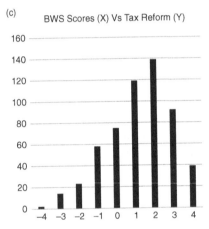

Figure 2.7c Histogram of individual BWS scores for tax reform

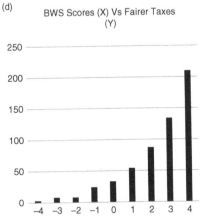

Figure 2.7d Histogram of individual BWS scores for fairer taxes

(e)

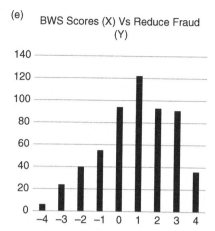

Figure 2.7e Histogram of individual BWS scores for reducing fraud

(f)

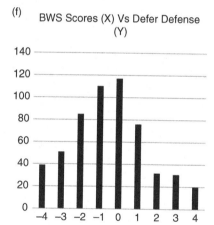

Figure 2.7f Histogram of individual BWS scores for deferring defense spending

(g)

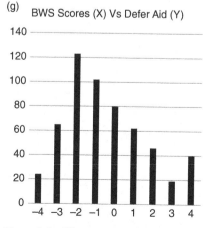

Figure 2.7g Histogram of individual BWS scores for deferring foreign aid spending

(h)

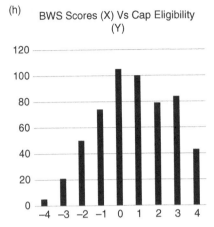

Figure 2.7h Histogram of individual BWS scores for capping eligibility for entitlement

(i)

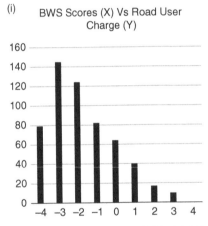

Figure 2.7i Histogram of individual BWS scores for road user charges for heavy vehicles

(j)

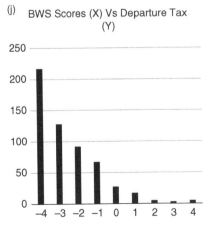

Figure 2.7j Histogram of individual BWS scores for increasing visitor Departure Tax

To avoid linear dependence, we pre-process the data to anticipate relevant predictors by cross-tabbing each saving or spending way with its cluster membership indicator (results omitted in the interests of space). The unconditional logistic regression model includes only potential predictors exhibiting differences across clusters. Statistical estimation results are in Tables 2.12a and 2.12b, which reveal that the BWS measures for saving and spending ways discriminate between clusters well, and both logistic regression models predict the cluster memberships highly accurately.

Table 2.12a *Unconditional logit regression results for ways to save money*

Model	Model fitting criteria −2 log likelihood	Likelihood ratio tests Chi-square	df	Sig.
Intercept only	708.448			
Final	134.373	574.075	7	0.000

Pseudo R-squares: Cox and Snell (0.645); Nagelkerke (0.894); McFadden (0.810)

Clusters for saving (2)	Est	S.E.	Wald	df	Sig.
Intercept	11.156	1.430	60.896	1	0.000
Tax reform	−1.402	0.203	47.469	1	0.000
Fairer taxes	−1.562	0.226	47.710	1	0.000
Defer defense	0.903	0.166	29.573	1	0.000
Defer foreign aid increases	0.769	0.144	28.428	1	0.000
Cap eligibility	−0.247	0.121	4.162	1	0.041
Road user charges	0.993	0.189	27.584	1	0.000
Visitor Departure Tax	1.827	0.258	50.267	1	0.000

The reference cluster is number 2

	Model classification table		
	Predicted		
Observed	1	2	% correct
1	171	16	91.4%
2	10	357	97.3%
Overall %	32.7%	67.3%	95.3%

Table 2.12b *Unconditional logit regression results for ways to spend money*

Model	Model fit criteria −2 log likelihood	Likelihood ratio tests Chi-square	df	Sig.
Intercept only	1441.887			
Final	286.309	1155.577	24	.000

Pseudo R-squares: Cox and Snell (0.876); Nagelkerke (0.946); McFadden (0.801)

Clusters for spending (4)		Est	S.E.	Wald	df	Sig.
1	Intercept	−6.661	1.079	38.139	1	0.000
	Spread boom	0.837	0.235	12.669	1	0.000
	Help vulnerable	1.143	0.260	19.332	1	0.000
	Aged care	1.687	0.276	37.444	1	0.000
	Help business	2.278	0.403	31.974	1	0.000
	Improve infrastructure	2.355	0.347	45.995	1	0.000
	Workforce productivity	2.455	0.380	41.718	1	0.000
	Health e-records	0.387	0.198	3.833	1	0.050
	Biosecurity	0.988	0.255	15.041	1	0.000
	Afghanistan, Middle East, etc.	0	.	.	0	.
2	Intercept	−2.791	0.531	27.598	1	0.000
	Spread boom	0.123	0.163	0.568	1	0.451
	Help vulnerable	0.462	0.178	6.707	1	0.010
	Aged care	1.235	0.187	43.524	1	0.000
	Help business	−0.976	0.211	21.350	1	0.000
	Improve infrastructure	0.178	0.179	0.988	1	0.320
	Workforce productivity	−0.616	0.208	8.754	1	0.003
	Health e-records	−0.158	0.139	1.297	1	0.255
	Biosecurity	−0.084	0.163	0.264	1	0.607
	Afghanistan, Middle East, etc.	0	.	.	0	.
3	Intercept	−15.383	1.966	61.224	1	0.000
	Spread boom	3.831	0.485	62.373	1	0.000
	Help vulnerable	4.223	0.516	66.987	1	0.000
	Aged care	2.928	0.341	73.700	1	0.000
	Help business	0.786	0.300	6.867	1	0.009
	Improve infrastructure	2.616	0.358	53.367	1	0.000
	Workforce productivity	3.187	0.444	51.484	1	0.000
	Health e-records	1.494	0.274	29.821	1	0.000
	Biosecurity	1.053	0.260	16.338	1	0.000
	Afghanistan, Middle East, etc.	0	.	.	0	.

The reference cluster is number 4

Classification table					
	Predicted				
Observed	1	2	3	4	% Correct
1	133	2	2	5	93.7%
2	2	152	3	7	92.7%
3	2	1	187	5	95.9%
4	7	11	3	32	60.4%
Overall %	26.0%	30.0%	35.2%	8.8%	91.0%

2.3.3 *More complex analyses including regression models*

The BWS scores used in the simple analyses above are likely to be novel even to many practitioners experienced in BWS, because they are not part of academics' or practitioners' typical "toolbox" of methods. Nevertheless, their versatility and ease of calculation means they should be a starting point for most (if not all) analyses. However, there often will be a need for more conventional regression and related statistical model analyses:

(1) to test whether BWS scores in fact have the attractive properties noted earlier;
(2) to test links between BWS scores and model estimates from DCEs, in order to provide confidence for researchers and practitioners familiar with DCEs in using them; and
(3) to provide a framework to model choices and deal with the (many) phenomena known to potentially impact discrete choice data.

In light of the above, we illustrate analyses of Case 1 BWS data with limited dependent variable regression models commonly used to analyze DCE choice data (conditional logit and its variants), and models that assume continuous numerical dependent variables (such as weighted least squares [WLS] regression).

DCE practitioners familiar with conditional logit (multinomial logit) regression often use it as a starting point for the analysis of DCE data. It also is available in many statistical software packages. Perhaps the simplest conditional logit model that can be estimated from Case 1 BWS data is one estimated only from the best choice data – that is, in each choice set only one object is chosen as best (over all others). To illustrate what those data would look like, we use an example from a study conducted in 2010 for the Sydney Independent Transport Inquiry. In that study 2,400 residents of Sydney completed a Case 1 BWS task to elicit relative priorities for nine short-term (relatively easily implemented) improvements to the transportation networks, as given in Table 2.13.

A BIBD in 12 sets of size 3 was used to design and implement the task that elicited preferences from survey respondents.

Table 2.13 *Short-term improvements in Sydney transport under consideration*

Object number	Object name (transport improvement)
1	Improved off-peak trains between major centers
2	Improved peak rail capacity
3	Improved bus services on major routes
4	Extensions of light rail services
5	Integrated fares
6	Integrated ticketing
7	Real-time arrival information
8	New cycleways; more bike and scooter parking
9	Trains using green power

Table 2.14 *Selection of raw data for conditional logit model of "best" choices*

				Presence (1)/absence (0) of objects								
ID	Total sets	Set	Option	Object #	O2	O3	O4	O5	O6	O7	O8	O9	Choice
1	1	1	1	2	1	0	0	0	0	0	0	0	1
1	1	1	2	4	0	0	1	0	0	0	0	0	0
1	1	1	3	8	0	0	0	0	0	0	1	0	0
1	2	2	1	1	0	0	0	0	0	0	0	0	0
1	2	2	2	4	0	0	1	0	0	0	0	0	1
1	2	2	3	5	0	0	0	1	0	0	0	0	0
2	13	1	1	2	1	0	0	0	0	0	0	0	1
2	13	1	2	4	0	0	1	0	0	0	0	0	0
2	13	1	3	8	0	0	0	0	0	0	1	0	0
2	14	2	1	1	0	0	0	0	0	0	0	0	1
2	14	2	2	4	0	0	1	0	0	0	0	0	0
2	14	2	3	5	0	0	0	1	0	0	0	0	0

Table 2.14 shows raw best data (set up for analysis in Stata MP10.0) for the first two choice sets of respondents ID 1 and 2.

In the table, *Set* is the set number (from 1 to 12), *Option* is the object's position in the set (1st, 2nd or 3rd), *Object #* is the object identifier (numbers 1 to 9 in the BIBD corresponding to a particular improvement), *O2* to *O9* are dummy variables corresponding to the objects that were available (1) or not (0) in each set. The code for object 1 (*O1*) is omitted, so regression estimates are with respect to this omitted object. *Total sets* is an indicator of all the choice sets created by combining ID and set (a unique person-choice set indicator) that tells Stata the composition of each person-choice set. In this particular case, it is worth noting that one must tell Stata that there is clustering by respondent, otherwise Stata will assume that the *Total Sets* variable for each set comes from a different person (in fact, 12 sets come from each person). In turn, this allows Stata to adjust the standard errors to properly reflect this. *Choice* is the dependent variable, indicating which object is chosen best in each set. One estimates a conditional logit regression from the worst data exactly the same way, with *Choice* now indicating the "least important" object in each set. One can multiply all dummy variables by −1 if one wishes to ensure that these estimates are on the same scale as those for "best"; otherwise, parameter estimates can be interpreted as "degree of low priority."

Flynn *et al.* (2007) set out the data (for Case 2) for conditional logit models that incorporate both best and worst choice data; the data are pooled, with the best data "stacked" above the worst data. Chapter 1 referred to this data pooling, noting that, under mild assumptions, we allow a single variable to capture two pieces of information, the best choice and the worst choice in each set. In fact, the worst data are "just extra choice sets"

Table 2.15 *Selection of raw data for conditional logit model of best and worst*

							Presence (1 or –1)/absence (0) of objects								
ID	Total sets	Set	New set	BW	Option	Object #	O2	O3	O4	O5	O6	O7	O8	O9	Choice
1	1	1	1	1	1	2	1	0	0	0	0	0	0	0	1
1	1	1	1	1	2	4	0	0	1	0	0	0	0	0	0
1	1	1	1	1	3	8	0	0	0	0	0	0	1	0	0
1	2	1	2	–1	2	4	0	0	–1	0	0	0	0	0	0
1	2	1	2	–1	3	8	0	0	0	0	0	0	–1	0	1
1	3	2	3	1	1	1	0	0	0	0	0	0	0	0	0
1	3	2	3	1	2	4	0	0	1	0	0	0	0	0	1
1	3	2	3	1	3	5	0	0	0	1	0	0	0	0	0
1	4	2	4	–1	1	1	0	0	0	0	0	0	0	0	0
1	4	2	4	–1	3	5	0	0	0	–1	0	0	0	0	1

added ("appended," to use Stata's terminology) to the best data. We again illustrate this for raw data from the first two choice sets, but only for person ID 1, in Table 2.15.

There are several important things to note about the above data set-up.

(1) Our original *Set* variable is now superseded by *New set*, which takes values from 1 to 24, indicating that there are now 24 choice sets, 12 best and 12 worst.
(2) The variable *BW* indicates whether an observation is from a best (+1) or a worst (−1) choice set, and basically is an intercept.
(3) *Total sets* is *not* the same as earlier: it is an interaction of respondent ID and *new set*. It increments from 1 to 24 for respondent ID 1, then from 25 to 48 for respondent ID 2, etc.
(4) There are only two observations for each worst choice set, which reflects the fact that the best choice is no longer available to be chosen. We *assume* that best is picked first, then worst; not the other way around. The implications of this assumption for the process that respondents followed will be discussed later.
(5) The "dummy" variables take values 0 and 1 for best choice sets and 0 and −1 for worst choice sets.

The same adjustments to standard errors should be made as for the best (or worst) only regression. This model is a *sequential* model, because we assumed one choice (best) first, followed by a second choice (worst).

Finally, some disciplines (such as economics) may want to analyze the choice data using the rank ordered logit (ROL) model. For sets of three objects, if we know best and worst then we know the full ranking (first, second and third).

Table 2.16 presents the data for the first two choice sets for respondent ID 1.

Table 2.16 *Selection of raw data for rank ordered logit model*

ID	Total sets	Set	Option	Object #	O2	O3	O4	O5	O6	O7	O8	O9	Rank
1	1	1	1	2	1	0	0	0	0	0	0	0	1
1	1	1	2	4	0	0	1	0	0	0	0	0	2
1	1	1	3	8	0	0	0	0	0	0	1	0	3
1	2	2	1	1	0	0	0	0	0	0	0	0	2
1	2	2	2	4	0	0	1	0	0	0	0	0	1
1	2	2	3	5	0	0	0	1	0	0	0	0	3

Table 2.17 *Estimates from all methods*

Object	ROL	CLB	CLW	SEQ	B	W	BW
Improved off-peak trains between major centers	0	0	0	0	0.466	0.272	0.194
Improved peak rail capacity	0.922	0.883	1.170	0.922	0.687	0.092	0.594
Improved bus services on major routes	0.514	0.372	0.750	0.514	0.557	0.137	0.419
Extensions of light rail services	−0.966	−1.263	−1.073	−0.966	0.163	0.486	−0.323
Integrated fares	−0.344	−0.494	−0.336	−0.344	0.294	0.287	0.006
Integrated ticketing	−0.445	−0.632	−0.433	−0.445	0.262	0.309	−0.047
Real-time arrival information	−0.876	−1.095	−0.969	−0.876	0.194	0.462	−0.268
New cycleways; more bike and scooter parking	−1.153	−1.174	−1.312	−1.153	0.162	0.546	−0.384
Trains using green power	−0.721	−0.981	−0.733	−0.721	0.217	0.409	−0.192
R-squared	**0.998**	**0.989**	**0.994**	**0.998**	**0.975**	**0.963**	**N/A**

All variables are defined in the same way as for the conditional logit model for best, except *Rank*, the rank order of the three objects (NB: Stata users should reverse the ranks so that "3" denotes the top rank, etc.).

Table 2.17 displays the regression estimates for all four models discussed above (ROL = rank ordered logit, CLB = conditional logit on best, CLW = conditional logit on worst, SEQ = sequential best-worst), together with B = the sample-level best choice frequency, W = sample-level worst choice frequency, and BW = sample-level best-minus-worst scores. The frequencies are simply the total number of times an object was chosen best (respectively, worst) across all 12 sets and all 2,400 people divided by the number of times it was available to be chosen: 4 × 2,400 = 9,600 (each object appears four times in the BIBD).

The bottom row gives the R-squared value for an ordinary least squares (OLS) regression of each set of estimates against the scores (BW, the final column). The two limited dependent variable models that make maximum use of the data (ROL and sequential models) produce estimates that are almost perfectly linear with the best-minus-worst scores.

2.3.4 Least squares analyses

Many choice modelers tend to immediately begin analyzing choice data with a limited dependent variable model, such as a conditional logit regression. Our experience is that this can lead to researchers being insufficiently familiar with their data prior to estimating models. For example, choice frequencies for each object often are ignored prior to analysis, but offer useful insights into the data structure and possibly the choice processes of the individuals. Indeed, data files for the choice models discussed above can be very large, so compact files of choice frequencies often provide a better way to learn more about one's data. In addition, least squares models often will give valid inferences (Flynn *et al.*, 2007; Flynn, Louviere, Peters *et al.*, 2008).

Table 2.18 contains the complete data set for a weighted least squares regression to estimate a "marginal" model. Marginal models are so named since they effectively "sum to the margins" the entries of a table containing the counts of all possible best-worst pairs. For example, a table of pairs for this case would be size 9 x 9; each cell contains a count of how many times each pair is chosen (row = best, column = worst), with zeros on the main diagonal (objects cannot be chosen as both best and worst). Summing across a row gives the marginal best total (inserted into one of the first nine rows of the *Count* variable) and summing down a column gives a marginal worst total (inserted into one of the bottom nine rows of the *Count* variable).

Table 2.18 *Raw data for weighted least squares "marginal" model for the nine ways to save money in Table 2.9*

Object #	BW	Count	Lcount	O1	O2	O3	O4	O5	O6	O7	O8	O9
1	1	779	6.658	1	0	0	0	0	0	0	0	0
2	1	1056	6.962	0	1	0	0	0	0	0	0	0
3	1	1589	7.371	0	0	1	0	0	0	0	0	0
4	1	867	6.765	0	0	0	1	0	0	0	0	0
5	1	525	6.263	0	0	0	0	1	0	0	0	0
6	1	609	6.412	0	0	0	0	0	1	0	0	0
7	1	867	6.765	0	0	0	0	0	0	1	0	0
8	1	301	5.707	0	0	0	0	0	0	0	1	0
9	1	139	4.934	0	0	0	0	0	0	0	0	1
1	−1	799	6.683	−1	0	0	0	0	0	0	0	0
2	−1	381	5.943	0	−1	0	0	0	0	0	0	0
3	−1	195	5.273	0	0	−1	0	0	0	0	0	0
4	−1	373	5.922	0	0	0	−1	0	0	0	0	0
5	−1	801	6.686	0	0	0	0	−1	0	0	−0	0
6	−1	877	6.777	0	0	0	0	0	−1	0	0	0
7	−1	442	6.091	0	0	0	0	0	0	−1	0	0
8	−1	1278	7.153	0	0	0	0	0	0	0	−1	0
9	−1	1586	7.369	0	0	0	0	0	0	0	0	−1

Thus, Table 2.18 is constructed by stacking the nine best object counts above the nine worst object counts. If the choice counts are associated with objects that occur different numbers of times in the design, then one must adjust the counts to reflect the availability of the object across the whole study. In the case of the nine ways to save money in the Australian federal budget, each object (way) occurs exactly the same number of times; hence, the counts do not need to be adjusted. More generally, choice counts can occur unequally often, as will be the case for BWS Cases 2 and 3 applications if and when attributes have unequal numbers of levels. Ln(*freq*) is the natural log of the frequency; due to an expected exponential relationship between choice probabilities and utilities in conditional logit models, it gives an estimate of the latent utility for each object. Choice counts are estimates of choice probabilities (can be transformed to be); hence, errors associated with each count cannot be independent and identically distributed (i.i.d.). Consequently, one can use WLS regression to estimate the parameters of a conditional logit model, as shown by Louviere and Woodworth (1983). The counts (or adjusted counts) are the weights in the WLS estimation.

Flynn *et al.* (2007) show how to apply WLS regression to sample-level best-worst *pairs* as in a maxdiff model. This model involves 9 × 8 = 72 observations for the nine ways to save money and also for the Sydney transport data. In other words, there are 36 best pairs and 36 worst pairs (9 × 9 − 9 = 72) in the design. It also is worth noting that Flynn, Louviere, Peters *et al.* (2008) show that *maxdiff* models typically add little extra statistical insights beyond those given by the marginal WLS model, but require much larger file sizes.

2.3.5 Expanding the data to obtain more choice information

The following material on data expansion is closely related to that given by Louviere, Street *et al.* (2008) and Marley and Islam (2012). In the following, given a set of objects {w,x,y,z}, we use the notation w>x,y,z to indicate that w is selected as best from that set, with parallel notation for all other best choices from the subsets of that set. As discussed earlier, asking for worst in addition to best provides more choice information from which to estimate models than is given by traditional first choice (best only). For example, assume that there is a set of four objects {w,x,y,z}, and the ranking from best to worst is w>x>y>z. Then we have the following information on the set and its subsets (regarding implied best choices):

> one choice set of size 4: w>x,y,z;
> three choice sets of size 3: w>x,y; w>x,z; w>y,z;
> six choice sets of size 2: w>x; w>y; w>z; x>y; x>z; y>z.

If there are five objects in a set, say {v,w,x,y,z}, and the ranking is v>w>x>y>z, then we have the following information (regarding implied best choices):

> one choice set of size 5: v>w,x,y,z;
> four choice sets of size 4: v>w,x,y; v>w,x,z; v>w,y,z; v>x,y,z;
> six choice sets of size 3: v>w,x; v>w,y; v>w,z; v>x,y; v>x,y; v>y,z;
> ten choice sets of size 2: v>w; v>x; v>y; v>z; w>x; w>y; w>z; x>y; x>z; y>z.

We do not need to obtain a full rank order for best-worst choice to give more information than simply asking best. For example, assuming a set of four objects {w,x,y,z} and knowing that w is best and z is worst, then we know (regarding implied best choices):

    one choice set of size 4: w>x,y,z;
    three choice sets of size 3: w>x,y; w>x,z; w>y,z;
    five choice sets of size 2: w>x; w>y; w>z; x>z; y>z;

For five objects {v,w,x,y,z}, with v best and z worst, we know (for implied best choices):

    one choice set of size 5: v>w,x,y,z;
    four choice sets of size 4: v>w,x,y; v>w,x,z; v>w,y,z; v>x,y,z;
    six choice sets of size 3: v>w,x; v>w,y; v>w,z; v>x,y; v>x,z; v>y,z;
    seven choice sets of size 2: v>w; v>x; v>y; v>z; w>z; x>z; y>z.

As described above, we can use repeated best and worst questions to obtain a partial or full rank ordering of the objects. We now illustrate this with five strategies that one can use to reduce carbon emissions. The objective of this example is to understand how effective citizens think each reduction strategy is; and we achieve this objective by using a BIBD to create five sets of four strategies, as shown in Table 2.19.

As previously discussed, a typical BWS experiment asks participants to choose only "most effective" and "least effective." However, we can get a full ranking of all four objects by asking an extra question, as shown in the screenshot in Figure 2.8.

Of course, one also could ask: "Of the other two ways, which do you think would be the least effective?" Indeed, one can ask as many best and/or worst choices as needed to get enough information to understand and analyze the data. However, typically, unless the comparison sets are fairly large (for example, ≥ 7), two rounds of best and worst choices (choose the best and the worst objects, then choose the best and the worst of the remaining objects) should provide enough information for most purposes.

More generally, if one wants a full ranking in each set and/or a full ranking of objects for each person, when comparison sets are larger than three, one needs additional best and worst questions to do this. For example, for five options one needs two extra questions, one additional best and one additional worst; for six options one needs three extra questions, two best and one worst (or vice versa); and for seven options one needs four additional

Table 2.19 *BIBD for five carbon emission reduction strategies*

Comparison set	Ways to reduce carbon emissions in BIBD (i.e., 1 to 5)			
1	1	2	4	3
2	5	1	3	2
3	2	4	5	1
4	3	5	1	4
5	4	3	2	5

Table 2.20 *Number of extra questions required for a full ranking*

Comparison set size	Basic best and worst questions	Extra best and worst questions
3	2	0
4	2	1
5	2	2
6	2	3
7	2	4
8	2	5
9	2	6
10	2	7
11	2	8

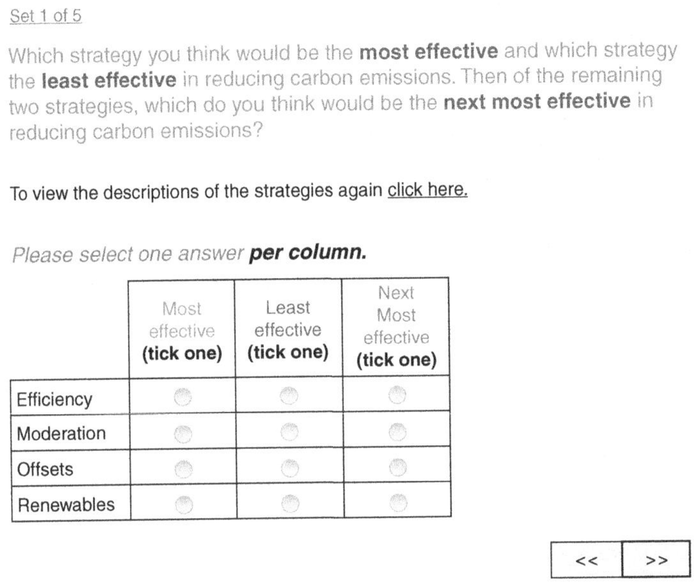

Set 1 of 5

Which strategy you think would be the **most effective** and which strategy the **least effective** in reducing carbon emissions. Then of the remaining two strategies, which do you think would be the **next most effective** in reducing carbon emissions?

To view the descriptions of the strategies again click here.

Please select one answer **per column.**

	Most effective (tick one)	Least effective (tick one)	Next Most effective (tick one)
Efficiency	○	○	○
Moderation	○	○	○
Offsets	○	○	○
Renewables	○	○	○

<<	>>

Figure 2.8 Screenshot of online survey task

questions, two best and two worst. Table 2.20 gives the number of questions needed for a complete order for comparison sets of sizes 3 to 11; extrapolating to set sizes larger than 11 should be obvious.

We now discuss expanding the data using the extra question for the five carbon emission reduction strategies. The strategies are energy efficiency (hereafter, "Efficiency"), "Moderation," using renewables (hereafter, "Renewables"), using carbon offsets (hereafter, "Offsets") and "Recycling." We begin by summarising the best and worst counts as in prior examples; these are in Table 2.21. The counts satisfy the assumption that most counts = 1/least counts, with the estimated constant of proportionality and $R^2 = 0.978$.

Table 2.21 *Summary counts and calculations for carbon reduction strategies*

Strategies	Most	Least	M–L	1 / (L)	1 / (L)*1M
Efficiency	1766	570	1196	0.0018	1754.386
Moderation	746	1389	−643	0.0007	719.9424
Renewables	1695	654	1041	0.0015	1529.052
Offsets	342	2763	−2421	0.0004	361.9254
Recycling	1471	644	827	0.0016	1552.795

Table 2.22 *BW measures for carbon emission reduction strategies*

Strategy	M–L	ROL	MNLmost	MNLleast	Lou(M–L)	HR(M–L)
Efficiency	1196	0.467	0.577	−0.590	0.458	0.399
Moderation	−643	−0.247	−0.343	0.335	−0.259	−0.226
Renewables	1041	0.389	0.530	−0.449	0.387	0.335
Offsets	−2421	−0.941	−1.137	1.169	−0.912	−0.791
Recycling	827	0.332	0.373	−0.465	0.325	0.283

Because we asked the extra "most" question, we know the full ranking in each comparison set. This allows us to expand the data in several ways: (1) the Beggs, Cardell and Hausman (BCH) approach of successive choice sets, which we then use as a basis for estimating the parameters of an ROL model; (2) the Horsky and Rao (HR) all pairs approach, which we use to calculate expected choice totals for each option in each set for each person and then aggregate the totals; and (3) the Louviere, Street *et al.* (Lou) approach, which we also use to calculate expected totals for each option in each set for each person and then aggregate the totals. We compare each of these approaches with the BWS scores (most-minus-least frequency counts) and conditional logit estimation of most and least choices separately. The aggregate sample summary results are in Table 2.22. Basically, each measure in Table 2.22 is almost perfectly proportional to the other measures, with all correlations above 0.98. A principal components analysis (PCA) returns an eigenvalue of 5.99, indicating that one factor accounts for all the data. So, as noted earlier, simple ways of calculating BWS scores, whether one uses extra best and worst choices to expand the data or not, produce aggregate measures that align well with those of more sophisticated methods.

We now illustrate the expansion methods using the example of ways to save money in the federal budget discussed earlier in this chapter. We begin by summarizing the best and worst choices in Table 2.22. The basic analysis is the same as before, namely counts of best and worst choices and differences in best and worst choices. The best and worst choice counts are summarized in earlier tables, so we display only the BWS scores. In this example only one round of best-worst choices is needed for a full ranking of the priority given to each way to save. We now introduce and discuss three expansion methods that have been proposed and applied in the choice modeling literature.

(1) **Calculate implied choices for each option from implied successive, independent (smaller) choice sets (Beggs, Cardell and Hausman, 1981).**

One can expand full or partial rankings implied by best and worst choices as follows: the option chosen as best is ranked first and the option chosen as worst is ranked last. For the ways to save example, one constructs a full choice set with all three objects as choice options, and the object chosen as best is the implied first choice. Next, one constructs an additional pair that contains the two objects not chosen as best or worst. The object ranked second is the implied choice. So, best and worst choices from a set of three objects can be expanded to two choice sets: one with all three objects and a second with the remaining pair of objects.

(2) **Calculate implied choices for each option from all pairs of options in each comparison set (Horsky and Rao, 1984).**

Horsky and Rao show that all the necessary choice information for estimating conditional logit models can be recovered from all possible pairs of choices. In the case of full or implied rankings from best and worst choices, the best and worst choices from the three objects in each set lead to three pairs: the object chosen as best is paired with each of the other two objects to make three pairs; the best option is the implied chosen object.

(3) **Calculate the implied number of choices for each option with the Louviere, Street *et al.* (2008) approach to produce expected choice totals for all possible subsets of J choice options.**

Any set of J objects can be decomposed into 2^J possible sets of choice sets (each option can be in/out of a set). Let the rank order of the options be x>y>z. Now use the ranking information for each comparison set to calculate the implied (expected) best choice for every 2^J subset in each comparison set. If J=3, there are seven forced choice comparison sets (1 triple, 3 pairs and 3 singles), as given in Table 2.23.

Table 2.23 *Implied choice sets from a $2^{J=3}$ expansion of three objects*

Sets	Object x	Object y	Object z	Choice
1	Absent	Absent	Absent	N/A
2	Absent	Absent	Present	Z
3	Absent	Present	Absent	Y
4	Absent	Present	Present	Y
5	Present	Absent	Absent	X
6	Present	Absent	Present	X
7	Present	Present	Absent	X
8	Present	Present	Present	X

Table 2.24 *BWS scores and expected choice counts by expansion method*

Attributes for saving items	BWS	Ln(BCH)	Ln(HR)	Ln(Lou)	Component
No Company Tax cut	−20	7.707	8.565	6.658	0.144
Reprioritize tax reform	675	7.979	8.735	6.962	0.762
A fairer tax system	1394	8.199	8.919	7.371	1.409
Prevent fraud and tax evasion	494	7.915	8.674	6.765	0.548
Defer defense spending/acquisitions	−276	7.585	8.463	6.263	−0.231
Defer foreign aid increases	−268	7.589	8.482	6.412	−0.157
Put in benefit eligibility caps	425	7.889	8.662	6.765	0.503
Raise road user charges	−977	7.144	8.246	5.707	−1.075
Raise Departure Tax	−1447	6.681	8.065	4.934	−1.904

We now continue the example of ways to save money in the federal budget. Recall there are 12 comparison sets of size 3. We compare each expansion method with BWS scores. The BCH expansion (approach 1) yields the following sets from a complete ranking for each comparison set: a set of three options, where rank 1 is implied chosen and a second set with the two remaining options, where rank 2 is implied chosen. The HR expansion (approach 2) gives all implied pairs from a complete ranking for each comparison set – 1,2; 1,3; 2,3 – where the numbers are the options ranked in that order, and the first number is the implied chosen option. The Lou expansion (approach 3) yields expected choice counts of 1, 2, 4, respectively, for ranks 1, 2, 3 in each comparison set. The BWS difference scores, and the natural log of the expected choice counts, are shown in Table 2.24.

As noted earlier in this chapter, the natural logarithm of the choice counts is an estimate of the utility associated with each way to save that is consistent with a conditional logit model (the denominator of the logit model is a constant for this set of nine choices treated as one choice set). We first subject the BWS scores and the log of each of the four expansion measures to a principal components analysis; the hypothesis is that one component should explain *all* the variance in the data. The PCA yields one eigenvalue equal to 3.955, which explains 98.9 percent of the variance in the four measures. We output the component scores, which are in the last column of the table. Figures 2.9a to 2.9d provide a graphical and statistical comparison; each graphs the PCA scores on the X-axis versus the other measures on the Y-axis. The graphs and associated regression fits for each expansion method clearly indicate that all give the same information about the relative priorities of each way to save money. Thus, as noted several times earlier in this chapter, simple BWS scores do an excellent job of measuring the relative priorities.

Now we turn our attention to discussing the analysis of best-worst data for situations in which it is reasonable to expect the choices to be probabilistic.

(a) PCA Scores (X) Vs BWS Scores (Y)

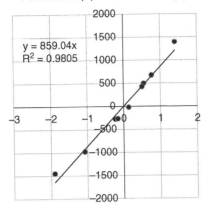

Figure 2.9a PCA scores versus BWS scores

(b)   PCA Scores (X) Vs Ln(BCH) (Y)

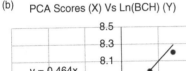

Figure 2.9b PCA scores versus Ln(BCH)

2.3.5 *Analyzing best and worst choices from larger comparison sets*

We focus on a larger problem involving seven objects, and analyze the results of the expansion methods statistically. The example in Table 2.25 is a BIBD for seven objects in 21 comparison sets of size 5 (design 7 in Table 2.3).

We assign utility values to each option (true values are, respectively, 1.7, 1.5, 0.7, 2.1, 1.2, 0.5, 0.3 for options 1 to 7), and add uniform random errors with range [0,1]. We now use each expansion method to construct extra implied choice sets and choices, and fit conditional logit models to the simulated choices. We consider the following cases. (1) Options are ranked from 1 to 5 in each set based on the relevant two best and two worst choices in Table 2.25; the resulting data are treated as five sets of 4 ranks. We estimate the parameters

(c)   PCA Scores (X) Vs Ln(HR) (Y)

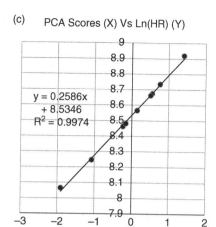

$y = 0.2586x + 8.5346$
$R^2 = 0.9974$

Figure 2.9c PCA scores versus Ln(HR)

(d)   PCA Scores (X) Vs Ln(Lou) (Y)

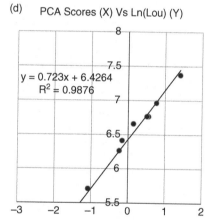

$y = 0.723x + 6.4264$
$R^2 = 0.9876$

Figure 2.9d PCA scores versus Ln(Lou)

using the rank order logit model. (2) We create all implied pairs in each of the 21 subsets of five options, and use the implied ranking in each comparison set to indicate the choices expected in each pair in each comparison set. We estimate a binary conditional logit model from these data. (3) We use the Louviere, Street *et al.* (2008) weighting approach to calculate choice counts expected for each of the J ranks in all possible 2^J choice sets, as discussed in the previous section. The expected choice counts are, respectively, 2^0, 2^1, 2^2, 2^4, ..., 2^{J-1} for ranks 1, 2, 3, 4, ..., J. The resulting data are "stacked," such that each choice option in each choice set is a data record. The dependent variable is the natural logarithm of the expected choice count; the choice counts are used as weights in a weighted least squares model to correct for non-constant error variances implied by using the choice counts as the dependent variable" (Louviere and Woodworth, 1983). One adds C−1 additional dummy

Table 2.25 *Example of seven objects in 21 sets of size 5*

Set	Comparison sets of size 5					Best1	Best2	Worst2	Worst1
1	3	4	5	6	7	3	4	6	7
2	2	4	5	6	7	2	4	6	7
3	2	3	5	6	7	2	3	6	7
4	2	3	4	6	7	2	3	6	7
5	2	3	4	5	7	2	3	5	7
6	2	3	4	5	6	2	3	5	6
7	1	4	5	6	7	1	4	6	7
8	1	3	5	6	7	1	3	6	7
9	1	3	4	6	7	1	3	6	7
10	1	3	4	5	7	1	3	5	7
11	1	3	4	5	6	1	3	5	6
12	1	2	5	6	7	1	2	6	7
13	1	2	4	6	7	1	2	6	7
14	1	2	4	5	7	1	2	5	7
15	1	2	4	5	6	1	2	5	6
16	1	2	3	6	7	1	2	6	7
17	1	2	3	5	7	1	2	5	7
18	1	2	3	5	6	1	2	5	6
19	1	2	3	4	7	1	2	4	7
20	1	2	3	4	6	1	2	4	6
21	1	2	3	4	5	1	2	4	5

variables for C total choice sets to capture differences in the choice set denominators associated with linearizing the conditional logit model. The choice set dummies are of no statistical interest per se; their role is to ensure that the model estimation is consistent with conditional logit

Statistical estimation results for these cases are shown in Table 2.26; we compare estimates graphically with true values in Figure 2.10. The graph shows that all are highly linearly related to the true values, as expected.

2.4 Sample size issues

Researchers may wish to calculate the power levels for proposed Case 1 BWS studies, and associated minimum desired sample sizes. The properties of some estimators (for example., BWS scores) have yet to be formally proved but, for estimation methods such as conditional or rank ordered logit, guidance from the DCE literature is available. For example, Rose and Bliemer (2009) reference papers that show how to calculate the minimum sample sizes needed to achieve a minimum asymptotic t-ratio for a given parameter estimate. It is worth noting that the cited work is relevant at a sample level (or a particular subgroup level); we

Table 2.26 *Estimation results for the three expansion cases*

		Binary logit:all pairs		Ranking		Weighting:conditional logit	
TRUE	ASC	Estimate	Std err.	Estimate	Std err.	Estimate	Std err.
0.3	alt1	−2.379	0.421	−7.376	1.055	−2.031	0.232
0.5	alt2	−2.01	0.373	−6.579	1.001	−1.779	0.208
1.2	alt3	0.006	0.251	−3.202	0.814	−0.886	0.146
2.1	alt4	3.414	0.552	1.453	0.771	0.262	0.105
0.7	alt5	−1.004	0.281	−4.696	0.899	−1.412	0.179
1.5	alt6	0.776	0.269	−0.954	0.707	−0.208	0.118
1.7	alt7	1.198		0		0	

Note: ASC = alternative specific constant.

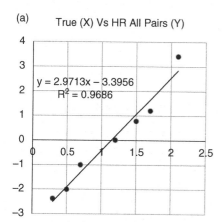

Figure 2.10a Comparisons of estimation results. (a) True vs H&R pairs

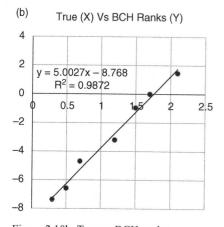

Figure 2.10b True vs BCH ranks

(c)   True (X) Vs Lou All Sets (Y)

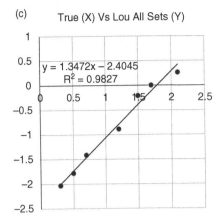

Figure 2.10c True vs Lou all sets

currently do not have such results at the level of the individual person (experimental participant).

2.5 Process issues: theory underlying best and worst choices

In Chapter 1 we noted that best-worst choice data can provide extra information about a respondent's utility function and/or can be used to better understand the process by which he/she makes choices. Thus far this chapter has focused on the first benefit, namely using extra information to provide better estimates of preferences. Now we summarize some of the theory and concepts underlying *process* – that is, how a person might make his/her best and worst choices. Theory for this case is provided by Marley and Louviere (2005), details of which are summarized in Chapter 5. This section provides a non-technical overview to try to make the theory and methods accessible to the widest possible audience.

Case 1 BWS theory is a theory of human cognitive processes; in other words, the theory relates to the process a person uses to solve the problem of how to make best and worst choices in each set. For example, a person may (1) evaluate the options in a set and simultaneously decide what option is best and what option is worst; (2) choose best first and worst second; (3) choose worst first and best second; (4) mentally rank all options to determine which is best and which is worst; (5) eliminate all options that are not best one at a time, and then select the best from the non-eliminated, returning to the eliminated options to select the worst; or (6) evaluate all possible pairs of different options, and choose the (one) pair that exhibits the largest positive difference on the underlying scale. Other ways of solving the problem also are possible. Generally, one can represent each process of interest as a statistical model; different statistical models can be estimated and compared with one another.

2.5.1 A simple view of the process: deterministic decision-making

Suppose people use a deterministic process to make best and worst choices – that is, they make no errors in choices. What process might they use? One possible process is for people to rank all J options in each comparison set from best to worst without errors. The table below shows eight objects (J = 8) ranked from 1 to 8, reflecting a latent dimension such as "preference"; object 1 is ranked first, object 2 ranked second, etc. Suppose a person can rank the eight objects without error in every possible subset. As noted earlier, all possible subsets of J things are given by a 2^J factorial expansion, producing 255 possible subsets of eight objects, plus one null (empty) set. If we give a person all 255 non-empty sets and ask him/ her to rank the objects in each set, and that person ranks them with perfect consistency, we would observe the choices shown in Table 2.27.

The choices in the table form a perfect base 2 series. The product of the best and worst choice counts is a constant, which is the total number of possible best choices that a top-ranked option can receive (or the total number of worst choices that a lowest-ranked option can receive). A few simple relationships can be stated based on this (possibly) unrealistic view of a person's ranking abilities.

From

Worst count = k / Best count

we obtain $\sqrt{(Bestcount)/(Worstcount)} = (1/\sqrt{k})$ *Best count*

For relatively simple BWS comparison tasks it may not be unreasonable to assume that a person behaves approximately consistently with the above relationships. For example, if the number of J objects is relatively few (say fewer than 8) and/or if comparison sets are relatively small (say fewer than 5), many people may choose approximately deterministically, in which case the above relationships may be a reasonable first approximation to a more complex process.

The relationship between the square root of the (best count/worst count) and the best counts results from deterministic choices. In fact, using both the best and the worst counts

Table 2.27 *Choice counts from deterministic decision-making*

Object	Rank (1 = best)	Best	Worst	B x W
1	1	128	1	128
2	2	64	2	128
3	3	32	4	128
4	4	16	8	128
5	5	8	16	128
6	6	4	32	128
7	7	2	64	128
8	8	1	128	128

should provide a better (more precise) estimate of the best counts, because we noted earlier that "raw" best counts are less precise estimates of the true scale values for objects at the lower end of the utility function. In real life people typically make errors, and it remains to be formally proved that under stochastic choices the expectation of the raw best counts is equal to the true "best" values. Nevertheless, empirically we typically find that this relationship holds to a close first approximation.

2.5.2 Probabilistic decision-making

The section above assumed a world in which people demonstrate no inconsistency ("errors") in their choices. Under those circumstances (probably unrealistic in many cases), individuals use a deterministic decision process to make the choices, such as "always choose Qantas; if Qantas is not available then always choose Virgin", etc. Naturally, different individuals can (and do) use different decision rules to make their choices – a state of affairs that applies whether choices are deterministic or stochastic. Any observed pattern of choice data may be more consistent with (better explained by) one process than another. To better understand such processes, we begin by assuming a complete ranking of the objects under consideration.

Assuming one has such a ranking, a classical approach would be to think in terms of a ranking model of repeated best (first) choices, which naturally leads to a rank ordered logit or probit statistical model (see, for example, Beggs, Cardell and Hausman 1981). The ROL model assumes a choice process in which a person makes a series of sequential choices down the rank order, from each (diminishing) choice set. Each choice in the sequential process also is consistent with a conditional logit model. Thus, the ranking process can be expressed as a product of independent probabilities of choosing best (subscript b) from successively smaller subsets, such as the probability of observing the full rank order from the set $\{w,x,y,z\}$, where $w>x>y>z$:

$$\Pr(w_b|w, x, y, z) \times \Pr(x_b|x, y, z) \times \Pr(y_b|y, z)$$

By way of comparison, let us contrast a ROL process with a process that reflects the sequential nature of some BWS tasks, such as online surveys that specifically ask for best first and worst second. We call the model of this sequential process a sequential best-worst (SBW) model, as discussed by Marley and Louviere (2005). The SBW model assumes that a person chooses options sequentially: best choice from the full set, followed by worst choice from the remaining set of non-first best options. Best choice and worst choice are represented by conditional logit models, and often the utility of an option for worst choices is assumed to be the negative of its value for best choices (see Chapter 6 for a discussion of this assumption). Note that this sequential model was introduced earlier in pooling the best and worst data from the Sydney transport example: best from three objects, worst from the remaining two. The process for the four-object ranking above is represented by a series of probability expressions, as shown below, with choosing best (subscript b) and choosing worst (subscript w):

$$\Pr(w_b|w, x, y, z) \times \Pr(z_w|x, y, z) \times \Pr(x_b|x, y)$$

We can graphically describe and compare the two processes as shown here; which process is more nearly correct in any applied case is an empirical issue:

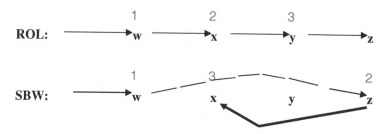

These expressions and diagrams make it clear that a sequential best-worst choice process is different from a straight ranking process by repeated (sequential) best. So, if a person uses a sequential worst-best choice process, the expression and diagram will also differ from ROL and SBW. Hopefully, it now is conceptually clear that a person may use any of several choice processes or "strategies"; which one of these is a closer approximation to a person's observed process in any application is an empirical question. We compare ROL and SBW in the chapter on the multi-profile case (Case 3, Chapter 4). However, at this stage we note that all models are approximations to reality, and some are better than others. Moreover, all models require researchers to make assumptions, and some or all of the assumptions may not be satisfied in any empirical application. Thus, typically, it is wise to test assumptions associated with particular model(s). As a final note about process, we will briefly explore two of the most common models of process used in BWS: the sequential model and the maxdiff model.

2.5.3 Sequential versus maxdiff models

The previous section focused on the process by which a person provides a complete ranking. For simplicity, we return to a single round of best-worst choices (that is, we have data for the "top" and "bottom" rank only in each choice set), although this generalizes to full ranking models. The sequential conditional logit model of section 2.3.3 assumes a particular process of respondents' decision-making, namely that they provide a best choice from n objects, and then a worst choice from the $n-1$ objects remaining after the best object has been removed. Alternatively, we can assume that best and worst choices are made in the reverse order, which also is a sequential model (albeit a different one).

The long-established competing maxdiff model assumes that a person simultaneously considers all possible $n(n-1)$ best-worst pairs in a choice set, and chooses that pair that exhibits the largest utility difference in the two objects relative to all other competing pairs in the set. The maxdiff model is less attractive than sequential models of such decisions because it assumes that a person considers all possible pairs, although an alternative interpretation is based on repeated independent best and worst choices (see Chapter 5). Nonetheless, some of the key results given by Marley and Louviere (2005) hold if and only if individuals use the maxdiff model. Despite such drawbacks, the maxdiff model has a number of attractive properties that have attracted attention from theorists and practitioners.

In practice, as shown (using Case 2) by Flynn, Louviere, Peters *et al.* (2008), estimates from maxdiff and sequential models are generally indistinguishable at a sample level. Thus, unless a researcher is an academic interested in particular issues in decision-making at the level of a single individual, our experience suggests that researchers can assume whichever model they find easier to deal with statistically. Usually, the sequential model is easier to work with than the maxdiff model. Indeed, the Latent GOLD Choice 4.5 software that supports BWS implements several variants of conditional logit models that assume sequential processes; it does not explicitly support any statistical model consistent with the maxdiff psychological model of decision-making. However, we refer readers interested in implementing such a model to Flynn *et al.* (2007), who discuss how to lay out and code the data.

2.6 Conclusions

We have introduced the BWS object case in this chapter, and shown how to apply it with hypothetical examples and actual illustrations. We have discussed the steps needed to design and implement a BWS study for Case 1, showing that the same principles apply across all applications. We have discussed and applied simple and somewhat more complex ways to analyze best and worst choice data obtained from BWS object experiments. Our discussion of analytical approaches provides some recommendations and cautions for practitioners.

(1) Marketers (and other practitioners interested in prediction) typically can use any of the analysis methods that we have discussed. Individuals who respond deterministically will cause convergence problems for maximum likelihood estimation methods, but the Louviere, Street *et al.* (2008) approach, the Frischknecht *et al.* (2014) approach and linear probability models (ordinary least squares estimation applied to the 0, 1 choice indicator dependent variable) are not affected by deterministic decision rules. For example, the Louviere, Street *et al.* (2008) approach uses weighted least squares regression to estimate conditional logit models from the expanded choice counts. The results of fitting these models show that the natural logarithm of the ratio of the observed best and worst choice counts, and the observed best-minus-worst choice counts, both give good (linear) approximations to the parameter estimates. The Frischknecht *et al.* (2014) approach uses penalized likelihood methods to ensure that one can estimate a reliable and accurate conditional logit model for each person.

Chapter 6 discusses another recent function of the best and worst counts that seems to have useful properties. We also discussed fitting linear probability models (ordinary least squares estimation applied to the 0, 1 choice indicator dependent variable) to the choice data generated by expanding the best and worst choices, which frequently gives estimates that are linearly related to the best-minus-worst counts (scores) (see Heckman and Snyder, 1997). Thus, our experience is that simple calculation and statistical estimation methods work well in practice with BWS choice data.

(2) Typically, one obtains considerable choice information from only one set of best and worst questions in each comparison set. Nevertheless, there are cases in which one needs and/or wants extra choice information, and we discussed how to do this by adding more best and worst choice questions to each comparison set (in the limit asking enough questions to obtain a full ranking of objects in each set). Generally, the extra information allows one to estimate BWS statistical models from the choices, but in some cases statistical models may not converge if individuals are deterministic. Some statistical models also will have difficulty converging in some stochastic cases without weighting. The Frischknecht *et al.* (2014) penalized maximum likelihood approach guarantees convergence for single individuals in all cases, and their simulations show that the approach is reliable and accurate.

(3) The feasibility of statistical estimation increases as the number of comparison sets increase relative to the numbers of objects compared. However, one may not be able to estimate models for single people in all cases unless one adopts the Frischknecht *et al.* (2014) approach, which ensures estimation 100 percent of the time.

(4) For the present, we suggest that economists and other researchers desiring welfare measures should use the estimates associated with conditional logit models. BWS "score-based" methods should be regarded as ways to check estimates, and, if necessary, stabilize algorithms (as in Chapter 12) to properly capture heterogeneity.

The basic features of Case 1 apply generally to the profile and multi-profile cases, as will be noted in those chapters.

Chapter 3

The BWS profile case

You are at your very best when things are worst.
Starman (Jeff Bridges), describing the human race to an Earth
scientist, in Starman *(1984: Raynold Gideon, screenwriter;*
John Carpenter, director)

3.1 Introduction

This chapter describes, discusses and illustrates the BWS profile case (Case 2). Researchers familiar with discrete choice experiments will recognize that this case has many features in common with DCEs. For example, like traditional DCEs, a good or service is described by a common set of attributes and levels; the descriptions are called *profiles* (hence, the name for this case). As in traditional ratings-based conjoint analysis (Green and Rao, 1971; Louviere, 1988a; 1994), the profiles are presented to experimental participants *one at a time*. In this sense, this case is somewhat like binary response DCEs that present profiles one at a time and ask for "Yes"/"No" (accept/reject, etc.) responses.

However, this case differs from traditional conjoint analysis and DCEs because experimental participants choose, respectively, the best and worst *attribute levels* in each profile. In other words, participants do not make holistic profile choices. Our experience is that this is an easier task for participants, as they evaluate only one profile at a time instead of choosing among two or more profiles, as in most DCEs. The one-profile-at-a-time aspect may be attractive in applications in which DCEs rarely have been used, such as the United Kingdom's National Health Service. Indeed, the authors have a fair amount of experience applying Case 2 to health-related research problems.

In the past researchers wanting to analyze data from Case 2 had to write special-purpose estimation software or develop a "work-around" in statistical software products such as SPSS, STATA and SAS. We suspect that the latter problem and the fact that formal proofs of the measurement properties appeared only recently (Marley, Flynn and Louviere, 2008) are responsible for less exposure for Case 2 than Case 1 or Case 3. Accordingly, we discuss these and other issues in this chapter to give this case more exposure; indeed, as we later discuss, Case 2 has unique advantages not shared by other conjoint, DCE or utility theoretic approaches for preference elicitation.

The plan of the rest of the chapter is as follows. We first describe and illustrate BWS profile case choice tasks (hereafter, "Case 2"). We then discuss issues associated with designing and implementing profile case projects. Next we discuss conceptual and estimation issues, drawing on our co-authored papers (Marley, Flynn and Louviere, 2008; Flynn *et al.*, 2007; Flynn, Louviere, Peters *et al.*, 2008). We close with a discussion of unresolved issues and potential topics on the research frontier.

3.1.1 The BWS Case 2 choice task

Case 2 focuses on processes by which individuals choose, respectively, the best and worst (most attractive, least attractive, would pay the most to have, would pay the least to have, etc.) attribute levels associated with a description of a good or service (also known as a "profile"). Therefore, like traditional DCEs, one must design profiles to describe particular configurations or specifications of a good or service. Each profile represents a combination of attributes and associated levels; each attribute has a particular level in each profile. Thus, each profile represents a unique and different combination of attribute levels. Profile case participants choose a level of one of the attributes that is best and a level of a different attribute that is worst from the levels presented in each profile. We illustrate the prototypical task with a dermatology example involving patient preferences for appointments (Coast, Salisbury *et al.*, 2006).

In the example question in Table 3.1, a person has indicated that the waiting time is best (probably because it's very short) and convenience is worst (probably because it's unattractive). These two choices yield a partial order because we know the person's first (best) and last (worst) of the four choices, but not the order of the other two choices. Table 3.2 contains a second example of preferences for quality of life states (profiles). This example illustrates the difficulty of anticipating a person's choices *à priori* because participants must prioritize all the attributes and levels relative to one another.

3.1.2 Information issues

Our experience suggests that profile case tasks generally are easier for people than traditional DCEs. However, this advantage has a downside, in that choices do not reveal the overall (un)attractiveness of any particular profile relative to some status quo or other

Table 3.1 *Profile case best-worst task for a dermatology study*

Best thing	The appointment with the specialist	Worst thing
☑	Your appointment will be this week	☐
☐	Getting to your appointment will be difficult and time-consuming	☑
☐	The consultation will be as thorough as you would like	☐
☐	The specialist has been treating skin complaints part-time for 1–2 years	☐

Table 3.2 *Profile case best-worst task for a quality of life study*

Best thing	Quality of life state	Worst thing
☑	You can have a lot of the love and friendship that you want	☐
☐	You can think about the future with only a little concern	☐
☐	You are able to do most of the things that make you feel valued	☐
☐	You can have most of the enjoyment and pleasure that you want	☑
☐	You are able to be independent in most things	☐

reference. For example, DCEs that elicit preferences for product descriptions such as for TV sets typically allow people to reject all the TV profiles offered in each choice set (opt out/buy none). In economic terms this means that the latter task provides unconditional demand information that reveals the decision *not* to choose. Choices in Case 2 reveal only conditional demand: choices are conditional on a particular sample of profiles. Whether or not researchers see the latter property as a limitation will depend on the particular research questions or study objectives. However, it is worth noting that one can overcome this limitation to some extent by asking one or more additional questions about each profile. For example, one can ask: "Would you actually choose this profile (scenario or appointment) if it was available to you now?" Naturally, including such additional questions raises issues as to how to combine best and worst choices with the answers to such questions. We discuss these issues later.

3.2 Design of BWS profile experiments

One can use design theory for linear models to construct attribute-level combinations (choice set of attribute levels); that is, choice options in Case 2 are the levels of each attribute presented as a holistic description (profile). Typically, these will be fractional factorial designs, but they need not be. For example, some research problems may be sufficiently small that one can use the complete factorial design, and each individual can be assigned to a block from that design.

3.2.1 Balanced incomplete block designs

Chapter 2 discussed how to use BIBDs to construct discrete choice experiments for the BWS Case 1. In principle, one also can do this for Case 2. However, a potential downside of doing so is that some comparison sets will have more than one level of the same attribute, and many attribute-level combinations will not describe holistic options – that is, will not be profiles. In other words, level combinations will not describe a good or service. To see this issue, consider a modified version of the airline ticket example from Chapter 1. There are now three 4-level attributes and two 2-level ones.

Table 3.3 *Example airline ticket profile problem*

Attribute	Level 1	Level 2	Level 3	Level 4
Airline	American (1)	Continental (2)	Delta (3)	United (4)
Flying time	4 hours (5)	5 hours (6)	6 hours (7)	7 hours (8)
Airfare (round trip)	$400 (9)	$500 (10)	$600 (11)	$700 (12)
Carry-on bag charge	$25 (13)	$50 (14)		
In-flight service	None (15)	Beverages only (16)		

Note: Numbers in parentheses represent levels 1 to 16, and are used in the BIBD example below.

Table 3.4 *Candidate BIBD for 16 attribute levels ("pseudo-objects")*

Block (set)	"Objects" in each set					
1	12	8	15	13	14	4
2	16	11	14	7	3	13
3	6	13	2	16	15	10
4	9	15	1	14	16	5
5	4	16	8	9	10	11
6	10	12	7	3	9	15
7	11	14	9	2	6	12
8	13	5	10	11	12	1
9	7	4	16	12	5	6
10	5	3	6	15	11	8
11	14	10	5	8	7	2
12	8	7	13	6	1	9
13	3	2	12	1	8	16
14	15	1	11	4	2	7
15	1	6	3	10	4	14
16	2	9	4	5	13	3

There are 256 possible tickets (combinations of the attribute levels in Table 3.3). If we denote the total population of possible combinations as P, a "design" represents a systematic and purposeful way to sample from P. Not surprisingly, different ways of sampling from P have different statistical properties. We consider ways to sample from P that ensure the identification of particular model specifications and yield efficient estimates of model parameters.

First consider using a BIBD to construct an "object case-like" study to observe best and worst attribute level choices. To do this, we treat every one of the 4+4+4+2+2=16 attribute levels from Table 3.3 as a different object, or "pseudo-object"; in other words, we ignore the attribute structure. A candidate BIBD is shown in Table 3.4, which has 16 comparison sets of size 6.

Table 3.5 *Comparison sets 3 and 15*

Set 3	Continental	5 hours	$500	$25	None	Beverages only
Set 15	American	Delta	United	5 hours	$500	$50

Consider sets 3 and 15 from Table 3.4, which give the comparison sets shown in Table 3.5. Comparison set 3 has two levels of in-flight service (none, beverages only), while comparison set 15 has three levels of airline (American, Delta, United).

This choice format may be less desirable than presenting one level of each attribute as a holistic profile. That said, the example shows that one can design a DCE for Case 2 using ideas in Chapter 2. We know of no examples using BIBDs for this purpose; a comparison with the approach we discuss below would therefore be interesting. However, it should be noted that the name of Case 2 (the profile case) was finally chosen because it is the profile nature of the options under consideration that defines it, *not* the attributes. So, a Case 2 task using a BIBD is effectively a Case 1 BWS study.

3.2.2 Sampling from the full factorial

We return to the idea of sampling from a population of P profiles. If one cannot use a full factorial design (that is, all P) for whatever reason, a typical way to sample from P is with a fractional factorial design. We denote a sample of profiles by T, and consider some ways to select T from P. Different fractional factorial designs have different statistical properties; some notable properties are the following (in order of statistical complexity).

- Independent estimation of only main effects (Resolution 3 designs). These designs allow one to estimate only the main effects of a strictly additive linear model, and often are called *orthogonal main effects plans* (OMEPs). To use OMEPs one *must* assume strictly additive underlying utility models. One cannot test if the assumption of additivity is satisfied after the fact, and estimates will be unbiased if the true model is strictly additive, but are *biased* if any omitted interactions are not zero. In Case 2, interactions represent departures from i.i.d. errors and/or the associated independence from irrelevant alternatives (IIA) property of choice models (defined below).
- Independent estimation of main effects in the presence of omitted two-way interactions (Resolution 4 designs). These designs allow one to estimate only the main effects of a strictly additive linear model. To use such designs, one *must* assume that the utility model contains only main effects and two-way interaction terms. Estimates are unbiased if one omits significant two-way interactions, but *biased* if omitted, higher-order interactions are not zero. Interactions have a similar interpretation as above.
- Independent estimation of all main effects and two-way interactions (Resolution 5 designs). These designs allow the estimation of main effects and two-way interactions independently of one another. To use these designs one *has to* assume that the utility

model contains only main effects and two-way interaction terms. Estimates are unbiased if *all* omitted effects are insignificant, but *biased* if significant high-order interactions are omitted. Interactions have a similar interpretation as above.

- Larger designs that allow independent estimation of main effects, two-way interactions and (some) higher-order interactions. Interactions have a similar interpretation to the above.

- Full (complete) factorials that allow the independent estimation of all effects. Interactions have a similar interpretation to the above.

The research objective in Case 2 is to measure each attribute level on a common scale (see Chapter 5). Thus, the underlying model is assumed to be additive – that is, utilities associated with each attribute level "add" to the total utility of a profile. Of course, this assumption may be wrong in an empirical data set. For example, the four levels of airfare should be correlated with one another, and (possibly) less correlated with the levels of in-flight service. If the errors associated with the latent quantities (the measures of each attribute level) are not independent, there will be violations of a key property that those familiar with choice modeling will recognize as the IIA property. This property requires the odds of choosing any two options to be unaffected by a third option in the choice set. Thus, if one uses a BIBD to design a profile DCE, as in Table 3.4, this may not hold for one or more comparison sets.

Therefore, we suggest using fractional factorial designs for linear models to design comparison sets, as this minimizes the chance that errors will be correlated. Naturally, it may well be that the errors will be correlated; hence, one may wish to test if this is true in a particular application. Another advantage of a fractional factorial approach is that designs are available for such tests. Put simply, if the process underlying choices of the best and worst attribute levels satisfies strict additivity (that is, the utility of each attribute level can be summed to give total utility), a simple OMEP will suffice. If one thinks that additivity may not hold for any reason, this can be tested by using larger designs that estimate all main and two-way interaction effects. One also may be able to do these tests with designs for the independent estimation of main effects in the presence of omitted two-way interactions, but we do not discuss this case.

Fractional factorial designs can be "balanced" or "unbalanced." A balanced design is one in which the levels of each attribute appear equally often and co-appear with the levels of other attributes equally often. This does not imply that all attributes have the same number of levels; it implies only that whatever number of levels each has will appear and co-appear equally often. Equal appearance and co-appearance properties give rise to independence properties because columns representing the attributes/levels must be probabilistically independent. With T the set of profiles in the design, this property means that all 2-level attributes appear equally often, namely $T/2$; all 4-level attributes appear equally often, namely $T/4$; and all 8-level attributes occur equally often, namely $T/8$. They co-occur as follows: 2-level and 4-level ($T/8$); 2-level and 8-level ($T/16$); and 4-level and 8-level ($T/$

32). Similarly, 3-level attributes and 9-level attributes occur T/3 and T/9 times, respectively, and co-occur T/27 times.

Designs that lack the balance in the previous paragraph are "unbalanced." We recommend avoiding unbalanced designs for Case 2 because they lead to some levels occurring more often than others within the *same* attribute, and also lead to correlations with constant terms (in some cases). Correlations with constant terms occur because unbalanced designs typically are constructed in ways that result in one or more levels of particular attributes appearing twice as often, or more than twice as often, as other levels, which leads to correlations with model intercepts. More specifically, unbalanced designs typically are constructed by collapsing levels to accommodate the imbalance. In other words, most fractional factorial designs are based on prime numbers or powers of prime numbers, so the numbers of levels are primes and/or powers of primes, such as 2, 4, 8, 16 or 3, 9, 27. We call such levels "compatible," meaning that they have a common divisor associated with the balance property.

In contrast, to mix incompatible levels, such as 2, 3, 4, 5, one uses designs that accommodate the largest levels (for example, "5"), collapsing some design column levels to accommodate attributes with fewer levels. For example, the $2 \times 3 \times 4 \times 5$ factorial (P=120) requires T to be at least 25. One candidate design is an OMEP or orthogonal latin square from the 5^6 factorial. This design can be used to construct a profile case DCE by (1) collapsing three of the five levels in one of the 5-level design columns to represent one of the levels of the 2-level attribute, using the other two levels in the column to represent the second level; (2) collapsing four of the five levels of a second 5-level design column to accommodate two levels of the 3-level attribute, using the third level to represent the other level; and (3) collapsing two of the five levels of a third 5-level column to accommodate one level of the 4-level attribute, and using the other three levels to represent the remaining three levels of the 5-level column.

This design is unbalanced because one level of a 2-level attribute occurs 3/5, the other 2/5 of the time; two levels of a 3-level attribute occur 2/5, the other level 1/5 of the time; and 3 levels of a 4-level attribute occur 1/5, the other level occurring 2/5 of the time. Co-occurrence also is unbalanced. The choice of levels to collapse is arbitrary, but may matter empirically: estimates for levels appearing relatively infrequently will have larger standard errors. Furthermore, one must adjust (reweight) choice counts to correct for imbalance. Additionally, imbalance may lead to what are known as "demand artifacts," which can occur if the participants "see" that certain levels appear more often and then assume that this occurs because these are levels to be chosen or avoided; the experiment is a test of whether the participant can learn this. Participants also may think of other possible reasons why some levels occur more frequently and change their choices in ways that do not reflect their true decisions. As a result, one should avoid these types of designs if possible.

We now describe two cases: (1) the $2^2 \times 4^3$ air ticket example; and (2) omitting one level of each 4-level air ticket attribute to get a $2^2 \times 3^3$. Attributes and levels are in Table 3.6; the omitted levels of each 4-level attribute are shaded.

Table 3.6 *Example airline ticket profile design with omitted levels*

Attribute	Level 1		Level 2		Level 3		Level 4	
Airline	1	American	2	Continental	3	Delta	4	United
Flying time	5	4 hours	6	5 hours	7	6 hours	8	7 hours
Airfare (round trip)	9	$400	10	$500	11	$600	12	$700
Charge to carry-on a bag	13	$25	14	$50				
In-flight service	15	None	16	Beverages only				

Table 3.7 *OMEP sampled from the 4^5 factorial*

Treatment	col. 1	col. 2	col. 3	col. 4	col. 5
1	0	0	0	0	0
2	0	1	1	2	3
3	0	2	2	3	1
4	0	3	3	1	2
5	1	0	1	1	1
6	1	1	0	3	2
7	1	2	3	2	0
8	1	3	2	0	3
9	2	0	2	2	2
10	2	1	3	0	1
11	2	2	0	1	3
12	2	3	1	3	0
13	3	0	3	3	3
14	3	1	2	1	0
15	3	2	1	0	2
16	3	3	0	2	1

We make both design examples with the same OMEP (Table 3.7) from the 4^5 factorial (P = 1024, T = 16).

Table 3.8 and Table 3.9 are balanced and unbalanced, respectively. In Table 3.8 the levels occur equally often within an attribute. In Table 3.9 six levels of the 3-level attributes occur four times (Continental, United, 5 hours, 7 hours, $500 and $700); the other levels occur eight times (Delta, 6 hours and $600). The 3-level attributes' co-occurrences also are unbalanced; all co-occurrences in Table 3.8 are balanced.

Thus, balanced fractional designs are a straightforward way to design profile case DCEs with reasonable statistical properties (for example, standard errors equal across levels of an attribute). However, it is worth noting that, if attributes differ in numbers of levels, level occurrence will differ by attribute; and one must account for this in analyzing best and worst choices. For example, in Table 3.9 the levels of a 2-level attribute occur *twice as often* as

Table 3.8 *Balanced design from OMEP*

Profile	Airline	Fly time	Fare	Bags	In-flight
1	American	4 hours	$400	$25	None
2	American	5 hours	$500	$50	Bev. only
3	American	6 hours	$600	$50	None
4	American	7 hours	$700	$25	Bev. only
5	Continental	4 hours	$500	$25	None
6	Continental	5 hours	$400	$50	Bev. only
7	Continental	6 hours	$700	$50	None
8	Continental	7 hours	$600	$25	Bev. only
9	Delta	4 hours	$600	$50	Bev. only
10	Delta	5 hours	$700	$25	None
11	Delta	6 hours	$400	$25	Bev. only
12	Delta	7 hours	$500	$50	None
13	United	4 hours	$700	$50	Bev. only
14	United	5 hours	$600	$25	None
15	United	6 hours	$500	$25	Bev. only
16	United	7 hours	$400	$50	None

Table 3.9 *Unbalanced design from OMEP*

Profile	Airline	Fly time	Fare	Bags	In-flight
1	Continental	5 hours	$500	$25	None
2	Continental	6 hours	$600	$50	Bev. only
3	Continental	6 hours	$600	$50	None
4	Continental	7 hours	$700	$25	Bev. only
5	Delta	5 hours	$600	$25	None
6	Delta	6 hours	$500	$50	Bev. only
7	Delta	6 hours	$700	$50	None
8	Delta	7 hours	$600	$25	Bev. only
9	Delta	5 hours	$600	$50	Bev. only
10	Delta	6 hours	$700	$25	None
11	Delta	6 hours	$500	$25	Bev. only
12	Delta	7 hours	$600	$50	None
13	United	5 hours	$700	$50	Bev. only
14	United	6 hours	$600	$25	None
15	United	6 hours	$600	$25	Bev. only
16	United	7 hours	$500	$50	None

levels of a 4-level attribute – that is, 2-level attribute levels are *available* to be chosen twice as often as 4-level attribute levels. Thus, one must weight up 4-level attribute levels or weight down 2-level attribute levels to calculate best and worst counts. Put another way, the opportunity to choose a level of a 2-level attribute is twice that of a 4-level attribute simply because it is available to be chosen twice as often. One reweights choice counts to reflect this; one can do this by dividing choice counts for 2-level attributes in half, as discussed later.

As in Chapter 2, we focus on models for single persons, and emphasize that level of analysis. In this spirit we list a few designs for single persons in Table 3.10 (in which a "*k* levels" column contains numbers of *k*-level attributes), and discuss how to use them to make many more balanced designs. The list in Table 3.10 is merely illustrative and not exhaustive, as many other designs exist.

The design examples in Table 3.10 have been constructed from a smaller set of OMEPs. For example, designs 1, 2 and 5 are all constructed from a 2^7 by omitting the relevant columns from the design. In fact, the smaller set of OMEPs consists of only

- 2^7
- 2^{11}
- 2^{15}
- 3^4
- 3^{13}
- 4^5
- 5^5
- 6×3^6
- 8×4^8

In addition to omitting columns, one can use the above OMEPs to make more designs by recoding levels. For example, each 4-level attribute column can make a 2×2 (2^2); a 6-level column can make a 2×3; an 8-level column can make a 2^3 or a 2×4. So, using the 8×4^8 OMEP as an example, an 8-level design column can make a 2, a 2^2 a 2^3 or even a 2^7 (see design 5 in Table 3.10); each 4-level column can make a 2^2 or a 2^3. Thus, if one wants as many 2-level columns as possible, one can make 31. Table 3.11 is an example of how to recode standard design codes for 4- and 8-level columns into 2- and 4-level columns.

Like Case 1, designs for Case 2 are available from websites, journal articles, catalogs and books. For example, orthogonal arrays can be found on the website of the SAS Institute (see www.sas.com) or Warren Kuhfeld's website (http://support.sas.com/techsup/technote/ts723.html). Case 2 designs differ from designs for traditional DCEs (the BWS multi-profile case). For example, Street and Burgess (2007) discuss using orthogonal arrays as "starting designs" to construct DCEs; Case 2 uses only a starting design.

Table 3.10 *Some example balanced fractional designs*

Design no.	2 levels	3 levels	4 levels	5 levels	6 levels	8 levels	T
1	3						8
2	4						8
3	5						8
4	6						8
5	7						8
6	8						12
7	9						12
8	11						12
9	12						16
10	15						16
1		3					9
12		4					9
13		5					18
14		7					18
15		8					27
16		12					27
17		13					27
18			3				16
19			5				16
20			6				32
21			9				32
22				3			25
23				4			25
24				5			25
25	2		1				8
26	3		1				8
27	4		2				16
28	4		3				16
29	1		4				16
30	2		4				16
31	3		4				16
32	15		4				32
33	2		1			1	32
34	3		2			1	32
35	8		4			1	32
36	12		4			1	32
37	2		6			1	32
38	3		7			1	32
39			8			1	32
40		2			1		18
41		4			1		18
42		5			1		18
43		6			1		18

Table 3.11 *Recoding an 8-level column*

Level	Makes this 4	Makes this 2	Makes this 2	Makes this 2	Makes this 2	Makes this 2
0	0	0	0	0	0	0
1	0	1	0	0	1	1
2	1	0	0	1	0	1
3	1	1	0	1	1	0
4	2	0	1	0	0	1
5	2	1	1	0	1	0
6	3	0	1	1	0	0
7^1	3	1	1	1	1	1

3.2.3 Orthogonal main effects plans

Researchers must decide how many profiles to administer in a profile case DCE. Returning to the dermatology example, one can use OMEPs that produce eight or 16 profiles. Flynn, Louviere, Peters *et al.* (2008) used both designs, randomizing patients to one of them. In principle, the 16-profile OMEP allowed the estimation of some two-way interactions, and recent work suggests gains in statistical efficiency and response surface coverage by choosing a larger subset of profiles T from the full set of profiles P. Coast, Flynn *et al.* (2006) and Louviere *et al.* (2011) provide empirical evidence that such gains pose little additional cost in terms of response rates, response variability or validity.

OMEPs identify and support the estimation of the main effects of each attribute level if the assumption of a strictly additive underlying process holds. If additivity is violated, inability to estimate interactions may be a liability, as one cannot test the IIA property underlying the BWS models. The estimation of all main effects and two-way interactions may require fairly large designs, as we now discuss. A minimum design to estimate all the main effects and two-way interactions requires T to be larger than the degrees of freedom (df) of all the main effects and two-way interactions (if T is only slightly larger than the total degrees of freedom, no design may exist). Table 3.12 gives a few examples that show the potential size of such designs. In most cases, these designs have more choice sets than one person can evaluate.

3.2.4 Recoding to avoid extreme profiles

One should not blindly construct DCEs using fractional factorials. Instead, one should check each profile to see if it makes sense. For example, one may want to avoid treatment combinations containing all bad or all good levels (for example, 0000 or 3333 in the case of a 4^4). A "Find and replace" operation is used to substitute/interchange coded levels to avoid

---

[1] In the case of the 8-level attribute, it can be used to construct a 4×2 or 2^3 factorial, or the following OMEPs: 4×2^2, 4×2^3, 4×2^4, 2^4, 2^5, 2^6, 2^7 (as discussed in section 3.2.4).

Table 3.12 *Degrees of freedom of selected designs*

Design	df for main effects	df for two-way interactions	Total df
2^4	4	6	10
3^4	8	24	32
4^4	12	54	66
2^6	6	15	21
3^6	12	60	72
4^6	18	135	153
2^8	8	28	36
3^8	16	112	128
4^8	24	252	276
2^{10}	10	45	55
3^{10}	20	180	200
4^{10}	30	405	435

Table 3.13 *Profile completion rates*

Profile	Completion rate (%)
Non-extreme	99.2
Worst conceivable profile	90.2
Best conceivable profile	89.4

extreme combinations. Alternatively, the codes in an OMEP (fractional factorial) design (such as 0, 1, 2, 3) do not imply quantitative levels; thus, one does not have to assign levels in numerical or other orders to design codes in a column of an OMEP (or fractional) design. For example, if the levels of a certain attribute are none, some, most and all, one can assign them design codes as follows: 0 = "none," 1 = "some," 2 = "most" and 3 = "all."

However, one need not do this; one can assign them design codes as follows: 0 = "all," 1 = "some," 2 = "none" and 3 = "most"; or 0 = "all," 1 = "most," 2 = "some" and 3 = "none." If levels are categorical and not ordered – for instance, different colors – one can assign levels to design codes arbitrarily as long as the assignment is consistent. In other words, if one assigns "green" to code = 1, then every code = 1 must be "green." Flexibility in assigning levels to design codes allows one to avoid profiles that pose relatively hard choices, such as coding profile "00000" as the worst conceivable quality of life. Table 3.13 shows that completion rates for extreme profiles differed from others in a quality of life study (Coast, Flynn, Natarajan *et al.*, 2008). Therefore, one might be well advised to recode accordingly to avoid such extremes.

To our knowledge, Table 3.13 is the first empirical completion rate result for extreme profiles in a design, so we need more empirical work to generalize these results. We suspect that lower completion rates for extreme profiles reflect difficulty in choosing the best or worst aspects of quality of life in profiles that are uniformly bad or good. Such profiles could (should!) be avoided at the coding stage; for example, Coast, Flynn, Natarajan *et al.* (2008) did *not* have to use 00000 to represent the lowest level of every attribute. It is worth noting that it may not be possible to avoid extreme profiles in all cases, but one at least should try to do so. For example, as there were only four attributes in the dermatology example, recoding [0, 1: hard, easy] to [1, 0: easy, hard] may simply have caused another profile (instead of 0000) to have the worst possible description.

3.2.5 *Higher-resolution designs*

Designs allowing the estimation of interaction effects rarely are used in Case 2 because of the focus on modeling single persons. However, those familiar with traditional multi-profile DCEs will know that such designs exist, but typically are much larger than OMEPs. So, few will be suitable to model individuals. One way to deal with this is to divide the T treatments in the master design into blocks or versions. For example, if a master design has T=256, but it is decided that no one should evaluate more than 16 profiles, one can randomly assign $t_i =$ 1 to 16 versions/blocks by randomly allocating profiles without replacement to each version, such that $T = t_1 + t_2 + \ldots + t_{16}$. It is worth noting that aggregating individuals in this way requires (strong) assumptions about homogeneity and/or distributions of attribute-level scale values etc. that may not be satisfied in empirical applications. Alternatively, one can use an OMEP (or other design) to make a design that has "extra" columns (that is, there are more columns in the design than one needs to make the basic design of interest). One then uses one or more of the orthogonal columns to create blocks. In other words, if the extra column has two levels, one creates two blocks; if it has four levels, one creates four blocks; and so on.

Blocked designs typically are used in traditional multi-profile DCEs if the design required to estimate all parameters of interest has more choice sets than any individual can evaluate. Similar issues apply to Case 2. In particular, one can include some common profiles in all blocks to test scale homogeneity across blocks. One also should test for block or version effects to determine if certain blocks have more (or fewer) best and worst choices of particular levels. Few researchers seem aware that "versions" can impact experimental outcomes, and one always should test this by effects-coding the versions and including them in the model analysis. A related issue is "individualizing DCEs" – common practice in marketing and transport. Again, few seem aware that differences in individual designs are confounded with differences between people. In other words, if each person receives a different design or different block of a design, then one confounds differences in individuals with differences in designs. Good practice suggests that one should include common profiles to allow for between-version and between-people tests of such effects.

3.3 Analysis

The analysis of Case 2 BWS data has strong parallels with that for Case 1 data. Indeed, in many respects, Case 2 can be considered to be a special case of Case 1 in which the objects have some "structure" to them (that is, profiles described by an attribute and level structure). We first discuss the calculation of best-minus-worst scores, then the estimation of regression models. Finally, we discuss data expansion techniques.

3.3.1 Calculating scores

As earlier noted, one must take differences in attribute-level occurrences into account in the analysis of best and worst choices in Case 2. We illustrate this issue with an OMEP from the $2^3 \times 4$ factorial in eight profiles in Table 3.14.

To make the example concrete, we use the OMEP to describe possible carbon trading programs in a new emissions trading market. Attributes and levels are: (1) annual cost increases to households ($200, $400, $600, $800); (2) how to use the revenues from the trades (invest 25 percent in research and development [R&D] on [i] energy-efficient vehicles and [ii] appliances, give 25 percent to [i] the poor and [ii] senior citizens); (3) exempt the transport sector for the first five years (no, yes); and (4) exempt the energy sector for the first five years (no, yes). We replace design codes in Table 3.14 with the corresponding attributes and levels to create the profiles in Table 3.15; we show a hypothetical person's best and worst choices (best aspect of plan; worst aspect of plan).

Table 3.14 *Example OMEP for BWS profile case*

Profile	Attribute 1	Attribute 2	Attribute 3	Attribute 4
1	0	1	0	1
2	0	0	1	0
3	1	1	0	0
4	1	0	1	1
5	2	1	1	0
6	2	0	0	1
7	3	1	1	1
8	3	0	0	0

Table 3.15 *Profiles created by OMEP*

Profile	Attribute 1	Attribute 2	Attribute 3	Attribute 4	Best	Worst
1	$200	Poor/seniors	No	Yes	1($200)	4(yes)
2	$200	R&D	Yes	No	2(R&D)	3(yes)
3	$400	Poor/seniors	No	No	1($400)	3(no)
4	$400	R&D	Yes	Yes	2(R&D)	4(yes)
5	$600	Poor/seniors	Yes	No	2(p/s)	3(yes)
6	$600	R&D	No	Yes	2(R&D)	4(yes)
7	$800	Poor/seniors	Yes	Yes	2(p/s)	1($800)
8	$800	R&D	No	No	2(R&D)	1($800)

Table 3.16 *Best and worst choice counts*

Option no.	Attribute	Level	Best	Worst	Best-worst
1	Increased yearly costs	$200	1	0	1
2	Increased yearly costs	$400	1	0	1
3	Increased yearly costs	$600	0	0	0
4	Increased yearly costs	$800	0	2	−2
5	How to use revenues	R&D	4	0	4
6	How to use revenues	Poor/seniors	2	0	2
7	Exempt transport	No	0	1	−1
8	Exempt transport	Yes	0	2	−2
9	Exempt energy	No	0	0	0
10	Exempt energy	Yes	0	3	−3

As a first approximation, we count how many times each attribute level is chosen as best (respectively, as worst), and subtract the worst count from the best count (see Table 3.16).

Note that the 4+2+2+2 attribute levels have been coded as 1 to 10 in the first column as option numbers. This is done purely for convenience, particularly when aggregating across respondents. It should be noted that "Use revenues for R&D" achieved a score of 4. However, this does not necessarily mean it is valued most; it was available to be picked twice as often as the cost levels (which each only appeared twice across the design). Thus, to properly compare the attributes, normalize them to range between −1 and +1 by dividing each difference by the availability (here = 4 or 2). The normalized difference scores are meaningful measures for individuals.

A useful measure for each individual is his/her sum of squared best-minus-worst scores across attribute levels. In particular, a low total sums of squares indicates a person who is either inconsistent (exhibits high variance) or has weak preferences, or both; high totals suggest the reverse. Thus, examining the distribution of the sum-of-squared scores is useful in characterizing heterogeneity. However, it should be noted that for certain statistical designs the maximum total sums of squares can be achieved when the respondent always chooses a given attribute as best and a (different) given attribute as worst. If this is the case then, depending on context, it may suggest that the person misunderstood the task (he/she ignored the levels).

As for Case 1, the best-worst scores can be used as inputs to clustering analyses, the distribution across the sample can be graphed for each attribute level (its empirical distribution) or other types of more sophisticated statistical analyses can be undertaken.

3.3.2 Limited dependent variable models

As for Case 1, we discuss the use of "traditional" limited dependent variable models (conditional logit and its variants) to demonstrate the links BWS has with traditional

DCEs. Models of sequential choices typically are easier to estimate with available statistical software than maxdiff models. However, it is worth noting that one must code and format data in certain ways to estimate such models correctly. For instance, if one assumes that the value for an object in a worst choice is the negative of its value for a best choice, then one must create sequential sets of choices and reverse-code the choices of best and worst when preparing data for estimation. The data are set up in exactly the same way as for Case 1. Indeed, the nine objects valued in the Sydney transport example used to illustrate Case 1 could have equally been (1) three 3-level attributes or (2) two 2-level attributes and a five-level attribute. Statistical estimation software such as Stata does not "care": there are $n-1$ dummy variables to be estimated (where n is the total number of attribute levels being valued across the study).

Earlier we discussed issues about the process a person might use to make best and worst choices; hence, it is natural to discuss the implications for choices of statistical models. As noted previously, some (appropriate) statistical models of choice processes are not available in commonly used statistical estimation software. For example, Flynn *et al.* (2007; Flynn, Louviere, Peters *et al.*, 2008) and Marley and Louviere (2005) note that prior BWS work assumed that the scale value for the "worst" choice of an object was the negative of the scale value for the "best" choice of that object. To estimate a model consistent with this assumption in Stata, one codes the independent variables similarly to the way described earlier (stacking best and worst choice counts) – that is, sequential best then worst choices can be coded with positive signs for best choices and negative signs for worst choices. However, it is worth noting that this assumption introduces a small error in the likelihood function on account of asymmetry in the (Gumbel) errors, which introduces a very minor bias.

This "small" error is compounded if one analyzes choices using the "marginal" method discussed by Flynn *et al.* (2007), as their approach assumes that best and worst choices are independent, which is not true. Thus, one should use caution with estimation test statistics. A more statistically accurate approach is what we call *the marginal sequential approach*, which allows for the modeling of best, then worst, or worst, then best. The present case explicitly models the best choice from a set of J options, and the worst choice as a choice from the remaining J–1 options; this approach was presented in Chapter 2 to illustrate our analysis of the Sydney transport data. Although the estimator in this approach is more accurate, a minor error introduced by the sign reversal assumption for best and worst choices remains.

The marginal sequential method assumes two conditional logit choices per set, similar to the marginal method given by Flynn *et al.* (2007). However, there is a first (best) choice from J attributes and a second (best) choice from J–1 attributes (best choice eliminated from set two), and the utility of each level is reverse-coded. Otherwise, the estimation details are the same: one estimates a series of conditional logit models.

The paired method of Flynn *et al.* (2007) addresses the incorrect independence assumption and error asymmetry, as it assumes that individuals use a maxdiff process model. However, coding the data for this estimation approach is more complex if one wants to use commonly available software such as Stata. At the time of this writing, more sophisticated analysis for maxdiff models (such as representing differences among people with latent class and related variants in Latent GOLD) is not possible in available software. Experience suggests that estimation errors associated with simpler estimation approaches are sufficiently small that it is hard to justify spending extra time and effort on more complex but slightly more accurate statistical models.

3.3.3 Weighted least squares summary analyses

One can estimate the scale values of the profile levels from the BWS profile choices with conditional logit estimation using maximum likelihood; one also can estimate conditional logit models from BWS choices with WLS regression, as noted by Flynn *et al.* (2007) and Flynn, Louviere, Peters *et al.* (2008). WLS is useful to gain familiarity with choice data, and is the first step of the maximum likelihood estimator using an iteratively reweighted least squares estimation approach (Green, 1984). WLS often produces estimates close to maximum likelihood estimates, therefore, and it is useful for identifying outliers, or attribute levels with large best and large worst choice frequencies.

Analyzing BWS choice data with WLS is discussed by Flynn *et al.* (2007) and Louviere, Street *et al.* (2008). For example, if one is willing to assume that utilities revealed by best choices are the negative of those revealed by worst choices, one can count best and worst choices, respectively, and stack them for analysis. Dummy-code or effects-code attribute levels associated with each best count, reversing the codes for worst. In other words, if the association of a particular level with a best count is coded $+1$, that level's association with a worst count is coded -1. For effects codes, if one codes $L-1$ levels associated with best as 1, and the Lth level uniformly -1, one reverses these codes for worst counts, namely -1 and 1. Table 3.17 illustrates this approach for the carbon trading example data.

For comparison we also use the Louviere, Street *et al.* (2008) approach to weight the rank order of the best-minus-worst counts in Table 3.16 to estimate the mean weight for each level and the mean natural log of the weights (the weight of each cost level × 2). The natural log of the weights is the dependent variable in WLS estimation; the WLS weight is the Louviere weight (Louviere and Woodworth, 1983). The means are OLS estimates of the scale values, and often are close first approximation to the true values. Indeed, one could argue that gains in accuracy/precision from more sophisticated estimation methods rarely are worth it. WLS estimation results and mean estimates are given in Table 3.19.

More specifically, the Louviere, Street *et al.* (2008) approach relies on the fact that if we know the ranking of the alternatives in a choice set, and we use this ranking to infer the implied choices in every possible choice set, we can anticipate the total number of best choices that should be observed over all the possible subsets of choice sets. Put another way, if there are J choice alternatives in a choice set, the total number of possible choice sets is 2^J. This base 2 series arises because an alternative either is or is not present in a choice set; hence, all possible sets are given by a 2^J factorial, in which the "2" refers to in/out of a set. A complete ranking implies that the alternative ranked "1" will be chosen J/2 times (that is,

Table 3.17 *Coding of stacked best and worst counts for levels*

Best/worst	Attribute	Level	Count	$200	$400	$600	$800	R&D	Poor and snrs	Tr no	Tr yes	En no	En yes
Best	Cost	$200	24	1	0	0	0	0	0	0	0	0	0
Best	Cost	$400	24	0	1	0	0	0	0	0	0	0	0
Best	Cost	$600	8	0	0	1	0	0	0	0	0	0	0
Best	Cost	$800	4	0	0	0	1	0	0	0	0	0	0
Best	Invest	R&D	20	0	0	0	0	1	0	0	0	0	0
Best	Invest	P/snrs	32	0	0	0	0	0	1	0	0	0	0
Best	Transport	No	11	0	0	0	0	0	0	1	0	0	0
Best	Transport	Yes	8	0	0	0	0	0	0	0	1	0	0
Best	Energy	No	14	0	0	0	0	0	0	0	0	1	0
Best	Energy	Yes	5	-1	-1	-1	-1	-1	-1	-1	-1	-1	-1
Worst	Cost	$200	6	-1	0	0	0	0	0	0	0	0	0
Worst	Cost	$400	6	0	-1	0	0	0	0	0	0	0	0
Worst	Cost	$600	16	0	0	-1	0	0	0	0	0	0	0
Worst	Cost	$800	32	0	0	0	-1	0	0	0	0	0	0
Worst	Invest	R&D	10	0	0	0	0	-1	0	0	0	0	0
Worst	Invest	P/snrs	4	0	0	0	0	0	-1	0	0	0	0
Worst	Transport	No	16	0	0	0	0	0	0	-1	0	0	0
Worst	Transport	Yes	22	0	0	0	0	0	0	0	-1	0	0
Worst	Energy	No	10	0	0	0	0	0	0	0	0	-1	0
Worst	Energy	Yes	28	1	1	1	1	1	1	1	1	1	1

every time it is "in" a set), the alternative ranked "2" will be chosen J/4 times (every time it is "in" a set that does not contain the alternative ranked "1"), and so forth. Tied rankings lead to the expectation that the total number of choices associated with these rankings will be equally divided among the ties.

The Louviere, Street *et al.* (2008) approach treats the anticipated 2^J choices as expected choice totals for best associated with each alternative in each choice set. This does not imply that individuals are deterministic, because any particular ranking of alternatives in a particular choice set can be subject to error. Thus, the implied choice counts have associated errors. These corresponding choice frequencies are the expected outcomes associated with the well-known Luce (1959) choice model, which is:

$$P(i|C_n) = V_i / \sum_j V_j, \ \forall j \in \text{in } C_n$$

where $P(i|C_n)$ is the probability of choosing alternative i in choice set C_n, V_i is the subjective value associated with alternative i, V_j is the subjective value associated with alternative j and "$\forall j \in \text{in } C_n$" denotes that the summation is computed over all of the j alternatives in the choice set, C_n. If one takes the log-form of the Luce model, namely:

$$Ln[P(i|C_n)] = Ln[V_i / \sum_j V_j]$$

and substitutes the inferred choice frequencies for the choice probabilities, the above expression becomes:

$$Ln(\text{choice frequency}_i) = LnV_i - Ln(K_{C_n})$$

where K_{C_n} is treated as a constant associated with each choice set that is the denominator in the logit model. This model can be estimated using WLS by taking $Ln(\text{choice frequency}_i)$ as the dependent variable and using the choice frequencies as the weight, as noted by Louviere and Woodworth (1983). In the example in Table 3.18 we treat tied ranks from the observed best-minus-worst scores by averaging the implied counts for the tied rank positions.

We summarize these data by simply calculating the means of each of the best-worst-related quantities in Table 3.18, which gives us Table 3.19. Also displayed are the true values (and the log of the true values) that were used to generate the best and worst choice data after assigning uniform random errors ranging between 0 and 1 (random errors above 0.5 are added to the true values; random errors below 0.5 are subtracted from the true value). Table 3.19 is accompanied by graphical comparisons of the mean quantities with the true and log true values, Figures 3.1 and 3.2, respectively. We provide two graphs because we expect the mean (average) of the ranks and the Louviere, Street *et al.* (2008) weights to be linearly related to the true values because we used a model of the Luce (1959) type to generate the choices; the best-minus-worst counts and the log of the Louviere weights should be linearly related to the log of the true values. As can be seen in Figure 3.1 and Figure 3.2, these expectations hold to a close first approximation.

The comparison strongly suggests that one can use several methods to estimate the attribute-level scale values that yield approximately the same statistical information. This result is similar to robustness arguments and empirical comparisons given by Louviere, Street *et al.* (2008). Now consider adding a third BWS choice – namely the attribute level that is the second best choice, as shown in Table 3.20. This gives a full ranking, although, as noted earlier, the implied process is (1) first best, (2) worst, and (3) second best.

3.3.4 More sophisticated analysis

More sophisticated estimation methods can be used to analyze best and worst choices. For example, as shown in Table 3.20, an extra best choice gives a full ranking; one can assign weights to the ranks, as did Louviere, Street *et al.* (2008). The weights are, respectively, rank 1 = 8, rank 2 = 4, rank 3 = 2, rank 4 = 1. Recall that one must account for the fact that the cost levels occur half as often; so, we reweight them by multiplying by two, giving the new calculations for best and worst counts in Table 3.21. We again use the data in Table 3.18, but now add weights to each observation to reflect the fact that the cost levels are available half as often (that is, weight them double). We now estimate two logical

Table 3.18 *Data layout for analyzing BWS data in example*

	Start with this basic data matrix				Calculate these quantities			
Set (Profile)	Attribute	Level	Best	Worst	Best minus worst	Rank	Louv wts	Ln(wts)
1	1	$200	1	0	1	1	8	2.079
1	2	Poor/seniors	0	0	0	2	3	1.099
1	3	No	0	0	0	2	3	1.099
1	4	Yes	0	1	−1	3	1	0.000
2	1	$200	0	0	0	2	3	1.099
2	2	R&D	1	0	1	1	8	2.079
2	3	Yes	0	1	−1	3	1	0.000
2	4	No	0	0	0	2	3	1.099
3	1	$400	1	0	1	1	8	2.079
3	2	Poor/seniors	0	0	0	2	3	1.099
3	3	No	0	1	−1	3	1	0.000
3	4	No	0	0	0	2	3	1.099
4	1	$400	0	0	0	2	3	1.099
4	2	R&D	1	0	1	1	8	2.079
4	3	Yes	0	0	0	2	3	1.099
4	4	Yes	0	1	−1	3	1	0.000
5	1	$600	0	0	0	2	3	1.099
5	2	Poor/seniors	1	0	1	1	8	2.079
5	3	Yes	0	1	−1	3	1	0.000
5	4	No	0	0	0	2	3	1.099
6	1	$600	0	0	0	2	3	1.099
6	2	R&D	1	0	1	1	8	2.079
6	3	No	0	0	0	2	3	1.099
6	4	Yes	0	1	−1	3	1	0.000
7	1	$800	0	1	−1	3	1	0.000
7	2	Poor/seniors	1	0	1	1	8	2.079
7	3	Yes	0	0	0	2	3	1.099
7	4	Yes	0	0	0	2	3	1.099
8	1	$800	0	1	−1	3	1	0.000
8	2	R&D	1	0	1	1	8	2.079
8	3	No	0	0	0	2	3	1.099
8	4	No	0	0	0	2	3	1.099

statistical models from the data: (1) a linear probability model (LPM), which is an OLS regression fit to the best choices (this regression includes dummy variables for each choice set to capture the fact that the denominator of each set is a constant); and (2) a WLS regression fit to the log of the Louviere, Street *et al.* (2008) weights, with the Louviere weights used as the weight. For each regression we use the observation weights as "case weights" to weight the data to correct for present/absence differences in the cost attribute

Table 3.19 *Best and worst choice counts*

Option no.	Attribute	Level	True	Ln (true)	B-W	Avgrank	AvgLouv	Avg Ln (Louvwts)	B-W/ avail	WLS	ROL
1	Cost increases	$200	1.6	0.47	1	1.5	5.5	1.589	0.5	1.82	0.74
2	Cost increases	$400	1.6	0.47	1	1.5	5.5	1.589	0.5	1.86	0.77
3	Cost increases	$600	0.5	−0.69	0	2	3	1.099	0	0.94	−0.16
4	Cost increases	$800	0.3	−1.20	−2	3	1	0.000	−1	−0.30	−1.30
5	Use revenues	R&D	2.1	0.74	4	1	8	2.079	1	2.17	1.09
6	Use revenues	Poor/ snrs	1.3	0.26	2	1.5	5.5	1.589	0.5	1.47	0.38
7	Exempt transport	No	0.7	−0.36	−1	2.25	2.5	0.824	−0.25	0.97	−0.12
8	Exempt transport	Yes	0.5	−0.69	−2	2.5	2	0.550	−0.5	0.63	−0.44
9	Exempt energy	No	0.9	−0.11	0	2	3	1.099	0	1.08	−0.02
10	Exempt energy	Yes	0.3	−1.20	−3	2.75	1.5	0.275	−0.75	0.26	−0.79

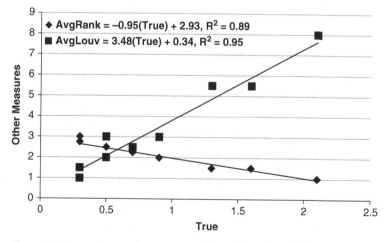

Figure 3.1 True values versus average ranks and Louviere weights

Table 3.20 *Adding extra best (or worst) choice questions*

Profile	Attribute 1	Attribute 2	Attribute 3	Attribute 4	Best	Worst	2nd Best
1	$200	Poor/seniors	No	Yes	1($200)	4(yes)	3(no)
2	$200	R&D	Yes	No	2(R&D)	3(yes)	1($200)
3	$400	Poor/seniors	No	No	1($400)	3(no)	4(no)
4	$400	R&D	Yes	Yes	2(R&D)	4(yes)	1($400)
5	$600	Poor/seniors	Yes	No	2(p/s)	3(yes)	4(no)
6	$600	R&D	No	Yes	2(R&D)	4(yes)	3(no)
7	$800	Poor/seniors	Yes	Yes	2(p/s)	1($800)	3(yes)
8	$800	R&D	No	No	2(R&D)	1($800)	4(no)

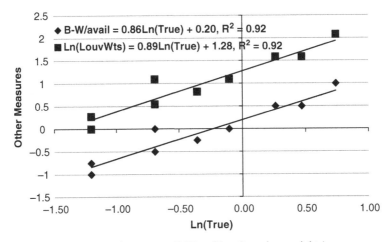

Figure 3.2 Log true values versus B-W and log (Louviere weights)

and the other three attributes of interest. The results of these analyses are shown in Table 3.22 and Figure 3.3.

This section described general issues in designing profile case DCEs, but did not address the issue of how exactly participants should be asked best-worst choice questions. This important issue has implications for the types of psychological choice models that participants may use, and statistical analyses appropriate to their choices. We now turn our attention to these issues.

3.4 Process issues: theory underlying best and worst choices

As discussed in Chapter 2, respondents can use several different psychological processes to make best and worst choices. Ideally, researchers should consider how the format of an

Table 3.21 *Data layout for analyzing BWS data*

	Start with this basic data matrix				Calculate these quantities				
Set (profile)	Attribute	Level	Best	Worst	B–W	Rank	Louv Wts	Ln(Wts)	Weight obs.
1	1	$200	1	0	1	1	8	2.079	2
1	2	Poor/seniors	0	0	0	2	3	1.099	1
1	3	No	0	0	0	2	3	1.099	1
1	4	Yes	0	1	−1	3	1	0.000	1
2	1	$200	0	0	0	2	3	1.099	2
2	2	R&D	1	0	1	1	8	2.079	1
2	3	Yes	0	1	−1	3	1	0.000	1
2	4	No	0	0	0	2	3	1.099	1
3	1	$400	1	0	1	1	8	2.079	2
3	2	Poor/seniors	0	0	0	2	3	1.099	1
3	3	No	0	1	−1	3	1	0.000	1
3	4	No	0	0	0	2	3	1.099	1
4	1	$400	0	0	0	2	3	1.099	2
4	2	R&D	1	0	1	1	8	2.079	1
4	3	Yes	0	0	0	2	3	1.099	1
4	4	Yes	0	1	−1	3	1	0.000	1
5	1	$600	0	0	0	2	3	1.099	2
5	2	Poor/seniors	1	0	1	1	8	2.079	1
5	3	Yes	0	1	−1	3	1	0.000	1
5	4	No	0	0	0	2	3	1.099	1
6	1	$600	0	0	0	2	3	1.099	2
6	2	R&D	1	0	1	1	8	2.079	1
6	3	No	0	0	0	2	3	1.099	1
6	4	Yes	0	1	−1	3	1	0.000	1
7	1	$800	0	1	−1	3	1	0.000	2
7	2	Poor/seniors	1	0	1	1	8	2.079	1
7	3	Yes	0	0	0	2	3	1.099	1
7	4	Yes	0	0	0	2	3	1.099	1
8	1	$800	0	1	−1	3	1	0.000	2
8	2	R&D	1	0	1	1	8	2.079	1
8	3	No	0	0	0	2	3	1.099	1
8	4	No	0	0	0	2	3	1.099	1

interview or survey may rule in or out some of these psychological models. In particular, if one asks questions in certain orders, web-based surveys ensure that a person uses a sequential best-worst choice process (for example, best, then worst) instead of a maxdiff model (simultaneous, independent choice of best and worst).

Marley and Louviere (2005) show that the set of best-minus-worst scores is sufficient for the likelihood of the maxdiff model. However, if that model holds, then the best and worst

Table 3.22 *LPM and WLS models fit to BWS choices*

Level	TRUE	Ln(true)	WLS	LPM
$200	1.6	0.470	1.438	1.370
$400	1.6	0.470	1.599	1.505
$600	0.5	−0.693	0.378	0.581
$800	0.3	−1.204	−0.071	0.004
R&D	2.1	0.742	2.182	2.220
Poor/seniors	1.3	0.262	1.182	1.170
No	0.7	−0.357	0.511	0.499
Yes	0.5	−0.693	0.217	0.293
No	0.9	−0.105	0.535	0.739
Yes	0.3	−1.204	−0.113	−0.048

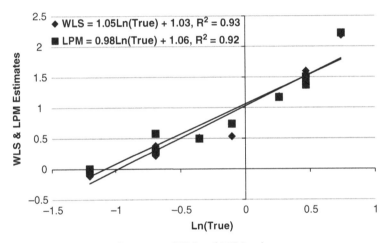

Figure 3.3 Log true values versus WLS and LPM estimates

scores and their differences are biased estimates of the true best and worst scale values. Normalized scores are calculated by dividing the (best and worst) choice counts by their availability (the total number of times that attribute level was available to be picked across the whole study). These are frequencies in the interval [−1, 1], and are also a weighted function of the differences between the estimated (marginal) best and worst choice probabilities when the data are fit by the maxdiff model (Flynn and Marley, 2014). It is obvious that such normalized scores are biased estimates of the true best and worst scale values, as their range is (−1, +1) and that of the scales is (−∞, ∞). On the other hand, *empirically*, the set of (normalized or not) score differences has been found to be highly correlated with the true scale values, as shown in the Sydney transport example.

Alternatively, one can write special-purpose estimation code in Matlab, Gauss or other software to maximize the likelihood of a model given the observed choice data. One also can estimate the parameters of this model using conditional logistic regression in readily available software, such as Stata. For example, Flynn *et al.* (2007) show how to estimate parameters using a pairwise expansion of the data for simultaneous best and worst choices.

Most estimation approaches for Case 2 assume that scale values for worst are the negative of scale values for best. One can relax this assumption, and it is an empirical issue whether a more general model fits the data better. For example, it may be that in Case 2 certain attribute levels represent a "total no-go," in that they do not influence the choice of best but, if present, they are chosen as worst because they make a profile totally unacceptable (Chapter 6 discusses such issues).

A sequential best-worst choice process may be more realistic for web-based or interviewer-administered or -assisted surveys in which participants choose in a particular order. BWS represents a partial ranking, so response data can be treated as a ranking with missing (or tied) middle ranks. Several sequential choice or ranking models will often fit an observed set of best-worst choices equally well, though most such models cannot be estimated with available statistical software packages.

Much of the exposition thus far has close parallels with that for Case 1. Apart from the need for the items under consideration to comprise a meaningful "profile," Case 2 methods of analysis are the same as those for Case 1. However, the *structure* inherent in Case 2, namely attributes with associated levels, introduces some new conceptual issues. These are issues that are vitally important when implementing certain analyses common to disciplines such as marketing and health economics, yet they have received little attention other than in the mathematical psychology literature. We discuss them in the next section.

3.5 Attribute impact versus attribute importance

Attribute-level parameters estimated in traditional DCEs confound the importance or weight of an attribute with the underlying latent measurement scale; the analogous result is well known in utility theory (Keeney and Raiffa, 1976; Anderson, 1970; Lynch, 1985; Louviere, 1988a). We find it somewhat surprising that few choice modeling researchers seem aware of this confounding effect; we therefore provide a brief overview of the details so that researchers can become more aware of the issue.

The importance or "weight" of an attribute in a person's choice (1) may be constant across an attribute's range, implying it is independent of the levels, or (2) may vary systematically with its levels. Anderson (1970; 1982) discusses these distinctions and Shanteau (1980) provides a more general discussion of attribute importance or weight; Marley, Flynn and Louviere (2008, sect. 6) give further discussion. Notions of attribute weight or importance are widespread in everyday life, and are exemplified by numerous "weighting schemes" used to compute overall indices, such as "attractiveness" or "utility," as in restaurant or wine quality ratings.

Attribute weights are *not* the same as attribute-level scale values. A scale value is the estimated position of an attribute level on an underlying latent dimension such as "utility." Many psychologists or social scientists measure weights and scale values independently, using some (integration) rule or function (such as an indirect utility specification) to combine them (Fishbein and Ajzen, 1975). Although widely used, the measures must satisfy certain mathematical operations to be valid. For example, if one asks people to rate several aspects of an environmental issue, and then one combines the ratings into an "overall attitude" towards the issue, the combination or "scoring" rule must satisfy the mathematical operations of addition, subtraction, multiplication and division to be sensible and valid. Often it is hard to see how this could be true.

For example, rating scales at the very best produce interval scales, the latter being measures such as the Fahrenheit temperature scale, with an arbitrary zero (scale origin) and unit; ratios of temperature difference are meaningful, but ratios of temperatures are not. So, a statement such as "It's twice as hot today as yesterday" is meaningless in measurement terms, even if it conveys meaning to another person. Therefore, if one has an attitude measure on two rating scales, say a_1 and a_2, and one wants to combine them with a "weighting function" into a new quantity such as "overall attitude," say $0.3a_1 + 0.7a_2$, we can determine if it is mathematically meaningful to do this. If a_1 and a_2 are measured on different interval scales, we can re-express them as $a_1^* = b_0 + b_1a_1$ and $a_2^* = c_0 + c_1a_2$, where b_0 and c_0 are arbitrary scale origins, and b_1 and c_1 are arbitrary measurement units – that is, a_1^* and a_2^* are linear transformations of a_1 and a_2, respectively (a valid operator for interval scales). Now, substituting expressions for a_1^* and a_2^* in the "weighting function," we have overall attitude = $0.3[b_0 + b_1a_1] + 0.7[c_0 + c_1a_2]$, which equals $0.3b_0 + 0.3b_1a_1 + 0.7c_0 + 0.7c_1a_2$, or = $(0.3b_0 + 0.7c_0) + 0.3b_1a_1 + 0.7c_1a_2$. While mathematically consistent, this result may not be what is intended.

Formalizing the above example, continue to assume that a_1 and a_2 are measured on different interval scales, and suppose that the weights in the "weighting function," say w_1 and w_2, are measured on an interval scale; hence, equivalent weights are w_1^* and w_2^*, linear transformations of w_1 and w_2. Substituting such linear terms in the weighting function gives $(p_0 + p_1 w_1)(b_0 + b_1a_1) + (q_0 + q_1)(c_0 + c_1 a_2)$. It now should be obvious that this makes no logical or mathematical sense. It would be best for the social and business sciences (not to mention medicine and engineering!) if practitioners stopped doing things such as this, because they cannot produce valid results except by accident; worse yet, one is likely to make seriously incorrect decisions using such "weighting schemes."

As an example that "works," consider choices of doctor appointments described by three attributes (appointment length, choice of doctor, location) that are measured on different interval scales,[2] each with two levels in the design. Suppose one wants to use an (additive) averaging rule to combine the attributes into an index of utility for doctor appointments such that each attribute has a weight that multiplies the scale values of each attribute level, and the utility index is a sum of the resulting products. For this rule to be mathematically meaningful,

---

[2] This might not be a very good assumption for the stated attributes, but it is satisfactory for illustrative purposes.

each weight must be measured on a ratio (or absolute) scale. Thus, for a linear averaging model, one might have the following overall index as a function of the three attributes:

$$U = w\_length * sc\_length + w\_dr * sc\_dr + w\_loc * sc\_loc \qquad (3.1)$$

where w_length, w_dr and w_loc are weights for length of consultation, choice of doctor and location, respectively; sc_length, sc_dr and sc_loc are scale values for each attribute, defined as:

$$sc\_length = \alpha_{length} + \beta_{length} * length\_level$$

$$sc\_dr = \alpha_{dr} + \beta_{dr} * dr\_level$$

$$sc\_loc = \alpha_{loc} + \beta_{loc} * loc\_level$$

If each attribute has two levels (low, high), the full factorial design has eight possible appointments (2^3 combinations of attributes and levels). Suppose scale values and weights for each attribute have the values in Table 3.23. Substituting the values and attribute levels for each of the eight appointments into Equation (3.1) produces the (hypothetical) total appointment utilities in Table 3.24.

The weight and scale associated with each attribute are known in this example, but if utilities are estimated from DCE choices one can only estimate a constant (= 0.68, representing the utility of an appointment defined by the lowest level of the attributes) and the

Table 3.23 *Scale value parameters and attribute weights*

Attribute				
	α	β_{low}	β_{high}	Weight
Appointment length	0.1	0.2	0.9	Weight_length: 0.2
Doctor	0.5	0.4	0.5	Weight_doctor: 0.3
Location	0.3	0.4	0.7	Weight_locate: 0.5

Table 3.24 *Utilities of attribute levels and appointments*

Appointment number	Length	Doctor	Location	Total appointment utility
1	0.06	0.27	0.35	0.68
2	0.06	0.27	0.50	0.83
3	0.06	0.30	0.35	0.71
4	0.06	0.30	0.50	0.86
5	0.20	0.27	0.35	0.82
6	0.20	0.27	0.50	0.97
7	0.20	0.30	0.35	0.85
8	0.20	0.30	0.50	1.00

utility difference of the two levels of each attribute. In the example, these are 0.14 for length (that is, 0.20–0.06); 0.03 for choice of doctor; and 0.15 for location. In other words, one cannot estimate separate weights and scale values. This is true in general for all axiomatic utility or conjoint elicitation procedures that involve a single task; the situation might be different if one has two or more different tasks using the same options (Marley, Flynn and Louviere, 2008, sect. 6).

An important consequence of this weight-scale confound is that the "effect" (or lack thereof) of an attribute across its levels in a DCE or conjoint preference elicitation exercise may be due to a large (small) weight relative to other attributes, or large (small) scale value differences associated with its levels, or a combination of both. Indeed, this applies to our example, as "large" utility differences in the levels of appointment length and location differ because the former has a relatively large scale difference, while the latter has a relatively large weight.

One cannot determine which case obtains in a DCE without extra information. Moreover, because of the attribute importance and scale value confound, one must be careful about making inter-dimensional utility comparisons, because these combine attribute importance and scale values.

For example, Flynn *et al.* (2007) note that Case 2 gives more insights into attribute/level utilities than conventional DCEs. Using our appointment example, the utility of the worst possible appointment (0.68) can be partly decomposed into constituent parts of 0.06, 0.27 and 0.35. Case 2 gives the additional utility of two levels compared with the third level, such as 0.21 and 0.29 (relative to 0.06). This allows one to estimate relative attribute impact, which we define to be the mean utility of an attribute across all its levels. Note that attribute impact is not equal to attribute importance; in particular, Marley, Flynn and Louviere (2008) show that importance weights are unrecoverable, except, as we now discuss, possibly in certain circumstances. Nonetheless, the concept may be useful to policy-makers.

Marley, Flynn and Louviere (2008) discuss how one might use BWS to estimate attribute importance weights. They conclude that one possible way to do this is to repeat a BWS task in different contexts when one expects that the importance of an attribute is likely to differ. An example they discuss is buying an air ticket for business or pleasure; it may be (conceptually) that the attribute-level scale values are identical in both contexts, but the attribute importance (for example, importance of fare, number of stops) likely differs. They note that asking a person to repeat a BWS task for both contexts (business, pleasure) allows one to separate attribute importance for business and pleasure (in principle).

3.6 Future research issues

3.6.1 Testing violations of assumptions: IIA

Conceptually, an interaction exists if the utility of one attribute level depends on another attribute level (or combination of other attribute levels). In Case 2, interactions are violations of the IIA property of Luce-type (1959) choice models – that is, profile case models assume additively separable utilities, and interactions violate that assumption. To test this property in Case 2 one must use designs that allow the independent estimation of all main effects and two-way interactions, or use what are called "availability designs" (Anderson and Wiley, 1992). We discuss such designs in the next section.

Designs for estimating main effects and two-way interactions allow the estimation of between-attribute-level interactions. If such interactions exist then, if attribute 1 is at – say – level 1 and attribute 2 is at – say – level 3, effects are sub- or super-additive, violating scale value addition. Availability designs assign some codes in a design column to attribute levels; the remaining codes are assigned to "not shown" (not available). If they are "not shown," no level is presented. Interactions are the effects of showing/not showing levels of one attribute on level choices of another attribute. Interactions violate additive separability, as they imply that estimates of attribute levels depend on what is shown/not shown, violating IIA. Those familiar with discrete choice models will recognize that this is similar to IIA tests for DCEs given by Louviere and Woodworth (1983). We provide no examples of availability designs nor discuss them further, because (1) they have not been used in Case 2 and (2) they create partial profiles that may create unintended demand effects. So, the role of availability designs in Case 2 should be considered to be a future research topic, but one should be cautious, because they create tasks in which the numbers of attributes per profile differ, requiring an "explanation" as to why this occurs.

For ease of exposition we return to the three 2-level attributes appointment example, reproducing the full factorial below. Table 3.25 shows that the factorial can be divided into two statistically equivalent OMEPs, each with four profiles (one with a gray background, the other with white). For each OMEP and the factorial, Table 3.26 shows mean weighted counts from the Louviere, Street *et al.* (2008) approach and the mean of the natural log of those counts. The estimates are identical for both OMEPs; therefore, the profile composition did not impact the outcomes, and IIA is satisfied.

Table 3.25 *Full factorial and two OMEPS with best and worst*

Appointment number	Length	Doctor	Location	Best	Worst
1	Tomorrow	Own GP	Nearby	Tomorrow	Nearby
2	Tomorrow	Own GP	Travel 1 hour	Tomorrow	1 hour
3	Tomorrow	Clinic	Nearby	Tomorrow	Clinic
4	Tomorrow	Clinic	Travel 1 hour	Tomorrow	1 hour
5	4 weeks	Own GP	Nearby	Own GP	4 weeks
6	4 weeks	Own GP	Travel 1 hour	Own GP	4 weeks
7	4 weeks	Clinic	Nearby	Nearby	4 weeks
8	4 weeks	Clinic	Travel 1 hour	Clinic	4 weeks

Table 3.26 *Choice counts for OMEPs and factorial*

Level	OMEP 1 (mean counts)		OMEP 2 (mean counts)		Both OMEPS (mean counts)	
	Wtd count	Ln(wtd count)	Wtd count	Ln(wtd count)	Wtd count	Ln(wtd count)
4 weeks	1.000	0.000	1.000	0.000	1.000	0.000
Clinic	2.000	0.693	2.500	0.693	2.250	0.693
Nearby	2.500	0.693	2.000	0.693	2.250	0.693
Own GP	3.000	1.040	3.000	1.040	3.000	1.040
Tomorrow	4.000	1.386	4.000	1.386	4.000	1.386
Travel 1 hour	1.500	0.347	1.500	0.347	1.500	0.347

3.6.2 Combining profile case choices with choices from other choice tasks

One may want to combine/compare results from profile case tasks with other choices, which is related to combining and comparing different sources of choice data; this topic is discussed by Swait and Louviere (1993), Hensher, Louviere and Swait (1998) and Louviere, Hensher and Swait (2000, chaps. 8, 13). Put another way, Case 2 is a type of DCE that produces choice data for attribute levels, not profiles. As discussed earlier in this chapter, attribute levels are mapped onto a common ratio or interval scale depending on how one analyzes/models the choices. The latter property of profile case scale value estimates is unique, because they do not require a common numeraire to be compared. Combining profile case choices with data from other types of DCEs remains a research opportunity, and, as of this writing, is unresolved.

Turning to a specific example, consider carbon trading profiles described by five attributes with extra choice information from repeated BWS questions. We use an OMEP from the 2^5 factorial to produce eight profiles. A person also is asked if he/she would vote for the plan in a binding referendum (yes, no), as shown in Table 3.27.

We show the BWS choice counts in Table 3.28; the repeated BWS choices allow us to use the Louviere, Street *et al.* (2008) weighting approach to calculate the square root of the ratio of best choices to worst choices. As Chapter 1 notes, this ratio should be proportional to best choices, and each attribute level is on a ratio scale.

The binary vote responses are insufficient for maximum likelihood estimation, so we use a linear probability model (ordinary least squares estimation applied to the 0, 1 choice indicator dependent variable) (Table 3.29) to illustrate how one might compare estimates (Heckman and Snyder, 1997). Typically, one has more choice data and can estimate a choice model using maximum likelihood. We use the estimated cost effect to convert other attributes to dollar units, as follows: start date ($297.62), investment ($297.62), transport ($297.62) and energy ($892.85). Using the BW differences, the implied cost slope is −0.05, which gives the following implied dollar differences for the attribute levels: start date ($200), investment ($200), transport ($280) and energy ($560). Thus, estimates from both procedures are reasonably monotonic.

Table 3.27 *Carbon trading example with repeated BWS choices and vote*

	Attribute no.					Repeated BWS choices				
	1	2	3	4	5					
Profile	Cost	Start date	Invest	Transport	Energy	Best 1	Best 2	Worst 2	Worst 1	Vote
1	$200	2010	R&D	No	Yes	1(R&D)	2(2010)	4(no)	5(yes)	no
2	$200	2010	Poor	Yes	No	1($200)	3(poor)	5(2010)	4(yes)	no
3	$200	2015	R&D	Yes	No	3(R&D)	1($200)	2(2015)	4(yes)	yes
4	$200	2015	Poor	No	Yes	1($200)	3(poor)	2(2015)	5(yes)	no
5	$800	2010	R&D	No	No	3(R&D)	2(2010)	5(no)	1($800)	yes
6	$800	2010	Poor	Yes	Yes	3(poor)	2(2010)	1($800)	5(yes)	no
7	$800	2015	R&D	Yes	Yes	3(R&D)	1($800)	4(yes)	5(yes)	yes
8	$800	2015	Poor	No	No	3(poor)	5(no)	2(2015)	1($800)	yes

Table 3.28 *Counts totals for BWS carbon example*

Level	Best 1	Best 2	Worst 2	Worst 1	Best sum	Worst sum	BW/diff	Sqrt(B/W)
$200	2	1	0	0	20	4	16	2.236
$800	0	1	1	2	8	22	−14	0.603
2010	0	3	1	0	14	10	4	1.183
2015	0	0	3	0	6	12	−6	0.707
R&D	4	0	0	0	32	4	28	2.828
Poor	2	2	0	0	24	6	18	2.000
Tr – no	0	0	1	0	2	4	−2	0.707
Tr – yes	0	0	1	2	4	20	−16	0.447
En – no	0	1	1	0	6	6	0	1.000
En – yes	0	0	0	4	4	32	−28	0.354

Table 3.29 *Linear probability model for vote response*

Effect	Estimate	Std. error	T-stat	P(T)
Constant	0.83333	.125	5.000	0.038
Cost	−0.00042	.125	−1.000	0.423
Start date	−0.12500	.125	−1.000	0.423
Investment	−0.12500	.125	−1.000	0.423
Exempt transport	−0.12500	.125	−1.000	0.423
Exempt energy	−0.37500	.125	−3.000	0.095

More generally, many DCEs include a numeraire (often money) that is used to convert all utility estimates to a common metric that is more meaningful to managers or policy-makers. Including a clearly "bad" attribute with several (assumed) "good" attributes to describe a product or service poses no issues for traditional DCEs. In other words, people must trade differences in money for differences in positive attributes. Case 2 potentially poses a problem because people no longer trade money or other numeraires for other attributes. There is no problem if all people make the same qualitative decision regarding "what money represents" compared to other attributes. However, this is unlikely, because some people may consider the price of a particular car as best because it represents "good value for money" but others might consider it worst as they have to give it up to get a car.

Nonetheless, numeraires are not needed in profile case DCEs when all the attribute levels are measured on a common scale, as is the case, for instance, when the maxdiff model holds (Marley, Flynn and Louviere, 2008). So, in such cases, no transformation is needed to equate attribute levels and permit inter-dimensional utility comparisons. However, it is worth noting that one still cannot estimate attribute weight or importance (as opposed to impact), but this is true for all choice experiments.

3.7 Conclusions

We introduced the BWS profile case, illustrating a number of conceptual and empirical issues. Many of the analysis issues are simple extensions of those for Case 1 of BWS: the best-minus-worst scores can be calculated easily in a spreadsheet and perform well empirically, though not all of their mathematical properties have yet been formally established. The profile nature of a Case 2 task differentiates Case 2 from Case 1 (hence the name "profile case"), but the possibility of dealing with Case 2 data in a Case 1 framework has been raised.

We discussed issues specific to Case 2, such as the ability to estimate attribute impact and the ability to estimate all levels for all attributes on a common scale. Future work should seek to establish under what circumstances such estimates differ from those from a traditional DCE. We next introduce the type of BWS that is an extension of a traditional DCE, namely the multi-profile case (Case 3).

Chapter 4

The BWS multi-profile case

The corruption of the best things gives rise to the worst.
David Hume (1711–1776) *(1889 [1757], sect. 10, 339)*

4.1 Introduction

This chapter describes and discusses the final BWS case (Case 3), which is the multi-profile case. This case is closely related to the literature on discrete choice experiments, with two key differences: (1) the response task associated with DCEs for this case is a choice of the best and the worst profile (and/or choices of the best and the worst profile plus second-best, second-worst, etc.); and (2) an emphasis on individual-level analysis. The plan of the chapter is as follows: we briefly review traditional DCE literature to provide some familiarity with this stream of research; we then show how Case 3 models logically extend prior work, and discuss departures noted above; we next describe, discuss and illustrate Case 3 design, implementation and analysis; and conclude with unresolved issues and future research opportunities.

DCEs are not new; the method of paired comparisons was formalized by Thurstone (1927). DCE developments since 1980 (1) concern multiple and paired choices, (2) rely on random-utility-theory-based probabilistic discrete choice models developed after 1970 (for example, McFadden, 1974), and (3) typically are constructed using principles from the design of statistical experiments. The latter stream of work was initiated by Louviere and Woodworth (1983), who pioneered a way to design multiple choice experiments consistent with McFadden's (1974) conditional logit model and more general models such as "mother logit" (McFadden, Train and Tye, 1978). Prior to Louviere and Woodworth (1983) there was little work on designed experiments for multiple choices, and researchers often used ad hoc combinations of pairs, triples, quadruples, etc. as choice experiments. Louviere and Woodworth provided a systematic way to design DCEs based on ideas from the design of statistical experiments. The focus in this chapter continues this tradition, and we describe and discuss relevant new developments when appropriate.

Recent reviews of DCE literature include those by Louviere, Hensher and Swait (2000), Louviere (2001), Louviere and Street (2000), Louviere, Street and Burgess (2003), Street, Burgess and Louviere (2005), Burgess *et al.* (2006), Street *et al.* (2008), Street and Burgess

(2007), Louviere and Lancsar (2009) and Rose and Bliemer (2009). Thus, there is no need to review what is already well known and well worn, so we give only brief details when they are relevant. As in prior chapters, we also minimize formalization so as to allow the widest possible access to the material.

As noted, Case 3 extends recent DCE design and modeling work to allow for best and worst choices. Like Cases 1 and 2, individuals face multiple choice options. Unlike Case 1, but like Case 2, choice options are described by attributes and associated levels. Unlike both Case 1 and Case 2, Case 3 DCEs can be classified as follows.

- Comparison (or choice) sets contain three or more profiles; each profile is described by a common set of attributes and levels as in Case 2. Therefore, choices are "generic," in the sense that profiles are choice options, and profiles are specific members of a general class. Profiles typically (but not always) differ from set to set. One typically decomposes choices into separate effects, such as main effects and (possibly) interactions of attributes and levels.
- Choice options also can be "objects," as in Case 1, and the objects have "names." For example, in marketing applications, names might be brands; in transport applications, names might be transport modes. Thus, one focuses on choices of specific members of a general class, and attributes and associated levels may or may not be common to all names offered for choice. For example, in mode choice applications in transport, petrol (gasoline) prices might apply only to private vehicle options, and fares might apply only to public transport options; but travel time might apply to both options. In this case, we say that such choices are not generic but are "alternative-specific." To date, Case 3 (best-worst) research has focused on the generic case.

The generic case relies on indirect utility functions that share a common set of terms or parameters for all options; the alternative-specific case relies on indirect utility functions in which one or more parameters and/or attributes/levels differ across choice options. For example, an indirect utility function for a private automobile may have parameters for the attributes of petrol cost, parking cost and travel time; an indirect utility function for public bus may have parameters for the attributes of fare, service frequency and travel time. It may or may not be the case that the travel time parameter is the same for automobile and bus. If it is the same, we say that the effect of travel time is "generic"; if it differs, we say that it is alternative-specific.

We focus on generic DCEs in this chapter, but note that, in principle, the basic ideas generalize to alternative-specific problems. To illustrate this, we later discuss an alternative-specific problem, and discuss how one might approach it in Case 3.

4.2 Design of BWS multi-profile experiments

Unlike Cases 1 and 2, there are many possible ways to design DCEs consistent with Case 3. To keep things as simple as possible, we focus on two design approaches: (1) using BIBDs to construct choice sets of three or more named things; and (2) using a Street and Burgess (2007) approach, or a similar optimal design approach, to design optimally efficient DCEs to test the null hypothesis that all the parameters of a generic indirect utility function in a conditional logit choice model are zero (not significant). While the second approach may sound restrictive, Street and Burgess note that, even if the null is false, such designs have good efficiency properties for a wide range of possible indirect utility function parameter values. Our empirical experience in using these designs for hundreds of applications since 2000 is that they produce accurate estimates of an assumed additive indirect utility function, and the model parameter estimates in turn produce highly accurate predictions of observed choice proportions (estimates of choice probabilities) in and out of the sample. However, as the literature cited above suggests, there is much ongoing work on the design of Case 3 DCEs, and there are several ways to design a DCE for Case 3 that one might consider.

4.2.1 BIBD example

We begin with an example BIBD application for two reasons: (1) BIBDs were previously discussed and illustrated in Chapter 2, and (2) designing a DCE with a BIBD is relatively straightforward, and so likely to interest many applied researchers. The steps required for this are common to all Case 3 applications.

(1) One must develop a list of suitable attributes and levels. As in prior chapters, we assume that one does this in an appropriate way (for example, with qualitative work, discussions with consumers/policy-makers); if not done appropriately, one is likely to get incorrect, or at least not particularly meaningful, results.

(2) Once a list of attributes and associated levels has been developed, in order to be able to estimate individual-level models, one uses a suitable design to (1) make profiles that describe competing choice options, and (2) assign the profiles to choice sets in such a way that the following two assumptions can be tested: that indirect utility functions are strictly additive and that underlying choice processes are well approximated by conditional logit models.

(3) One uses a "find and replace" operator to translate the design codes into the attributes and levels.

(4) One lays out choice sets and formats a response task in a suitable way; the response task is some variant of a Case 3 task.

(5) One recruits a suitable sample of experimental participants and administers the DCE to the participants to obtain best and worst choices (including more than one round of best and worst choices if desired and/or practical).

(6) One analyzes the best and worst choices in a suitable manner.

We use delivered pizza products to illustrate the approach; four 4-level attributes and two 2-level attributes are shown in Table 4.1.

Table 4.1 *Attributes/levels for delivered pizza example*

Attribute	Level 0	Level 1	Level 2	Level 3
Brand	Dominos	Eagle Boys	Pizza Haven	Pizza Hut
Price	$12	$14	$16	$18
Number of toppings	1	2	3	4
Delivery time	10 mins.	20 mins.	30 mins.	40 mins.
Free Coke/Pepsi	No	Yes		
Free dessert	No	Yes		

Table 4.2 *16 treatment OMEP from the $4^4 \times 2^2$ factorial*

Treatment	Column 1	Column 2	Column 3	Column 4	Column 5	Column 6
1	0	3	0	3	0	1
2	0	2	1	1	1	0
3	0	1	2	0	0	0
4	0	0	3	2	1	1
5	1	3	1	2	0	0
6	1	2	0	0	1	1
7	1	1	3	1	0	1
8	1	0	2	3	1	0
9	2	3	2	1	1	1
10	2	2	3	3	0	0
11	2	1	0	2	1	0
12	2	0	1	0	0	1
13	3	3	3	0	1	0
14	3	2	2	2	0	1
15	3	1	1	3	1	1
16	3	0	0	1	0	0

There are two steps in constructing a design. First, one needs a "starting" design with the appropriate statistical properties – in this case an orthogonal main effects plan. Second, one needs another design that tells us how to use the profiles from the OMEP to construct the choice sets (that is, the second design provides a way to *assign* profiles to choice sets). The first step, to create the starting design, is exactly the same as that for Case 2. We use an OMEP from the $4^4 \times 2^2$ factorial in 16 treatments to do this (Table 4.2).

A find and replace operation produces the pizzas in Table 4.3.

The second step, putting subsets of these 16 pizzas (profiles) into choice sets, uses a suitable BIBD to make the choice sets, as shown in Table 4.4. It has 20 blocks (choice sets). Each choice set has four choice options. Each option occurs five times and co-occurs once with once each other option.

Table 4.3 *Translating design codes to profiles*

Profile	Brand	Price	Toppings	Delivery time	Coke/Pepsi	Dessert
1	Dominos	$18	1 topping	40 mins	No	Yes
2	Dominos	$16	2 toppings	20 mins	Yes	No
3	Dominos	$14	3 toppings	10 mins	No	No
4	Dominos	$142	4 toppings	30 mins	Yes	Yes
5	Eagle Boys	$18	2 toppings	30 mins	No	No
6	Eagle Boys	$16	1 topping	10 mins	Yes	Yes
7	Eagle Boys	$14	4 toppings	20 mins	No	Yes
8	Eagle Boys	$142	3 toppings	40 mins	Yes	No
9	Pizza Haven	$18	3 toppings	20 mins	Yes	Yes
10	Pizza Haven	$16	4 toppings	40 mins	No	No
11	Pizza Haven	$14	1 topping	30 mins	Yes	No
12	Pizza Haven	$142	2 toppings	10 mins	No	Yes
13	Pizza Hut	$18	4 toppings	10 mins	Yes	No
14	Pizza Hut	$16	3 toppings	30 mins	No	Yes
15	Pizza Hut	$14	2 toppings	40 mins	Yes	Yes
16	Pizza Hut	$142	1 topping	20 mins	No	No

Table 4.4 *BIBD for 20 choice sets, four options per set*

Set	4 options in each choice set			
1	2	5	8	14
2	1	5	6	7
3	5	9	12	16
4	4	5	11	15
5	3	5	10	13
6	1	2	3	4
7	2	6	9	11
8	2	7	13	16
9	2	10	12	15
10	1	8	9	10
11	6	8	13	15
12	4	7	8	12
13	3	8	11	16
14	1	14	15	16
15	3	6	12	14
16	7	10	11	14
17	4	9	13	14
18	1	11	12	13
19	4	6	10	16
20	3	7	9	15

Table 4.5 *Translating profiles into choice sets with a BIBD*

Choice set 1	Profiles (choice options)			
attribute	2	5	8	14
Brand	Dominos	Eagle Boys	Eagle Boys	Pizza Hut
Price	$16	$18	$142	$16
Number of toppings	2 toppings	2 toppings	3 toppings	3 toppings
Delivery time	20 mins.	30 mins.	40 mins.	30 mins.
Free Coke/Pepsi	Yes	No	Yes	No
Free dessert	No	No	No	Yes
Choice set 2	Profiles (choice options)			
attribute	1	5	6	7
Brand	Dominos	Eagle Boys	Eagle Boys	Eagle Boys
Price	$18	$18	$16	$14
Number of toppings	1 topping	2 toppings	1 topping	4 toppings
Delivery time	40 mins.	30 mins.	10 mins.	20 mins.
Free Coke/Pepsi	No	No	Yes	No
Free dessert	Yes	No	Yes	Yes
Choice set 20	Profiles (choice options)			
attribute	3	7	9	15
Brand	Dominos	Eagle Boys	Pizza Haven	Pizza Hut
Price	$14	$14	$18 •	$14
Number of toppings	3 toppings	4 toppings	3 toppings	2 toppings
Delivery time	10 mins.	20 mins.	20 mins.	40 mins.
Free Coke/Pepsi	No	No	Yes	Yes
Free dessert	No	Yes	Yes	Yes

Table 4.4 lists the four options (pizzas) that appear in each of the 20 sets. Each pizza is represented by the code (1 to 16) used in Table 4.3. We show the first two and last one of the choice sets in Table 4.5.

After assigning profiles to choice sets, one lays out and formats the choice sets as a Case 3 best and worst choice task, as illustrated in Table 4.6.

Next one implements the task as a survey, which typically includes other questions, as noted in previous chapters. For example, one can program the survey with special-purpose web survey software and administer it over the web, using a panel provider. This automates the collection of choice response data, and produces a data file, eliminating human error in coding and data collection/reporting. Our experience is that such errors account for between 5 percent and 25 percent of data errors, so automating the design, task formatting and

Table 4.6 *One way to format choice sets and BWS questions*

Scenario 1	Options you can choose			
Pizza features	A	B	C	D
Brand	Dominos	Eagle Boys	Eagle Boys	Pizza Hut
Price	$16	$18	$142	$16
Number of toppings	2 toppings	2 toppings	3 toppings	3 toppings
Delivery time	20 mins.	30 mins.	40 mins.	30 mins.
Free Coke/Pepsi	Yes	No	Yes	No
Free dessert	No	No	No	Yes
(1) I most prefer	□	□	□	□
(2) I least prefer	□	□	□	□
(3) I next most prefer	□	□	□	□

Scenario 2	Options you can choose			
Pizza features	A	B	C	D
Brand	Dominos	Eagle Boys	Eagle Boys	Eagle Boys
Price	$18	$18	$16	$14
Number of toppings	1 topping	2 toppings	1 topping	4 toppings
Delivery time	40 mins.	30 mins.	10 mins.	20 mins.
Free Coke/Pepsi	No	No	Yes	No
Free dessert	Yes	No	Yes	Yes
(1) I most prefer	□	□	□	□
(2) I least prefer	□	□	□	□
(3) I next most prefer	□	□	□	□

Scenario 3	Options you can choose			
Pizza features	A	B	C	D
Brand	Dominos	Eagle Boys	Pizza Haven	Pizza Hut
Price	$14	$14	$18	$14
Number of toppings	3 toppings	4 toppings	3 toppings	2 toppings
Delivery time	10 mins.	20 mins.	20 mins.	40 mins.
Free Coke/Pepsi	No	No	Yes	Yes
Free dessert	No	Yes	Yes	Yes
(1) I most prefer	□	□	□	□
(2) I least prefer	□	□	□	□
(3) I next most prefer	□	□	□	□

survey administration eliminates a potentially large source of errors. A hypothetical example of one person's answers is shown in Table 4.7, with the ranking of options in each choice set in Table 4.8 being that implied by the choices of most preferred (rank 1), least preferred (rank 4), next most preferred (rank 2) and the remaining option (rank 3).

Table 4.7 *Choice sets, choice options and best and worst choices*

Choice set	Option A	Option B	Option C	Option D	1st Best	2nd Best	Worst
1	2	5	8	14	2	8	5
2	1	5	6	7	6	7	5
3	5	9	12	16	12	16	5
4	4	5	11	15	4	15	5
5	3	5	10	13	3	13	5
6	1	2	3	4	4	3	1
7	2	6	9	11	2	6	11
8	2	7	13	16	13	16	7
9	2	10	12	15	12	15	10
10	1	8	9	10	8	9	10
11	6	8	13	15	13	15	8
12	4	7	8	12	4	12	7
13	3	8	11	16	3	16	11
14	1	14	15	16	16	15	1
15	3	6	12	14	3	12	14
16	7	10	11	14	7	11	10
17	4	9	13	14	4	13	14
18	1	11	12	13	12	13	1
19	4	6	10	16	4	16	10
20	3	7	9	15	3	15	9

One combines the profile design codes with the BIBD to produce a design matrix that supports various analyses of the best and worst choice data, as shown in Table 4.9. We simulate the best and worst choices of one person using the true utilities ("True util."), disturbed by uniform random errors in the range [0,1]. Table 4.9 also shows the expected best (bestct) and worst (worstct) counts associated with the Louviere, Street *et al.* (2008) rank expansion approach explained and illustrated earlier. The table also contains differences in the best and worst counts (B-W). We (1) estimate an OLS regression with differences in simulated best and worst counts as the dependent variable; the predictor variables are effects-coded attribute levels in the design matrix ("Brand," "Price," "Topping," "Del. time," "Coke/Pepsi," "Dessert"), and (2) estimate a WLS regression of $\log_e$ of the Louviere, Street *et al.* (2008) expected (best) choice counts in Table 4.9 on the effects-coded attribute levels in Table 4.9. The results of these analyses are given in Table 4.10.

The estimation results are graphed in Figure 4.1 and shows that all OLS and WLS attribute-level utility estimates are proportional. The constant of proportionality is the ratio of the error variances associated with each estimation approach; a ratio less than one implies that the approach graphed on the X-axis has higher error variability (see, for

Table 4.8 *Implied ranking of choice options in Table 4.7*

	Ranking of Options			
Set/block	A	B	C	D
1	1	4	2	3
2	3	4	1	1
3	4	3	1	2
4	1	4	3	2
5	1	4	3	2
6	4	3	2	1
7	1	2	3	4
8	3	4	1	2
9	3	4	1	2
10	3	1	2	4
11	4	4	1	2
12	1	4	4	2
13	1	3	4	2
14	4	3	2	1
15	1	3	2	4
16	1	4	2	3
17	1	3	2	4
18	4	3	1	2
19	1	3	4	2
20	1	3	4	2

Table 4.9 *Design matrix for 20 BIBD choice sets*

Set	Profile	True util.	Bestct	Worstct	B-W	Brand	Price	Topping	Del. time	Coke/ Pepsi	Dessert
1	2	0.75	8	1	7	0	2	1	1	1	0
1	5	−1.9	1	8	−7	1	3	1	2	0	0
1	8	0.5	4	2	2	1	0	2	3	1	0
1	14	−0.25	2	4	−2	3	2	2	2	0	1
2	1	−0.85	2	4	−2	0	3	0	3	0	1
2	5	−1.9	1	8	−7	1	3	1	2	0	0
2	6	0.5	8	1	7	1	2	0	0	1	1
2	7	0.5	4	2	2	1	1	3	1	0	1
3	5	−1.9	1	8	−7	1	3	1	2	0	0
3	9	0.2	2	4	−2	2	3	2	1	1	1
3	12	1.6	8	1	7	2	0	1	0	0	1
3	16	0.95	4	2	2	3	0	0	1	0	0
4	4	2.65	8	1	7	0	0	3	2	1	1
4	5	−1.9	1	8	−7	1	3	1	2	0	0
4	11	−0.1	2	4	−2	2	1	0	2	1	0

Table 4.9 (*cont.*)

Set	Profile	True util.	Bestct	Worstct	B-W	Brand	Price	Topping	Del. time	Coke/ Pepsi	Dessert
4	15	0.85	4	2	2	3	1	1	3	1	1
5	3	1.75	8	1	7	0	1	2	0	0	0
5	5	−1.9	1	8	−7	1	3	1	2	0	0
5	10	−1	2	4	−2	2	2	3	3	0	0
5	13	1.55	4	2	2	3	3	3	0	1	0
6	1	−0.85	1	8	−7	0	3	0	3	0	1
6	2	0.75	2	4	−2	0	2	1	1	1	0
6	3	1.75	4	2	2	0	1	2	0	0	0
6	4	2.65	8	1	7	0	0	3	2	1	1
7	2	0.75	8	1	7	0	2	1	1	1	0
7	6	0.5	4	2	2	1	2	0	0	1	1
7	9	0.2	2	4	−2	2	3	2	1	1	1
7	11	−0.1	1	8	−7	2	1	0	2	1	0
8	2	0.75	2	4	−2	0	2	1	1	1	0
8	7	0.5	1	8	−7	1	1	3	1	0	1
8	13	1.55	8	1	7	3	3	3	0	1	0
8	16	0.95	4	2	2	3	0	0	1	0	0
9	2	0.75	2	4	−2	0	2	1	1	1	0
9	10	−1	1	8	−7	2	2	3	3	0	0
9	12	1.6	8	1	7	2	0	1	0	0	1
9	15	0.85	4	2	2	3	1	1	3	1	1

Set	Profile	True util.	Bestwt	Worstwt	B-W	Brand	Price	Topping	Del. time	Coke/ Pepsi	Dessert
10	1	−0.85	2	4	−2	0	3	0	3	0	1
10	8	0.5	8	1	7	1	0	2	3	1	0
10	9	0.2	4	2	2	2	3	2	1	1	1
10	10	−1	1	8	−7	2	2	3	3	0	0
11	6	0.5	1	8	−7	1	2	0	0	1	1
11	8	0.5	2	4	−2	1	0	2	3	1	0
11	13	1.55	8	1	7	3	3	3	0	1	0
11	15	0.95	4	2	2	3	1	1	3	1	1
12	4	2.65	8	1	7	0	0	3	2	1	1
12	7	0.5	2	4	−2	1	1	3	1	0	1
12	8	0.5	1	8	−7	1	0	2	3	1	0
12	12	1.6	4	2	2	2	0	1	0	0	1
13	3	1.75	8	1	7	0	1	2	0	0	0
13	8	0.5	2	4	−2	1	0	2	3	1	0
13	11	−0.1	1	8	−7	2	1	0	2	1	0
13	16	0.95	4	2	2	3	0	0	1	0	0
14	1	−0.85	1	8	−7	0	3	0	3	0	1

Table 4.9 (*cont.*)

Set	Profile	True util.	Bestwt	Worstwt	B-W	Brand	Price	Topping	Del. time	Coke/ Pepsi	Dessert
14	14	−0.25	2	4	−2	3	2	2	2	0	1
14	15	0.85	4	2	2	3	1	1	3	1	1
14	16	0.95	8	1	7	3	0	0	1	0	0
15	3	1.75	8	1	7	0	1	2	0	0	0
15	6	0.5	2	4	−2	1	2	0	0	1	1
15	12	1.6	4	2	2	2	0	1	0	0	1
15	14	−0.25	1	8	−7	3	2	2	2	0	1
16	7	0.5	8	1	7	1	1	3	1	0	1
16	10	−1	1	8	−7	2	2	3	3	0	0
16	11	−0.1	4	2	2	2	1	0	2	1	0
16	14	−0.25	2	4	−2	3	2	2	2	0	1
17	4	2.65	8	1	7	0	0	3	2	1	1
17	9	0.2	2	4	−2	2	3	2	1	1	1
17	13	1.55	4	2	2	3	3	3	0	1	0
17	14	−0.25	1	8	−7	3	2	2	2	0	1
18	1	−0.85	1	8	−7	0	3	0	3	0	1
18	11	−0.1	2	4	−2	2	1	0	2	1	0
18	12	1.6	8	1	7	2	0	1	0	0	1
18	13	1.55	4	2	2	3	3	3	0	1	0
19	4	2.65	8	1	7	0	0	3	2	1	1
19	6	0.5	2	4	−2	1	2	0	0	1	1
19	10	−1	1	8	−7	2	2	3	3	0	0
19	16	0.95	4	2	2	3	0	0	1	0	0
20	3	1.75	8	1	7	0	1	2	0	0	0
20	7	0.5	2	4	−2	1	1	3	1	0	1
20	9	0.2	1	8	−7	2	3	2	1	1	1
20	15	0.85	4	2	2	3	1	1	3	1	1

example, Swait and Louviere, 1993). So, WLS estimates are more efficient than OLS estimates.

It is important to note that both regression results include dummy codes for each choice set (omitted to save space); when one linearizes a conditional logit model by taking the natural logs of both the left-hand and the right-hand sides, the right-hand side includes the systematic component (utilities) plus the log of the denominator of each choice set. One captures these denominators by including effects-coded dummy variables. These dummy variables can be viewed as "nuisance" parameters, and can be ignored after estimation.

Recall that the starting design is an OMEP; therefore, the columns of that design are independent. Recall also that the BIBD ensures that each profile, and hence the associated attribute levels, occur equally often and co-occur equally often. Thus, one can simply

Table 4.10 *OLS and WLS regression results for attribute-level effects*

	BW difference scores				Ln(bestcounts)			
Effect	Estimate	Std err	T-stat	P(T)	Estimate	Std err	T-stat	P(T)
Intercept	−1.4879	1.5184	−0.9799	0.3324	0.9413	0.1923	4.8939	0.0000
Dominos	2.8552	0.6320	4.5180	0.0000	0.4416	0.0849	5.1988	0.0000
Eagleboys	−2.4659	0.6184	−3.9877	0.0002	−0.3692	0.0976	−3.7811	0.0005
PizzaHaven	−2.0000	0.6073	−3.2931	0.0019	−0.3015	0.0939	−3.2112	0.0024
Price18	4.6108	0.6101	7.5572	0.0000	0.7137	0.0784	9.1046	0.0000
Price16	1.3750	0.6073	2.2640	0.0284	0.2263	0.0879	2.5762	0.0133
Price14	−2.8466	0.6184	−4.6031	0.0000	−0.4124	0.0983	−4.1952	0.0001
Toppings1	−1.7500	0.6073	−2.8815	0.0060	−0.2448	0.0889	−2.7542	0.0085
Toppings2	0.4034	0.6184	0.6524	0.5175	0.0498	0.0918	0.5426	0.5901
Toppings3	−0.0909	0.6184	−0.1471	0.8837	−0.0441	0.0952	−0.4630	0.6456
Deltime40	4.5625	0.6073	7.5124	0.0000	0.7386	0.0781	9.4596	0.0000
Deltime30	0.4802	0.6320	0.7598	0.4513	0.0456	0.0852	0.5348	0.5954
Deltime20	−2.1534	0.6184	−3.4823	0.0011	−0.3238	0.1012	−3.2011	0.0025
Coke/Pepsi	1.2642	0.3554	3.5567	0.0009	0.2120	0.0528	4.0136	0.0002
Freedessert	0.3366	0.3518	0.9568	0.3438	0.0268	0.0501	0.5347	0.5955

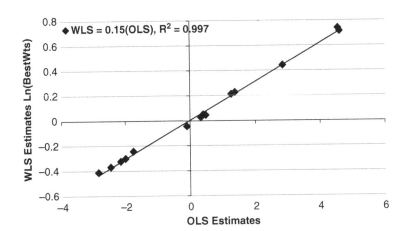

Figure 4.1 OLS versus WLS estimates

calculate the means of each attribute level that are useful in gaining a preliminary understanding of the data. We transform the best and worst choices into a ranking, and then apply
the Louviere, Street *et al.* (2008) weights (derived from expansions to all non-empty
subsets) to obtain the expected best and worst choice totals in each choice set, as shown
in Table 4.9. Based on previous empirical results, we expect the natural log of the weighted
best (respectively, worst) totals (counts) to be linearly related to the true values. Similarly,

Table 4.11 *Means and regression estimates calculated from Table 4.9*

Attribute	Level	True util	OLS	WLS	Bestwt	Worstwt	B–W	L -w	LnBwt	LnWwt
Brand	0	1.08	2.86	0.44	5.25	2.85	2.40	0.35	1.66	1.05
	1	−0.10	−2.47	−0.37	2.80	4.85	−2.05	−0.31	1.03	1.58
	2	0.18	−2.00	−0.30	2.95	4.55	−1.60	−0.24	1.08	1.52
	3	0.78	1.61	0.23	4.00	2.75	1.25	0.21	1.39	1.01
Price	0	1.43	4.61	0.71	5.65	2.00	3.65	0.56	1.73	0.69
	1	0.76	1.38	0.23	4.15	3.05	1.10	0.17	1.42	1.12
	2	0.00	−2.85	−0.41	2.65	4.85	−2.20	−0.35	0.98	1.58
	3	−0.25	−3.14	−0.53	2.55	5.10	−2.55	−0.38	0.94	1.63
Toppings	0	0.13	−1.75	−0.25	2.90	4.30	−1.40	−0.21	1.07	1.46
	1	0.33	0.40	0.05	3.95	3.55	0.40	0.07	1.37	1.27
	2	0.55	−0.09	−0.04	3.60	3.75	−0.15	−0.04	1.28	1.32
	3	0.93	1.44	0.24	4.55	3.40	1.15	0.17	1.52	1.22
Del. time	0	1.35	4.56	0.74	5.65	2.00	3.65	0.56	1.73	0.69
	1	0.60	0.48	0.05	3.70	3.20	0.50	0.07	1.31	1.16
	2	0.10	−2.15	−0.32	3.15	4.95	−1.80	−0.28	1.15	1.60
	3	−0.12	−2.89	−0.46	2.50	4.85	−2.35	−0.35	0.92	1.58
Drink	0	0.10	−1.26	−0.21	3.38	4.43	−1.05	−0.16	1.22	1.49
	1	0.87	1.26	0.21	4.13	3.08	1.05	0.16	1.42	1.12
Dessert	0	0.31	−0.34	−0.03	3.70	3.95	−0.25	−0.04	1.31	1.37
	1	0.65	0.34	0.03	3.80	3.55	0.25	0.04	1.34	1.27

following discussions in earlier chapters, we expect the natural log of the square root of the expected best counts divided by the expected worst counts to be linearly related to the true utilities. The results are shown in Table 4.11 and graphically compared in Figure 4.2.

Figure 4.2 clearly shows that the means of each of the measures provides an estimate of each scale value that is linearly related to its true value.

One often uses choice models estimated from DCEs to predict the choice probabilities associated with products, policies or profiles. Each choice set of options lies on an absolute probability scale, although the scale is relative only to the set of choice options being considered. Change the set – or, better put, change options in the set – and the choice probabilities associated with the options change. Currently, Case 3 assumes an additive underlying utility model and a conditional logit or Luce (1959) choice model. If these assumptions are true, ratios of choice probabilities of any two options are invariant to choice sets (the IIA property).

Lest one object that it is well known that the IIA property rarely is ever satisfied, recall that our focus in this and prior chapters is on *individuals*, not aggregates of individuals. Very few (if any) studies have been conducted with DCEs to test whether IIA holds for single individuals, and current state-of-the-art, random-utility-theory-based, discrete choice models *all* assume i.i.d. extreme value type 1 (EV1) errors for individuals, implying that IIA

Table 4.12 *True profile utilities versus simple best-worst estimates*

Profile	True utilities	Best-minus-worst	Stacked B–W
1	−0.85	−5.00	−2.50
2	0.75	1.60	0.80
3	1.75	6.00	3.00
4	2.65	7.00	3.50
5	−1.90	−7.00	−3.50
6	0.50	−0.40	−0.20
7	0.50	−0.40	−0.20
8	0.80	−0.40	−0.20
9	0.20	−2.20	−1.10
10	−1.00	−6.00	−3.00
11	−0.10	−3.20	−1.60
12	1.60	5.00	2.50
13	1.55	4.00	2.00
14	−0.25	−4.00	−2.00
15	0.85	2.00	1.00
16	0.95	3.00	0.00

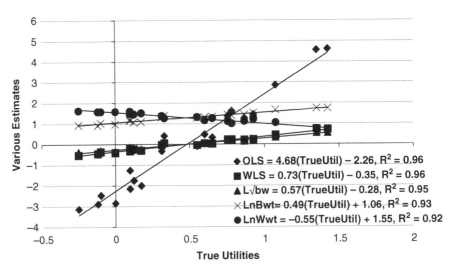

Figure 4.2 Comparison of true attribute-level means with various estimates

holds for individuals. Indeed, almost all published results associated with latent class and random parameter models assume i.i.d. EV1 errors. So, an area for future research is the extent to which i.i.d. EV1 errors for single people can be relaxed and the implied choice models estimated given whatever restrictions are relaxed.

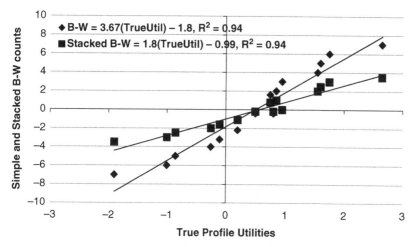

Figure 4.3 True utilities versus simple and stacked best-minus-worst counts

We now return to the topic of *profiles*, and show that in fact the profiles are measured on a common scale, and one can compare various ways to estimate Case 3 models for these quantities. Table 4.12 shows the true utility value of each of the 16 pizza profiles that we designed at the start of the example, and shows estimates of the true utilities produced by (1) an OLS regression on the differences in best and worst counts with "profile" as the predictor; and (2) an OLS regression on a matrix of stacked differences in best and worst counts, with 15 effects-coded dummies for "profile," with the effects codes reverse-coded for worst counts (that is, 1, 0, −1 for best counts; −1, 0, 1 for worst counts), as discussed later in this chapter. Figure 4.3 graphs the true utilities against the best-minus-worst counts in Table 4.12.

These show that simple differences in best and worst choice counts provide a reasonable first approximation (that is, up to linearity) to the utilities of each profile.

4.2.2 Street and Burgess example

Now we redo the same example using a Street and Burgess (hereafter, "S&B") design that is optimally efficient if two assumptions are satisfied: (1) a strictly additive indirect utility function; and (2) i.i.d. EV1 errors (resulting in a conditional logit model). As previously noted, this design is optimally efficient for testing the null hypothesis that all the utility parameters equal zero, but, as also noted earlier, Street and Burgess (2007) show that the design is reasonably efficient for utility parameter values associated with choice probabilities at the extremes of the distribution. The design specifications (attributes and levels) are given in Table 4.1; a suitable S&B design that creates 16 choice sets instead of the 20 choices sets for the BIBD approach is shown in Table 4.13. We repeat the same steps for this design as for the BIBD example, using the same "true" utility values.

Table 4.13 Burgess and Street design for pizza specifications

Set	Alt	Brand	Price	Tops	Deltime	Drinks	Dessert
1	1	1	1	1	1	1	1
1	2	2	2	2	2	1	2
1	3	3	3	3	3	2	1
1	4	4	4	4	4	2	2
2	1	2	2	2	2	1	1
2	2	3	3	3	3	1	2
2	3	4	4	4	4	2	1
2	4	1	1	1	1	2	2
3	1	3	3	3	3	1	1
3	2	4	4	4	4	1	2
3	3	1	1	1	1	2	1
3	4	2	2	2	2	2	2
4	1	4	4	4	4	1	1
4	2	1	1	1	1	1	2
4	3	2	2	2	2	2	1
4	4	3	3	3	3	2	2
5	1	2	3	4	1	2	2
5	2	3	4	1	2	2	2
5	3	4	1	2	3	1	1
5	4	1	2	3	4	1	2
6	1	1	4	3	2	2	2
6	2	2	1	4	3	2	2
6	3	3	2	1	4	1	1
6	4	4	3	2	1	1	2
7	1	4	1	2	3	2	2
7	2	1	2	3	4	2	1
7	3	2	3	4	1	1	2
7	4	3	4	1	2	1	2
8	1	3	2	1	4	2	1
8	2	4	3	2	1	2	2
9	1	3	4	2	1	1	2
9	2	4	1	3	2	1	1
9	3	1	2	4	3	2	2
9	4	2	3	1	4	2	1
10	1	4	3	1	2	1	2
10	2	1	4	2	3	1	1
10	3	2	1	3	4	2	2
10	4	3	2	4	1	2	1
11	1	1	2	4	3	1	2
11	2	2	3	1	4	1	1
11	3	3	4	2	1	2	2
11	4	4	1	3	2	2	1
12	1	2	1	4	1	1	2
12	2	3	2	1	2	2	1
12	3	4	3	2	3	2	2
12	4	1	4	3	1	2	1
13	1	2	4	4	1	2	2
13	2	3	1	1	2	2	1
13	3	2	3	2	3	1	2
13	4	4	4	1	4	1	1
14	1	2	2	4	2	2	2
14	2	3	3	1	3	2	1
14	3	4	4	2	4	1	2
14	4	1	1	3	1	1	1
15	1	4	4	1	3	2	2
15	2	1	1	2	4	2	1
15	3	2	2	3	1	1	2
15	4	3	3	4	2	1	1
16	1	1	3	2	4	2	2
16	2	2	4	3	1	2	1

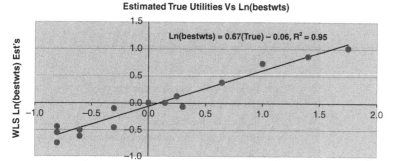

Figure 4.4 Estimated true utilities versus bests

As with the BIBD example, one can graph the true utilities against various ways of estimating/calculating the scale values for each attribute level. Figure 4.4 shows one of these comparisons, excluding the others to save space. The other comparisons produce similar results to those for the BIBD. As before, the true utility values are highly linearly related to the natural log of the Louviere, Street *et al.* (2008) weights (based on expansions to all non-empty subsets) associated with the implied ranking of options in each choice set (Ln(bestweights)).

4.3 Empirical examples for Case 3

We focus on two empirical examples, one for emissions trading schemes (ETSs) and one for delivered pizzas. Both are based on the BIBD approach described earlier in this chapter. In other words, we first generate 16 profiles from a $3^4 \times 2^5$ design for eight attributes, and then we use the same BIBD discussed earlier to make 20 sets of four choice options. In the interests of space, we do not reproduce these designs but simply note that the procedure is exactly as described earlier. We analyze the data using several estimation and calculation methods for each individual in the sample separately, and for the sample aggregate choice data. The attributes and levels for this example are shown in Table 4.14.

The data for this example are a random sample of 55 people from the Pureprofile online panel in Australia. This particular example is one of 32 versions of a much larger study, but is adequate to illustrate the analysis and results. We begin by estimating WLS models for each of the 55 people, following the Louviere, Street *et al.* (2008) approach. The descriptive statistics that summarize the statistical results for the 55 WLS models are shown in Table 4.15. The results suggest that there is considerable homogeneity across respondents with respect to the size of the emission reductions that we should introduce now, with much less agreement, or possibly little effect, in terms of other attributes/levels.

The delivered pizza example involves a sample of 20 randomly drawn Pureprofile panelists in Australia. We designed the DCE using the Street and Burgess (2007) approach,

Table 4.14 *Emissions trading attributes and levels*

Attribute	Levels
Start year	2011
	2013
Revenue allocation	Lower Goods and Services Tax (GST)
	Give to low-incomes and seniors
	Reduce business taxes
	Improve govt. services and reduce debt
Invest 20% of revenue in R&D	No
	Yes
Exempt transport for three years	No
	Yes
Exempt energy sector for three years	No
	Yes
How to implement carbon reductions	Carbon trading scheme
	Carbon tax
	Technology standards
	Hybrid scheme
Initiating the scheme	Begin large carbon reductions now
	Wait for China and United States
2020 emission reduction target	5%
	10%
	20%
	25%

Table 4.15 *Emissions trading results*

Effect	N	Mean	Std err	T-stat	Std dev
Start in 2011	55	0.022	0.015	1.511	0.108
Use revenues to reduce the GST	55	0.087	0.038	2.296	0.282
Use the revenues for the poor and elderly	55	0.121	0.045	2.652	0.337
Use the revenues to reduce business taxes	55	−0.197	0.037	−5.372	0.272
Do not allocate 20% of revenues to R&D	55	−0.033	0.016	−1.990	0.121
Do not exempt transport	55	−0.008	0.015	−0.535	0.114
Do not exempt energy-intensive industries	55	−0.007	0.016	−0.430	0.115
Implement as a carbon trading scheme	55	−0.075	0.029	−2.570	0.216
Implement as a carbon tax	55	−0.017	0.035	−0.475	0.258
Implement as technology standards	55	0.019	0.030	0.632	0.222
Do not wait for US and China – act now	55	0.190	0.035	5.413	0.260
Reduce emissions by 5% in 2030	55	1.114	0.046	24.165	0.342
Reduce emissions by 10% in 2030	55	1.237	0.031	40.137	0.229
Reduce emissions by 20% in 2030	55	1.376	0.025	55.753	0.183
Reduce emissions by 30% in 2030	55	1.409	0.036	39.296	0.266

Table 4.16 *Delivered pizza products attributes and levels*

Attribute	Level
Brand of delivered pizza	Pizza Hut, Dominos, Eagle Boys, Pizza Haven
Price of a large pizza	$12, $14, $16, $18
Number of toppings	1, 2, 3, 4
Free garlic bread/bread sticks	No, yes
Free Coke or Pepsi	No, yes
Free dessert	No, yes

which produces 16 choice sets with four options per set. The delivered pizza attributes and levels are shown in Table 4.16.

We note that both examples represent one experimental condition taken from a much larger experiment with 32 (ETSs) and 44 (pizzas) conditions. Except for most-minus-least counts or the log of the square root of most/least, attribute-level utilities are estimated by effects-coding coding attribute levels. Omitted attribute levels are coded −1 with effects codes; so, omitted level estimates equal $-1 \times (\beta_{level1} + \beta_{level2} + \beta_{level3})$ for a four-level attribute, and $-1 \times b_{level1}$ for a two-level attribute.

We analyze the best-worst Case 3 data in seven different ways, showing that all give approximately the same results. The seven procedures are as follows: (1) a simple best-minus-worst count (M–L); (2) the natural logarithm of the square root of best counts divided by worst counts (Ln[Sqrt(M/L)]); (3) estimating individual-level linear probability models (LPMs) (ordinary least squares estimation applied to the 0, 1 choice indicator dependent variable); (4) estimating individual-level weighted least squares regressions of the linearized conditional logit model using the Louviere, Street *et al.* (2008) approach (WLS), using expansions to all non-empty subsets; (5) a linear regression fit to simple best-minus-worst counts for each individual (B–Wreg); (6) a one-size-fits-all aggregate conditional logit model estimated by maximum likelihood using the individual choice data in the usual way (Clogit) by estimating across all the individuals in the sample; and (7) a one-size-fits-all aggregate rank order logit model (ROL) estimated by maximum likelihood using the individual rankings in all choice sets. The results for the ETS example are given in Table 4.17; the results for the delivered pizza example are given in Table 4.20, which we discuss later.

We first test the hypothesis that all the methods produce approximately the same estimates of the attribute-level utilities in the ETS example. We do this by subjecting the estimates in Table 4.17 to a principal components factor analysis. If the seven methods all produce the same estimates of the attribute-level utilities, they all should be proportional to one another, implying that one component (factor) should explain virtually all the data. The results of this analysis are given in Table 4.18, which clearly shows that one factor accounts for approximately 97 percent of all the variance in the table columns. Thus, the columns are linearly dependent, and can be summarized by extracting the factor scores from the

Table 4.17 *Descriptive stats for ETS options*

Effects	Aggregate counts		Individual (mean estimates)			Aggregate estimates	
	M–L	Ln(SQRT(M/L))	LPMs	WLSs	B–Wreg	Clogit	ROL
Start 2011	48	0.044	0.0097	0.0220	0.0273	0.041	0.079
Reduce GST	68	0.128	0.0295	0.0872	0.0773	0.110	0.211
Poor/elderly	86	0.151	0.0625	0.1205	0.0977	0.210	0.272
Reduce business tax	−144	−0.283	−0.0977	−0.1972	−0.1636	−0.365	−0.457
Invest in R&D – no	−42	−0.038	−0.0131	−0.0325	−0.0239	−0.006	−0.069
Exempt transport – no	−2	−0.002	−.00023	−0.0082	−0.0011	−0.015	0.000
Exempt energy – no	−16	−0.014	0.0028	−0.0067	−0.0091	0.031	−0.027
Carbon trading scheme	−76	−0.142	−0.0500	−0.0748	−0.0864	−0.158	−0.252
Carbon tax	−4	−0.007	0.0136	−0.0165	−0.0045	0.088	−0.013
Technology standard	10	0.021	−0.0364	0.0189	0.0114	−0.044	0.027
Reduce carbon now	306	0.270	0.1040	0.1896	0.1739	0.339	0.509
5%	−126	−0.239	−0.0784	−0.1698	−0.1432	−0.213	−0.422
10%	−28	−0.054	−0.0341	−0.0471	−0.0318	−0.072	−0.102
20%	58	0.100	0.0511	0.0921	0.0659	0.060	0.208

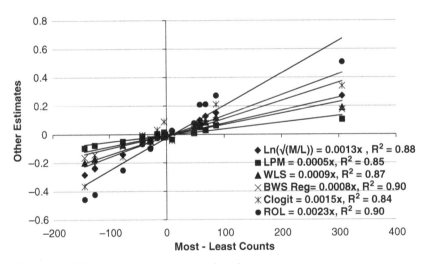

Figure 4.5 Utility estimates versus most-minus-least counts

principal components analysis, which are shown in Table 4.19. Figure 4.5 is a graph of the estimates in columns 2 through 7 of Table 4.17, plotted against the aggregate most-minus-least choice frequency counts. Both Table 4.18 and the associated graph support the null hypothesis.

Table 4.18 *Principal components factor analysis of ETS estimates*

Component	Initial eigenvalues	
	Total	% of variance
1	6.781	96.872
2	0.1	1.426
3	0.08	1.145
4	0.033	0.465
5	0.006	0.085
6	0	0.005
7	0	0.002

Table 4.19 *Factor scores extracted from principal components analysis*

Effects	Factor score
Start 2011	0.287
Lower GST	0.750
Poor/seniors	1.078
Reduce business tax	−1.813
Invest in R&D – no	−0.245
Exempt transport – no	−0.033
Exempt energy – no	−0.037
Carbon trading scheme	−0.881
Carbon tax	0.062
Technology standard	−0.035
Reduce carbon now	2.048
5%	−1.482
10%	−0.409
20%	0.712

The results in Table 4.19 together with the associated standard errors for the effects in Table 4.18 (not shown to save space) indicate that the effects associated with reducing emissions are very large and significant, with utility generally increasing with larger reductions. The question of how to use the revenues raised by an ETS is also significant: using it (1) to reduce the GST and/or to assist the poor and seniors is positive, (2) to reduce business taxes is very negative. There also are large effects for acting now to reduce emissions (2011), whereas waiting to see what the United States and China do is highly negative. Implementing the ETS as a carbon trading scheme or a hybrid scheme is negative.

The results suggest that the sample wants the government to act now, use the revenues to reduce the GST and/or assist the poor and seniors and make the highest emission reductions

Table 4.20 *Summary results for delivered pizza example*

Effect	Aggregate counts		Mean (individual estimates)			Aggregate model	
	M–L	Ln[SQRT(M/L)]	LPMs	WLS	B–Wreg	Clogit	ROL
Pizza Hut	−1	−0.005	0.056	0.079	−0.003	0.161	0.119
Dominos	22	0.140	0.031	0.121	0.069	0.118	0.174
Eagle Boys	−35	−0.243	−0.075	−0.263	−0.109	−0.336	−0.270
$12.00	30	0.168	0.078	0.115	0.094	0.265	0.258
$14.00	14	0.090	0.016	0.162	0.044	0.097	0.191
$16.00	12	0.087	−0.016	0.121	0.038	−0.011	0.124
1 topping	−105	−0.704	−0.144	−0.789	−0.328	−0.725	−0.930
2 toppings	−17	−0.133	−0.075	−0.071	−0.053	−0.221	−0.200
3 toppings	41	0.287	0.044	0.345	0.128	0.294	0.424
Free bread	−44	−0.137	−0.031	−0.207	−0.069	−0.138	−0.214
Free drink	−52	−0.162	−0.038	−0.191	−0.081	−0.112	−0.259
Free dessert	−34	−0.103	−0.019	−0.148	−0.053	−0.109	−0.169

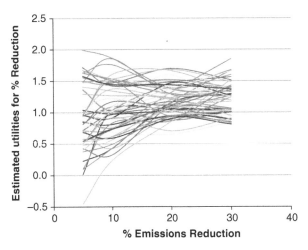

Figure 4.6 Emission reduction utilities versus emission reduction levels

possible. The distribution of individual utilities for emission reduction levels is shown in Figure 4.6. The figure shows how one can visualize the individual-level parameter estimates from Case 3 using the WLS estimates for each person for emission reduction percentages; similar figures are possible for the other attributes. The figure indicates more preference heterogeneity for smaller than larger reductions, and shows that the sample was fairly consistent in preferring higher reductions.

Now we turn our attention to the delivered pizza results. We follow the same analytical procedure that we used for the ETS attributes and levels – that is, we calculate/estimate the

Table 4.21 *Eigenvalue extraction from principal*
components factor analysis

Component	Initial eigenvalues	
	Total	% of variance
1	6.781	96.872
2	0.1	1.426
3	0.08	1.145
4	0.033	0.465
5	0.006	0.085
6	0	0.005
7	0	0.002

Table 4.22 *Factor scores from principal*
components factor analysis

Effect	Factor score
Pizza Hut	0.470
Dominos	0.752
Eagle Boys	−0.696
$12.00	0.994
$14.00	0.645
$16.00	0.489
1 topping	−2.401
2 toppings	−0.323
3 toppings	1.296
Free bread	−0.434
Free drink	−0.530
Free dessert	−0.261

attribute level utilities in seven ways, as shown in Table 4.20. Because the procedure is the same that was used for the ETS example, we simply note that we once again test the null hypothesis that all seven methods give estimates of the utilities that are approximately proportional. We conduct a principal components factor analysis of the seven columns in Table 4.20, and these results are shown in Table 4.21, followed by the extracted factor scores sin Table 4.22. As with the ETS example, these results strongly support the null hypothesis, and suggest that all seven methods give approximately the same utility estimates. In fact, the differences in the seven methods are that some provide more statistically efficient estimates than others (see Figure 4.7). Indeed, relative to the most-minus-least counts, higher slopes in the graphs represent more efficient (less error variability) in the estimates.

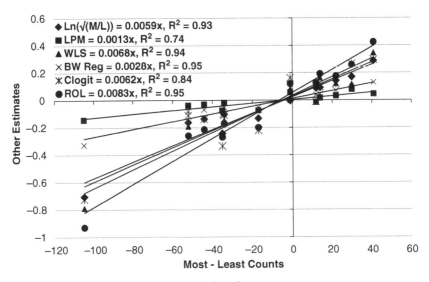

Figure 4.7 Utility estimates versus most-minus-least counts

For delivered pizzas, the largest effects in this sample are for the number of toppings, followed by free bread, free drinks and free dessert; the price and brand have minor effects. The distribution of estimated effects is shown in Figure 4.8a and Figure 4.8b for the price and the number of toppings, respectively. The lack of significance for the price clearly can be seen in the graph, whereas strong significance for the number of toppings also can be seen in the consistently positive utility functions.

4.4 Discussion and conclusions

We discussed the use of best-worst (most-least) responses as a way to obtain more preference information, which in turn allows one to estimate more accurate models for individuals and aggregates of individuals. We discuss potentially fruitful areas for future research in later chapters.

This chapter emphasized simple analysis and simple statistical models. It culminated with an example that demonstrated that several relatively simple ways of analyzing best (most) and worst (least) choices from DCEs all produce approximately the same results. Thus, researchers should choose an analytical method that they feel comfortable with and know how to use, and with which they can be relatively confident that they will get reliable and accurate results. These examples also serve to demonstrate that recent trends in applied economics, marketing and other fields to introduce and apply ever more sophisticated and advanced statistical choice models and/or ways of analyzing choice data do not add much when one can model single individuals and/or can observe a complete set of choices for a single person sufficient to estimate a unique model for that person. In turn, this provides

(a) Price functions for twenty people

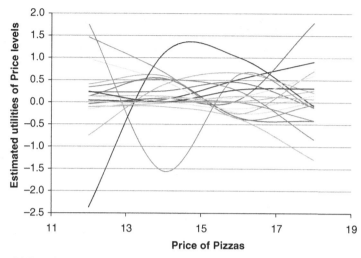

(b) Toppings function for twenty people

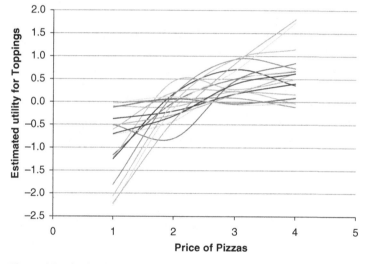

Figure 4.8 Distribution and shape of individual utility curves (pizzas)

researchers with a powerful new way to "look at" and visualize choice information for individuals, including distributions of model estimates across people. It also enables researchers to understand whether assumptions being made in aggregate, top-down models about distributions of utilities and distributions of error variances are, in fact, correct.

Chapter 5

Basic models

Everything should be made as simple as possible, but not simpler.

Attributed to Albert Einstein (1879–1955)

5.1 Introduction

Louviere and Woodworth (1990) and Finn and Louviere (1992) developed the best-worst scaling method and developed and evaluated a probabilistic model of their Case 1 data. Recent research in this area has two rather distinct foci. The first is on the use of BWS as a method of collecting, say, ranking data, which is then modeled in various ways related to the multinomial logit for best choices or to weighted versions of the rank ordered logit for repeated best choices; the first four chapters of this book illustrate this approach.

The second focus is on developing mathematical models that might describe processes underlying the best and/or worst choices made by a person; this approach is well illustrated by Marley and Islam (2012), Marley and Louviere (2005), Marley and Pihlens (2012), Marley, Flynn and Louviere (2008) and Scarpa *et al.* (2011). This approach explores models in addition to the multinomial logit and weighted rank order logit for data collected by BWS. Many such models have different specifications and potentially different parameter values associated with the choice options and/or the attribute levels on latent scales.

Ideally, one should estimate using a statistical model suitable to a particular psychological process underlying the choices. This point is recognized in some (but by no means all) contexts, thanks to warnings in statistical software manuals. For example, the Stata manual cautions that, when one estimates an (exploded) rank ordered logistic regression model that assumes choices are ranked from top to bottom (best from n items, best from remaining n–1 items, . . ., best from the last two items), one will get slightly different results compared with a model that assumes that choices are ranked from bottom to top. Our experience suggests that differences in estimates are fairly small at an aggregate or subgroup level (for example, Louviere, Street *et al.*, 2008; Flynn, Louviere, Peters *et al.*, 2008), but individual-level models may require one to pay more attention to this issue. For example, a model might assume simultaneous, independent best and worst choices, but web-based or

114

interviewer-administered surveys might use a structured sequential task that requires sequential choices. So, researchers should pay attention to task structures and, when possible, estimate model forms consistent with the way in which people make their choices. In particular, by asking questions in certain orders, web-based or interviewer-administered surveys can increase the likelihood that a person uses a repeated best, then worst, choice process rather than, say, simultaneous, independent choice of best and worst. On the other hand, a "free" choice of best and worst might be more appropriate when one is interested in the relative strengths of the two processes (see section 5.5).

Section 5.2 presents verbal descriptions of various such models, and section 5.3 presents the corresponding mathematical representations. We refer forward to the mathematical representations when presenting the verbal descriptions; however, our intent is that the latter can stand alone. Up to the present, many of the mathematical models of (repeated) best and/or worst choice are very closely related to the MNL, and are likely difficult to differentiate by choice data alone. Therefore, section 5.5 discusses recent related models based on both choices and the time to make them.

We talk of choice between "options," as the ideas we present apply equally to Cases 1, 2 and 3. Of course, the mathematical details (section 5.3) differ for the three cases.

5.2 Process descriptions of some models

5.2.1 The maxdiff model

We begin with the model introduced by Louviere and Woodworth (1990) and Finn and Louviere (1992), both because it was the first best-worst model applied to data and because it can be used in a relatively natural way to motivate various earlier (Marley, 1968; Yellott, 1977) and later (Marley and Louviere, 2005; Marley and Pihlens, 2012) models. The name "maxdiff" has become popular for this model, especially in the United States, as it can be motivated in terms of a process of choosing the maximum of a set of (random) differences. Section 5.4 presents the mathematical structure of this model for Cases 3, 2 and 1.

Finn and Louviere (1992) described the process of choosing the best, and the worst, option in a presented set of options as one in which a person evaluates all (ordered) pairs of options and chooses one pair exhibiting the largest (positive) difference on the underlying, latent scale. They interpreted this process as being based on random utility maximization, with independent extreme value (Gumbel) distributions for the random component differences. This leads to an MNL-type representation, in which the utility values[1] are differences (see section 5.4.5).

Marley and Louviere (2005) presented a description of a different process that leads to the same formula for best-worst choice as the above random utility approach. We now present that approach, as variants on it lead to the class of sequential (repeated) best and/or

---

[1] Throughout this chapter, when we say "utility value" we mean the deterministic component of that value.

worst models (see Marley and Louviere, 2005; and section 5.2.2), and to natural choice and response time models (section 5.5).

The process is based on independent best and worst choices, each represented by an MNL model; even though the processes are independent, the utility value for an option in the worst process is the negative of its value in the best process; for Case 3, the relevant formulae are (2) (respectively, (3)), in section 5.4. Based on these MNL representations (equivalently, underlying random utility processes with i.i.d. extreme value "error" terms), the person chooses the best option in the available set of options and, independently, chooses the worst option in the available set; if these two options are different, this pair is the chosen best-worst pair; if the two options are the same, the process is repeated (with resampling from all the available options) until a pair of distinct options is selected.[2] Marley and Louviere (2005) show that this process terminates provided there is no option that is certain to be chosen as both best and worst; under this assumption, the probability of choosing option i as the best and option $i' \neq i$ as the worst is given by the maxdiff model; for Case 3, the relevant formula is (4) in section 5.4.2.

Estimation of the parameters of the maxdiff model

We now describe some basic estimation procedures for the maxdiff model. We continue to talk of the choice of an "option" and describe the results as they apply to Case 1. However, exactly parallel results hold for Cases 2 and 3 (though the notation and terminology need to be extended in those cases: see Marley, Flynn and Louviere, 2008; Marley and Pihlens, 2012).

We consider estimating the parameters in two ways: (1) a "simple first approximation" approach that can be implemented with most commonly available statistical software (or even MS Excel) by calculating "scores" (means); or (2) a more sophisticated approach.

Simple first approximation

Calculate the availability of each option – that is, the total number of times that it appears across the whole study. Then divide the number of times each option is selected as best (respectively, worst) by its availability, giving frequencies on a scale of zero to one. However, these best (respectively, worst) frequencies are not unbiased estimates of parameters in the maxdiff model, although, interestingly, the set of best-minus-worst frequencies across the options in the study is a sufficient statistic for the maxdiff model (Marley and Louviere, 2005; Marley and Pihlens, 2012). As noted by Marley and Louviere (2005), it would be preferable to use some combination of these best and worst scores (frequencies) to provide better parameter estimates, but to date there is no obvious combination for which the mathematical properties have been proved. Certainly the best-minus-worst frequency differences are biased estimates of the (random utility) scale u in the formula for the choice probabilities in the maxdiff model (in, say, Case 1, (5)) – the range of the best-minus-worst score frequencies is $(-1, 1)$, whereas the range of

---

[2] Earlier descriptions of this process assumed that the two choices (of best and worst) were "simultaneous," without adequate definition of that term. However, the choices can be sequential – that is, one after the other – as long as they are independent, and both choices are from the full set of available options.

u is the real numbers. Lipovetsky and Conklin (2013) have suggested the alternative measure $ln[(1 + b - w)/(1 + w - b)]$, where $b - w$ (respectively, $w - b$) is the relevant normalized best-minus-worst (respectively, worst-minus-best) score; this measure is extremely close to being a linear function of the normalized best-minus-worst scores except at the ends of the range – that is, 1 (respectively, –1) – where it goes to ∞ (respectively, $-\infty$). On the other hand, empirically, the set of score differences (equivalently, the set of score frequencies) has been found to exhibit a high linear correlation with the true values of the (random utility) scale *u*. This result may be due, in part, to the fact that, for the maxdiff model, ranking the scale values in descending order of the scores, breaking ties at random, has "minimal average loss" among all ("permutation-invariant") ranking procedures that depend on the data only through the set of scores (see section 5.4.7 for more details on these properties).

More sophisticated estimation approaches

One can write special-purpose estimation code in Matlab, Gauss or other software to maximize the likelihood of the maxdiff model given the observed best-worst choice data; the likelihood is given by Marley and Louviere (2005, eq. 30) for Case 1 and by Marley and Pihlens (2012) for Case 3. One also can estimate the parameters of this model using conditional logistic regression in readily available software such as Stata. For example, Flynn *et al.* (2007) show how to estimate parameters using a pairwise expansion of the data that assumes simultaneous best and worst choices.

Most estimation approaches for the maxdiff model assume that the (random) utility value for worst is the negative of the scale value for best; in Cases 2 and 3, the assumption is for attribute levels. One can relax this assumption, and it is an empirical issue if a more general model fits the data better. For example, it may be that, in Case 2, certain attribute levels represent "a total no-no" in that they do not influence choice of best but, if present, they are chosen as worst because they make a profile totally unacceptable. Various researchers have recently begun exploring the extent to which the restrictive assumption is reasonable and how to interpret the data when it is not; see Chapter 6.

5.2.2 Models based on repeated best and/or worst choice

A (process) model that is interpreted in terms of a constrained sequence of repeated best and/or worst choices may be more realistic for web-based or interviewer-administered or assisted surveys, when participants can be forced to choose in a particular order. Marley and Louviere (2005) motivate numerous sequential choice models (that is, those based on repeated best and/or worst choices); however, there are few, if any, statistical software packages available for various of those models.

It is (disturbingly?) easy to think up sequential models for best and/or worst choice, and ranking by repeated such choice. For instance:

(1) rank ordered logit for best choices: the person makes repeated best choices, with each such choice satisfying a common MNL model;

(2) rank ordered logit for worst choices: the person makes repeated worst choices, with each such choice satisfying a common MNL model;

(3) the person makes repeated best-worst choices, with each such best-worst choice pair satisfying a common maxdiff model;

(4) the person makes repeated best, then worst, choices, with, for example, each such best (respectively, worst) choice satisfying a common MNL model in which the utility value for each option in the MNL model for the worst choice is the negative of the corresponding value for the best choice; or

(5) the person makes repeated worst, then best, choices, with, for example, each such worst (respectively, best) choice satisfying a common MNL model in which the utility value for each option in the MNL model for the worst choice is the negative of the corresponding value for the best choice.

Published work to date on BWS has relied heavily on (1), the ROL for best choices – that is, BWS is used a data collection method. We note that published Case 2 health studies have tended not to elicit complete rankings (typically because of the studies being by post or interviews of limited length on account of resource constraints). These data have typically been analyzed using a version of models (3) or (4), with only one round of best-worst choice. Since these models require the data to be manipulated (for example, worst data must be stacked below best data for model (4)), we routinely compare estimation results from custom-written Stata do-files with estimation results from Stata's rologit procedure (which allows the missing interior ranks to be set equal). For instance, with four objects, and one best-worst pair, the best option would have rank 1, the worst object rank 3, and each of other two objects would have rank 2. However, we have not published these comparisons.

5.3 Mathematical models of best, worst and repeated best and/or worst choice

The majority of the applications of best worst scaling in the chapters of this book are based on models related to the multinomial logit; this is also the case in many recent publications. Therefore, we restrict the theoretical material in this chapter, by and large, to such models.

We first describe the constant utility version of the MNL model for best (respectively, worst) choice between profiles (Case 3), which allows us to introduce the usual notation for multiattribute options. We then extend this model to best and worst choices for all three cases, followed by a presentation, and discussion, of random utility versions of these models and of plausible empirical and theoretical relations between the parameters in the models for each case. Next, we discuss some properties of simple "score" summaries of best-worst data. Finally, section 5.5 extends the models for best (respectively, worst, best-worst) choice to rankings and response times in repeated best and/or worst choice.

5.3.1 Notation for multiattribute option (profiles)

There are m attributes, usually with $m \geq 2$. We let $M = \{1, \ldots, m\}$ and assume that attribute i, $i = 1, \ldots, m$, has $q(i)$ levels. A profile (traditionally called a multiattribute option) is an m-component vector with each component i taking on one of the $q(i)$ levels for that component. A typical profile j is denoted by

$$\mathbf{x}_j = (x_{j1}, \ldots, x_{jm}), \tag{5.1}$$

where x_{ji}, $i = 1, \ldots, m$, denotes the level of attribute i in profile j. We call each x_{ji} an attribute level. We also have a vector

$$\boldsymbol{\beta} = (\beta_1, \ldots, \beta_m),$$

which is the utility coefficient of each attribute $i = 1, \ldots, m$. For most of this chapter, we assume that this vector is the same for all respondents. In fact, we present the models as if they are for single participants.

Finally, the probability of choosing profile i as the best (respectively, worst) alternative in choice set X is denoted $P_B(i|X)$ (respectively, $P_W(i|X)$), and the probability of choosing profile i as the best and profile $i' \neq i$ as the worst alternative in choice set X is denoted $P_{BW}(ii'|X)$. Later, we adapt the notation $P_{BW}(ii'|X)$ for choice in profiles (Case 2) and choice among things (Case 1).

5.4 Multinomial logit models for best and/or worst choice among profiles

5.4.1 Mulitinomial logit

The multinomial logit model assumes that the probability of choosing profile i as the best option in choice set X is[3]

$$P_B(i|X) = \frac{\exp \boldsymbol{\beta}' \mathbf{x}_i}{\sum_{j \in X} \exp \boldsymbol{\beta}' \mathbf{x}_j}. \tag{5.2}$$

and, here, we assume that the probability of choosing profile i' as the worst option in choice set X is

$$P_W(i'|X) = \frac{\exp - \boldsymbol{\beta}' \mathbf{x}_{i'}}{\sum_{j \in X} \exp - \boldsymbol{\beta}' \mathbf{x}_j}. \tag{5.3}$$

Thus, we are assuming that the utility coefficient for each attribute of a profile when choosing the worst profile is the negative of that coefficient when choosing the best profile.

---

[3] The following is based on interpreting each vector as a column vector, and letting "'" stand for the transpose.

One can illustrate this assumption as follows. Consider a choice set with four options x_i, $i = 1, 2, 3, 4$, with respective overall utility 2, 4, 7 and 10 (that is, $\beta'x_1 = 2, \beta'x_2 = 4$, $\beta'x_3 = 7, \beta'x_4 = 10$) and another choice set with four options y_i, $i = 1, 2, 3, 4$, with respective overall utility -2, -4, -7 and -10 (that is, $\beta'y_1 = -2, \beta'y_2 = -4, \beta'y_3 = -7$, $\beta^{ce'}y_4 = -10$). Then the probability of choosing x_i, $i = 1, 2, 3, 4$, as best in the set $\{x_1, x_2, x_3, x_4\}$ is the same as the probability of choosing y_i, $i = 1, 2, 3, 4$, as worst in the set $\{y_1, y_2, y_3, y_4\}$. This is a reasonable theoretical, and conceptual, assumption, which yields models with half the number of parameters of the full model. To date, the constrained models have generally been considered adequate. However, Bednarz (2006) provides Case 1 data that show that deriving best choice probabilities in the above manner from worst choices does not produce the same results as deriving best choice probabilities from the best choices. Various researchers have recently begun exploring the extent to which the restrictive assumptions is reasonable and the interpretations of the data when it is not (see Chapter 6).

In this chapter, we confine our attention to models for the choice of the best and/or the worst option in a set of available options. To the extent that these choices are reliable, it is of interest to consider the use of repeated choices of the best and/or worst option to generate a rank order of the available options, and to develop models for such rankings. Marley and Louviere (2005) present various theoretical results for this general class of ranking models, and the corresponding tasks are studied in Chapter 4, by Marley and Islam (2012) and in various of the papers cited in the latter paper.

An interesting fact about ranking models based on repeated best and/or worst choice is that even if two models are of the same general form, and have the same number of parameters, they will not necessarily predict the same ranking probabilities. A well-known example is ranking by repeated best choices, versus ranking by repeated worst choices, where the best and the worst choice probabilities satisfy the MNL model, with the worst scale value the negative of the best scale value (Luce and Suppes, 1965; Yellott, 1977). In fact, there is, essentially, only one model based on using repeated best and/or worst choices to produce rankings that gives the same ranking probabilities independent of the particular order of best and/or worst choices used to generate the rank orders: Marley's (1968) reversible ranking model; the proof of this fact is given by Marley and Islam (2012, corollary 7).

5.4.2 Maxdiff model for best-worst choice among profiles

As mentioned previously, the maxdiff model for best-worst choice among profiles (Case 3) can be motivated as follows (later, we present a description of it as a random utility model). The probability of choosing profile i as the best (respectively, worst) option in choice set X is given by the MNL model of (5.2) (respectively, (5.3)). The person chooses the best option in X and, independently, chooses the worst element in X; if these two options are different, this pair is the chosen best-worst pair; if the two options are the same, the process is repeated (with resampling from all of X) until a pair of distinct options is selected. Marley and Louviere (2005) show that this process terminates provided there is no option i with $P_B(i|X) = P_W(i|X) = 1$. With this proviso, the probability of choosing profile i as the best option in choice set X and profile $i' \neq i$ as the worst option in choice set X is

$$P_{BW}(ii'|X) = \frac{\exp \boldsymbol{\beta}'(\mathbf{x}_i - \mathbf{x}_{i'})}{\sum_{\substack{j,j' \in X \\ j' \neq j}} \exp \boldsymbol{\beta}'(\mathbf{x}_j - \mathbf{x}_{j'})}. \qquad (5.4)$$

This is the maxdiff model for choice among profiles.

5.4.3 Maxdiff model for best-worst choice in a profile

For Case 2, choice in profiles, the presented set X is a single profile $\mathbf{x}_k$, and the choice options are the attribute levels $x_{kr}, r = 1, \ldots, m$, of that profile. The natural adaptation of the notation, and process, introduced above (for Case 3) results in the maxdiff model assuming that the probability of choosing attribute level x_{ki} as the best option in profile $\mathbf{x}_k$ and attribute level $x_{ki'}$, $i' \neq i$, as the worst option in profile $\mathbf{x}_k$ is

$$P_{BW}(ii'|\mathbf{x}_k) = \frac{\exp(\beta_i x_{ki} - \beta_{i'} x_{ki'})}{\sum_{\substack{j,j' \in M \\ j' \neq j}} \exp(\beta_j x_{kj} - \beta_{j'} x_{kj'})}.$$

5.4.4 Maxdiff model for best-worst choice among things

For Case 1, choice among things, the presented set X consists of options that do not usually have a multiattribute structure that is studied by the task, nor are the options the attributes of a single profile. Thus, we replace the notation $\mathbf{x}_k$ for a profile by k, for a generic object. Then, the natural adaptation of the notation, and process, introduced above (for Case 3) gives the result that the maxdiff model assumes that the probability of choosing thing i as the best option in choice set X and thing $i' \neq i$, as the worst option in choice set X is

$$P_{BW}(ii'|X) = \frac{\exp[u(i) - u(i')]}{\sum_{\substack{j,j' \in M \\ j' \neq j}} \exp[u(j) - u(j')]}, \qquad (5.5)$$

where u is the utility (value) function, which is to be estimated.

5.4.5 *Random utility representation of the maxdiff model for Case 1*

We now present random utility representations of the maxdiff model for best-worst choice among things (Case 1). We also use Case 1 to discuss some conceptual (scaling) issues that arise from it; related issues arise for the constant utility representations of the maxdiff model given above, but many readers are likely more familiar with random utility representations. Exactly parallel random utility representations (and issues) arise for Case 2 and Case 3 of the maxdiff model, and for random utility representations of the MNL model for best (respectively, worst) choices. We use utility values, rather than attribute levels and utility coefficients ("beta weights"), as the results can be more clearly stated, and proved, in this form.

Assume that for every pair of distinct things kk' there is an independent Gumbel random variable $\varepsilon_{kk'}$ in standard form.[4] Then a random utility representation of best-worst choice probabilities in Case 1 is given by: there are utility values $v(j)$ and constants ("scale factors") $\alpha > 0$ such that

$$P_{BW}(ii'|X) = \Pr\Big([v(i) - v(i')] + \alpha\varepsilon_{ii'} \geq v(j) - v(j')] + \alpha\varepsilon_{jj'}, \forall j, j' \in M, j' \neq j\Big). \quad (5.6)$$

Standard calculations yield

$$P_{BW}(ii'|X) = \frac{\exp\frac{[v(i) - v(i')]}{\alpha}}{\sum_{\substack{j, j' \in M \\ j' \neq j}} \exp\frac{[v(j) - v(j')]}{\alpha}}, \quad (5.7)$$

(in other words, with $u(j) = v(j)Â/Â\,\alpha$, we have the maxdiff model for Case 1). Since α is not identifiable from the choice probabilities without additional assumptions, we omit it when we later discuss the maxdiff model for Case 2 and Case 3. However, first we discuss the scale properties of v, hence of u, and recent work on conditions under which α is identifiable.

The most common property of such a scale u is that it is either:

ordinal: a scale f can be replaced by any strictly monotonic increasing function of f;
interval: a scale f can be replaced by $Af + B$, where $A > 0$ and B are any constants;
ratio: a scale f can be replaced by Af, where $A > 0$ is any constant;
difference: a scale f can be replaced by $f + B$, where B is any constant; or
absolute: f cannot be replaced by any other scale.

If we assume that the random component has no scale properties (that is, α and the $\varepsilon_{kk'}$ in (5.6) are unchanged when a scale transformation is applied to v,) then, looking at (5.7), it is clear that, of the above possibilities, v, and hence u, is at most a difference scale – since the value of the quantity on the right-hand side of the equation is unchanged if v is replaced by $v + B$, where B is any constant, whereas it would be changed if v were a ratio, interval or ordinal scale.

---

[4] This means that $Pr(\varepsilon_{kk'} \leq t) = e^{e^{-t}} (\infty < t < \infty)$, which has variance $\pi^2/6$.

Clearly, α still cannot be identified in the above expression, as we can replace $v(j)/\alpha$ throughout by $u(j)$. However, if there are circumstances in which α varies and v does not – such as in different individuals – then both may be identifiable (see section 5.4.6). The elimination of the above (potential) confusion between the properties of the utility scale (u above) and of the variance of the assumed random variables is leading to important new theoretical and empirical results: see Marley, Flynn and Louviere (2008) for the set-dependent maxdiff model, which involves such scales; regarding the general issue of the scale parameter in random utility models, see Louviere and Swait (2010), Salisbury and Feinberg (2010a) and Swait and Louviere (1993); and for utility versus scale interpretations of temporal discounting data, see Hutchinson, Zauberman and Meyer (2010) and Salisbury and Feinberg (2010b).

5.4.6 *Random utility representation of the maxdiff model for Case 2 and Case 3*

Proceeding in a manner exactly parallel to that for Case 1, we develop random utility representations, and properties, for Case 2 and Case 3, with utility functions replacing the product of utility coefficients and attribute levels.

For Case 2, we have a difference (utility) scale u and independent Gumbel random variables $\varepsilon_{ii'}$ in standard form such that

$$
\begin{aligned}
P_{BW}(ii' \mid \mathbf{x}_k) &= \Pr\Big([u(x_{ki}) - u(x_{ki'})] + \varepsilon_{ii'} \geq u(x_{kj}) - u(x_{kj'})] + \varepsilon_{jj'}, \forall j, j' \in M, j' \neq j \Big) \\
&= \frac{\exp - [u(x_{ki}) - u(x_{ki'})]}{\sum\limits_{\substack{j,j' \in M \\ j' \neq j}} \exp - [u(x_{kj}) - u(x_{kj'})]}.
\end{aligned}
\tag{5.8}
$$

The assumption of a single difference scale u across all the attributes follows from the results of Marley, Flynn and Louviere (2008). As an exercise, using arguments similar to those in section 5.4.5, the reader can persuade him-/herself that these are necessary restrictions for the representation to "make sense."

For Case 3, we have independent difference (utility) scales u_i, $i = 1, \ldots, m$, and independent Gumbel random variables $\varepsilon_{ii'}$ in standard form such that

$$
\begin{aligned}
&P_{BW}(ii' \mid X) \\
&= \Pr\Big(\sum\nolimits_{k=1}^{m} [u_i(x_{ki}) - u_i(x_{ki'})] + \varepsilon_{ii'} \geq \sum\nolimits_{k=1}^{m} [u_i(x_{kj}) - u_i(x_{kj'})] + \varepsilon_{jj'}, \forall j, j' \in M, j' \neq j \Big) \\
&= \frac{\exp - \sum\nolimits_{k=1}^{m} [u_i(x_{ki}) - u_i(x_{ki'})]}{\sum\limits_{\substack{j,j' \in X \\ j' \neq j}} \exp - \sum\nolimits_{k=1}^{m} [u_i(x_{kj}) - u_i(x_{kj'})]}.
\end{aligned}
$$

$$
\tag{5.9}
$$

The assumption of independent difference scales u_i, $i = 1,\ldots, m$, on each attribute follows from results found by Marley and Pihlens (2012). As above, as an exercise, using arguments similar to those in section 5.4.5, the reader can persuade him-/herself that these are necessary restrictions for the representation to "make sense."

Note that, in Case 2, we have a common difference scale u on all the attributes, whereas, in Case 3, we have an independent difference scale u_i on each attribute i. Since these scales are derived in different (types of) experiments, there is no necessary empirical relation between them. Nevertheless, one would hope that such (Case 2 and Case 3) experiments are not measuring totally different properties of the attributes. One theoretical (and, potentially, empirical) property one could hope for is that, for each attribute i, the scale u_i of Case 3 is strictly monotonic, increasing with respect to the scale u of Case 2. However, we are also assuming that the u_i, $i = 1,\ldots, m$, and u are independent difference scales. Then, under weak mathematical conditions,[5] the relation between u_i and u has to be linear; in other words, there are constants $a_i > 0$ and b_i such that, for each attribute-level x_{ki}, we have $u_i(x_{ki}) = a_i u(x_{ki}) + b_i$ (see Aczél, Roberts and Rosenbaum, 1986). The interested reader can get a feeling for why this result is true by trying to make a strictly monotonic increasing function, other than a linear one, "work" in preserving the difference scale properties of u_i and u.

Finally, if one has data from both a Case 2 and a Case 3 experiment in which the above results hold, then substituting the expressions $u_i(x_{ki}) = a_i u(x_{ki}) + b_i$ in the Case 3 representation gives

$$P_{BW}(ii'|X) = \frac{\exp - \sum_{k=1}^{m} a_i[u(x_{ki}) - u(x_{ki'})]}{\sum_{\substack{j,j' \in X \\ j' \neq j}} \exp - \sum_{k=1}^{m} a_i[u(x_{kj}) - u(x_{kj'})]}.$$

In this expression, the "importance weights" are known (from the relation between the data in the two experiments). However, from a Case 3 (or Case 2) experiment alone, such weights are not identifiable (see Marley, Flynn and Louviere, 2008).

The above results relating the Case 2 scale to the Case 3 scale were based on the assumption that, for each attribute i, the scale u_i of Case 3 is strictly monotonic increasing with respect to the scale u of Case 2. Although this is an interesting, and possibly desirable, result, the data may be otherwise. Weaker, but still interesting, theoretical relations are obtained with weaker assumptions (Flynn and Marley, 2014).

5.4.7 Score properties for maxdiff models

We now present theoretical results for best-minus-worst scores (defined below) for the maxdiff model of best-worst choice. Some of these results were proved by Marley and

---

[5] The function is continuous; alternatively, it is bounded from above on an interval.

Pihlens (2012), the rest by Marley and Islam (2012). The latter proofs were for (partial or full) ranking probabilities that belong to the class of weighted utility ranking models. This class includes the maxdiff model of best-worst choice as a special case, along with the MNL model for best choice and the MNL model for worst choice; however, it also includes many interesting ranking models, such as the reversible ranking model (Marley, 1968). For simplicity and relevance, we state the results for the maxdiff model – that is, for Case 1 we have (5.7); for Case 2, we have (5.8); and for Case 3 with additivity we have (5.9). Nonetheless, we know that, empirically, the score measures used in these results are useful for preliminary analyses of the data, independent of the model that is eventually fit to the data (see Flynn and Marley, 2014).

We first state results that hold in common for Cases 1, 2 and 3; these are results that do not depend on the actual structure (type) of the "choice options" – whether a (choice) option is to be interpreted as an object (Case 1), an attribute level (Case 2) or a profile (Case 3).

Using notation paralleling that of Marley and Louviere (2005) for Case 1, for each option x in the design, let $\hat{b}(x) - \hat{w}(x)$ denote the number of times option x is chosen as best in the study minus the number of times option x is chosen as worst in the study. We call this the score for x (in this particular design) and refer to "the scores" for these values across the options in the design.

Scores: property 1 (for Cases 1, 2 and 3)

Using general language (with undefined terms in quotation marks), the following states a result due to Huber (1963) in such a way that it applies to the maxdiff model for options; Marley and Islam (2012) state the terms and results exactly. Assume that one is interested in the rank order, only, of the utility values in the maxdiff model. An acceptable loss function is a "penalty" function that depends only on the order of the utility values and the order of the scores (that is, the loss remains the same if both the scale values and the scores are reordered in the same way) and that increases if the ranking is made worse by misordering a pair of scale values. Let S be a master set with $n \geq 2$ elements and assume that, for some k with $n \geq k \geq 2$, every subset of S with exactly k elements appears in the design[6] $D(S)$. Then, given the maxdiff model, ranking the scale values in descending order of the (best-minus-worst) scores, breaking ties at random, has "minimal average loss" among all ("permutation-invariant") ranking procedures that depend on the data only through the set of scores.

Comment 1 The above result actually holds for the class of weighted utility ranking models, a class that includes the MNL for best; MNL for worst; and the maxdiff model for best-worst choice (Marley and Islam, 2012).

Comment 2 Given the above property of the scores, they are likely useful starting values in estimating the maximum likelihood values of the utilities $u(x)$, $x \in S$. In fact, various empirical work on the maxdiff model gives a linear relation between the (best-minus-worst)

---

[6] Further work is needed to extend the theoretical result to, say, balanced incomplete block designs. See Marley and Pihlens (2012) for related discussions of *connected designs*.

scores and the (maximum likelihood) estimates of the utilities[7] (Louviere, Street *et al.*, 2008). In addition, Marley and Islam (2012) show similar results for weighted utility ranking models applied to the ranking data of a Case 3 study of attitudes towards the microgeneration of electricity.

Scores: property 2 (for Cases 1, 2 and 3)

The set of (best-minus-worst) scores is a sufficient statistic.

Comment 1 The above result actually holds for the class of weighted utility ranking models, a class that includes the MNL for best; MNL for worst; and the maxdiff model for best-worst choice (Marley and Islam, 2012, theorem 3).

The following result shows that, in the sense stated, the best-minus-worst scores reproduce the difference between the best and the worst choice probabilities given by the maximum likelihood estimates of the maxdiff model.

Scores: property 3 (for Cases 1, 2 and 3)

For the maxdiff model, the (best-minus-worst) score for an option x equals the sum over $X \in D(S)$ of the weighted difference between the (marginal) best and the (marginal) worst probability of choosing option x in set X, with those probabilities evaluated at the values of the maximum likelihood parameter estimates; the weight for a set X is the number of times X occurs in the design $D(S)$ (Marley and Pihlens, 2012, prove this for Case 3; the result for Case 1 and Case 2 is then immediate).

The following result applies to the attribute levels in Case 3; there is no equivalent result in Case 1 or Case 2, as there are no "implied" choices of attribute levels in those cases.

Scores: property 4 (for Case 3, with the preference independent maxdiff model, (9))

Using notation from Marley and Pihlens (2012) for choice among profiles (Case 3), $\hat{b}_i(p) - \hat{w}_i(p), p \in Q(i), i \in M$, denotes the number of times attribute level p is "chosen"[8] as best minus the number of times p is "chosen" as worst. Then Marley and Pihlens show that, for the preference independent maxdiff model (5.9),

(1) the set of values $\hat{b}_i(p) - \hat{w}_i(p)$ is a sufficient statistic; and
(2) $\hat{b}_i(p) - \hat{w}_i(p)$ equals the sum over all $X \in D(S)$ of the weighted difference between the (marginal) best and (marginal) worst probability of "choosing" attribute level p in set X, with those probabilities evaluated at the values of the maximum likelihood parameter estimates; the weight for a set X is the number of times X occurs in the design $D(S)$.

---

[7] Assume that the maxdiff model holds, and a BIBD is used for the survey. If the utility values are in a small range – say $[-1/2/1/2]$ – then a linear relation holds under a first-order Taylor expansion of the maxdiff choice probabilities (unpublished, available from Marley).

[8] Of course, in this Case 3, attribute level p is "chosen" (only) as a consequence of its being a component of the profile chosen on a given choice opportunity.

5.5 Models of choice and response time

Many models that predict both the choices made and the time to make them[9] – the response time – are essentially random utility models as used in the study of choice (best, worst, etc.) with a temporal structure imposed on the random variables. Here we summarize context-free accumulator models. As with all random utility models, these models cannot handle the classic context effects on choice, such as those called the attraction effect, the similarity effect and the compromise effect; Marley and Regenwetter (in press) summarize those choice data and their explanation by recent context-dependent accumulator models. Here, we summarize the (context-free) linear ballistic accumulator (LBA) model (Brown and Heathcote, 2008). Like other multiple accumulator models, the LBA is based on the idea that the decision-maker accumulates evidence in favor of each choice, and makes a decision as soon as the evidence for any choice reaches a threshold amount. The time to accumulate evidence to threshold is the predicted decision time, and the response time is the decision time plus a fixed offset (t_0), the latter accounting for processes such as response production. The LBA shares this general evidence accumulation framework with many models (as summarized by Busemeyer and Rieskamp, 2014) but has a practical advantage, namely that the LBA model assumes linear accumulation of evidence and, consequently, has an easily computed expression for the joint likelihood of a given response time and response choice among any number of options. We also show that a special case of the LBA yields choice probabilities that agree with those of standard MNL models for best, worst and best-worst choice.

Figure 5.1 gives an example of an LBA decision between two options, A and B. The A and B response processes are represented by separate accumulators that race against each other. The vertical axes represent the amount of accumulated evidence, and the horizontal axes the passage of time. Response thresholds (*b*) are shown as dashed lines in each accumulator, indicating the quantity of evidence required to make a choice. The amount of evidence in each accumulator at the beginning of a decision (the start point) varies independently between accumulators and randomly from choice to choice, usually assumed to be sampled from a uniform distribution: $U(0, A)$, with $A \leq b$. Evidence accumulation is linear, as illustrated by the arrows in each accumulator of the figure. The rate of accumulation is traditionally referred to as the drift rate, and this is assumed to vary randomly from accumulator to accumulator and decision to decision according to an independent distribution for each accumulator, reflecting choice-to-choice changes in factors such as attention and motivation. Rate means, *d*, and standard deviations, *s*, can differ between accumulators and options, though at least one value of *s* is usually fixed as a scaling constant.

Here, we consider a class of LBA models that assumes multiplicative drift rate variability, as this gives choice probabilities of the MNL form. The original LBA model assumed additive drift rate variability (Marley and Regenwetter, in press, summarize both classes of model).

---

[9] The material in section 5.5 is adapted from Marley and Regenwetter (in press), reproduced with kind permission from Cambridge University Press.

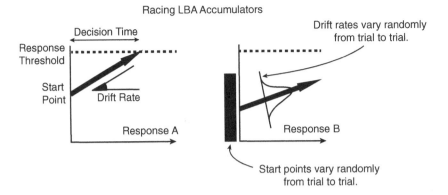

Figure 5.1 Illustrative example of the decision processes of the linear ballistic accumulator
Source: *Adapted from Hawkins* et al. *(2014a, fig. 1) (reproduced with kind permission from John Wiley & Sons).*

To agree with published papers, we use $\mathbf{B}_x$ (respectively, $\mathbf{W}_x$) to denote the distribution of time for option x to reach threshold, when the task is to choose the best (respectively, worst) of the available options, with parallel notation $\mathbf{BW}_{x,y}$, $x \neq y$, when the task is to choose the best (x) and worst (y) option. We also use a generic notation for the options, as we do not discuss results that differ between Cases 1, 2 and 3.

In the following summaries, we ignore the fixed offset (t_0). Let $\boldsymbol{\Delta}$ be a random variable on the positive reals; this will be the distribution of the (multiplicative) drift rate variability. Let, for $r > 0$,

$$\Pr(\boldsymbol{\Delta} < r) = G(r), \tag{5.10}$$

where G is a cumulative distribution function (CDF). Let b be the threshold and let x be a typical choice option with drift rate $d(x)$, and let $\boldsymbol{\Sigma}$ be a second random variable on $[0, A]$ with $A \leq b$; this will be the distribution of the start point. Let, for $h \in 0, A]$,

$$\Pr(\boldsymbol{\Sigma} < h) = H(r).$$

For option x, the start point has distribution $\boldsymbol{\Sigma}$ and the drift rate multiplier has distribution $\boldsymbol{\Delta}d$ (x); in addition, assume the samples of $\boldsymbol{\Sigma}$ and $\boldsymbol{\Delta}$ for different xs are independent, which we denote by $\boldsymbol{\Sigma}_x$ and $\boldsymbol{\Delta}_x$; thus, the subscripts do not imply dependence on x beyond the assumption of independent samples for different xs. Then, with $\mathbf{B}_x = \dfrac{b - \boldsymbol{\Sigma}_x}{\boldsymbol{\Delta}_x d(x)}$ the random variable for the time taken for the LBA with (mean) drift rate $d(x)$ to reach threshold, we have

$$\Pr(\mathbf{B}_x < t) = Pr\left(\frac{b - \boldsymbol{\Sigma}_x}{\boldsymbol{\Delta}_x d(x)} \leq t\right). \tag{5.11}$$

The major LBA applications to date have assumed that the starting point variability is given by a random variable $\mathbf{p}$ with uniform distribution on $[b - A, b]$, in which case (5.11) can be rewritten as

$$\Pr(\mathbf{B}_x < t) = \Pr\left(\frac{\mathbf{p}_x}{\mathbf{\Delta}_x d(x)} \leq t\right). \tag{5.12}$$

The above representation is a perfectly plausible multiplicative LBA model for any cumulative distributions G on the nonnegative reals and H on $[0, A]$ with $A \leq b$. However, a major argument advanced in favor of LBA models is their computational tractability in terms of probability density functions (PDFs) and cumulative distribution functions. In particular, it is usually assumed that the accumulators are independent, and therefore the main need is for the PDF and CDF of, say, (5.11) to be tractable.

As illustration, we now present a multiplicative LBA with no start point variability and Fréchet drift rate variability that leads to a standard set of models for best, worst and best-worst choice. Consider the special case of (5.12) when there is no start point variability (that is, $A = 0$,), and so p has a constant value b; in this case, without loss of generality, we can set $b = 1$. Then (5.12) reduces to

$$\Pr(\mathbf{B}_x < t) = \Pr\left(\frac{1}{\mathbf{\Delta}_x d(x)} \leq t\right).$$

We also assume that $\mathbf{\Delta}$ has a Fréchet distribution – that is, there are constants $\alpha, \beta > 0$, such that, for $r \geq 0$,

$$\Pr(\mathbf{\Delta} < r) = G(r) = e^{-(\alpha r)^{-\beta}}. \tag{5.13}$$

The following is then an obvious manner to obtain a set of models for best, worst and best-worst choice, respectively, and the corresponding response times.[10] Let $B_X(x, t)$ denote the probability of choosing x as the best option in X before time; the corresponding notation for worst is $W_X(x, t)$ and for best-worst $B_X(x, t; y, t)$ with $x \neq y$. We also assume that the drift rates are related and of the form $d(x), 1/d(x), d(x)/d(y)$; these restrictions can be removed as needed by data. Because a decision is made when the first accumulator reaches the threshold, we have the following.

(1) Best, with drift rates $d(z), z \in X$:

$$B_X(x, t) = \Pr\left(\frac{1}{\mathbf{\Delta}_x d(x)} = \min_{z \in X} \frac{1}{\mathbf{\Delta}_z d(z)} \leq t\right), \tag{5.14}$$

---

[10] Remember that the subscript on $\mathbf{\Delta}_z$, $\mathbf{\Delta}_{x, y}$, etc. indicates independent samples, not other dependence on z or x, y.

(2) Worst, with drift rates $1/d(z), z \in X$:

$$W_X(y,t) = \Pr\left(\frac{1}{\Delta_y \frac{1}{d(y)}} = \min_{z \in X} \frac{1}{\Delta_z \frac{1}{d(z)}} \le t\right), \tag{5.15}$$

(3) Best-worst, with drift rates $d(p)/d(x)$ and for all $p, q \in X p \ne q$:

$$BW_X(x,t;y,t) = \Pr\left(\frac{1}{\Delta_{x,y} \frac{d(x)}{d(y)}} = \min_{\substack{p,q \in Y \\ p \ne q}} \frac{1}{\Delta_{p,q} \frac{d(p)}{d(q)}} < t\right) (x \ne y). \tag{5.16}$$

Note that (16) implies that the best and the worst options are chosen at the same time; this is an unreasonably strong assumption, which we weaken later.

For $t \ge 0$, let

$$F(t) = 1 - \exp - \left(\sum_{z \in X} d(z)^\beta (\alpha t)^\beta\right).$$

Then routine calculations (paralleling those given by Marley, 1989) give, for $X \subseteq A$ and $x, y \in X$,

$$B_X(x;t) = \frac{d(x)^\beta}{\sum_{z \in X}^n d(z)^\beta} F(t), \tag{5.17}$$

$$W_X(y,t) = \frac{1/d(y)^\beta}{\sum_{z \in X}^n 1/d(z)^\beta} F(t), \tag{5.18}$$

and

$$BW_X(x,t;y,t) = \frac{d(x)^\beta/d(y)^\beta}{\sum_{\substack{r,s \in X \\ r \ne s}}^n d(r)^\beta/d(s)^\beta} F(t) \ (x \ne y). \tag{5.19}$$

The corresponding choice probabilities $B_X(x), W_X(y), BW_X(x,y)$ are given by these formulae in the limit as $t \to \infty$ – that is, as $F(t) \to 1$. Now, for $z, p, q \in A, p \ne q$, let $u(z) = \ln d(z), \varepsilon_z = \ln \Delta_z, \varepsilon_{p,q} = \ln \Delta_{p,q}$. Then the choice probabilities can equally well be written as: for all $x, y \in X \in D(A)$,

$$B_X(x) = \Pr\left(u(x) + \varepsilon_y = \max_{z \in X}[u(z) + \varepsilon_z] \right), \tag{5.20}$$

$$W_X(y) = \Pr\left(-u(y) + \varepsilon_y = \max_{z \in X}[-u(z) + \varepsilon_z] \right), \tag{5.21}$$

and for all $x, y \in X \in D(A)$, $x \neq y$,

$$BW_X(x,y) = \Pr\left(u(x) - u(y) + \varepsilon_{x,y} = \max_{\substack{p,q \in X \\ p \neq q}}[u(p) - u(q) + \varepsilon_{p,q}] \right). \tag{5.22}$$

However, given that Δ_z and $\Delta_{p,q}$ are generated by Fréchet drift rate variability (that is, (13)), we have it that $\varepsilon_z = \ln\Delta_z$ and $\varepsilon_{p,q} = \ln\Delta_{p,q}$ satisfy extreme value distributions.[11] When treated as a single model, the three models (5.20), (5.21) and (5.22) then satisfy an inverse extreme value maximum[12] random utility model (Marley and Louviere, 2005, def. 11). Standard results (summarized by Marley and Louviere, 2005,[13] and (5.17), (5.18) and (5.19) with $F(t) \to 1$, show that the expression for the choice probabilities given by (5.20) (respectively, (5.21), (5.22)) agrees with standard multinomial logit forms. Note that β is not identifiable from the choice probabilities, but it is, in general, identifiable when response times are also available (though the form predicted above for the response time distribution is not suitable for data). Note that, when (5.17) and (5.18) both hold with $F(t) \to 1$, we have that for all $x, y \in X, x \neq y, B_{\{x,y\}}(x) = W_{\{x,y\}}(y)$; empirically, this relation may not always hold (Shafir, 1993), nor is it a necessary property of this class of models when the $w(z) \neq 1/b(z)$ for each option z. See Chapter 6 for further discussion.

Equations (5.17), (5.18) and (5.19) show that each of these models (for best, worst and best-worst choice) has the property that the option chosen is independent of the time of choice; that property would not hold for (most) distributions other than the Fréchet for drift rate variability. Moreover, although the underlying utility maximization process may be cognitively plausible for best (or worst) choices, that for best-worst choice in (5.16) appears to require the participant to "simultaneously" compare all possible discrete pairs of options in the choice set, leading to a significant cognitive load; as already noted, it also implies that the best option and the worst option are chosen at the same time. Fortunately, as noted earlier, Marley and Louviere (2005, sect 4.1.2, case 2) present the following plausible process involving separate best and worst choice processes that generates the same choice probabilities: the person chooses the best option in X and, independently, chooses the worst option in X; if the resulting choices differ, then they are given as the responses; otherwise,

---

[11] With, in this case: for $-\infty < t < \infty \, Pr(\varepsilon_z \leq t) = \exp - (\alpha e^t)^{-\beta}$ and $Pr(\varepsilon_{p,q} \leq t) = \exp - (\alpha e^t)^{-\beta}$.
[12] We have added *maximum* to Marley and Louviere's definition to emphasize that the random utility models of *choice* are written in terms of maxima, whereas the equivalent accumulator models of *response time* are written in terms of minima.
[13] Marley and Louviere used the case $\alpha = \beta = 1$.

the person repeats the process until the selected pair of options do differ. The next section summarizes a parallel LBA model that extends this process to response times.

5.5.1 *Additive drift rate variability*

In contrast to the multiplicative drift rate model presented above, the linear ballistic accumulator model assumes additive drift rate variability generated by independent normal random variates, truncated at zero – that is, constrained to be nonnegative.[14] This is a random utility model that does not have the undesirable property that the choices made and the time to make them are independent. Nonetheless, it has been shown to make extremely similar predictions for best, worst and best-worst choice probabilities to those made by the multiplicative LBA model with no start point variability and Fréchet drift rate variability (Hawkins *et al.*, 2014a). The derivations for the additive model exactly parallel those described above with $\Delta d(x)$ replaced by $trunc(\mathbf{D}_z + d(z))$, with a major advantage of the additive model being that all formulae for cumulative distribution functions and probability density functions are computationally very tractable when the start point distribution is uniform. We now briefly summarize recent applications of this model to some standard data on best, worst and best-worst choice; Marley and Regenwetter (in press) summarize its extension to handle context effects in best choice and response times.

Hawkins *et al.* (2014a) fit four best-worst LBA models to each of three sets of data: two sets of best-worst choice data obtained in DCEs, the first involving choice between aspects of dermatology appointments, the second between mobile phones; and one set of best-worst choice and response time data in a perceptual judgment task: choosing the rectangle with the largest (respectively, smallest) area in a set of four rectangles presented on a trial, with multiple presentations of various sets of rectangles. Each additive LBA model is based on processes that follow naturally from a corresponding MNL model, with the latter as described above. In each fit of the models to only the best and/or worst choices, an essentially linear relationship was found between the log drift rate and utility estimates for the MNL model; and goodness of fit, as determined by the log-likelihood and root mean square error, was comparable. However, participants in the perceptual judgment task were free to make the best (largest) and worst (smallest) choice in whatever order they wished.

When both the choice and response time data from this experiment are fit, three of the models are inappropriate – one because it implies that best choices are always made before worst choices, the second because it implies the reverse and the third because it implies that the best and worst choices are made simultaneously. The relevant one of the first two models might be appropriate in experiments in which participants are forced, by the design, to respond in the order best, then worst (respectively, worst, then best); however, the third is implausible (for response times) under any reasonable circumstances. The data from the perceptual judgment task show: large differences between participants in best-then-worst

---

[14] In their data analyses, Brown and Heathcote (2008) ignored the small percentage of times that the normal distributions could take on negative values; Heathcote and Love (2012) present the correct analysis in terms of truncated normals.

versus worst-then-best-responding, but normally with both orders for each participant; changes in the proportion of response order as a function of choice difficulty; and changes in inter-response time because of choice difficulty. As noted above, these data are incompatible with three of the models, and, as Hawkins *et al.* (2014a) show, they cannot be satisfactorily fit by mixtures of these models. Therefore, we restrict our (brief) presentation to the fourth model, called the parallel (additive) LBA model, which is an extension of Marley and Louviere's (2005, sect. 4.1.2, case 2; and above) process model for choice to response time.

The parallel (additive) LBA model for best-worst choice assumes concurrent best and worst races, with, in general, different (drift rate) parameters in the two sets of races; the data analysis by Hawkins *et al.* (2014a) assumed that the worst drift rate is the reciprocal of the corresponding best race. The option chosen as best (respectively, worst) is that associated with the first accumulator to reach threshold in the best (respectively, worst) race. For computational convenience, Hawkins *et al.* presented, and tested, an approximation to the full model, in that they allow the same option to be selected as both best and worst, which was not allowed in their experiment; their model also allows for vanishingly small inter-response times, which are not physically possible. These predictions affect a sufficiently small proportion of their data that they were acceptable. The parallel model overcomes the drawbacks of the other three models described above by accounting for all general choice and response time trends observed in data; for instance, the model is able to capture inter- and intra-individual differences in response style, reflected by the data of those participants who tend to respond first with the best option, or first with the worst option.

The fact that data on best-worst choice could be well fit by each of the four best-worst LBA models but data on both choice and response time could be well fit only by the parallel LBA model gives support to the trend in consumer research to collect both the choices made and the time to make them. Moreover, the addition of response time data allows the estimation of scale parameters that cannot usually be estimated from best-worst choice data.

Chapter 6

Looking forward

Remember, today is the tomorrow you worried about yesterday,
and all is well.

Anon.

6.1 Introduction

This chapter is a positioning one, acknowledging the existing limitations of best-worst scaling (BWS), as a theory and/or as a method of data collection. As such, it should alert the reader to current areas of methodological research and provide a research agenda for the future. It touches upon innovative avenues of research that seek to better understand the psychological processes that might underpin random utility theory. Such work is of key importance in providing physiological and clinical justifications for the (statistical) random utility model. In many cases it refers to work that has begun in the field of health: this simply reflects the fact that stated preference data are both commonly used in that field and lacking in revealed preference counterparts to validate them. Thus, the reader should not conclude that the arguments are relevant only to health.

6.2 Best versus worst

Almost all applications of best-worst scaling in the preceding chapters (see Chapter 15 for an exception) and in the wider BWS literature have assumed, implicitly or explicitly, that the best and worst choices made by a particular individual reflect *mirror image* values (see Chapter 5 for specific meanings of this term); this enables *data pooling* ("stacking") of the worst data below (or above) the best data, and (with a sign change) treating the worst data as just more best data. Effectively, this also is the method for the popular maxdiff model of best and worst choices (see, for example, Sawtooth Software [www.sawtoothsoftware.com] and Chapter 5). The maxdiff model assumes that individuals compare every pair of best-worst and worst-best outcomes, and choose the pair with the largest positive difference. Recent empirical studies that include both the best-worst choices made and the time to make them find that the maxdiff model gives excellent fits to the choices, but the response times show that no individual uses a maxdiff process (Hawkins *et al.*, 2014a).

The fact that few (if any) individuals use a maxdiff process raises interesting and important questions as to the nature of the true underlying cognitive process that individuals use to make best and worst choices; in other words, it is likely that different individuals make these choices in different ways. Individuals must evaluate the information provided to them using an evaluation function, decision rule or indirect utility function, and, based on their evaluation(s), they must use some process to make a choice. In addition, different individuals are likely to be more (less) consistent in applying their rules or processes. Such potential differences imply there will be heterogeneity in the population of people making best and worst choices, and this heterogeneity can (and will) be attributable to both differences in rules and differences in the consistency of applying them (choice consistency or error variance). Thus, it is likely naïve and misleading to assume that best and worst choices reflect "mirror image values"; researchers should dig more deeply into the underlying processes and choice consistency of individuals.

In fact, there is prior work on different process models. In particular, there has been much recent work on best-worst models that assume that individuals sequentially evaluate the choice options – that is, they choose best first, then worst, then next best, or they choose worst, then second worst, then best, etc. Recent examples include the studies by Marley and Islam (2012), Marley and Louviere (2005), Marley and Pihlens (2012), and Scarpa *et al.* (2011). Despite a good start on the problem, these studies pay less attention to scale differences than is needed. So, while work on scale effects has begun, researchers such as Marley and Flynn (2015) note the need for further research on these effects. Specifically, scale effects were considered by Bednarz (2006), Marley and Islam (2012); and Scarpa *et al.* (2011) study both scale and stage effects.

Three recent papers criticize a focus on simple models: Dyachenko, Walker Reczeck and Allenby (2014); Giergiczny *et al.* (2013); and Rose (2013). In his concluding remarks, Rose alludes to a distinction that we have made in this book, namely that between using BWS as a data collection method and as a modelling framework. One might be somewhat agnostic about appropriate modeling assumptions applied to data when BWS is used as a data collection procedure; however, one might suspect that, when best choices are made before worst choices, a model that respects that form might be more appropriate. Nonetheless, when one aggregates best and worst data the underlying model properties become important. For example, the properties of best-minus-worst scores were proved under the assumption that the maxdiff model holds. However, it would likely require considerable Monte Carlo tests to check whether those properties continue to be useful if (say) a best, then worst, MNL model holds with different scale factors and/or utility values in the first (best) and second (worst) stages. In other words, it may very well be the case that the best-minus-worst scores continue to be linearly related to each of the best and worst utility values, but with different slopes (and intercepts) in the two cases.

It also is possible to draw incorrect conclusions regarding differences in best and worst values or underlying choice consistency as a result of aggregating choices over differences in people; that is, it may be that, if one can identify groups of individuals who use the same or similar rules or processes, individuals within these groups may more closely conform to the notion of best and worst values being "mirror images." Clearly, more research is needed to determine if finite groups of individuals can be identified reliably and accurately, and the extent to which such identification reveals similarities or differences in best and worst choice processes and values. Promising approaches currently available include archetypal analysis (Cutler and Breiman, 1994), scale-adjusted latent class models (Magidson and Vermunt, 2007) and bagged clustering (Dolničar and Leisch, 2004). However, there has been insufficient empirical experience with these approaches to know if and when one should (or should not) apply them and whether some are more appropriate for the three different BWS cases or not. Systematic research on these issues would therefore be welcome.

As discussed in Chapter 5, the possible models proliferate considerably when one considers various possible combinations of sequential best and/or worst choices, and those models probably can mimic each other. Indeed, even out-of-sample predictions may not provide strong differentiation in such models.

To date, most model tests have been applied to aggregate choice data, and, as previously noted, one might suspect different participants to have different values (preferences), and/or to use different decision rules and/or to be more (or less) consistent in how they choose. Several case studies in this book illustrate approaches based on individual participant choices in which best and/or worst scores appear to play a useful role in initial clustering of participants with similar preferences.

It is likely to be the case that it will be fairly difficult, if not impossible, to capture and separate these differences in typical survey and related field applications of BWS. The reasons for this are straightforward, in so far as one rarely collects very many choice observations per individual, which makes it difficult to statistically discriminate between possible underlying differences in individuals. Thus, one potentially useful way forward might be to combine data from surveys or field applications (usually involving few choices for each of a large number of participants) with a more typical experimental approach in psychology (often involving many choices for a smaller number of participants). In this way, experimental data may illuminate the extent to which certain simplifying assumptions do or do not hold for individual participants. We illustrate this approach with recent collaborative work between members of the Institute for Choice at the University of South Australia and the Department of Psychology at the University of Newcastle.

In particular, Hawkins *et al.* (2014b) aimed to determine whether choices made under a single instruction set – that is, most preferred (best) and least preferred (worst) – can be explained with a single latent variable, such as the utility (or valence) of different attributes and options. For instance, when asked to sequentially consider a series of multi-attribute options such as automobiles or job candidates, respondents tended to arrive at the same final preference (as shown by Huber, Neale and Northcraft, 1987; Levin, Jasper and Forbes, 1998; Levin *et al.*, 2001; the first paper used accept/reject, the other two include/exclude). However, explicit instruction to consider external factors, such as selection-related costs in personnel selection, may result in different choice outcomes (Huber, Neale and Northcraft, 1987). It is possible that, in the absence of manipulations designed to lead them to do otherwise, people might base best and worst choices on the same cognitive information.

Consequently, Hawkins *et al.* (2014a) examined whether selecting both the best and the worst option gives different data for best (respectively, worst) than when only a best (respectively, worst) choice is made; and whether best and worst choices are based on a common latent variable (summaries of the data and models are given in Chapter 5). They tested three groups of participants with identical choice sets. One group was asked to choose only their most preferred (best) option; a second group was asked to choose only their least preferred (worst) option; and a third group was asked to choose both their most and least preferred options.

Data from two experiments (one perceptual and one consumer) were analyzed using three statistical approaches (Bayesian analysis, state-trace analysis and cognitive modeling); all analytical methods reached the same conclusion, namely that deliberation involved in choosing the worst option from a set does not influence preferences for the best option; equally, choosing which option is best does not influence preferences for the worst option. Furthermore, the best and worst choices appear to reflect judgments that arise from a single latent variable. The result for best choices is important, since the best response is usually of greater interest in certain applied domains. For instance, for a marketer it is likely more profitable to know which product consumers might purchase (include in their consideration sets), rather than the (potentially many) products they likely will not purchase (will reject). The results suggest that data on best or worst choices can be used interchangeably to yield similar conclusions about preference strengths, although combining the best-worst procedure with response times likely produces more reliable parameter estimates for model-based inference.

6.3 Best/worst versus accept/reject

Suppose you seek to purchase a new eReader, and the local computer store has six models available.[1] The models will differ across multiple attributes, such as size of screen, memory size, weight, back-lit or not, clarity, etc. In making your decision, you could eliminate by aspects until a single option remains (Tversky, 1972), or choose the best and worst options based on the same (or different) weighted sums of the value to you of the various attribute levels of each option. As a result of various such decision rules, you might end up knowing which is your most preferred (best) and least preferred (worst) of the available options. However, you might then either accept (that is, purchase) the best available option, or not purchase (that is, reject) it because all the eReaders are too expensive. This illustration shows that best and/or worst choices do not give the same information as accept and/or reject decisions, as has been well known in the DCE literature

---

[1] The material in section 6.3 is adapted from Hawkins et al. (2014b). Copyright © 2014 by the American Psychological Association. The use of this information does not imply endorsement by the publisher.

since the paper by Louviere and Woodworth (1983), who introduced the concept of allowing participants to choose "none" of the available options. Orme (2009) discusses the use of such "anchors" and supports the use of Louviere's dual-response approach of adding an "all/none/some" question after the best-worst choices.

To further support the above distinctions, we briefly discuss the literature in psychology and consumer choice on accept and/or reject choices relative to that on best and/or worst choices. In these areas, accept/reject choices have been studied mainly from the perspective of "framing effects" in judgment. In this paradigm, decision tasks are designed in such a way that they can lead to inconsistent preferences under different experimental conditions. For example, Shafir (1993) presented hypothetical award (accept) and deny (reject) choices regarding the two parents in a case of an only child and sole custody. The choice involved one "impoverished" low-variance option (parent A), with mostly average attributes; and one "enriched" high-variance option (parent B) with some excellent and some awful attributes; two sets of respondents saw the same two options, but were given different instructions. Respondents asked to which parent they would *award* sole custody tended to accept the "enriched" option, yet respondents asked to which parent they would *deny* sole custody again tended to select the "enriched" option.

Similar patterns of preferences have been observed in investment decisions (Cheng and Chiou, 2010), choices among job candidates (Ganzach, 1995) and even in a psychophysical judgment task (Tsetsos, Chater and Usher, 2012). Such reversals might arise because respondents focus on different attributes when accepting and rejecting (for example, van Buiten and Keren, 2009), or perhaps the reversals are mediated by the amount of elaboration of attribute information (Ganzach and Schul, 1995; Juliano and Wilcox, 2011). The statistical principle commonly used in this research is the logic of dissociations: if one experimental manipulation (for example, high- versus low-variance choice options) has different effects under different levels of another manipulation (such as decisions to accept versus reject), we might conclude that two different cognitive processes are at work (for example, different cognitions about accepting versus rejecting). Although this logic is common in psychology, and can appear compelling, it also can be misleading (Loftus, 1978; Wagenmakers *et al.*, 2012), and one also must beware of aggregation fallacies involved in making inferences from between-subject designs. Additionally, the vast majority of prior studies in these paradigms failed to consider the possibility that the experimental manipulations can impact not only the mean of the response distributions but also on the variance of these distributions (as well as other moments); this fact is now well known in the discrete choice experiment and modeling literature (see, for example, Salisbury and Feinberg, 2010a; Fiebig *et al.*, 2010).

Another possible explanation for the discrepancy between the results obtained by Shafir (1993) and Tsetsos, Chater and Usher (2012) and many of the results from best/worst studies is the divergent goals of researchers using process-based versus measurement-based models. For example, Busemeyer and Rieskamp (2014) describe how researchers using measurement models (such as MNL) apply them to small samples of (discrete) choice data aggregated over many people, to efficiently estimate parameters (which can be important in applied contexts), while process-focused researchers collect larger amounts of data for a few participants to try to understand the cognitions underlying choice by individuals (which are important to psychologists). This focus has led psychologists to construct particular experimental situations that yield interesting context effects, which in turn reveal subtle cognitive biases. In contrast, applied researchers tend to focus on measurement using designs that minimize such effects.

It is likely that recent process models, such as the *parallel best-worst linear ballistic accumulator* (Hawkins *et al.*, 2014a; see Chapter 5) can be extended to account for known context effects in accept/reject tasks. For example, Shafir (1993) found that the sum of the proportion of times that an option is accepted under one instruction and rejected under a second instruction can be greater than one; this might be explained by a weighted multi-attribute model in which the weights change across tasks but the underlying utilities do not.

6.4 Aggregation (or not) of best and worst data

6.4.1 Best and worst differ only in variance scale factor

In cases in which worst data differ "only" in their scale factor from best, there are well-established methods for data pooling. These date from the seminal article by Swait and Louviere (1993), and largely rely on rescaling the independent variables up or down in order to control for heteroskedasticity between the two (or more) data sets. So, for example, if worst choices were more consistent (possessed smaller variances, leading to larger estimates in absolute size) than best, then, instead of the −1 factor applied to the worst data, a "more negative" number could be used, before data pooling with best data. Alternatively, one can directly estimate the variance scale ratio between the two or more data sets simultaneously using full-information maximum likelihood estimation or a similar Bayesian estimation approach.

As is obvious, differences in scale present few problems statistically, although they may have policy implications. For instance, in the field of health, clinicians should be aware that patients may be "better" (more consistent) in their best (or worst) choices, and that more time and/or patient education may be required when eliciting worst (or best) if statistical power is not to be compromised. Across various fields there is also the possibility that the "wrong" policy options are eliminated from consideration at too early a stage when consumers/citizens are simply very unsure of their preferences and require public information campaigns.

6.4.2 Best and worst differ in terms of nature of the decision rule (process)

A potentially more serious problem emerges when best and worst arise from different processes. Assume a study has been conducted using a traditional DCE or a Case 3 BWS study, involving choices between complete ICECAP-O quality-of-life states.[2] Suppose

---

[2] This is a modified example from Chapter 12; see that chapter for explanations of the abbreviation "ICECAP-O," and related ones on subsequent pages.

citizens choose their best state in a conventional utility maximization framework but use elimination by aspects (EBA) in their choice of worst state. It is far from clear that there is a single capability (utility) scale on which all the impaired quality-of-life states can be placed. If EBA is being used "from the bottom" and conventional utility maximization is being used "from the top," where, if anywhere, do the scales meet in the middle, and how is any discrepancy to be reconciled? Disciplines such as health economics require a single scale in order to quantify changes in outcomes, and it is unclear when and if one could pool such best and worst data in a theoretically acceptable way.

Similarly, economists working in a welfarist paradigm could confront serious problems trying to aggregate such choices. Under the conditions mentioned in the previous paragraph, willingness to pay is likely to vary according to whether best or worst data are used, although the nature of the policy decision (that is, whether it is a policy expansion or a policy withdrawal) might be helpful in informing the decision as to which data (best or worst) should be used. Nevertheless, all researchers must move their focus away from statistical issues arising from differences in elicitation methods and consider the conceptual underpinnings of each – namely, what is the policy problem, and what is the theoretically correct tool to address it?

6.5 Comparisons of the three cases of BWS

Further research into the relationships between estimates from the three cases of BWS is needed, particularly since Cases 2 and 3 are being used interchangeably (without suitable caveats) in fields such as health economics. To set the scene, it is helpful at this point to summarize some decisions that were made in the early days of Case 2 in health economics. Members of the UK ICEPOP team decided early on to use Case 2 to elicit preferences. The decision was informed on practical grounds: it was quickly realized that a (DCE or Case 3 BWS) task involving choices between whole ICECAP-O profiles would be too difficult for large numbers of the vulnerable (older) group who were the subjects of the study. This decision was subsequently vindicated by a re-analysis of the (pairwise) DCE data also collected (Flynn, Peters and Coast, 2013).

The decisions to use Case 2 were also supported for statistical reasons. Because Case 2 tasks are generally "easier" than multi-profile ones, they tend to exhibit smaller variances on the latent scale, producing larger, more precise, estimates of utility parameters (Flynn, Peters and Coast, 2013). Of course, this advantage becomes a problem if non-trivial numbers of respondents begin to exhibit deterministic (non-probabilistic) decision making as a result of an excessively easy task, an issue discussed by Flynn (2010b). However, this issue was largely seen as theoretical among the vulnerable groups sampled in the ICECAP and CHU-9D studies.

Marley and Pihlens (2012) have subsequently shown that, under weak mathematical conditions, Case 3/DCE estimates should be linearly related to those obtained from an "equivalent" Case 2 study (see Flynn and Marley, 2014, 193–4, for a summary). However, there are a number of caveats that have been ignored, partly because of the *practical* reasons used to justify Case 2 in the early days of ICEPOP. These deserve a more complete exposition here.

6.5.1 Case 2 versus Case 3/DCE estimates

There are some possibly strict conditions that must hold for Case 2 estimates to be the same (up to scale) as those obtained from a multi-profile task (such as Case 3 or a DCE).

(1) Respondents must not "become deterministic" (or vice versa) as a result of doing the two different types of task.
(2) There must be no interactions.
(3) The context must not change as a result of the change in choice task.

The first condition has already been discussed. The second condition has received some attention from Flynn (2010b). The Case 2 task effectively moves the profile "out of context," in that there is no longer a comparator that might change the utility associated with the attribute levels in the profile on offer. Indeed, it raises the conceptual issue of what exactly an interaction in a Case 2 task is. Furthermore, as discussed by Flynn, in certain studies (most notably those with attributes that all have ordered levels) it becomes impossible to present certain profiles that are necessary to estimate interactions, because these profiles also induce deterministic decision making: "best" and/or "worst" is trivially easy.

The third condition is perhaps the most crucial, but least well appreciated, certainly among economists. It concerns choice context. Marley, Flynn and Louviere (2008) provide an example of how changing the context of the task – for example, from choosing a flight for business reasons to choosing it for pleasure – might alter the "importance" weights applied to the attributes. The distinction between importance weights (associated with attribute but varying by context) and level scales (invariant to context) is one made in mathematical psychology, but it is not part of traditional economic theory. Whitty *et al.* (2014) reference the appropriate literature but appear not to understand the implications when attempting to explain why they obtained such different estimates from Case 2 compared to those from a standard (best) DCE task. Their study elicited the relative importance of sociodemographic and health factors (as attributes) in a priority setting in a Case 2 BWS task. However, the DCE task was by its nature radically different: it required respondents to choose which of two interventions was more deserving of funding. It is easy to imagine situations in which the level of an attribute is not perceived to be high or low in utility terms in the Case 2 task, but in which the attribute as a whole has a large importance weight, in the context of *comparisons between interventions*. The authors nowhere state which, if any, of the tasks is closest to how decision making is actually conducted in practice; in this case that is the criterion that should determine the choice task to be used.

Indeed, in terms of implications for choice of task, it is hard to see at this time how to make simple recommendations. Generally speaking, the context of how the estimates will ultimately be used should guide the decision as to which type of BWS to use. The use of a within-profile task such as the Case 2 BWS by Coast and Flynn shows them to be somewhat relaxed about its use, despite the fact that it is fundamentally a different type of task from that used in health economics evaluations to date (in which multi-profile tasks predominate). First, the estimates in this context (quality of life) do not appear to change much, depending on the type of task. Second, multi-profile tasks effectively disenfranchise large numbers of respondents because of task complexity. Third, the nature of Case 2 estimates in this context, as a measure of "unmet need," is more in line with what Sen (1982) wished capabilities to measure than as a tool for economic evaluation. It must be acknowledged that he would likely be uncomfortable with the use of individual preferences *at all*; but Case 2 estimates come closer to the spirit of how he intended to measure capabilities. The fact the estimates are not markedly out of line with those from multi-profile tasks (Flynn, Peters and Coast, 2013) suggests that the published estimates can still be used in economic evaluation.

A final point can be made concerning the difficulty of multi-profile tasks. Both the ICECAP and CHU-9D teams chose Case 2 tasks because of the perceived inability of significant numbers of respondents to complete multi-profile tasks (although the latter were time trade-off/standard gamble tasks). The state of the art at that point vindicated such decisions: although multi-profile tasks might be argued to be more appropriate, given the economic evaluations for which the instruments were designed, so many respondents were obviously unable to conduct the valuation tasks that representativeness would have been compromised. Studies by Flynn (within subject) and Louviere (between subject) that are to be submitted for publication have confirmed warnings made by Rose and Bliemer (2009) that the maximally efficient designs in use at the time in DCEs also make choice tasks as difficult as possible for respondents: the modulo arithmetic ("rotation of attribute levels") used to construct choice sets ensured zero overlap across profiles, making the task extremely difficult for vulnerable groups. Currently, we suggest that one may want to consider a design that represents a compromise between statistical and respondent efficiency, so as to make DCEs "doable" by vulnerable groups.

6.5.2 *Case 1 versus multi-profile estimates*

Case 1 has been used by the authors in a number of applied research projects when resources to conduct full qualitative studies to identify the most relevant attributes for a DCE were not available. Specifically, when clients provide a large list of attributes it is necessary to reduce this quickly and cheaply, without risking omitting any key attributes that influence choice.

Case 1 pilot studies seem to work quite well for this purpose. Respondents are presented with the range of levels relevant to each attribute of interest in the study preamble. Then a Case 1 study is conducted to identify the attributes that are likely to influence their choices in a full DCE/Case 3 study, given those likely levels. Clearly, such an approach confounds estimates of the levels themselves with their range. However, if it is done carefully, it enables attributes with little likely effect on choice to be identified and eliminated.

Research is needed to better understand the conditions under which this approach is valid and unlikely to omit important attributes. Such research may also contribute to the agenda that seeks to better separate attribute importance from level scale values.

6.6 BWS driving forward the research agenda in applied psychology and economics

BWS has already begun to drive forward the research agenda in applied psychology (for example, segmenting the population on the basis of personality type) and economics (for example, valuing highly impaired health/social care states).

6.6.1 Limitations of asking worst after best

In all these cases the power of BWS to exploit the fact that respondents already have considered the choice set before choosing "worst" has been pertinent. This makes BWS surveys more cost-effective (reducing the number of choice sets that are presented). However, it also complicates a number of analyses, including investigation of the size of the variance scale factor (choice consistency) and the time taken to make a worst choice. More controlled psychological studies of worst are needed if issues specific to such choices are to be better understood and modeled.

6.6.2 What does the addition of response times give us?

As summarized in section 6.2, Hawkins *et al.* (2014a; 2014b) have shown that data with both choice and response times essentially give us the "same" inferences as best-worst choice data, though possibly with more accurate estimates of the parameters. While this is an important validation of the MNL model as a psychological model of choice, it raises questions over what the addition of such response time data provides.

Health economists may have one answer: as a key validation of stated preference data when there are no revealed (real market) data. They may also yet identify circumstances in which stated preference data provide unreliable results. Early analysis of a Case 1 BWS study of attitudes towards end-of-life care in Australia (see Chapter 7 for the results of analysis of the choice data) has identified certain attitudes whose response times are inconsistent with the MNL applied to the choice data alone (that is, without response times). Such attitudes tend to be "gut" instincts that induce fast responses and involve little thought; hence, they are unlikely to provide explanatory power in an associated DCE. Such work is continuing and is likely to help identify attitudes with predictive power by acting as proxies for more difficult DCE choices.

6.6.3 Are there different "worst" decision rules and what does this mean for design?

We earlier noted the possibility of different decision rules for worst. This has implications for design: to what extent must design be a compromise between optimizing for best and optimizing for worst (if worst is a different type of choice)? Work on this potentially challenging design problem would be welcome.

6.7 Data expansion methods

Earlier chapters demonstrated analytical methods that relied on "expanding the data," such as including all implied subsets of the choice set actually answered and assuming that the choice the respondent actually made holds true in all the implied choice sets. The primary purpose of data expansion methods is to improve the precision of parameter estimates and enable one to estimate logit or other statistical choice models when the number of degrees of freedom is otherwise too few. However, such expansions make particular assumptions about "what the respondent would have done"; in particular, they assume respondents would have answered deterministically (without error) in the implied choice sets together with the same mean he/she derived from options in the actual (full) choice set answered. This has the effect of propagating a certain variance (zero) in the conventional random utility model to the larger model that includes the "pseudo choice sets." While this probably gives more precise estimates, it is likely to make many researchers uncomfortable. In other words, if the error variance is a function of choice set size, such expansion method assumptions may be unwarranted and have implications for the correct estimation of willingness to pay. Marley and Islam (2012) develop valid (probabilistic) interpretations of several such "expansions" of best-worst and/or (partial) ranking data, and test them on stated preferences for the local solar generation of electricity. Further work, including simulation studies (at the least), is required.

6.8 Final thoughts

It is hoped that this book will provide the definitive guide to BWS. It confirms the names for the three cases chosen by Louviere for the review by Flynn (2010b) and makes clear that BWS can be used as a theory of process and/or as a method of data collection. At the very least, future studies can make clear what type of BWS approach is being used and for what purpose(s). Various methods of analysis have been introduced, and the empirical chapters provide case studies illustrating them.

We have tried to be candid in identifying areas in need of further work. Some of these areas already are being investigated in current research projects, but many remain potential opportunities and unresolved problems. Finally, it is likely that our proposed future research agenda will complement other research agendas currently under way to achieve a better understanding as to why people make the choices they do. For example, Marley and Swait are trying to better understand and model mixed choice strategies; Marley, Louviere and Flynn, together with colleagues at the University of Newcastle, are continuing work that incorporates response times. There also is work combining BWS and eye-tracking methods with electroencephalogram data in choice contexts (Khushaba *et al.*, 2013). Together, it is likely that these streams of research will form the next generation of choice models.

Applications: Case 1

Chapter 7

BWS object case application: attitudes towards end-of-life care

Terry N. Flynn, Elisabeth Huynh and Charles Corke

7.1 Introduction

This chapter uses Case 1 – the object case – to elicit the views of older Australians towards different, and potentially competing, end-of-life care strategies. In addition to the empirical aims of the original article, this chapter aims to illustrate to those working in health how Case 1 BWS techniques used previously in personality assessment can be used to elicit attitudes towards health care. The proportion of the Australian population aged 65 and over grew from 8.5 percent in 1961[1] to 13.3 percent in 2009.[2] This proportion is predicted to rise to 21.3 percent in 2031,[3] which has implications for health and social care service provision, particularly if there are continuing reductions in the proportion of an Australian's life that is spent contributing to the system in tax. This aging issue is common to most of the developed world. Costly, and burdensome, interventions to preserve life are increasingly used. While advances in medical care mean that such highly interventionist strategies return some patients to a health state approximating that experienced before the deterioration, in many cases these treatments serve only to prolong the dying process or return the patient to a highly impaired state in which activities of daily living cannot be performed. Many individuals do not want this expensive and potentially intrusive care (SUPPORT investigators, 1995).

Doctors and family members generally choose interventionist treatment for patients who cannot make their own choice, unless patients make their wishes clear in advance. However, the process of thought leading to the creation of an advance care plan is difficult for most patients (Baker *et al.*, 2013), and only a minority complete plans at present, so clinicians often have little information about an individual patient's treatment preferences.

Advance care planning (ACP) is typically conducted in an interview that is necessarily long and complex, because of the need to consider various medical interventions that might be applied singly, or in combination, in different circumstances. Outcomes can vary, in terms of chance of survival, treatment burden and quality of life. Therefore, traditional ACP

---

[1] www.abs.gov.au/ausstats/abs@.nsf/2f762f95845417aeca25706c00834efa/a2cd8d204f84e882ca2570ec001117a1!Open Document.
[2] www.abs.gov.au/AUSSTATS/abs@.nsf/Previousproducts/3235.0Main%20Features32009?opendocument&tabname= Summary&prodno=3235.0&issue=2009&num=&view=#PARALINK2.
[3] www.abs.gov.au/ausstats/abs@.nsf/2f762f95845417aeca25706c00834efa/a2cd8d204f84e882ca2570ec001117a1!Open Document.

interviews have typically been qualitative in nature (Singer, Martin and Kelner, 1999),[4] making them impossible to scale up to the population level.

However, ACP has to be scaled up to this level, not least because end-of-life care is both emotive and resource-intensive to society. There have been attempts recently to standardize ACP interviews, using more traditional survey questions, in order to reduce their length. One such attempt is the Medical Treatments Preferences Profile (MTPP) in Australia. Unfortunately, most of the questions are Likert scale questions, with the potential vulnerabilities detailed in other chapters of this book.

However, very recent work has introduced a form of discrete choice experiment, although several of the authors were unaware of this reinvention and used the term "clinical vignettes" (Beattie, Flynn and Clark, 2013; Dodson *et al.*, 2013; Louviere, Hensher and Swait, 2000). In the ACP context their research offers a cost-effective solution to the informational problem detailed above: by using statistical design matrices, the DCE framework enables patient responses to a relatively small number of "What if?" scenarios potentially to be generalized to a wider range of situations (Louviere and Street, 2000). However, one issue that a conventional DCE does not solve is the fact that respondents must consider complex clinical scenarios. Some people find this difficult and, indeed, confronting and would be more comfortable having their *attitudes* elicited. Should it be possible to reliably predict a patient's DCE preferences for specific treatments from his/her attitudes – whether to life generally or ACP specifically – this could greatly help the planning process.

Thus, this study[5] had two primary aims: first, to elicit preferences for end-of-life care scenarios using the simplest type of DCE – namely, presenting single profiles requiring binary choice (yes/no) answers; and, second, to elicit attitudes using Case 1 BWS in order to understand whether there was broad agreement between preferences and attitudes. A secondary aim was to ascertain whether these more easily quantified attitudes elicited from the BWS study could predict the preferences elicited from the DCE. Since Case 2 BWS had previously been used to understand the preferences of older people in the United Kingdom (Coast, Flynn, Natarajan, *et al.*, 2008; Coast, Flynn, Sutton, *et al.*, 2008), it was not thought infeasible to use it among older residents of Australia (those aged fifty-five and over), as in this study.

7.2 Methods

This was the first ever study to use DCEs to elicit not only specific population treatment preferences but general attitudes towards care scenarios in health care. The attitudinal study was intended to follow methods used previously in the field of personality assessment in which subsets of attitudinal statements form the objects in a Case 1 BWS study.

[4] This includes, in Australia, www.respectingpatientchoices.org.au.
[5] Funding: the study was funded by the Australian Victoria State Department of Health, which had no influence on any of the design and conduct of the study; the collection, management, analysis and interpretation of the data; the preparation, review or approval of the chapter; or the decision to submit it for publication.
 Ethical approval: since the respondents were anonymous, ethics approval was covered by the institutional survey approval of the University of Technology, Sydney, which conducted the study before the first two authors changed affiliation.

7.2.1 Participants

A total of 1,166 older adults aged 55 and over (including 402 aged 75 and over) resident in Australia were recruited from two general population online panels, following requests to participate to 1,881 respondents (62 percent response rate). The second specialist "older respondent" panel (from the ORU company) was used when it became clear that the main panel administered by Pureprofile, although extremely large (covering 3 to 5 percent of the Australian population), was unlikely to provide an adequate number of older (over 75 years) respondents within the study timeframe.

7.2.2 Administration of surveys

The treatment preference survey was a conventional DCE involving a full factorial of 16 ($2 \times 2 \times 4$) hypothetical clinical scenarios defined by levels (amounts) of three attributes: decline in cognitive health (two levels – no impairment or dementia), heath impairment (two levels – stroke or coma) and life-saving treatment on offer (four levels – antibiotics, ventilation, tube feeding or major surgery).

The four treatments were chosen on the basis of their predictive ability in prior research suggesting that people who reject antibiotics reject everything, while people who accept major surgery accept everything (Kass-Bartelmes, Hughes and Rutherford, 2003). The DCE was split into two versions of eight scenarios, with respondents randomized to one version. Respondents were required to state, in each scenario, whether they would wish the particular life-saving treatment on offer to be administered or not.

The attitudinal survey that participants completed was a Case 1 BWS survey that elicited the degree of agreement with each of 13 attitudes (or "values") towards medical treatment. The 13 statements were refined from two pilot studies, with some based on existing literature (Kaldjian *et al.*, 2009; Mack *et al.*, 2010). A balanced incomplete block design (Street and Street, 1987) for the 13 objects in 13 blocks was used, each with four of the attitudes. Figure 7.1 gives subset three of the 13 to illustrate the nature of the task.

This choice-based question format had three principal benefits. First, it forced respondents to discriminate between attitudes that likely compete in clinical practice, unlike a Likert scale, which permits the respondent to (for instance) indicate "complete agreement" with both a statement prioritizing life extension over symptom management and one prioritizing the opposite. Second, it was immune to differences in response styles that are known to affect both within- and between-population studies using Likert scales (Lee, Soutar and Louviere, 2007; Steenkamp and Baumgartner, 1998). Third, it allowed statements to be made about the odds of choosing one statement over another at the level of the individual respondent, to measure uncertainty quantitatively.

Respondents also answered a number of sociodemographic, health and other questions relevant to any experience they may have had of end-of-life care. These questions were included in an attempt to explain any observed heterogeneity in attitudes and/or preferences (true differences in views) and variances (choice consistency, most likely arising because of differences in a respondent's "sureness" or certainty of views).

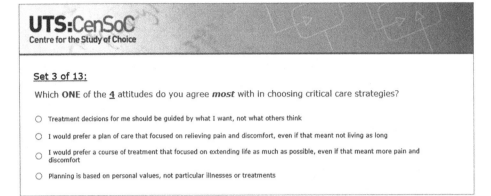

UTS:CenSoC
Centre for the Study of Choice

Set 3 of 13:

Which **ONE** of the **4** attitudes do you agree *most* with in choosing critical care strategies?

○ Treatment decisions for me should be guided by what I want, not what others think

○ I would prefer a plan of care that focused on relieving pain and discomfort, even if that meant not living as long

○ I would prefer a course of treatment that focused on extending life as much as possible, even if that meant more pain and discomfort

○ Planning is based on personal values, not particular illnesses or treatments

Figure 7.1 Example BWS task for one of 13 choice sets for a BIBD to value 13 attitudinal statements

7.2.3 Outcome measures

Analysis was conducted using Stata MP11 and Latent GOLD Choice 4.5 with Syntax Module to quantify preference and variance heterogeneity (Flynn *et al.*, 2010). Primary analyses consisted of:

(1) reporting of sample-level treatment rejection rates under all 16 scenarios in the DCE;
(2) a segmentation analysis conducted to identify "types" of respondent based on treatment preferences elicited from the DCE using (variance) scale-adjusted latent class (SALC) analyses; the main hypothesis tested was that increases in age would be associated with stronger (more certain), and possibly greater numbers of, views; and
(3) reporting of average attitudinal scores from the BWS study.

Secondary analyses:

(1) repeated the segmentation analysis using the BWS data to ascertain whether common segments explained both attitudes and preferences;
(2) reported treatment rejection rates in the DCE by attitudinal score to understand the extent to which differences in general attitudes were associated with differences in specific treatment preferences; and
(3) reported rates of discussion with friends/relatives/doctors according to treatment acceptance rates; it was hypothesized that people who had had such discussions were less likely to accept treatment.

7.3 Results

Of the 1,166 respondents, the 75+ age group (n=402) was disproportionately male (64.2 percent) compared with the age 55–74 age group (45.9 percent), probably because of the initial recruitment method to the panel (of internet users almost two decades ago).

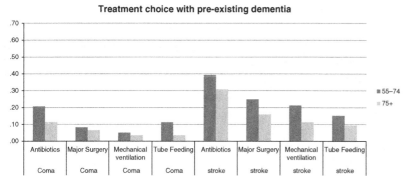

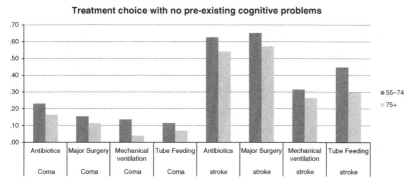

Figure 7.2 DCE results showing proportion of respondents accepting life-saving treatment

7.3.1 Primary analysis 1

Figure 7.2 shows the proportion of respondents (by age group) who would accept treatment in each of the 16 hypothetical scenarios. As expected, imagining living with pre-existing dementia was associated with lower acceptance rates generally, and experiencing irreversible coma caused a large number of treatment rejections. The older age group consistently rejected treatment more often than the younger age group.

7.3.2 Primary analysis 2

The averages in the first analysis concealed heterogeneity within the population, which was identified using logit-based models. For results to be valid, respondents with perfect single-attribute predictors had to first be eliminated: this was the case for 75 respondents (5 percent of those aged 75 and over and 7.2 percent of those aged 55 to 74), the majority of whom used the rule "Reject treatment if health deterioration = coma." In a scale-adjusted latent class analysis of the remaining DCE data, examination of the log-likelihood and Bayes information criterion statistics suggested that there were no more than three materially different classes among the group as a whole, but there was an additional fourth class among the younger age group. The classes were described as follows.

(1) This type was strongly opposed to any intervention that prolongs life in poor health or quality-of-life state. They had a particular aversion to being kept alive when experiencing extreme cognitive or mental impairments. It comprised 61 percent of respondents aged 75 and over and 42 percent of those aged less than 75.

(2) This type was in favor of medical interventions no matter what the chances of success and/or degree of impairments following the avoidance of death, and comprised 7 percent of respondents aged 75 and over and 6 percent of those aged less than 75.

(3) This type was mildly "anti-treatment" but was willing to trade off aspects of treatment and outcomes; thus they "took each decision on its own merits" and comprised the remaining 32 percent of respondents aged 75 and over and 33 percent of those aged less than 75.

(4) This class had very weak preferences, with no discernible patterns. It existed only in those aged under 75 and comprised the remaining 19 percent of these younger respondents.

7.3.3 Primary analysis 3

Figure 7.3 shows the average attitudinal scores from the BWS survey. These represent the average frequency of choosing an attitude as "most agreed with" minus the average frequency of choosing it as "least agreed with." They were calculated by:

(1) subtracting the number of times an attitude was picked as "least" from the number of times it was picked as "most" (since every attitude appeared four times across the study, this produced a number bounded by $+/- 4 \times 1166 = +/- 4664$); and

(2) normalizing these to be on the $[-1, +1]$ interval to produce the "best-minus-worst scores" (the "scores") by dividing each number by the total availability (4664).

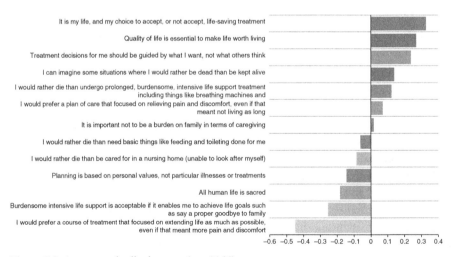

Figure 7.3 Average attitudinal scores (n = 1166)

It is clear that, on average, the overall sample strongly agree that quality of life should take precedence over life extension and believe that that their views should not be over-ridden. Those aged 75 and over had exactly the same ordering of the 13 attitudes; for those aged 55 to 74, the ordering of "Planning is based on personal values, not particular illnesses or treatments" and "All human life is sacred" was swapped.

7.3.4 Secondary analyses

Secondary analysis A

Latent class solutions were qualitatively similar to those from the DCE: the algorithm found large "pro quality of life" classes very quickly, and that "pro life extension classes" were smaller. In most cases attitudes expressing a desire for control and autonomy were important.

However, cross-tabulations of the statistically preferred solution against that from the DCE did not exhibit strong associations, because the SALC attitudinal solution did not properly recognize the structure of the data: "pro treatment classes" were not the same when driven by "Strong agreement with pro-survival attitudes" versus "Strong disagreement with pro-quality of life attitudes."

Secondary analysis B

Table 7.1 shows DCE treatment acceptance rates split according to the attitudinal BWS score (which can be calculated at the level of the individual respondent). Thus, respondents with a BWS score of -1 always picked that attitude as the one they agreed with least on all four occasions it appeared, and never picked it as most; those with a score of $+1$ did the opposite. Respondents with a score of zero might never have picked the attitude at all, or might have picked it as most the same number of times as they picked it as least.

The data reveal that strong "anti-treatment" attitudes are associated with anti-treatment preferences: a respondent can say "Yes" to treatment up to eight times but a large majority always said "No" to certain treatments. However, the discriminatory power of attitudes at the other end of the scale is poor: strong "pro-treatment" attitudes are associated with approximately 50 percent treatment acceptance rates for treatments that are of key relevance to the attitude under consideration, which is no better than chance.

Thus, the BWS attitudinal survey can identify "generally anti-treatment" respondents well, but provides much poorer discriminatory power among those respondents whose treatment preferences depend upon the circumstances of the clinical scenario.

Secondary analysis C

Table 7.2 shows the percentage of respondents who discussed / hadn't discussed end-of-life care with a relative, friend or doctor, by the number of times he/she said yes to treatment. It is clear that reduced propensity to accept treatment is associated with prior discussion about end-of-life care.

Table 7.1 *Percentage of respondents accepting mechanical breathing to save one's life by agreement with each of two opposite attitudes*

Attitudes and scores	Mechanical breathing accepted			
I would rather die than undergo prolonged, burdensome, intensive life support treatment...	Zero times	Once	Twice	Number
−1	50.0%	34.6%	15.4%	26
−0.75	38.7%	46.8%	14.5%	62
−0.5	50.5%	31.7%	17.8%	101
−0.25	66.0%	22.0%	12.0%	150
0	69.6%	25.3%	5.1%	217
0.25	83.3%	14.4%	2.3%	222
0.5	87.3%	12.7%	0.0%	197
0.75	90.0%	9.2%	0.8%	130
1	93.4%	6.6%	0.0%	61
Total	74.5%	19.8%	5.7%	1166

Attitudes and scores	Mechanical breathing accepted			
I would prefer a course of treatment that focused on extending life as much as possible	Zero times	Once	Twice	Number
−1	87.3%	11.5%	1.2%	244
−0.75	81.3%	18.0%	0.7%	294
−0.5	76.7%	21.4%	1.9%	206
−0.25	71.9%	24.4%	3.7%	135
0	67.6%	18.2%	14.1%	170
0.25	51.7%	32.8%	15.5%	58
0.5	24.3%	45.9%	29.7%	37
0.75	38.9%	27.8%	33.3%	18
1	25.0%	25.0%	50.0%	4
Total	74.5%	19.8%	5.7%	1166

7.4 Discussion and conclusions

It is common for older patients to receive highly interventionist care in order to keep them alive. This study shows that such care often conflicts with their wishes, with only a small minority of people wishing for treatment virtually no matter what. It shows that general attitudes towards treatment can usefully predict treatment preferences among those with "anti-treatment" attitudes. Although this is less so for respondents expressing strong "pro-treatment" attitudes, these constitute a much smaller group in society. Treatment preference prediction from attitudes is important, as people generally find it easier, and less confronting, to consider their attitudes than to contemplate specific treatment options. The observation that any discussion about end-of-life care with friends, family or clinicians is

Table 7.2 *Percentage of respondents having discussed/not discussed end-of-life views according to how many times they said "Yes" to life-saving treatment*

Number of "Yes" responses to life-saving treatment	Have discussed	Haven't discussed	Number of respondents
0	61.4%	38.6%	376
1	60.3%	39.7%	219
2	45.3%	54.7%	245
3	40.2%	59.8%	117
4	40.4%	59.6%	99
5	40.5%	59.5%	37
6	9.5%	90.5%	21
7	25.0%	75.0%	4
8	22.9%	77.1%	48
Overall	**50.6%**	**49.4%**	**1166**

associated with lower rates of treatment acceptance is important. It is difficult to infer causation: anti-treatment people may make more effort to have their views recorded.

The magnitude of the choice-model-estimated probabilities provides estimates of the degree of "certainty" or "sureness" of the respondent: his/her answers to a series of interrelated questions can alert clinicians to preferences that are uncertain or have not stabilized. For example, cross-sectional data from this study identified a segment of people aged 55 to 74 who have weak attitudes and preferences, but this segment does not exist among those aged 75 and over. This suggests that greater caution is warranted in interpreting the responses of the under 75s.

Some of the attitudes tested elicited weak preferences in most respondents and had limited independent discriminatory power. This suggests that the list could be reduced further. The attitude statements that were selected may not be ideal, and further refinement might result in better discrimination. It is possible that attitudes that are less skewed towards "anti-treatment views" might allow a larger number of patterns of choices exhibiting "pro-treatment" and "potentially pro-treatment" attitudes to be possible; this might improve the BWS model's ability to predict those with "it depends" preferences.

The DCE was necessarily simplistic; richer insights might be drawn if more treatments are offered. However, the gains in statistical efficiency might be offset by the cognitive overload associated with more choice.

The study was conducted among the general population, most of whom do not complete advance care plans. Therefore, the extent to which patients who actually do so have similar attitudes and preferences is unknown (Gill, Griffin and Hesketh, 2013). A second arm of this study is evaluating the tool among patients attending an ACP clinic. Preliminary analysis suggests that these patients have even more anti-treatment, pro-control views and have sought out the clinic to document such views that they might have as much legitimacy as possible. Longitudinal data are needed to establish the extent to which attitudes and treatment preferences are stable over time. In particular, there is a need to understand whether, and to what extent, attitudes and preferences change in response to:

- becoming a patient and transitioning along an end-of-life care pathway (Singer, Martin and Kelner, 1999);
- the provision of specific information (for example, a description of what ventilation involves from a patient perspective) and how the information is provided (for example, whether via verbal, pictorial or multimedia means) (Waller, Currow and Lecathelinais, 2008);
- the extent to which the individual can rely on carers to support him/her (Abernathy *et al.*, 2008);
- the concordance between patient, family member and clinician views (Steinhauser et al., 2000); and
- the provision of information about the attitudes and/or preferences of other individuals and how this might assist surrogate decision-making (for family and doctors).

Patients attending the ACP clinic have been receiving a personalized report, containing their own individual BWS scoring – the best-minus-worst scores – providing an overall picture of their views, and how they compare to the wider population. This could be usefully uploaded to e-health records; it is anticipated that knowledge of attitudes and treatment preferences will help clinicians and families deliver better, more patient-centered care.

The online surveys have also recorded how long each respondent took to answer "most" and "least" (response times). It is now known that such data provide independent verification of the strength of views elicited in choice experiments (Hawkins *et al.*, 2014b). Preliminary analysis of the response time data from this study has suggested additional constructs consistent with the "fast" (emotional) and "slow" (deliberative) thinking proposed in the literature (Kahneman, 2011). If this is confirmed in formal analyses, it will provide further confirmation of the validity of these results and provide insights into the degree to which emotional factors influence ACP.

The tools developed here, particularly the BWS attitudinal one, are effective at eliciting advance care plans. General anti-treatment attitudes, elicited in simpler Case 1 BWS discrete choice surveys, can be used as predictors for specific treatment preferences in those expressing "anti-treatment" attitudes. This is important, because among the older (Australian) general population there is widespread aversion to interventionist treatment, a focus on high-quality outcomes and a desire for control over decision making. There is only a small minority who wish for life-extending care at all costs.

Chapter 8

How consumers choose wine: using best-worst scaling across countries

Larry Lockshin and Eli Cohen

8.1 Introduction

This chapter presents an example of the application of BWS to an issue in wine marketing, and by doing so illustrates the steps in using the BW attribute model across multiple countries. At the same time the chapter demonstrates some of the strengths of the BW attribute model in allowing the easy comparison of consumer behavior across a number of countries, whereas traditional Likert scaling often provides little discrimination between the attributes. The approach taken in this chapter is categorized as Case 1 (object case), and follows the topics as discussed below.

First, the issue of marketing wine to multiple countries is explored as a basis for the research. The formulation of the attributes and the issues involved in choosing both the number of attributes to compare and their composition is discussed next. Then the survey instrument is described, including the demographic and other variables collected, which help interpret the results. The formulation of the data for analysis and the actual analysis come next, showcasing the ease of comparing the attributes across the whole sample. Comparing the countries and illustrating the graphical approach for finding differences between how consumers choose wine across countries follow this. Another positive of the BW approach is that it tends to reduce method and respondent variability, which makes the use of multivariate methods, such as clustering, easier to interpret. This is illustrated by using latent class analysis to derive clusters across the countries. These clusters show that there are three overall schemes that wine buyers use to decide on their purchases in each country, but the number of buyers in each segment differs greatly by country. These final results are discussed, and the example concludes with some recommendations for further application of BWS to cross-national research.

8.2 The problem

Wine provides an instructive area in which to use BWS, because it is a complex category that has developed quite differently around the world. There are countries, such as France, Italy and Spain, that have been growing grapes and making wine for well over 1,000 years. Wine for them has been a local drink, usually made and consumed within 50 kilometers. At the same time these countries have exported some of their production to neighboring countries, especially the United Kingdom, where grapes cannot be grown easily. This history has resulted in a culture and a set of institutions that have evolved over this long period. These countries, along with Germany and much of eastern and southern Europe, are known as the Old World wine producers.

Grapes were taken by most of the European explorers in the sixteenth through nineteenth centuries to every country they visited. In many of them, grapes could be grown and wine made. Thus, we have newer wine sectors in countries such as the United States, Chile, Argentina, South Africa, Australia and New Zealand. These, too, developed both domestically and as export industries, but quite differently from their European parents. Now, in the early twenty-first century, grapes have been planted and wine is being made in a third new group of countries, such as China, India and Brazil.

Wine use, along with newer countries producing and consuming, has grown around the world, even in countries that do not grow grapes or make wine. Initially the trade in wine was restricted to the main European producers and to their neighbors who could not produce wine, such as the United Kingdom, Scandinavia, and Russia. Now, the trade in wine has grown substantially over the past 20 years, although total world consumption has changed little. The Old World is drinking less wine while the New World and many newly developing countries are drinking wine more and more.

These changes present a problem to wine producers used to making and selling a product to their domestic market or to an educated and discerning international market. Wine was typically made by small producers, who grew the grapes and made the wine in a way particular to their specific region. Because of local customs that determined how wine was grown and made, it has not usually been seen as something that could be adapted to different markets. This has changed in recent years as larger and larger wine companies emerged and began buying grapes from different regions and producing different brands, all in the same winery. This is more akin to how most fast-moving consumer goods (FMCG) companies operate, but it is very new to the wine sector.

The problem stemming from these changes is to make and market wine that can be sold in a number of different markets by understanding the differences and similarities about how consumers buy wine. Traditional European thinking would be that buyers use the region, such as Bordeaux or Burgundy, as the most important aspect of their wine choice, while producers in the United States and Australia tend to focus on the grape variety, such as Chardonnay or Cabernet, as the key to how consumers buy. Many consumers see wine purchasing as a complex choice, with so many attributes (brand, region or country, grape variety, price, bottle shape, etc.) that at least some of them look to experts or other objective sources to gain information, while others may display more typical supermarket shopping behavior by buying the wines from the most prominent displays or those on special offer (Mitchell and Greatorex, 1988). Wine marketers would like to better understand the aspects of their product that are most important to buyers in different countries. Are the people pretty much the same everywhere, so that the same marketing mix can be used, or are there strong differences between countries, so that different packaging and different marketing techniques would make better sense?

8.3 Methods

8.3.1 Factors in wine choice

The issues illustrated above show that, in order to understand what things are important in buying wine, more than just the product attributes are important. Wine is a complex product with many different attributes and levels. Wine bottles typically have a front label that includes a brand or producer name, the region and country where the grapes were grown, often the grape variety (though this is not true for many Old World wines) and the alcohol level, which is required by law. Many wine bottles also have a back label, on which more about the winery, the wine, what foods it matches and other details are provided. Besides the information on the label, there are many different styles and colors used for labeling, which can make the package either more or less attractive to some consumers. Most wine is sold through supermarkets, which use displays and sometimes information on the shelf to help consumers make their purchase decisions.

Casini, Corsi and Goodman (2009) looked at choice attributes for wine using best-worst scaling in Italy. The most important attributes were previous experience, personal recommendations and the taste of the wine. The authors also found some differences in respondents' preferences based on age, involvement level and the geographical part of Italy they were from.

The following section details the 13 items used to create the BWS choice sets on the basis of factors important in the decision process in a retail store. When a product has a high proportion of attributes that can be assessed only during consumption (experience attributes), as with wine (Chaney, 2000), then the ability of consumers to assess quality prior to purchase is severely impaired, and consumers will fall back on extrinsic cues, such as packaging, price and labels in the assessment of quality (Speed, 1998). Chaney (2000) found that there is very little external search effort undertaken prior to entering the store to purchase wine, with the two highest-ranked information sources in her study being point-of-sale material and labels, but these were found to rate at only the "Somewhat important" level. Little research has been done on direct label influences on consumer wine choice, but Orth and Malkewitz (2008) show differential consumer responses in liking and purchase intent for different wine label archetypes. Mueller *et al.* (2010) looked at the influence of back label statements on choice; winery history and elaborate taste descriptions were found to be the most positive influences on choice, while ingredient labelling was the only negative influence on choice.

Keown and Casey (1995) found that the taste of the wine was a dominating factor for wine consumers. Thompson and Vourvachis (1995) found that taste was the most highly correlated attribute relating to wine choice, noting that this is to be expected, as it is frequently found to be the key attitudinal factor in studies of wine choice. The taste of the wine represents one of the major perceived risks presented by Mitchell and Greatorex (1988). They found that the taste of the wine was the risk that concerned consumers most. However, virtually no purchase situations include the opportunity to taste the wine before purchase, so having previously tasted the variety has been shown to be important in wine selection (Goodman, Lockshin amd Cohen, 2006).

Keown and Casey (1995) found that pricing was extremely important to all respondents in a study of wine-purchasing influences. Similarly, in a study conducted by Jenster and Jenster (1993), price was an overriding criterion in making the purchase decision among European wine consumers. Generally, price is an important cue to quality when there are few other cues available, when the product cannot be evaluated before purchase and when there is some degree of risk of making a wrong choice (Monroe and Krishnan, 1985). Lockshin *et al.* (2006) used discrete choice experiments to show that price was most important, followed by brand name, awards and medals, then region.

Lockshin, Rasmussen and Cleary (2000) highlight the fact that the brand name acts as a surrogate for a number of attributes, including quality. The brand name by itself is usually not a strong enough cue for the purchase decision, as much more information is available on the label, but brand is important for wine purchase in all New World countries and is growing in the Old World wine markets.

Batt and Dean (2000) found that the origin of the wine was the third most important variable influencing consumers' decision to purchase wine in Australia. In Europe, research by Skuras and Vakrou (2002), Dean (2002), Keown and Casey (1995) and Gluckman (1990) suggests that the country of origin is a primary and implicit consideration of consumers in their decision to purchase wine. Research by Tustin and Lockshin (2001) in Australia confirmed that the region of origin has a major impact on wine purchase. Other authors have studied the region of origin as a cue to wine purchasing and found it usually to be in the top four cues (Angulo *et al.*, 2000; Gil and Sanchez, 1997; Lockshin *et al.*, 2006; Quester and Smart, 1998).

Landon and Smith (1998) suggest that, given incomplete information on quality, consumers rely heavily on both individual firm reputation based on the past quality of the firm's output and collective or group reputation indicators and characteristics, which allow consumers to segment firms into groups with differing average qualities to predict current product quality. To help deal with that uncertainty, quality-conscious consumers process various perceived signals of quality, mainly of an extrinsic nature, such as price, producer, brand, vintage, region, awards, ratings and recommendations (Lockshin *et al.*, 2006; Lockshin, Rasmussen and Cleary, 2000).

It is clear that there are many potential extrinsic attributes consumers might consider in choosing wine: brand name, price, origin, grape variety, label design and medals or awards (usually displayed as stickers on the front label). Wine bottles typically have a back label, which provides more detail about the wine. Different back labels can convey a range of information, such as the taste of the wine, the method of production, the history of the winery and food matching. Consumers were shown in one study to make different

Table 8.1 *Possible factors influencing wine choice*

1. Tasted the wine previously
2. Someone recommended it
3. Grape variety
4. Origin of the wine
5. Brand name
6. Medal/award
7. I read about it
8. Matching food
9. Information on back label
10. Information on the shelf
11. An attractive front label
12. Promotional display in store
13. Alcohol level below 13%

evaluations of wine bottles on the basis of the back label statements (Shaw, Keeghan and Hall, 1999). Further research (Goodman, Lockshin and Cohen, 2006) explored factors influencing wine choice using interviews with consumers and the wine trade. As noted above, wine is often consumed with food, and some consumers choose their wines on the basis of the food they are planning to drink it with it. Food and wine magazines are full of recommendations for food and wine matching. Goodman, Lockshin and Cohen, (2006) found that other ways consumers use to reduce risk are to read articles about wine, or to ask someone to recommend which wines to buy. Finally, little research has been conducted about the effect of the legal requirement to put the level of alcohol in the wine on the label; however there is growing concern about the effects of overconsuming alcohol, and this study offered a chance to see if consumers paid any attention to that information.

The research cited above was used to select 13 different factors that might influence wine choice (Table 8.1). This number was selected as large enough to cover a wide range of possible influences but not so large that a best-worst design would become too long and tiring, especially since it would be used in multiple countries. The 13 items would be too many to have each individual rank each item separately, but it does allow the testing of extrinsic as well as shelf display and other factors that might influence a person's wine choice based on previous research.

8.3.2 Segmentation and cross-national studies in wine marketing

In marketing terms, segmentation is the process of dividing the market (buyers) into groups such that the preferences are more similar within the group than between the groups (Smith, 1956). It is predicated on the assumption that there are efficiencies to be gained by developing products and marketing activities geared to one group at the expense of not suiting another. We know people are different, and, although we all have the same basic needs, we often prefer to satisfy those needs with different products. The problem lies with the idea of segmenting buyers on the basis of these preferences.

Some previous research has attempted to measure wine drinker segmentation by means of lifestyle segments (Bruwer and Li, 2007; Bruwer, Li and Reid, 2002). Although the segments are reported to be robust, each time the survey has been run, different segments have occurred. This could be because of changes in the market, which means the segments themselves were not very robust; or it could be due to the problems with measurement error discussed in Chapters 1 and 2. Research conducted by Lockshin, Spawton and Macintosh (1997) and Aurifeille *et al.* (2002) using Likert-type items also failed to find the same segments in two different countries using involvement as the means of segmentation. Wine provides a fertile ground to test whether segments occur between countries or whether countries act as segments, and therefore companies need to adapt their marketing country by country.

Moskowitz and Rabino (1994) used the sensory attributes of flavored soda to find cross-national segments based on ideal points. However, their segments had larger variance than within the countries. Another study utilized BWS to segment consumers from six countries based on product benefits (Cohen and Neira, 2003). The study compared BWS plus latent class analysis (LCA) to standard Likert measures of the same benefits followed by PCA and k-means clustering. The results showed the superiority of BWS plus LCA to produce managerially relevant clusters.

Several cross-national studies have been published for wine in a retail environment (Casini, Corsi and Goodman, 2009; Cohen, 2009; Goodman, 2009; Mueller and Rungie, 2009) and in an on-premise environment (Cohen, d'Hauteville and Sirieix, 2009).

The goal of this research is to look for segments across countries by utilizing the criteria consumers use to make purchase decisions, because these are likely to be more robust and to yield managerially useful criteria for marketing across different countries. This BW research provides a unique test of the method by utilizing both product attributes and the most likely retail and interpersonal influences to measure their relative influence (importance) on choice within a very complex consumer category.

8.3.3 Implementation

Hall and Lockshin (2000) found that the composition of means–end chains was related to the situation in which the consumer intended to drink the wine. Different consumption situations amplified or muted the importance of different wine attributes, therefore these must be taken into account in wine research. For this survey, respondents were asked to imagine they were shopping at their favorite retail store to buy a bottle of wine to have at home that night with friends or family. How typical this situation is may differ in the different countries surveyed, but specifying a consumption situation reduces variability as a result of respondents imagining different usage situations.

8.3.4 Design of the choice sets

We applied a balanced incomplete block design to allocate the 13 attributes presented in Table 8.1. One advantage of BIBDs is that large numbers of items can be studied in order to get the full ranking of all items in a relatively small number of subsets. Furthermore, these designs control the number of times each pair is compared, and, by increasing the number of times each item is compared with every other item, the total number of subsets is increased and/or the number of items in each subset is increased. The simplest design is the one such that each item appears only once with each other. Comparing each item with each other item more frequently increases the internal validity of the survey, but makes it longer and more repetitive for the respondent. We used a 13,4,4,1 design for the 13 attributes, which means that there are 13 choice sets, each attribute appears four times across all choice sets, each choice set contains four attributes, and each attribute appears once with each other. The design is presented in Table 8.2.

The design in Table 8.2 contains 13 choice sets; each choice set was presented in the questionnaire as a separate table. The 13 tables contain four attributes in each table. An example of one choice set (table) is presented in Figure 8.1; and it represents choice set no. 4 in Table 8.2 and contains attributes 4, 5, 7 and 13. In the choice sets that are presented to the subjects, the number of the attribute in the choice set is substituted with its description as in Table 8.1. The respondents were asked to choose the "best" (most important) attribute and the "worst" (least important) attribute while considering purchasing a bottle of wine in a retail store. Note that a specific usage occasion is provided to reduce the variance that would occur if each respondent considered a different occasion. The questionnaire is designed to include 13 choice sets (tables) based on the design in Table 8.2 and a range of questions concerning the habits of drinking wine and demographic data as planned by the researchers.

Table 8.2 *Balanced incomplete block design for 13 attributes*

v = 13 choice set #	13,4,4,1 attribute #			
1	1	2	4	10
2	2	3	5	11
3	3	4	6	12
4	4	5	7	13
5	5	6	8	1
6	6	7	9	2
7	7	8	10	3
8	8	9	11	4
9	9	10	12	5
10	10	11	13	6
11	11	12	1	7
12	12	13	2	8
13	13	1	3	9

Remember the last time you purchased a bottle of wine to have with friends for dinner.

For each of the following tables, tick the ONE reason that **MOST** influenced your choice and the ONE that **LEAST**.

Least/Worst	Attribute	Most/ Best
☐	1 Origin of the wine	☐
☐	2 Brand name	☐
☐	3 I read about it	☐
☐	4 Alcohol level below13%	☐

Figure 8.1 An example of a best-worst choice set as presented to respondents

8.3.5 Data collection

Each respondent competed a survey including all 13 choice sets plus demographic and product category usage questions. Since each respondent saw all 13 choice sets, we can compute a best-worst score for each of the 13 items for each person by subtracting the number of times each item was chosen worst from the number of times it was chosen best. As each attribute appears four times in the 13 choice sets, the scores for each item for each person could range from +4 to –4. Therefore, the average best-worst scores range from positive to negative values, but the interpretation is one of a continuous scale from most to least important.

The data were collected as part of a research project sponsored by the Australian wine industry in 11 different countries: Australia, Austria, Brazil, France, Germany, Israel, Italy, New Zealand, Taiwan, the United Kingdom and the United States. Although the country choice was based on the existence of ongoing academic collaboration, these countries represent both New and Old World wine-producing and some developing wine-consuming countries on five continents speaking six different languages.

The survey was translated by a different native academic speaker from English into each of the languages for our 11 countries. It was then back-translated and corrected for any errors before the final version was used. The target for this research was wine drinkers in each country. Sampling was limited to those consuming wine at least once per month, so the data represent wine drinkers, but not the overall population. Therefore, most of the surveys were collected face to face near wine retail stores. The data from the United Kingdom and part of the Australian data were collected using an online survey sponsored by Wine Intelligence, a market research firm for the wine sector. The aim was not to develop an instrument that could project to a national sample but to measure the important factors that wine drinkers in each country used to make their selections from retail wine stores.

8.3.6 Data handling

The first step before the analysis of the data is transforming the item numbers in each choice set to the original items numbers as in Table 8.1. One possibility is using an Excel© spreadsheet that also is used for calculations and graphical presentations. After transforming the best and the worst in each choice set to the original item numbers and sorting by item, the best-minus-worst (B–W) for each item is calculated; so for each respondent we have 13 new variables (B–W), one for each item.

The ranking of the attributes for all the subjects in the survey is obtained by ordering the best-worst scores of the attributes for each item for each person, then summing them. A positive value of best-minus-worst for an attribute means that it was chosen more frequently as "Best" than "Worst," and a negative value is the opposite. The average B–W scores are calculated by dividing the totals of B–W scores by the number of respondents.

Another way to compare attribute importance is to derive ratio scores by taking the square root after dividing the total best (B) scores by the total worst (W) scores for each person. We added 0.5 to each W to avoid dividing by zero (Auger, Devinney and Louviere, 2007; Flynn *et al.*, 2007; Lee, Soutar and Louviere, 2008; Marley and Louviere, 2005). The square root of (B/W) for all attributes (SQRT(B/W)) is scaled by a factor such that the most important attribute with the highest SQRT(B/W) becomes 100. All attributes can then be compared to each other by their relative SQRT(B/W) ratio. The result is interpreted as X percent (for example, 60 percent) as likely to be chosen best as the most important attribute.

8.4 Results

Table 8.3 shows the demographics of the 11 country samples. The proportions in each group are not equal, but represent the wine-consuming groups in the countries. Thus, the United Kingdom is overrepresented for those above 55 years old, while Taiwan has a much younger skew. We used three items to measure wine involvement across the countries, because it has been shown to be related to wine consumption and even more to the attributes consumers use in their wine choices in Australia and in France (Aurifeille *et al.*, 2002; Lockshin *et al.*, 2006; Lockshin, Spawton and Macintosh, 1997). With three items summed for each person, low involvement ranged from 3–9; medium involvement was 10–12 and high involvement ranged from 13–15. Frequency of wine consumption is separated into those who drink more than once per week and those who drink less often. The samples overall provide a range of demographics and wine consumption behaviors within and between countries, which will allow us to see whether these characteristics are linked to segments based on BW scores.

We can see that there are some differences in the make-up of the samples from each country. Taiwan has a larger number of males and Germany more females. The US sample skews quite young, while Italy, New Zealand, Taiwan and the United Kingdom skew older.

Table 8.3 *Sample characteristics for each country in percentages*

Country (sample size)	Gender		Age				Frequency of drinking wine		Wine involvement		
	Male	Female	18–24	25–40	41–55	over 55	Low	High	Low	Medium	High
Australia (305)	52	48	14	34	30	21	42	58	24	37	39
Austria (182)	49	51	10	27	35	27	63	37	30	37	32
Brazil (293)	49	51	20	23	21	35	75	25	83	15	2
France (158)	58	42	15	20	34	31	72	28	30	46	24
Germany (129)	35	65	12	60	19	9	76	24	39	38	23
Israel (184)	59	41	18	50	18	14	64	36	50	33	17
Italy (314)	50	50	4	30	35	31	39	61	25	32	42
NZ (364)	46	54	2	24	39	35	37	63	16	53	31
Taiwan (317)	62	38	8	55	29	8	58	42	18	53	29
UK (303)	50	50	0	25	24	51	71	29	43	38	19
US (195)	48	52	47	18	8	26	51	49	27	34	39
Average (2744)	51	49	12	33	28	28	56	44	34	38	28

Source: Lockshin and Cohen (2011) (courtesy of Emerald Group Publishing).

New Zealand, Australia and Italy have larger percentages of frequent wine drinkers. Australian, Italy and New Zealand have the most frequent wine drinkers in their sample, while Australia, Italy and the United States have the greatest proportion of high-involvement wine consumers. The demographics will be used further along to help identify the segments, but for now we move to comparing the countries on their best-worst scores for each of the 13 wine choice factors (Tables 8.4 and 8.5).

It is clear from these two tables that there are some similarities and some differences between the mean best-worst scores for each country. The negative weights are not negative influences, but just less important on the scale of +4 to –4. Tasting the wine previously is most important for nine of the 11 countries, with brand most important in Brazil and origin in France. Larger differences are apparent when we look at the second and third most important factors. The second most important factor in Australia is "Someone recommended it," but this is half as important as tasting the wine previously. In France, matching with food is almost as important as the origin (99 compared to 100, or 1.54 compared to 1.41). In Austria, the grape variety and the origin are also highly important. In Italy, matching food is very important. Australia, Israel, New Zealand, the United Kingdom and the United States all rank tasting the wine previously the most important factor, with a very large gap to the next item. The other countries have several items that seem to have probabilities of 70 percent or greater compared to the most important one, which means that there is a combination of factors influencing wine choice.

Table 8.4 *Average BW rating of wine choice factors in each country (ranked by Australia)*

	Australia	Austria	Brazil	France	Germany	Israel	Italy	NZ	Taiwan	UK	US
Tasted the wine previously	2.60	1.37	1.58	1.41	2.04	3.04	1.89	2.58	2.26	2.23	2.19
Someone recommended it	1.25	0.03	0.81	0.49	1.53	0.73	0.34	0.90	1.44	0.89	1.32
Grape variety	0.91	1.43	0.55	0.70	0.54	0.68	0.41	1.50	0.03	-0.13	0.60
Origin of the wine	0.62	1.02	0.74	1.54	0.98	-0.85	0.76	0.75	0.74	0.47	0.25
Brand name	0.60	-0.27	2.38	0.25	-0.85	0.72	0.00	0.99	0.17	0.10	0.41
Medal/award	0.48	-0.29	-1.48	0.46	-0.59	-0.14	-0.22	1.09	0.53	-0.45	0.14
I read about it	0.00	-0.69	-0.42	0.01	-0.17	0.66	0.65	-0.34	.077	-0.12	0.09
Matching food	-0.26	0.97	1.04	1.73	1.33	0.92	1.70	-0.74	-0.72	-0.19	0.31
Information on back label	-0.27	0.19	-0.79	-0.89	0.27	-0.69	0.43	-0.95	-0.62	0.43	-0.69
Information on the shelf	-0.87	-0.73	-.077	-1.68	-0.09	-1.28	-1.21	-1.06	-0.89	-0.28	-0.49
An attractive front label	-1.02	0.23	-1.74	-1.58	-0.40	-1.21	-1.49	-1.00	-0.96	-0.77	-0.23
Promotional display in store	-1.40	-2.01	-0.96	-0.72	-1.84	-0.73	-1.72	-0.88	-0.78	-0.41	-1.06
Alcohol level below 13%	-2.66	-1.26	-.93	-1.71	-2.75	-1.85	-1.55	-2.84	-1.97	-1.76	-2.84

Source: Lockshin and Cohen (2011) (courtesy of Emerald Group Publishing).

Table 8.5 *Probability of each wine attribute been chosen best by country (ranked by Australia)*

	Australia	Austria	Brazil	France	Germany	Israel	Italy	NZ	Taiwan	UK	US
Tasted the wine previously	100.0	100.0	70.8	80.5	100.0	100.0	100.0	100.0	100.0	100.0	100.0
Someone recommended it	47.8	49.1	42.4	45.0	77.0	22.4	40.6	33.9	66.4	51.3	64.1
Grape variety	36.2	99.6	41.4	52.0	44.1	22.9	42.4	37.9	31.7	29.8	41.8
Origin of the wine	33.0	85.4	46.9	100.0	56.1	9.0	52.2	29.6	47.8	40.1	36.1
Brand name	31.2	41.8	100.0	39.8	20.4	23.1	33.9	33.2	34.2	33.2	36.2
Medal/award	29.8	41.5	11.9	45.5	24.3	14.7	30.5	33.7	41.3	24.6	31.6
I read about it	23.0	31.7	21.5	35.3	28.6	23.2	51.3	15.0	48.2	29.5	30.7
Matching food	20.2	81.5	50.9	99.0	65.1	25.1	87.1	12.7	21.5	29.1	34.0
Information on back label	19.3	53.3	18.9	18.4	39.2	9.2	45.3	10.2	21.4	40.8	18.0
An attractive front label	12.1	54.9	9.5	14.2	26.4	7.1	14.0	9.2	16.5	20.5	24.8
Information on the shelf	12.0	29.8	18.9	10.9	31.1	6.1	14.5	8.2	17.4	26.4	23.3
Promotional display in store	9.4	11.8	18.4	24.5	11.4	10.8	14.0	10.9	20.5	26.2	18.9
Alcohol level below 13%	3.5	25.0	15.8	10.8	4.2	4.9	13.1	2.6	11.0	10.4	4.5

If we look only at mean values by country, we might consider segmenting the market by countries, because there seem to be groups of countries with somewhat similar patterns of choosing wine in retail stores. From a marketing perspective, it seems that in nine of the countries promoting trial of the wines is very important, but the secondary factors differ. A useful question to ask is whether there are similar segments across the 11 countries, or whether marketing strategies are best implemented on a country-by-country basis.

8.4.1 *Latent class segmentation*

We used Latent GOLD software, version 4.0 (Vermunt and Magidson, 2005) to estimate a latent class cluster model based on the individual best-worst scores. We estimated models ranging from two to nine clusters plus one in which 11 clusters were specified using country membership, and compared the log likelihoods (LL) and Bayesian information criterion of each. Decreasing BIC (closer to zero) and increasing LL indicate improving fit. It is clear from examining Figures 8.2 and 8.3 that the forced 11-country cluster solution has the worst fit of all the models tested. Thus, the differences between countries are greater than those between the latent segment models. Cluster solutions, in which membership is allowed to vary according to the importance of each of the 13 wine choice attributes, produce much better-fitting models. There is no clear number of clusters for which the solution begins to decrease in fit. The largest improvement in fit occurs between two and three clusters, and the improvement is less but approximately the same for each successive model. The choice of the optimum cluster number is then based on the lowest number of interpretable clusters (Cohen and Neira, 2003; Ruta, Garrod and Scarpa, 2008). After examining the solutions for three, four and five clusters, we chose the three-cluster solution, because there was no overlap between the loadings of each of the 13 items on each cluster (data available from the

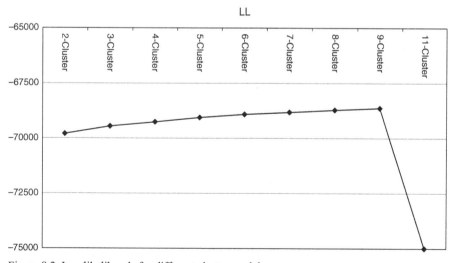

Figure 8.2 Log likelihoods for different cluster models

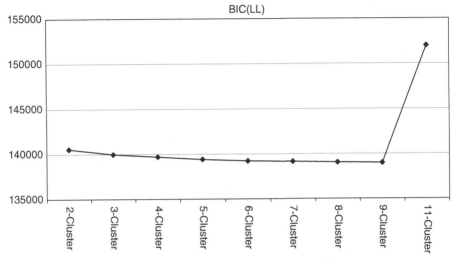

Figure 8.3 Bayesian information criterion for different cluster models

authors). The four and larger cluster solutions each had several attributes that loaded on multiple clusters and very small final clusters, making interpretation difficult. The three-cluster solution is easily interpretable and leads to "actionable" segmentation (Swait, 1994).

Table 8.6 shows the three-cluster solution. The loadings of each of the 13 attributes are significantly different between the clusters (p-values < 0.05) except for matching wine with food. This item is not very important in any cluster and its importance does not differ between clusters. The correct classification using this model is 86 percent, which is far higher than the random classification expectation of 33 percent. The results show that the three clusters represent the core attributes as follows. Cluster 1 is labeled as "cognitive cues" and focuses on the extrinsic factors (Jacoby and Olson, 1977; Lockshin *et al.*, 2006), which indicate wine quality and taste based on the cognitive understanding of how these factors relate to the actual wine. These people choose their wines by considering objective information on the label. The key attributes used are the grape variety, the origin of the wine, the brand, and medals and awards, which can be seen as objective measures of quality.

The second cluster is labeled "assurance cues" and consists of attributes indicating previous knowledge (tasted before), learning (read about it) or recommendation by someone else. These wine purchasers choose on the basis of previous experience or recommendation and seem to be avoiding the risk of choosing an unknown wine. The third cluster focuses on the package and display without thinking deeply about the cues are their indication of quality, and is named "in-store cues." These people do not assess the information on the label, or use previous experience to make their purchase decisions. They use shelf-based promotions and the packaging to make their decision. This is also the only segment that looks to wines with lower alcohol levels.

Table 8.6 *Latent class cluster parameter values for 11 countries*

	Cluster 1: cognitive cues	Cluster 2: assurance cues	Cluster 3: in-store cues	p-value	R^2
Origin of the wine	0.45	−0.31	−0.14	0.00	0.26
Grape variety	0.43	−0.23	−0.21	0.00	0.27
Medal/award	0.11	0.04	−0.15	0.00	0.03
Brand name	0.10	0.05	−0.14	0.00	0.02
Matching food	0.02	−0.02	0.00	0.24	0.00
Alcohol level below 13%	−0.02	−0.20	0.22	0.00	0.06
Information on back label	−0.03	−0.19	0.22	0.00	0.05
I read about it	−0.05	0.30	−0.25	0.00	0.09
Tasted the wine previously	−0.06	0.44	−0.38	0.00	0.16
An attractive front label	−0.20	−0.03	0.23	0.00	0.07
Promotional display in-store	−0.29	−0.02	0.31	0.00	0.14
Someone recommended it	−0.30	0.73	−0.42	0.00	0.34
Information on the shelf	−0.43	−0.19	0.62	0.00	0.22

Source: Lockshin and Cohen (2011) (courtesy of Emerald Group Publishing).

We can see in Table 8.7 that, although the segmentation is truly cross-national, membership is quite different by country (chi-square of 241.1 with p < 0.00). Austria, France, Italy and New Zealand have the largest percentage membership in the cognitive cluster. This does not seem to be driven by the typical Old World/New World dichotomy but perhaps by having a greater number of more interested wine buyers. Israel, Taiwan and the United States are overrepresented in cluster 2, the ones needing assurance in purchasing wine. This may reflect the recent development of a wine-drinking culture in these countries. Austria, Germany and the United Kingdom are the biggest countries by percentage in cluster 3, which may be because of the high percentage of discount grocery stores selling wine in these countries (Euromonitor International, 2008).

The demographic composition of the clusters is presented in Table 8.8. There are some demographic differences between the clusters as measured by chi-square. Cluster 1, the cognitive-based cluster, is slightly more male, while the other two are slightly more female. Clusters 1 and 3 are older than cluster 2. Perhaps their experience reduces the need for risk-reducing choice strategies. Cluster 3 has more infrequent wine drinkers and more low-involvement wine drinkers, which makes sense, since these people seem to choose wine by the promotional displays rather than by experience or knowledge. The more highly involved wine consumers are in cluster 1, which also makes sense, since higher wine involvement is more associated with complex cognitive choosing (Perrouty, d'Hauteville and Lockshin, 2006). However, the differences in cluster membership by demographics are not really large enough to utilize in marketing to the distinct segments. There are different sizes of the segments in the countries surveyed (Table 8.7). This could lead some marketers to focus on specific segments in different countries.

["

Considering the cross-national pattern of segmentation we found leads to valuable managerial insights. The biggest segment in every country except Taiwan and the United States (and tied for largest in Israel) is that of cognitive-based buyers. This segment averages about 50 percent of those surveyed. These buyers read the label and make decisions based on grape variety, origin, brand name and awards. Interestingly, the grape variety is normally used on wines from the New World, but not wines from traditional wine-producing countries, such as France and Italy. Wine marketers concerned with cognitive choosers should clearly show these attributes on the label, as well as in their market communications.

The second biggest segment focuses on risk-reducing strategies, such as recommendations and previous experience. Recommendations are a well-regarded means of reducing the implicit risk in buying a wine (Mitchell and Greatorex, 1988). These can stem from wine reviews or from personal recommendations by salespeople and friends (Lockshin, Spawton and Macintosh, 1997). This is the largest group in the United States and Taiwan; it averages about 34 percent of all those surveyed. Marketers aiming at this group need to provide sampling where it is legal and other means for potential wine buyers to have a taste of the wine, such as by-the-glass promotions in restaurants.

The third segment is the smallest, but represents a substantial group of buyers in Austria, Germany, Brazil, the United Kingdom and the United States. These buyers use displays, attractive front labels and back labels to help them make their wine choice decisions. However, the relatively small size of this segment suggests that expensive efforts into retail displays and wine label design are not directed at the majority of wine consumers. There is very little information on what makes a wine label attractive to different segments of consumers (Orth and Malkewitz, 2008). However, these findings should be tempered by Mueller, Lockshin and Louviere (2010), who showed that consumers' response to labels is mainly subconscious and therefore not likely to be reported under direct questioning. More research needs to be conducted in order to provide wine companies with clear ideas of label designs for specific segments of consumers.

A different interpretation of the results would suggest that wine marketers could develop a range of packaging and promotion to reach each of the segments simultaneously. In a sense, this is mass marketing, but with a varied assortment on the shelf to attract buyers, who use different purchasing strategies. Smaller wineries, which do not have the resources to follow this strategy, could decide to target only specific countries, with a single marketing program, where the largest segments fit with their marketing mix. In contrast, larger wineries would likely have a brand portfolio across multiple countries with different wines aimed at the different segments. There are also implications for channel strategy, whereby wines aimed for supermarket or discount shelves would be packaged differently from wines sold through independent retailers. At the moment this does not seem to be the case (Orth and Malkewitz, 2008).

Segmenting consumers by the way they choose a product is more likely to result in actionable segments than the more typical use of values and lifestyle or secondary characteristics collected for other purposes (Cohen and Neira, 2003; Steenkamp and Ter Hofstede, 2002). This research showed that BWS can be used across a wide range of countries to measure the relative importance of different attributes used in product choice in retail stores. This resulted in a simple yet powerful segmentation scheme that highlights similarities among wine buyers around the world. The key contribution has been the demonstration that best-worst scaling has properties that make it easier to implement than, and enable it to overcome most of the technical difficulties that have plagued, other international comparative research in marketing. Using this method will allow a wider range of international researchers to make valid comparisons and thus advance international marketing management. Another contribution is our use of choice attributes for comparisons across countries. How people choose is more basic and easier to interpret than many of the previous studies focusing on attitudes and brand perceptions (Cohen and Neira, 2003; Salciuviene, Auruskeviciene and Lydeka, 2005).

Best-worst scaling provides ratio-level scales for the items included in the survey, provided that none of the best-worst choice probabilities equals one or zero (Marley, Flynn and Louviere, 2008). The resulting scale provides the relative importance of each item tested. If an important item is not included in the research, the results will not be indicative of actual preferences in the marketplace. This limitation occurs with any choice task, and the interpretation has to take this into account (Marley and Louviere, 2005). In our case, there is extensive literature on wine choice and long-term practical experience. Nonetheless, it is possible that there are some important features that were not included, especially in the newer wine-drinking countries. The omitted alternative problem can be circumvented only through good literature reviews, practical experience and in-depth interviews or focus groups in the intended markets.

Chapter 9

Best-worst scaling: an alternative to ratings data

Geoffrey N. Soutar, Jillian C. Sweeney and Janet R. McColl-Kennedy

9.1 Introduction

The purpose of this chapter is to compare best-worst scaling with rating scales in an organizational research application. Category rating scales are commonly used in organizational research, as they are easy for respondents to answer, allow one to ask questions about more items and have reasonable statistical properties (Gupta and Govindarajan, 1984). However, respondents can use different parts of ratings scales (for example, the middle point or end points) or display "response styles" that affect the items' means and variances (Craig and Douglas, 2000; Baumgartner and Steenkamp, 2001; Diamantopoulos, Reynolds and Simintiras, 2006; De Jong *et al.*, 2008). Consequently, ratings scales may be poor measures of the relationships of interest.

Indeed, social desirability bias, acquiescence bias and extreme response bias can affect results obtained from rating scales (Paulhus, 1991). While social desirability bias has often been ignored in organizational research, it is recognized as a potential source of bias that needs to be considered (Banerjee, 2002; Luo, Rindfleisch and Tse, 2007; Tan and Peng, 2003). Similarly, acquiescence bias may be an issue if people rate most items positively (Paulhus, 1991), as this "heightens the correlations among items that are worded similarly, even when they are not conceptually related" (Winkler, Kanouse and Ware, 1982). This has led some researchers to suggest the use of positive and negative items as a way to reduce acquiescence bias (for example, Baumgartner and Steenkamp, 2001; Saxe and Weitz, 1982; Srinivasan, Rangaswamy and Lilien, 2005). However, others have argued that this approach can confound construct unidimensionality (Herche and Engelland, 1996), especially in cross-cultural research (Wong, Rindfleisch and Burroughs, 2003). Consequently, an approach that reduces acquiescence bias without introducing other measurement problems is needed.

In particular, perceptions should be measured in ways that do not affect associations between constructs of interest (for example, job satisfaction and performance). Response biases can distort rating scale values, so they do not represent true scores; hence, it seems desirable to measure these perceptions in ways that avoids such distortion. BWS (Finn and Louviere, 1992; Lee, Soutar and Louviere, 2008; Louviere, Swait and Anderson, 1995) can overcome such problems; specifically, researchers select a list of relevant aspects (such as

* This study was supported by an Australian Research Council Discovery Grant (DP0450736).

possible organization culture issues), assign them to sets using a suitable experimental design and ask a target sample of people to choose the best (or most appropriate) and the worst (or least appropriate) aspect in each set. The experimental design, a balanced incomplete block design, controls for context effects (each aspect occurs with every other aspect an equal number of times), and certain types of BIBDs (such as Youden designs: Gupta, 2005) can control for order effects (each item occurs in the first, second, third, etc. position across the different subsets).

Cohen and Markowitz (2002) note that this approach forces respondents to choose only one item as the most important or least important; as a result, respondents cannot consistently use mid-points, end points or one end of a scale, forcing them to discriminate between the items, which reduces various response biases. A key advantage of BWS is that one can derive a unidimensional interval-level scale from the simple nominal choices made by the respondents (Marley and Louviere, 2005). Further, if all aspects included in the scaling exercise are viewed as similar (that is, valued approximately the same), all scores will be similar (close) on the best-worst scale; but, if the various aspects differ significantly, the obtained scores will vary considerably.

The BWS approach also has an operational advantage over rating scales, in that the task is simple and undemanding because respondents choose one item for best and one item for worst, ultimately improving data quality (Drolet and Morrison, 2001). The objective of our study is to compare and test rating scales and Case 1 BWS scales in a typical organizational context to see if the aforementioned advantages obtain.

9.2 The present study

9.2.1 Competitive positioning

Competitive positioning is a key management decision, as it involves choices about where an organization will compete (via the identification of target markets) and how it will compete (via the development of competitive advantage to serve such targets) (Blankson and Kalafatis, 2004; Hooley, Saunders and Piercy, 2004). Such choices are central to the activities that organizations undertake in order to achieve a differential advantage. A well-defined marketplace position is fundamental to an organization's long-term success (Porter, 1996), particularly when it is built on assets and resources that are difficult to imitate (Barney, 1991). Consequently, they are important constructs to study.

Successful positioning differentiates an organization from its competitors on one or more dimensions important to customers (Porter, 1985; 1996). In management and marketing, different competitive positioning options and frameworks have been identified, including Porter's (1985) view of positional advantage through cost leadership or differentiation and, more recently, the six positioning dimensions (price, quality, service, innovation, customization and uniqueness) of Hooley, Broderick and Moller (1998) and Hooley, Saunders and Piercy (2004). Many researchers have considered differential positional advantage forms, such as Day and Wensley's (1988) suggestion that brand name, innovativeness and superior quality can create a market position that helps an organization achieve its objectives.

There is also empirical support for a link between positioning strategies and performance (see, for instance, Doyle and Wong, 1998; Fahy *et al.*, 2000; McAlexander, Schouten and Scammon, 1991). For example, Hooley and Greenley (2005) found that organizations with clear positioning strategies (such as being seen as "service leaders") report greater levels of customer satisfaction, loyalty and sales volume than organizations with undefined or "stuck-in-the-middle" strategies. However, despite the importance of positioning, little attention has been paid to the impact that the scaling approach used to measure an organization's adoption of a competitive position has on the findings and conclusions of such research. As noted earlier, this may have important implications when examining relationships between these constructs.

The need for industry-specific research has also been highlighted, with claims that competitive positioning varies between business and consumer markets, goods and services markets and even across service industries. For example, it has been suggested that the positioning of services is more challenging than the positioning of goods, because of services' distinguishing characteristics – such as intangibility and inseparability – and the need to communicate intangible benefits effectively (Blankson and Kalafatis, 1999a; 1999b; Ellis and Mosher, 1993). There is also a general view that business services have less time and opportunity to purposely employ positioning strategies, while consumer services (such as retail) and goods producers have more developed and sophisticated positioning strategies (Dibb and Simkin, 1993; Kalafatis, Tsogas and Blankson, 2000; Reeder, Brierty and Reeder, 1987).

Correspondingly, competitive positioning research has received more attention in consumer service and product contexts. Indeed, even though its relevance and importance to business marketing has been recognized (for example, Dibb and Simkin, 1993; Kalafatis, Tsogas and Blankson, 2000), there has been little attempt to understand the competitive positions business firms try to create (especially business and professional services). Consequently, we study the impact that positioning strategies, as measured by alternative measurement approaches, have on performance.

Professional services constitute an appropriate industry for such an investigation. Not only is it the fastest-growing sector in most economies worldwide, including international trade (Australian Trade Commission, 2007; United Nations Conference on Trade and Development, 2004), but professional services are also distinct from other services, as they have unique characteristics and face unique marketing challenges. For example, professional service firms (PSFs) often face short deadlines and constant demands, have limited marketing knowledge (particularly smaller firms) and view the time spent on marketing as time deducted from billable hours, rather than as investments in future cash flows (Ellis and Mosher, 1993; Herbig and Milewicz, 1993; Kotler, Hayes and Bloom, 2002). PSFs also have been slow to adopt formal planning procedures (Barr and McNeilly, 2003; Crane, 1993; Hodge, Brown and Lumpkin, 1990; Yavas and Riecken, 2001). Thus, knowledge of positioning is likely to be even more crucial for professional service providers than for other service providers.

9.3 Research approach

9.3.1 Selection of positions

Qualitative interviews with professional service providers (Amonini *et al.*, 2007), which extended research into marketing practices that has been conducted by Coviello, Brodie and Munro (1997) and Coviello *et al.* (2002), identified 10 market positions that professional service firms seek that we used in the present study, namely:

(1) perceived value;
(2) high-quality communication through databases;
(3) service quality;
(4) a strong brand;
(5) commitment to clients;
(6) developing networks among firms;
(7) innovation;
(8) a transactional (one off/discrete) approach to customers;
(9) a strong relationship with clients; and
(10) high-quality interactions with clients.

9.3.2 Data collection

We compared two data collection approaches (that is, ratings and BWS) to compare and assess the importance of the 10 positioning strategies in assisting organizations reach their goals. We collected data from two separate samples of professional service providers to ensure the independence of the measurement approaches. In both cases data were collected via a large Australian national online panel whose members complete online surveys in exchange for small incentives in the form of points. Online panels have rapidly gained recognition as a way to obtain representative samples (see, for example, MacDonald and Uncles, 2007; Wyner, 2006), so we saw them as an appropriate sampling frame in this case. We wished to obtain 200 responses in each case; so we invited more than 1,000 panel members in selected careers such as accounting, banking, law, consulting engineers, insurance, advertising and marketing to participate in the surveys. We screened respondents to be professional people who worked in a business and who had at least a moderate level of client contact. We used quota sampling to match the sample characteristics with the population of various Australian states. In the case of both survey samples, we achieved the desired target sample size, with usable samples of 199 and 203, respectively. Sample profiles are shown in Table 9.1.

Table 9.1 *Sample profile*

		Sample 1 n = 199	Sample 2 n = 203
Industry	Accounting	20%	29%
	Banking and finance	12%	18%
	Law	7%	8%
	Management/consultancy	10%	10%
	Engineering/architecture	27%	14%
	Management/marketing research	7%	8%
	Other (none above 3.4%)	18%	17%
Location	Metropolitan	83%	82%
	Regional	17%	18%
Size of firm	Up to 49 employees	40%	44%
	50–499 employees	278%	26%
	500%	31%	28%
	Not stated	1%	2%
Gender	Male	61%	57%
	Female	39%	43%

9.3.3 Measures

As earlier noted, we collected two types of measures: ratings and BWS. Ratings of the 10 competitive-positioning strategies were obtained using a seven-category rating scale; Specifically, respondents were asked about the importance of each strategy in achieving the organization's goal (where 1 was "Not very important" to the organization and 7 was "Extremely important" to the organization). For the BWS task, the 10 strategy types were assigned to subsets based on a balanced incomplete block design for 11 options that had 11 subsets, each including five strategy items. Respondents saw each strategy item six times, and each pair of items co-occurred in three sets. For each of these sets, respondents were asked to choose the strategy that was most important and the strategy that was least important to their organization achieving its goals.

9.4 Results

Before comparing the results of the ratings and best-worst data sets, the best-worst scores were converted to seven-point scales to make the comparisons easier, because such scales are commonly used in organizational research (for example, Hooley and Greenley, 2005; Jones, Mothersbaugh and Beatty, 2002; Slater and Narver, 1994) and the rating scales we used were seven-category scales. Descriptive statistics for each sample are given in Table 9.2. As can be seen from the table, the ratings standard deviations were larger than the best-worst standard deviations, but both approaches suggested a similar importance

Table 9.2 *Descriptive statistics, based on rating scales and best-worst scales*

Positioning aspect	Mean * (rating)	SD (rating)	Rank (rating)	Mean * (B-W)	SD (B-W)	Rank (B-W)
Service quality	6.14	1.22	1	5.53	1.05	1
Commitment to clients	6.00	1.32	2	4.96	0.94	3
High-quality interactions	5.96	1.34	3	4.23	0.71	4
A strong relationship	5.91	1.37	4	5.04	0.93	2
Perceived value	5.49	1.62	5	3.97	1.12	7
Strong brand	5.11	1.91	6	3.98	1.08	6
Innovation	4.85	1.69	7	4.10	1.03	5
Developing networks	4.09	1.82	8	2.95	0.99	9
Transactional approach	4.04	1.96	9	2.64	1.07	10
Databases	3.84	1.93	10	2.96	0.98	8

Note: * = based on a seven-point scale.

ordering, with service quality provision and commitment to clients seen as the most important positioning aspects, withe taking a transactional approach and using databases seen as the least important positioning aspects. The Spearman rank correlation between the two orders was 0.88, which was significant well beyond the 1 percent level, suggesting that the BWS approach did not alter the relative (ordinal) importance attached to the various positioning aspects suggested by the ratings data.

Mean scores for the strategies all were significantly higher for the ratings data than the BWS data (with t statistics ranging from 5.40 to 16.26), and seven of the 10 strategies were significantly negatively skewed, suggesting "endpiling" that can result from response bias (Lee, Soutar and Louviere, 2007). The remaining three strategies were not significantly skewed. The BWS data had only one significant skew (for high-quality interactions with clients), which was positive – a result that suggests that BWS better controlled response bias, as anticipated.

However, of more interest is the pattern of relationships between the various positioning approaches, because this is most likely to be impacted by response biases that can affect rating scales. Consequently, we computed correlations between the 10 positioning approaches for each data collection approach, with the results shown in Table 9.3. As expected, all the correlations from the ratings data are positive, ranging from 0.14 ("Perceived value" and "Developing networks") to 0.75 ("High-quality interactions" and "A strong relationship"), and all are significant at the 5 percent level, with 41 of the 45 correlations being significant at least at the 1 percent level. There were no strong distinctions between the strategies, supporting our earlier suggestion that ratings data may suffer from response biases that lead to "a tendency (for scales) to correlate positively" (Diamantopoulos, Reynolds and Simintiras, 2006).

On the other hand, the BWS correlations were both positive and negative, ranging from – 0.31 ("A strong relationship" and "Transactional approach") to 0.14 ("Databases" and

Table 5.5 *Correlations between importance of positioning approaches*

Positioning approach	Value	Commit	Networks	One-off	Quality interactions	Innovation	Relationships	Service quality	Strong brand	Databases
Rating scales										
Perceived value	1.00									
Our commitment to clients	0.52	1.00								
Developing networks	0.14	0.28	1.00							
A one-off approach to clients	0.17	0.19	0.46	1.00						
The quality of our interactions with clients	0.42	0.62	0.21	0.21	1.00					
Innovative organization	0.31	0.25	0.45	0.34	0.22	1.00				
Strong relationships	0.41	0.67	0.28	0.19	0.75	0.20	1.00			
The service quality we provide to clients	0.61	0.72	0.15	0.18	0.66	0.23	0.64	1.00		
The strength of our brand	0.26	0.38	0.48	0.29	0.23	0.42	0.28	0.32	1.00	
Using databases to communicate with clients	0.21	0.20	0.64	0.50	0.23	0.39	0.26	0.16	0.47	1.00
Best-worst scales										
Perceived value	1.00									
Our commitment to clients	-0.21	1.00								
Developing networks	-0.30	-0.05	1.00							
A one-off approach to clients	0.05	-0.13	-0.04	1.00						
The quality of our interactions with clients	-0.02	-0.23	-0.07	-0.03	1.00					
Innovative organization	-0.08	-0.31	-0.07	-0.15	0.06	1.00				
Strong relationships	-0.12	0.22	-0.01	-0.31	-0.13	-0.26	1.00			
The service quality we provide to clients	0.00	-0.07	-0.26	-0.18	0.06	-0.08	-0.01	1.00		
The strength of our brand	-0.10	-0.11	-0.05	-0.16	-0.28	-0.04	0.01	-0.18	1.00	
Using databases to communicate with clients	-0.23	-0.03	0.14	0.08	-0.05	-0.19	-0.16	-0.24	-0.12	1.00

"Developing networks"). In all, just over half the correlations (24 of the 45) were significant, with only 10 being significant beyond the 1 percent level. This result also suggests that BWS can overcome response bias problems evident in the ratings data, as well as providing a logical set of relationships. For example:

• people who attributed more importance to one-off transactions attributed less importance to strong relationships;
• people who saw developing networks as important were less likely to offer clients' value (which seems sensible, as the time required to develop relationships reduces the time available to add value); and
• people who saw databases as important also saw networking as important, suggesting that the two strategies might reinforce each other.

Thus, the various relationships were intuitively appealing, in contrast to the invariably positive and significant correlations obtained from the ratings data.

Now we assess whether response biases exist in a different way: whether, if the types of response biases suggested earlier exist, the underlying structure produced by factor-analyzing the data often will be less complex than it is in reality. The reason for this is that an underlying general factor created by the response biases will explain a large proportion of the variance (Podsakoff, MacKenzie and Podsakoff, 2003). Consequently, we conducted a principal components analysis on each data set to examine this issue. The PCA of the ratings data resulted in two eigenvalues greater than one that (together) explained 63 percent of the variance, with the first component explaining 43 percent of the variance. This suggests a single strong underlying factor, and likely response bias. Indeed, as one might expect from the correlational analysis results of the rating scale data, six of the nine positioning approaches loaded most highly on the first component.

In contrast, the PCA of the BWS data produced eigenvalues greater than one that (together) explained 59 percent of the variance in that data set. In this case, the first component explained only 17 percent of the variance, and the other three factors had almost equal impacts: 16 percent, 13 percent and 13 percent, respectively). Further, most of the strategies did not load highly on the first component, with high loadings spread across the four factors. These results suggest that response biases may mask more complex factor structures, which can provide additional insights into organizations' positioning strategies.

We also compared the interrelationships between the items by "mapping" them with multidimensional scaling (MDS) (Lee, Soutar and Louviere, 2008; Padgett and Mulvey, 2007). We used the PERMAP scaling program (Heady and Lucas, 1997) to obtain MDS maps for each of the two correlation matrices. In both cases, stress measures used to determine dimensionality (Dröge and Darmon, 1987; Green and Rao, 1972) suggested a two dimensional map was appropriate. However, the two maps, shown in Figures 9.1 and 9.2, suggest quite different relationships between the positioning aspects. For example, five of the 10 positioning aspects group closely together in the southwest quadrant of the ratings map, with no aspects located in the northwest quadrant, while the BWS mapping results show much greater spread.

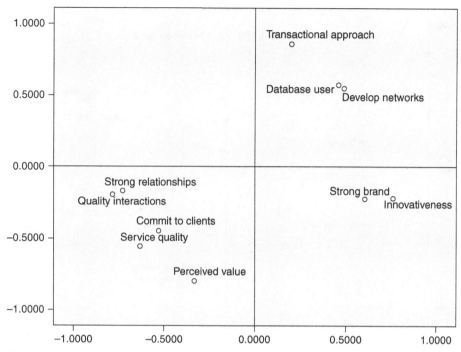

Figure 9.1 Positioning map obtained from the ratings data

There also are some similarities in the two MDS maps. First, databases and networking positioning strategies are very close in both. This is consistent with Coviello and her various co-authors' suggestions that there are conceptual distinctions between such marketing practices, despite the practices being empirically indistinct. Coviello and her co-authors argued that database marketing involved the use of technology-based tools to target and retain customers, while network marketing involved the development of interfirm relationships that led to mutual benefits. The three positioning strategies seen as least important for achieving firm outcomes (which are shown in Table 9.2) clustered in a single quadrant in both maps.

A further similarity is seen in the "Service quality" and "Perceived value" map positions. Perceived value typically implies a trade-off between quality and price (Monroe, 1990; Zeithaml, 1988) and, hence, a close relationship between the two would be expected. However, quality and value are conceptually distinct, as quality is a cognitive evaluation, while value is an evaluation of what is received compared to what is given, and is inherently more personal (Sweeney and Soutar, 2001; Zeithaml, 1988). This is consistent with the close, yet different, positions of these two positioning aspects on the MDS maps.

"Service quality" is close to "Commitment to clients" in Figure 9.1, yet distinct from "Commitment to clients" in Figure 9.2. Previous researchers argued that there is a distinction between the two approaches from a customer perspective, as service quality measures

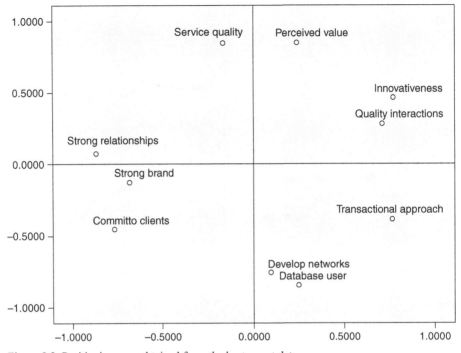

Figure 9.2 Positioning map obtained from the best-worst data

performance along transactional dimensions, whereas commitment is a core component of relationship quality that emphasizes the intangible aspects of ongoing relationships (see, for example, Roberts, Varki and Brodie, 2003; Wetzels, de Ruyter and Birgelen, 1998). Hence, high commitment is related to strong relationships. Figure 9.2 supports this notion, and shows that "Strong brand," "Commitment to clients" and "Strong relationships" are similar in the importance of such strategies in achieving firm goals. A strong brand is important for professional services, as the perceived risk of making an incorrect purchase decision is high, and the brand is a key risk reduction component (Hill and Neeley, 1988; Verhage, Yavas and Green, 1990). Amonini *et al.* (2007) found that the development of a strong professional service brand implied building a reputable brand that involved employees in "acting the brand," because brand images are developed via those employees with whom customers came into contact. This is also supported in Figure 9.2, in which "Strong brand" is similar to "Strong relationships" and "Commitment to clients."

Notwithstanding the fact that one can note such similarities and differences, a visual comparison of these maps is highly subjective, because of the arbitrary origins and orientation of the configurations. Consequently, we used Cliff's (1966) matching program to further assess the maps' congruency. Cliff's procedure fixes a matrix to a "target," rotates the two matrices to a common orientation and computes the goodness of fit between the two (Green and Rao, 1972). Cliff (1966) suggested that matrices with a goodness-of-fit index of less than 0.80 were not congruent. In this case, the goodness-of-fit index was 0.45, which suggests that, while there is some similarity, the maps cannot be considered congruent. A further measure of congruence is the correlation between the inter-point distances within the map (Green and Rao, 1972). In this case, the inter-point correlation was 0.20, again suggesting little congruency between data sets. Moreover, this result suggests that the measurement approach itself impacts the positioning aspects' interrelationships, which implies that subsequent analysis is influenced by the measurement approach, because correlations between various positioning strategies differ depending on the scaling approach used.

9.5 Conclusions

We compared best-worst scales to rating scales for measuring managers' perceptions of their respective firm's market positions. This comparison matters, because BWS can overcome response biases often associated with the rating scales typically used in organizational and other social science and business research (Ward and Lewandowska, 2005). We found that BWS and rating scales produced the same pattern of relative (ordinal) importance that the sample of managers attached to the various positioning aspects in achieving their goals. However, BWS overcame the response biases inherent in rating scales. Specifically, BWS scores were generally not skewed and had negative and positive correlations, whereas most ratings scores were negatively skewed and all the ratings data correlations were positive.

BWS also provided insights into interrelationships between the positioning strategies not evident from the rating scales. For example, the most important five of the 10 positioning aspects in achieving the firm's goals ("Strong relationships," "High-quality interactions," "Commitment to clients," "Service quality" and "Perceived value") grouped closely together in the ratings map but were clearly differentiated in the BWS map. This finergrained distinction provides more insight for managers, particularly as many professional service firms use a number of positions simultaneously (Amonini *et al.*, 2007). For example, based on the BWS results, managers do not view a service quality positioning strategy as similarly effective in achieving firm goals as showing their commitment to clients, because these are distinct and unrelated strategies. In contrast, developing strong relationships and a strong brand are positions viewed to be similar in effectiveness to showing commitment to clients.

In summary, we have provided evidence for changing how one measures managers' perceptions – namely, shifting from rating scales(typically used) to BWS. Importantly, BWS creates simpler tasks for respondents, generates more powerful measurement scores in terms of utility measures, reduces response bias, provides greater differentiation between constructs and is likely to provide more insights into interrelationships between strategies. Thus, BWS is a useful and potentially valuable way to measure perceptions in organizational research, such as the positioning strategies we studied.

Applications: Case 2

Chapter 10

When the ayes don't have it: supplementing an accept/reject DCE with a Case 2 best-worst scaling task

Richard T. Carson and Jordan J. Louviere

10.1 Introduction

Accept/reject and other questions with binary alternatives, such as favor/oppose and like/dislike, are common in the discrete choice experiment literature. They usually take the form of offering respondents a binary choice, in which the two alternatives are the current status quo and an alternative. There can be a single choice set or a sequence of choice sets. A recent example is the study by Day *et al.* (2012), who investigated whether consumers would pay an additional charge to have a public water supply that had fewer days with lower-quality taste/smell and color.

A common difficulty with such questions is that a sizable fraction of the population of interest may not shift from choosing one alternative to the other for any plausible difference in attribute values. For example, with a new product, there may be a limited number of people prepared to try it initially, although the larger potential fraction of the population who may buy the product in the longer run might have clear preferences over possible attribute levels that would influence a firm's design decisions. Another common example comes from politics. In places with a well-established two-political-party system, most voters are unlikely to switch their vote from their current party to the other party in the current election cycle. However, this does not mean that voters are indifferent to the candidates/positions of the opposing party. In environmental valuation studies, it is common to see a sizable fraction of the public opposed to an improvement in the status quo level of the environmental good being studied because they ideologically oppose additional government action. What is important to recognize is that, when a consumers are forced to pay for a good or experience a policy change, it cannot be inferred that they are indifferent to specific attribute levels even though they favor or oppose all the alternatives to the current status quo. Common to all these situations is an inability to extract as much information about preferences as researchers would like, because of constraints on either the range of plausible attribute levels or the rate of adoption/switching in the short run. In situations such as these, a Case 2 best-worst scaling task can be a valuable addition to a binary or multiple choice task.

Table 10.1 *Attributes and levels in the voting task*

Attribute	Level
Year in which the scheme begins	Start 2010
	Start 2012
How the revenues raised are used	Redistribute to poor and seniors
	Reduce GST
Invest 20% of revenues in R&D	Do not invest in R&D
	Invest 20 in R&D
Exempt transport-related activities	Do not exempt transport
	Exempt transport
Exempt energy-intensive industries	Do not exempt energy
	Exempt energy

10.2 Australian climate policy alternatives

This chapter considers data from a survey involving 388 people randomly sampled from a weighted version of the Pureprofile online panel designed to be representative of voting-age Australians. It is useful to first look at the sequence of binary-choice voting questions, because our implementation of a Case 2 BWS task served as a natural prequel to this more familiar and commonly used voting task. In this case respondents were asked if they would vote for each of 16 emissions trading schemes paired against the status quo of no ETS. Each emissions trading plan was described by a combination of five attributes, each of which has the two possible levels shown in Table 10.1. Since each of the five attributes has two levels, there are 2^5 (32) possible ETSs. We divided the 32 possible schemes into two sets of 16, each of which had the statistical property that all main effects and two-way interactions for the five attributes can be estimated (under the assumption that all higher-order interactions equal zero).

Graphs of all the main effects and two-way interactions are shown in Figure 10.1.[1] It is important to note that the ranges on the Y-axis (aggregate sample choice proportions) differ slightly from graph to graph. Nonetheless, a common feature of all graphs is that the *range* of effects displayed on the Y-axis is relatively small. Mean choice proportions for each of the main effects are shown in Table 10.2 and are consistent with the graphs: they have a narrow range, with only "Start year" and "20% in R&D" displaying a difference in mean choice proportions. In turn, this result suggests the sample respondents were (1) largely indifferent to attributes when voting for schemes, (2) very heterogeneous in their responses to the attributes when voting for the schemes,[2] or (3) a combination of both.

---

[1] Carson, Louviere and Wei (2010) provide a discussion about why these attributes were central to the policy debate that took place in Australia and look at data from an earlier survey using these attributes to define a possible emissions trading scheme. Their results are similar to those reported here, suggesting temporal stability at the aggregate level over about a one-year time period.

[2] From a political science median voter perspective, it not surprising to see the public split into roughly equal proportions on these attributes, as they are the ones that the major parties decided to contest with respect to competing visions of the details of an emissions trading scheme. A Liberal Party leadership shift in 2009 resulted in the party being opposed to the implementation of any ETS.

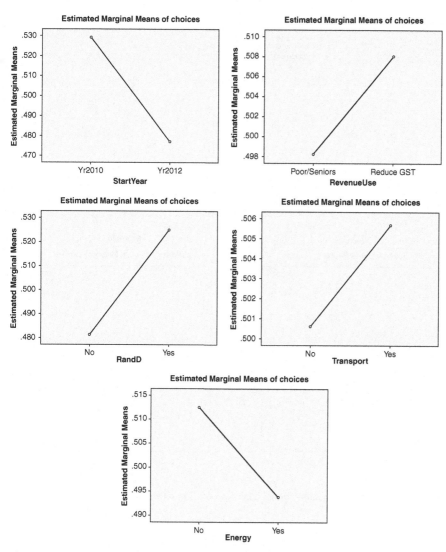

Figure 10.1a Attribute main effects: emissions trading schemes

One way to illustrate the narrow range of choice proportions (the percentage voting "Yes" for a particular ETS paired with the status quo) is to calculate the proportion voting "Yes" for each of the 32 possible ETS options in the survey. Table 10.3 sorts the 32 schemes from highest to lowest voting percentage, and shows that 13 of the possible schemes got majority support. We suggest some caution in interpreting these proportions, as 93 people voted "Yes" in every scenario (which makes sense if a respondent is concerned about climate change but does not care a lot about the details of the particular ETS to be implemented).

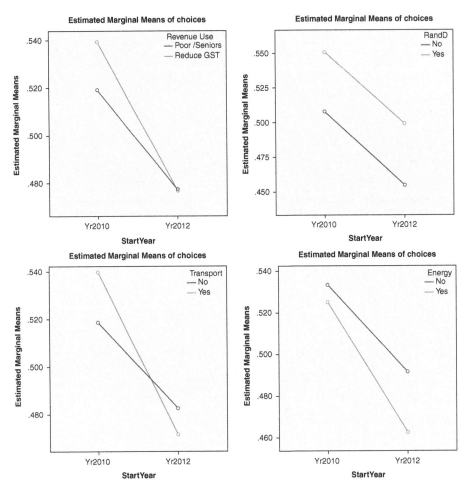

Figure 10.1b Attribute two-way interactions: emissions trading schemes

One can count the attribute levels for each of the majority-supported schemes to "suggest" what may underlie the choices. For example, all 13 majority schemes were to start in 2010. Six would reduce the Goods and Services Tax, while the rest (seven) would redistribute revenues to poor and senior citizens. Ten of the majority schemes invest 20 percent of revenues in R&D related to reducing carbon emissions. Seven schemes do not exempt transport-related activities or industries, and nine schemes do not exempt energy-intensive industries. This suggests that the sample was most homogeneous about the starting year (2010 versus 2012), and was fairly homogeneous towards investing 20 percent in R&D and not exempting energy-intensive industries. In turn, this suggests that other attributes matter very little and/or a large fraction of respondent are indifferent to differences in them.

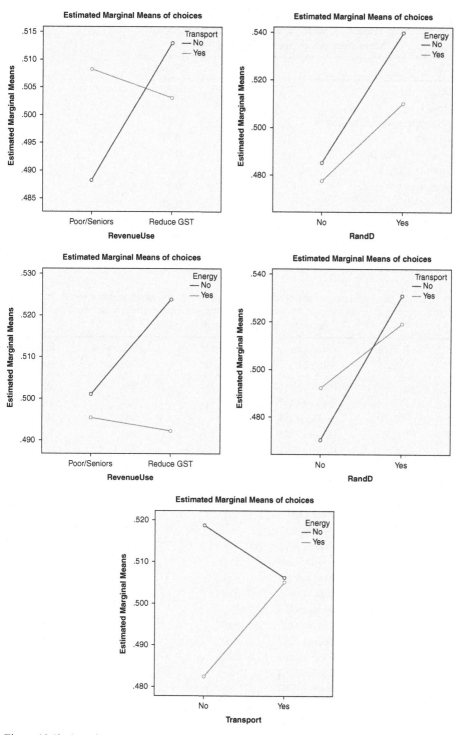

Figure 10.1b (cont.)

Table 10.2 *Attribute main effect means from the voting task*

Mean votes percentage by level	
Level	Vote %
Start 2010	0.53
Start 2012	0.48
Redistribute to poor and seniors	0.50
Reduce GST	0.51
Do not invest in R&D	0.48
Invest 20% in R&D	0.53
Do not exempt transport	0.50
Exempt transport	0.51
Do not exempt energy	0.51
Exempt energy	0.49
Total	0.50

Table 10.3 *All possible emissions trading schemes sorted by proportion voting "Yes"*

	Sorted vote percentage by design matrix				
Vote	1. Plan begins	2. Income will go to	3. Invest 20% in R&D	4. Exempt transport	5. Exempt energy
0.660	Yr2010	Poor/seniors	No	Yes	Yes
0.613	Yr2010	Reduce GST	Yes	Yes	Yes
0.603	Yr2010	Reduce GST	Yes	No	No
0.588	Yr2012	Reduce GST	Yes	No	No
0.582	Yr2010	Reduce GST	No	Yes	No
0.572	Yr2010	Poor/seniors	Yes	Yes	No
0.562	Yr2010	Reduce GST	Yes	No	Yes
0.546	Yr2010	Poor/seniors	Yes	No	Yes
0.546	Yr2012	Poor/seniors	Yes	Yes	No
0.546	Yr2010	Poor/seniors	No	No	No
0.531	Yr2010	Reduce GST	Yes	Yes	No
0.510	Yr2010	Poor/seniors	Yes	No	No
0.505	Yr2012	Poor/seniors	Yes	No	Yes
0.490	Yr2012	Poor/seniors	Yes	No	No
0.485	Yr2010	Reduce GST	No	No	No
0.485	Yr2010	Reduce GST	No	No	Yes
0.479	Yr2012	Reduce GST	Yes	Yes	No
0.474	Yr2012	Poor/seniors	Yes	Yes	Yes
0.474	Yr2012	Reduce GST	No	No	Yes
0.469	Yr2012	Reduce GST	Yes	Yes	Yes
0.469	Yr2010	Poor/seniors	Yes	Yes	Yes
0.464	Yr2012	Reduce GST	No	No	No

Table 10.3 (*cont.*)

Vote	1. Plan begins	2. Income will go to	3. Invest 20% in R&D	4. Exempt transport	5. Exempt energy
			Sorted vote percentage by design matrix		
0.464	Yr2012	Poor/seniors	No	No	No
0.464	Yr2012	Poor/seniors	No	Yes	Yes
0.459	Yr2012	Reduce GST	No	Yes	No
0.454	Yr2010	Reduce GST	No	Yes	Yes
0.443	Yr2012	Poor/seniors	No	Yes	No
0.443	Yr2012	Reduce GST	Yes	No	Yes
0.438	Yr2012	Reduce GST	No	Yes	Yes
0.438	Yr2010	Poor/seniors	No	Yes	No
0.433	Yr2012	Poor/seniors	No	No	Yes
0.412	Yr2010	Poor/seniors	No	No	Yes

Table 10.4 *Observed numbers of "Yes" votes in the sample*

Total "Yes" votes	Frequency	Percentage in sample
0	40	0.103
1	24	0.062
2	20	0.052
3	20	0.052
4	24	0.062
5	30	0.077
6	17	0.044
7	19	0.049
8	21	0.054
9	14	0.036
10	17	0.044
11	11	0.028
12	18	0.046
13	9	0.023
14	17	0.044
15	29	0.075
16	58	0.149

We next consider the total number of "Yes" votes for the sample displayed in Table 10.4, which shows that about 25 percent of the sample always voted "No" or always voted "Yes," providing no preference information for attributes/levels. A further 24 percent voted "No" or "Yes" almost every time, again giving little attribute/level preference information. Thus, almost 50 percent of the sample in the voting task responded extremely, providing little information about how the sample is likely to respond to changes in attribute levels; however, schemes that will attract majority support (a majority "Yes" vote) can clearly be identified. This suggests that some (perhaps many) of the 49 percent with extreme responses were using accept/reject rules that are not well approximated by additive indirect utility functions, and, indeed, some (perhaps many) may have behaved deterministically.

10.3 Case 2 best-worst scaling task

We combined the binary-choice voting task with a Case 2 best-worst scaling task, such that each of the 388 survey respondents reported the attribute levels that they thought were, respectively, the best and worst aspects of each scheme described. An example of this task is depicted in Figure 10.2, which shows that survey respondents were asked to tick one box for the best and a second box for the worst attribute level. Each respondent completed this task in conjunction with the accept/reject task – that is, we showed respondents one emissions trading scheme description at a time, and they were asked to choose the best and worst aspects of each scheme description and then tell us whether they would vote "Yes" or "No" for it. Thus, despite the fact that many respondents made extreme choices in the voting task, they each provided a complete set of Case 2 BWS choices. This allows us to analyze the choice data for the aggregate sample and each person.

We begin with the attribute level choices for the aggregate sample. Table 10.5 contains the mean best and worst choice sample proportions and their associated standard deviations. These results suggest that there may be more to the voting preferences than meets the eye. Specifically, we can immediately "see" large differences in best and worst choice proportions for levels of start year, redistribution of revenues and investing in R&D. By way of contrast, exemptions for transport and energy show much smaller differences.

Marley, Flynn and Louviere (2008) showed that the best and worst choices in Case 2 BWS tasks can be placed on a common scale (see Chapter 3). Thus, we can use the results in Table 10.5 to calculate additional sample measures, such as (1) best-minus-worst choice proportion differences, (2) the square root of best divided by worst choice proportions and (3) the natural logarithm of the square root of best divided by worst choice proportions. The first measure is a difference scale of the latent "bestness" of a level centered at zero. Ratios

The best aspect of this plan is (tick one box below):	Aspects of plan 1	The worst aspect of this plan is (tick one box below):
☐	Start plan in 2012	☐
☐	Use revenues to reduce GST	☐
☐	Do not invest 20% in R&D	☐
☐	Exempt transport	☐
☐	Exempt energy	☐

Figure 10.2 Example Case 2 BWS task for emissions trading scheme options

Table 10.5 *Aggregate sample mean best-worst choices by attribute level*

Level	Best mean %	Worst mean %	Best SD	Worst SD
Start 2010	0.33	0.17	0.471	0.377
Start 2012	0.14	0.36	0.349	0.479
Redistribute to poor and seniors	0.38	0.17	0.486	0.376
Reduce GST	0.43	0.09	0.496	0.291
Do not invest in R&D	0.07	0.25	0.249	0.434
Invest 20% in R&D	0.23	0.10	0.421	0.305
Do not exempt transport	0.09	0.22	0.293	0.416
Exempt transport	0.12	0.23	0.321	0.423
Do not exempt energy	0.09	0.20	0.280	0.398
Exempt energy	0.12	0.20	0.323	0.401

Table 10.6 *Calculation of best and worst measures from Table 5 results*

Level	Best mean %	Worst mean %	B% – W%	SQRT (B% / W%)	Ln(SQRT (B% / W%)
Start 2010	0.330	0.170	0.160	1.393	0.332
Start 2012	0.140	0.360	−0.220	0.624	−0.472
Redistribute to poor and seniors	0.380	0.170	0.210	1.495	0.402
Reduce GST	0.430	0.090	0.340	2.186	0.782
Do not invest in R&D	0.070	0.250	−0.180	0.529	−0.636
Invest 20% in R&D	0.230	0.100	0.130	1.517	0.416
Do not exempt transport	0.090	0.220	−0.130	0.640	−0.447
Exempt transport	0.120	0.230	−0.110	0.722	−0.325
Do not exempt energy	0.090	0.200	−0.110	0.671	−0.399
Exempt energy	0.120	0.200	−0.080	0.775	−0.255

of differences are meaningful quantities on this scale, but differences between levels cannot be directly compared. The second measure is a ratio scale of "bestness" that should be proportional to the best choice proportions, which we test below. This scale allows one to compare differences between levels and make meaningful statements about ratios of measures (for example, this level is twice as "best" as that level). Measure three also is a difference scale centered around zero, and should be proportional to the best-minus-worst difference scores, which we also test below. Finally, the measures in Table 10.5 are choice proportions; as such, they are estimates of choice probabilities on an absolute scale ranging between zero and one, allowing one to make meaningful statements about ratios of choice proportions (for example, level A is half as likely to be chosen best as level B).

The calculations are given in Table 10.6, with relationships between the measures graphically displayed in Figures 10.3a, 10.3b and 10.3c. The figures indicate that the

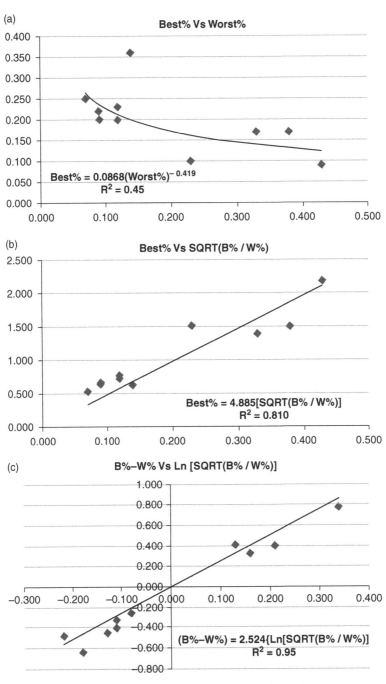

Figure 10.3 Relationships between calculated BWS measures for aggregate sample

assumption that aggregate-sample best choice proportions are inversely related to their worst proportion counterparts is not well satisfied. However, the relationships between (a) best proportions minus worst proportions and the natural log of the square root of the ratio of best proportions to worst proportions and (b) best proportions and the square root of the ratio of best proportions divided by worst proportions better satisfy the assumption of proportionality of measures. Possible reasons for the unsatisfactory fit of the relationship between best and worst proportions are (1) preference heterogeneity (that is, the choices of attribute levels differ across respondents), (2) differences in choice consistency (error variability) in best and worst choices and/or (3) different rules (choice processes) for making best and worst choices.

We consider choice (preference) heterogeneity by calculating best and worst choice totals for each attribute level for each person and then cluster-analyzing them. This allows us to test differences in best and worst choices of attribute levels to determine if this is at least partially responsible for the poor fit of the assumed relationship between best and worst proportions. Additionally, the cluster analysis is interesting in its own right, as it can reveal potentially meaningful differences in respondents that can shed light on the voting choices. Work by Dimitriadou, Dolničar and Weingessel (2002) and Dolničar and Leisch (2010) suggests that, if there is structure underlying the data of interest (here, the individual best and worst choices), all cluster procedures will find it; however, they also showed that, if there is no structure underlying the data, many methods will give results suggesting that there is structure. We use Ward's hierarchical tree clustering approach, as this allows us to see where clusters form and how they agglomerate and separate (that is, if we go from three to four clusters, we know exactly where the people who become cluster four come from). Table 10.7 contains the aggregate summary results of a six-cluster solution for the 388 respondents in our sample; we stopped at six clusters because additional clusters had few respondents.

The columns in Tables 10.7a to 10.7c are labeled C1 to C6, representing the six clusters. Each of the three tables (a to c) has a different measure; for example, Table 10.7a displays best-minus-worst difference scores. We graphed (not shown here) clusters 1 to 6 against the sample averages, which strongly suggested that the cluster differences were not large (in other words, it is likely that there is no real multi-modal structure underlying the best-worst choices). Thus, the sample is very homogeneous but displays large variability in the choice consistency, or the sample differences can be represented by some type of probability distribution. We begin by testing cluster differences in a simple but compelling way with principal components analysis. The null hypothesis of interest is that only one component underlies each set of measures, and the collection of all 18 measures (3 BWS measures × 6 clusters).

The results of this analysis suggest that only one component underlies the data. Table 10.8a provides a singular value decomposition in terms of the three measures used with the first component in all cases explaining over 90 percent of the variance. Table 10.8b looks at the same type of analysis but now using all three measures in Table 10.8a together. It seems clear that there is no underlying structure beyond one component.

Table 10.7 *Calculations derived from the most and least Case 2 BWS choices*

a *Best-minus-worst difference scores*

Means	Best-minus-worst difference scores					
Alt	C1	C2	C3	C4	C5	C6
Start 2010	0.140	0.077	0.213	0.175	0.136	0.183
Start 2012	−0.123	−0.304	−0.163	−0.295	−0.216	−0.169
Poor and seniors	0.213	0.240	0.098	0.267	0.245	0.187
Reduce GST	0.360	0.369	0.321	0.295	0.436	0.277
Not invest R&D	−0.211	−0.115	−0.213	−0.183	−0.219	−0.144
Invest R&D	0.113	0.093	0.187	0.089	0.139	0.135
Not exempt transport	−0.076	−0.163	−0.175	−0.094	−0.102	−0.179
Exempt transport	−0.221	−0.064	−0.075	−0.099	−0.175	−0.063
Not exempt energy	−0.032	−0.125	−0.138	−0.065	−0.120	−0.194
Exempt energy	−0.164	−0.006	−0.054	−0.089	−0.125	−0.031

b *Square root of best choices (counts) divided by worst choices (counts)*

Means	SQRT(best/worst)					
Alt	C1	C2	C3	C4	C5	C6
Start 2010	1.316	1.165	1.688	1.414	1.358	1.396
Start 2012	0.777	0.529	0.661	0.545	0.593	0.724
Poor and seniors	1.607	1.572	1.189	1.792	1.550	1.400
Reduce GST	2.184	2.143	2.116	2.100	2.483	1.902
Not invest R&D	0.521	0.661	0.495	0.554	0.383	0.528
Invest R&D	1.367	1.300	1.693	1.323	1.647	1.672
Not exempt transport	0.776	0.540	0.553	0.750	0.699	0.544
Exempt transport	0.512	0.816	0.813	0.744	0.591	0.816
Not exempt energy	0.876	0.539	0.616	0.793	0.642	0.485
Exempt energy	0.514	0.979	0.843	0.744	0.688	0.910

c *Natural log of the square root quantities in Table 4b*

Means	Ln[SQRT(best/worst)]					
Alt	C1	C2	C3	C4	C5	C6
Start 2010	0.274	0.153	0.524	0.347	0.306	0.334
Start 2012	−0.253	−0.636	−0.414	−0.607	−0.522	−0.323
Poor and seniors	0.474	0.452	0.173	0.583	0.438	0.337
Reduce GST	0.781	0.762	0.750	0.742	0.910	0.643
Not invest R&D	−0.652	−0.413	−0.703	−0.591	−0.961	−0.639
Invest R&D	0.312	0.263	0.526	0.280	0.499	0.514
Not exempt transport	−0.253	−0.616	−0.593	−0.287	−0.359	−0.610
Exempt transport	−0.669	−0.203	−0.207	−0.295	−0.527	−0.203
Not exempt energy	−0.132	−0.617	−0.485	−0.232	−0.443	−0.724
Exempt energy	−0.666	−0.021	−0.170	−0.296	−0.374	−0.094

Table 10.8a *Singular value decomposition results for measures (principal components analysis)*

Component	Best–worst differences		SQRT(best/worst)		Ln[SQRT(best/worst)]	
	Eigenvalue	% of variance	Eigenvalue	% of variance	Eigenvalue	% of variance
1	5.581	93.013	5.629	93.817	5.444	90.738
2	0.202	3.368	0.207	3.442	0.360	5.997
3	0.151	2.514	0.108	1.807	0.127	2.109
4	0.041	0.681	0.029	0.475	0.039	0.653
5	0.022	0.362	0.022	0.360	0.020	0.335
6	0.004	0.061	0.006	0.099	0.010	0.168

Table 10.8b *Principal components analysis results for all three measures*

	Analysis combining all three measures	
Component	Eigenvalue	% of variance
1	16.486	91.588
2	0.737	4.092
3	0.456	2.534
4	0.170	0.947
5	0.081	0.448
6	0.043	0.240
7	0.011	0.062
8	0.008	0.046
9	0.007	0.041
10 to 18 = 0		

We now produce histograms for the 10 attribute levels for the best-minus-worst difference scores; the PCA results indicate that results are the same for all measures, so we discuss only the BWS scores. Histograms are calculated for the entire data set, which is why there are so many observations (80 observations × 388 people), but the graph would be identical for one observation per person. In Figure 10.4, look at the first row of the figure that has the two start date attribute levels, 2010 and 2012. The average difference scores for 2012 are lower than those for 2010. The data also are multi-modal, with spikes at −1 and +1, but the mass of the distribution is concentrated near zero, suggesting that many people were indifferent about start year. In the case of how to use the revenues collected by the scheme, many people chose to give the revenues to the poor and seniors every time that choice was available (+1), although on average the mean for reducing the GST is higher. So, there seem to be many individual differences as well as a lot of indifference (mass again centered near zero). For investing in research and development, the sample clearly favors investing 20

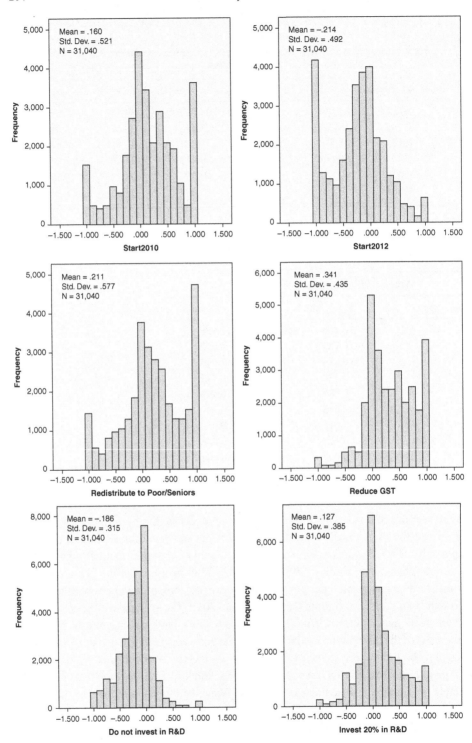

Figure 10.4 Histograms for BWS scores for each attribute level

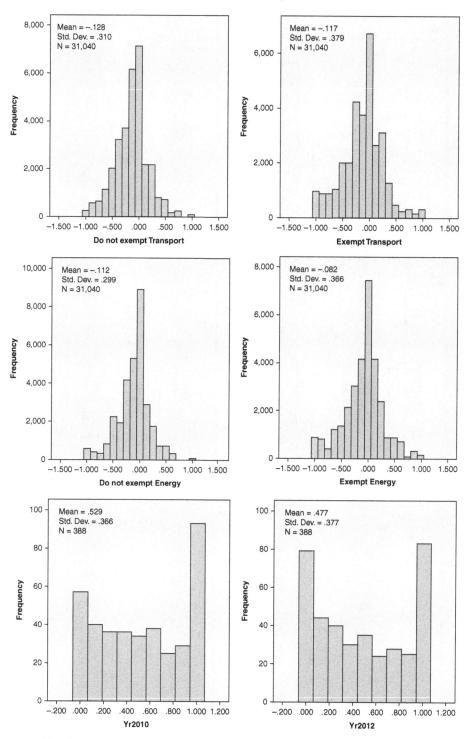

Figure 10.4 (cont.)

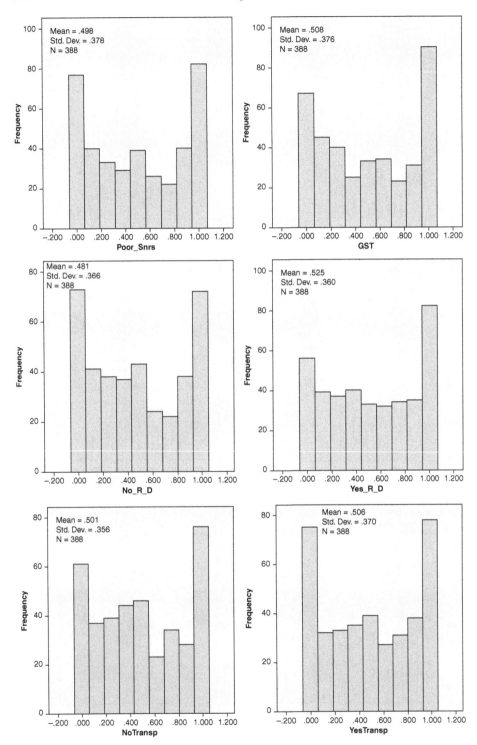

Figure 10.4 (cont.)

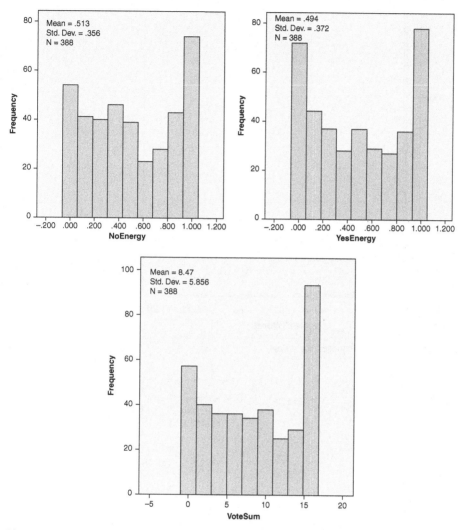

Figure 10.4 (cont.)

percent of the revenues raised in R&D, with a clear mode at +1 for the latter level, together with a large proportion of indifferent people. Both transport exemption levels were relatively unpopular (both have negative means), and only a few people chose either level consistently as best or worst, with many indifferent to both levels. Both energy attribute levels also have negative means, but a few people consistently chose them as the worst levels (−1), with many indifferent (near zero).

We also investigate the degree to which respondents were consistent in their choices by fitting linear probability models to each person's best and worst choices, and calculating the residuals from these regressions for each person. We then square the residuals and display their distribution in a histogram in Figures 10.5a and 10.5b, which are, respectively, the

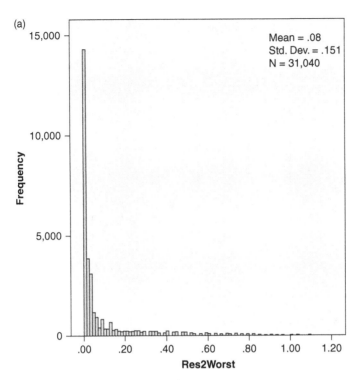

Figure 10.5(a) Residuals squared for worst

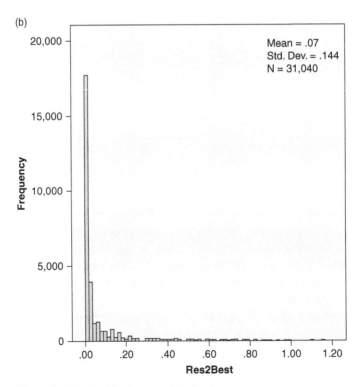

Figure 10.5(b) Residuals squared for best

mean squared residuals for best and worst choices. These histograms suggest that the vast majority of people were very consistent in their choices, and that they were slightly more consistent in making best choices than worst choices. Taken together, the histograms suggest that many people were deterministic or nearly so in their best and worst choices of attribute levels. The histograms also indicate that it would be difficult to tell a well-behaved random coefficient story for this sample. In other words, although one can estimate statistical choice models from these data that allow for a distribution of utility estimates over the respondents, it is unclear (1) why one would want to do that in this case and (2) whether such a statistical representation would be stable over space and time in any meaningful way.

10.4 Relationship to covariates

Therefore, it is likely that a more insightful approach is to determine if one can capture "observable" (as opposed to "unobservable") preference heterogeneity in the sample by allowing choices of attribute levels for the two tasks to differ by particular covariate measures in the survey, as we now show.

We begin by calculating simple best-minus-worst difference scores. We use the 1, 0 choice indicator measures in the data to construct a new variable that takes on the values −1 (level chosen worst), 0 (level not chosen as either best or worst) and +1 (level chosen best). Ultimately, we wish to ask if we can predict these three outcomes statistically using available covariates as predictors. Two obvious statistical models that can be used for this purpose are (1) unconditional (polychotomous) multinomial logit regression and (2) ordinal regression. We do not illustrate using these statistical models to test for relationships with the covariates because the number of possible terms is too large.

In any case, before fitting models one should "look" at one's data, which we do by cross-tabbing the best-minus-worst difference scores with the covariates. We examine these results and the associated chi-square tests. There are many cross-tab tables for this data set, so, in the interests of space and because this is a case study chapter, we present only a few results (tables). Specifically, we cross-tab the BWS difference scores with available covariate measures, for each attribute level. We now discuss a few of the more interesting results.

We categorize the tables by the attribute level to which they pertain. For example, the first set of three tables relates to the attribute level "Starting the scheme in 2010." Table 10.9a indicates that respondents who agreed that global warming probably has been happening were much more likely to choose that level as most (+1), while those who disagreed were more likely to choose it as least (−1). Table 10.9b looks at political parties, and shows that Greens were more likely to choose 2010 as most (+1) and Liberals were most likely to choose it as least (−1).[3] So, more left-leaning voters favored starting in 2010, but more right-leaning voters favored starting in 2012.

[3] Labour is the major center-left party and, at the time of the survey, formed the government with the Greens, who have an environmentalist orientation. The Liberal Party is the mainstream center-right party, and is often in a coalition with the Nationals, who are strong in rural areas. The (Liberal) Democrats have a libertarian orientation.

Table 10.9 *Cross-tab plans that start in 2010*

a *Start in 2010*

		BWS			
		−1	0	+1	Total
Do you think global warming probably has been	Has been	14.8%	49.5%	35.6%	100.0%
happening, or it probably hasn't been happening?	Has not been	29.3%	51.0%	19.7%	100.0%
Total		17.1%	49.8%	33.1%	100.0%

Notes: Pearson chi-square = 82.142; df = 2; Sig < 0.000.

b *Start in 2010*

		BWS			
		−1	0	+1	Total
Which political party do you identify the most with:	Labour	16.6%	47.1%	36.3%	100.0%
	Liberals	23.1%	52.6%	24.4%	100.0%
	Greens	6.3%	52.4%	41.3%	100.0%
	Nationals	15.0%	55.0%	30.0%	100.0%
	Democrats	14.6%	45.8%	39.6%	100.0%
	None	17.4%	50.9%	31.7%	100.0%
Total		17.1%	49.8%	33.1%	100.0%

Notes: Pearson chi-square = 62.439; df = 10; Sig < 0.000.

The next tables relate to giving part of the revenues raised to help the poor and senior citizens. Table 10.10a tabulates BWS scores with age, which indicates that the older the respondent, the more likely he/she was to choose this level as most, while at the same time being less likely to choose it as least. Table 10.10b tabulates household income with the BWS scores, suggesting that the higher the household income, the less likely a respondent was to choose this level as most (+1), and instead he/she is more likely to choose it as least (−1). Conversely, poorer respondents were more likely to choose it as most (+1).

The next results refer to using the revenues to reduce the GST. Table 10.11a tabulates those agreeing with implementing a scheme that reduces more emissions even if it costs more. Respondents who disagreed were much more likely to choose this level as most (+1). Table 10.11b tabulates political affiliation with the level, showing that those most likely to choose reducing GST (+1) had no political affiliation, those least likely to choose reducing GST as most were the Greens, while the Nationals were least likely to choose reducing GST as least (−1).

The next set of tables give results for investing 20 percent of the revenues in research and development related to reducing emissions and sustainable technologies. Table 10.12a looks at how serious respondents think global warming will be for Australia's future

Table 10.10 *Cross-tab giving the revenues to the poor and senior citizens*

a *Giving revenues to poor and seniors*

		BWS			
		−1	0	+1	Total
Which age group are you in?	18–19	20.1%	50.7%	29.2%	100.0%
	20–24	26.6%	41.0%	32.4%	100.0%
	25–29	23.5%	42.6%	33.8%	100.0%
	30–34	22.1%	46.3%	31.6%	100.0%
	35–39	11.0%	45.3%	43.8%	100.0%
	40–44	16.1%	51.4%	32.5%	100.0%
	45–49	12.5%	43.6%	43.9%	100.0%
	50–54	11.0%	51.9%	37.1%	100.0%
	55–59	18.5%	38.6%	42.9%	100.0%
	60–64	9.5%	47.0%	43.5%	100.0%
	65–69	0.0%	14.6%	85.4%	100.0%
	70+	0.0%	31.3%	68.8%	100.0%
Total		17.0%	44.9%	38.1%	100.0%

Notes: Pearson chi-square = 169.371; df = 22; Sig < 0.000.

b *Giving revenues to poor and seniors*

		BWS			
		−1	0	+1	Total
Household income	Below $25,000	5.7%	29.8%	64.6%	100.0%
	$25,000 to $50,000	9.1%	47.2%	43.7%	100.0%
	$50,000 to $75,000	13.3%	41.2%	45.5%	100.0%
	$75,000 to $100,000	23.4%	46.6%	30.0%	100.0%
	$100,000 to $125,000	24.6%	45.3%	30.1%	100.0%
	$125,000 to $150,000	20.1%	56.4%	23.5%	100.0%
	$150,000 to $200,000	26.6%	54.9%	18.5%	100.0%
	Above $200,000	20.3%	47.7%	32.0%	100.0%
Total		17.0%	44.9%	38.1%	100.0%

Notes: Pearson chi-square = 252.268; df = 14; Sig < 0.000.

crossed with investing in R&D. It indicates that the more serious respondents think the problem will be, the more they are likely to choose this level as most (1), whereas the less serious respondents thought it was, the more likely the level chosen was least (−1). Table 10.12b looks at attitudes towards technological breakthroughs fixing global warming with choice of the level as most or least, and shows that the more faith is expressed in technological advances solving the problems, the more likely investing in R&D is chosen as

Table 10.11 *Cross-tab using the revenues to reduce the GST*

a *Using revenues to reduce the GST*

		BWS		
		−1	0	+1	Total
Should Australia adopt a plan that requires an 80% reduction Yes		10.2%	51.8%	38.0%	100.0%
in greenhouse gases by 2050 instead of a 60% reduction No		8.1%	41.0%	51.0%	100.0%
even if the plan will have substantially higher costs?					
Total			9.3%	47.2%	43.5%	100.0%

Notes: Pearson chi-square = 51.984; df = 2; Sig < 0.000.

b *Using revenues to reduce the GST*

		BWS		
		−1	0	1	Total
Which political party do you identify the most with:	Labour	9.6%	49.7%	40.7%	100.0%
	Liberal	9.6%	45.5%	44.9%	100.0%
	Green	12.8%	64.2%	22.9%	100.0%
	National	2.5%	52.5%	45.0%	100.0%
	Democrats	10.4%	62.5%	27.1%	100.0%
	None	7.6%	37.5%	54.9%	100.0%
Total		9.3%	47.2%	43.5%	100.0%

Notes: Pearson chi-square = 105.436; df = 10; Sig < 0.000.

most (+1). Conversely, the less faith is expressed, the more likely it is chosen as least (−1). Table 10.12c shows that professionals were most likely to choose the level as most (1), while production and transport workers were least likely to choose it as most (1). Laborers and related workers were most likely to choose the level as least (−1). Finally, Table 12d shows that Greens were most likely to choose this level as most (+1), whereas Nationals were more likely to choose it as least (−1).

The final set of tables pertains to exempting energy-intensive industries. Table 10.13a tabulates where respondents live in connection with this question. Respondents in Brisbane and Perth were most likely to choose this level as most (+1), while respondents in the Australian Capital Territory (ACT) and Tasmania were least likely to choose it as most (+1). Conversely, respondents in South Australia other than in Adelaide and respondents in the Northern Territory were most likely to choose the −1 level, while Brisbane respondents were least likely to choose the −1 level. Table 10.13b shows that respondents affiliated with Greens and Democrats were least likely to choose this level as most (1). Nationals were

Table 10.12 *Cross-tab investing 20 percent of the revenues in R&D*

a *Investing 20 percent of revenues in R&D*

		BWS			
		−1	0	+1	Total
If nothing is done to reduce global warming in the future, how serious a problem do you think it will be for Australia?	Extremely serious	7.5%	64.2%	28.3%	100.0%
	Very serious	10.4%	64.8%	24.8%	100.0%
	Somewhat serious	11.6%	73.1%	15.2%	100.0%
	Slightly serious	14.7%	66.5%	18.8%	100.0%
	Not serious at all	18.1%	69.0%	13.0%	100.0%
Total		10.4%	66.6%	23.1%	100.0%

Notes: Pearson chi-square = 74.010; df = 8; Sig < 0.000.

b *Investing 20 percent of revenues in R&D*

		BWS			
		−1	0	+1	Total
How much faith do you have that technological breakthroughs will solve major environmental problems in the future?	A lot	9.7%	55.2%	35.0%	100.0%
	Some	9.8%	69.2%	21.0%	100.0%
	Little	11.7%	69.5%	18.8%	100.0%
	None	14.6%	74.3%	11.1%	100.0%
Total		10.4%	66.6%	23.1%	100.0%

Notes: Pearson chi-square = 77.503; df = 6; Sig < 0.000.

c *Investing 20 percent of revenues in R&D*

		BWS			
		−1	0	+1	Total
Which of the following best describes your current occupation?	Manager or administrator	11.2%	55.4%	33.5%	100.0%
	Small business owner/partner	10.4%	62.1%	27.5%	100.0%
	Professional (e.g. doctor, architect, solicitor, etc.)	7.7%	55.3%	37.0%	100.0%
	Associate professional (e.g. police, nurse, technician)	10.7%	73.2%	16.1%	100.0%
	Tradesperson or related worker	11.0%	71.3%	17.6%	100.0%
	Clerical, sales and service worker	12.3%	66.7%	21.1%	100.0%
	Production and transport worker	6.3%	85.4%	8.3%	100.0%
	Laborer or related worker	15.6%	69.5%	14.8%	100.0%
	Other	9.8%	73.7%	16.5%	100.0%
Total		10.4%	66.6%	23.1%	100.0%

d *Investing 20 percent of revenues in R&D*

		BWS			
		−1	0	1	Total
Which political party do you	Labor	11.3%	67.2%	21.4%	100.0%
identify the most with?	Liberals	8.3%	67.9%	23.7%	100.0%
	Greens	7.3%	49.3%	43.4%	100.0%
	Nationals	32.5%	50.0%	17.5%	100.0%
	Democrats	4.2%	56.3%	39.6%	100.0%
	None	10.8%	71.9%	17.3%	100.0%
Total		10.4%	66.6%	23.1%	100.0%

Notes: Pearson chi-square = 117.501; df = 10; Sig < 0.000.

most likely to choose it as most (1). Democrats and Greens were most likely to choose this level as least (−1), and Nationals were least likely to choose it as least (−1).

One might well ask why one rarely sees tests of unobservable heterogeneity that extend beyond a few covariates. The answer is that (1) there is little to no theory to guide hypothesis testing and model selection, and (2) there typically are many possible effects that could be estimated. For example, if you consider only the tables above, there are several binary attitudinal measures (two categories), political party (six), age (nine), location (13), occupation (nine), two questions about how much faith one has in technological solutions to climate change (four) and how serious global warming might be (five), and household income (eight), to name only the ones illustrated. There are 10 attribute levels that could be chosen as most or least or not chosen as either (three). Thus, if we want to test the covariates mentioned against whether or not each attribute level is chosen as most or least, there are three response outcomes (−1, 0, +1) × 10 attribute levels × (several 2s), × 6 × 9 × 13 × 9 × 4 × 5 × 8, or 242,611,200 possible cells that could be observed if we fully cross all the measures. Typically, one considers only the main effects; hence, there are (two non-referenced outcome categories × 10 levels) × (3 + 5 + 8 + 12 + 8 + 3 + 4 + 7) = 20 × 50 = 1,000. Each covariate main effect has degrees of freedom equal to the number of categories minus one, so the total covariate's main effects are the additive component of the expression. They are estimated for each attribute level and two of the response outcome categories. We, in fact, estimated an unconditional (polychotomous) multinomial logit model for each level. Appendix 10.A contains statistical estimation results for giving the revenues to the poor and senior citizens and using the revenues to reduce the GST. The size and complexity of these tables should make it obvious why we do not report results for the other eight levels or attempt to interpret the results here but, instead, leave it to those who may be interested to peruse.

Table 10.13 *Crosstab exempting energy-intensive industries*

a *Exempting energy-intensive industries*

		BWS			
		−1	0	+1	Total
In which location do you live?	Sydney	19.6%	68.1%	12.3%	100.0%
	Other NSW	15.8%	70.7%	13.5%	100.0%
	Melbourne	24.2%	64.6%	11.2%	100.0%
	Other Victoria	16.9%	70.0%	13.1%	100.0%
	Brisbane	8.6%	71.9%	19.5%	100.0%
	Other Queensland	19.3%	72.4%	8.3%	100.0%
	Adelaide	21.6%	68.5%	9.9%	100.0%
	Other South Australia	33.0%	59.1%	8.0%	100.0%
	Perth	15.8%	68.2%	16.1%	100.0%
	Other WA	25.0%	67.9%	7.1%	100.0%
	ACT	30.1%	67.0%	2.8%	100.0%
	Tasmania	22.1%	70.2%	7.7%	100.0%
	Northern Territory	41.7%	41.7%	16.7%	100.0%
Total		20.1%	68.1%	11.8%	100.0%

Notes: Pearson chi-square = 96.795; df = 24; Sig < 0.000.

b *Exempting energy-intensive industries*

		BWS			
		−1	0	+1	Total
Which political party do you identify the most with?	Labor	19.0%	70.3%	10.7%	100.0%
	Liberals	15.7%	68.3%	16.0%	100.0%
	Greens	38.9%	53.5%	7.6%	100.0%
	Nationals	20.0%	55.0%	25.0%	100.0%
	Democrats	45.8%	52.1%	2.1%	100.0%
	None	16.9%	71.3%	11.8%	100.0%
Total		20.1%	68.1%	11.8%	100.0%

Notes: Pearson chi-square = 116.025; df = 10; Sig < 0.000.

10.5 Discussion and concluding remarks

The purpose of this chapter was to provide a case study comparison of Case 2 and Case 3 best-worst tasks. We focused on a comparison of emissions trading schemes in Australia based on a study of a random sample of voting-age Australians in 2009. We compared a more traditional DCE (Case 3) format whereby survey respondents decided whether or not to vote for a particular ETS described by five 2-level attributes with a Case 2 task in which they chose, respectively, the best and worst attribute levels in each ETS profile (description, treatment combination). We noted that Cases 2 and 3 are complementary in so far as they provide different measures and insights into the values of attribute levels. For example, Case 2 places each of the 10 attribute levels on a common scale, whereas Case 3 measures each attribute level on separate scales for each attribute. In fact, the latter property of Case 3 measures is a key reason that economists developed Hicksian welfare measures such as willingness to pay; it puts these quantities on a common scale (such as dollars), allowing attribute-level comparisons with a common numeraire.

We showed that the Case 3 aggregate sample results actually had large underlying differences in respondents on some attributes/levels, such as start year and distribution of revenues. There also were many people who always voted "No" or "Yes" – a common result in binary discrete choice DCE tasks. We also showed that there were common attribute levels associated with the sample of emissions trading schemes that received more than 50 percent "Yes" votes, such that all had a starting year of 2010, a majority had an investment of 20 percent of revenues raised in R&D activities and a majority did not exempt energy-intensive industries. We compared these results to the Case 2 BWS results, which showed non-continuous, multi-modal distributions of choices on most attributes. We also showed that we could identify statistical differences in the choices made in the Case 2 task that were related to individual covariate differences such as age, gender and income. Thus, the Case 2 results provided more nuanced, complementary insights into the distribution of choices and their relationship with observable individual differences measured by the covariates.

Appendix 10.A MNL estimation of least and most choice for two attribute levels

Table 10.A1 *Listing and description of covariates used in analyses*

Covariates and associated levels used in the MNL estimation		N
	−1	527
BWS	0	1395
	1	1182
Q1. Which of the three ways is the one that you most	Taxes	760
prefer the government to use to reduce greenhouse gas	Permits	744
emissions?	Technical standards	1600
	Internet	896
	Magazines	112
	Meetings	80
Q10. From what source do you get most of your infor-	Newspapers	520
mation about global warming?	Radio	80
	Television	1008
	Other	408

Table 10.A1 (*cont.*)

Covariates and associated levels used in the MNL estimation		N
	Getting people to conserve more energy at home	680
Q11. Which one of these options do you think that the government should most concentrate on to reduce carbon dioxide emissions?	Getting people to take public transport rather than drive	464
	Installing more wind and solar power	1648
	Building nuclear power plants	312
	Sydney	552
	Other NSW	304
	Melbourne	520
	Other Victoria	160
	Brisbane	256
	Other Queensland	192
DX3. In which location do you live?	Adelaide	232
	Other South Australia	88
	Perth	336
	Other WA	56
	ACT	176
	Tasmania	208
	Northern Territory	24
	Single	880
DX5. What is your marital status?	Married/couple	1840
	Separated/divorced/widowed	384
	Own home with mortgage	1264
DX7. Which of the following best describes your current home ownership status?	Own home without mortgage	592
	Rent	960
	Other	288
	Single person	632
	Single adult with children at home	176
	Peer group flatting together	224
	Young couple – no children	384
	Young family – mainly pre-school children	440
DX8. Which of the following best describes your household?	Middle family – mainly school-aged children	368
	Mature family – mainly teenage children or older	488
	Middle aged couple –no children/ no children at home	224
	Older couple –no children/no children at home	168

Table 10.A1 (*cont.*)

Covariates and associated levels used in the MNL estimation		N
	Full-time work – self-employed	312
	Full-time work – employee	1304
	Part-time work (less than 35 hours a week)	584
DX9. Which of the following best describes your work status?	Unemployed – looking for work	144
	Unemployed – not looking for work	48
	Full-time student	144
	Retired	200
	Household duties	368
	Manager or administrator	448
	Small business owner/partner	280
	Professional (e.g. doctor, architect, solicitor, etc.)	416
	Associate professional (e.g. police, nurse, technician)	224
DX10. Which of the following best describes your current occupation?	Tradesperson or related worker (e.g. plumber, carpenter, etc.)	136
	Clerical, sales or service worker	456
	Production or transport worker	96
	Laborer or related worker	128
	Other	920
DX11. Which of the following statements best describes you?	English is my main language	2936
	English is not my main language	168
DX12. Are you the main income earner in your household?	Yes	1384
	No	1040
	Joint/equal	680
	Labor	1288
	Liberal	624
DX19. Which political party do you identify the most with?	Green	288
	National	40
	Democrats	48
	None	816

Table 10.A2 *Summary MNL model estimation results for levels 3 and 4 (poor and seniors + GST)*

Effect	Give revenues to poor and seniors				Use revenues to reduce the GST			
	−2 LL	Chi-sq.	df	Sig	−2 LL	Chi-sq.	df	Sig
Intercept	3041.305	0.000	0	–	2686.809	0.000	0	–
Q3_1	3041.786	0.481	2	0.786	2693.743	6.934	2	0.031
Q3_2	3042.740	1.434	2	0.488	2690.885	4.076	2	0.130
Q3_3	3046.034	4.728	2	0.094	2688.554	1.745	2	0.418
Q3_4	3043.866	2.560	2	0.278	2687.126	0.317	2	0.853
Q3_5	3047.914	6.609	2	0.037	2704.385	17.576	2	0.000
Q4	3050.231	8.926	2	0.012	2696.575	9.766	2	0.008
Q5	3070.832	29.527	2	0.000	2699.773	12.964	2	0.002
Q6	3055.514	14.208	2	0.001	2703.989	17.180	2	0.000
Q7	3050.475	9.170	2	0.010	2713.450	26.641	2	0.000
Q8	3054.643	13.338	2	0.001	2688.617	1.808	2	0.405
Q9	3042.226	0.921	2	0.631	2697.987	11.178	2	0.004
Q12	3041.374	0.069	2	0.966	2697.156	10.347	2	0.006
Q13	3046.818	5.512	2	0.064	2693.651	6.842	2	0.033
Q14	3053.514	12.209	2	0.002	2699.642	12.833	2	0.002
Q15	3075.189	33.883	2	0.000	2697.384	10.575	2	0.005
DX1	3053.640	12.334	2	0.002	2687.049	0.240	2	0.887
DX2	3057.049	15.744	2	0.000	2707.686	20.877	2	0.000
DX6	3048.702	7.397	2	0.025	2689.338	2.529	2	0.282
DX14	3107.223	65.917	2	0.000	2695.395	8.586	2	0.014
DX15	3055.979	14.673	2	0.001	2694.105	7.296	2	0.026
DX16	3058.219	16.913	2	0.000	2687.931	1.122	2	0.571
DX17	3044.340	3.035	2	0.219	2697.667	10.858	2	0.004
DX18	3044.391	3.086	2	0.214	2690.823	4.014	2	0.134
Q1	3074.336	33.030	4	0.000	2697.039	10.230	4	0.037
Q10	3069.640	28.335	12	0.005	2720.417	33.608	12	0.001
Q11	3066.051	24.745	6	0.000	2700.644	13.835	6	0.032
DX3	3179.257	137.951	24	0.000	2755.015	68.206	24	0.000
DX5	3048.528	7.222	4	0.125	2696.316	9.507	4	0.050
DX7	3080.969	39.664	6	0.000	2710.881	24.072	6	0.001
DX8	3117.930	76.625	16	0.000	2756.130	69.321	16	0.000
DX9	3163.770	122.464	14	0.000	2716.691	29.882	14	0.008
DX10	3221.552	180.246	16	0.000	2749.562	62.753	16	0.000
DX11	3042.038	0.732	2	0.693	2697.571	10.762	2	0.005
DX12	3056.647	15.341	4	0.004	2689.497	2.688	4	0.611
DX19	3097.129	55.824	10	0.000	2734.930	48.121	10	0.000

Table 10.A3 *MNL model parameter estimation results for two levels (poor and seniors + GST)*

BWS outcome		BWS outcome = least (−1)				BWS outcome = most (+1)			
		Est.	S.E.	Wald	Sig	Est.	S.E.	Wald	Sig
−1	Intercept	−0.974	1.414	0.475	0.491	−0.237	1.874	0.016	0.899
	Q3_1	0.159	0.236	0.454	0.500	0.553	0.290	3.625	0.057
	Q3_2	−0.240	0.240	0.996	0.318	−0.370	0.291	1.613	0.204
	Q3_3	0.190	0.145	1.711	0.191	0.212	0.175	1.455	0.228
	Q3_4	0.089	0.189	0.224	0.636	−0.092	0.235	0.154	0.694
	Q3_5	0.131	0.213	0.379	0.538	0.301	0.257	1.377	0.241
	Q4	−0.673	0.230	8.586	0.003	0.232	0.271	0.733	0.392
	Q5	−0.017	0.075	0.050	0.823	−0.106	0.094	1.285	0.257
	Q6	−0.199	0.183	1.184	0.277	−0.825	0.216	14.531	0.000
	Q7	0.134	0.121	1.222	0.269	−0.178	0.143	1.551	0.213
	Q8	0.571	0.157	13.309	0.000	−0.044	0.197	0.051	0.822
	Q9	−0.052	0.082	0.399	0.528	0.095	0.096	0.975	0.324
	Q12	0.014	0.159	0.007	0.931	0.069	0.200	0.119	0.730
	Q13	0.221	0.094	5.483	0.019	−0.194	0.119	2.648	0.104
	Q14	0.509	0.153	11.091	0.001	−0.248	0.175	1.998	0.157
	Q15	−1.080	0.224	23.297	0.000	−0.228	0.241	0.900	0.343
	DX1	0.160	0.160	1.002	0.317	0.047	0.181	0.068	0.794
	DX2	−0.151	0.046	10.919	0.001	−0.014	0.055	0.063	0.802
	DX6	0.003	0.005	0.388	0.533	−0.010	0.007	2.111	0.146
	DX14	0.200	0.043	21.758	0.000	0.146	0.052	7.813	0.005
	DX15	−0.322	0.104	9.621	0.002	−0.320	0.124	6.626	0.010
	DX16	−0.058	0.043	1.861	0.172	0.052	0.049	1.118	0.290
	DX17	0.020	0.025	0.640	0.424	0.087	0.032	7.569	0.006
	DX18	0.037	0.033	1.230	0.267	−0.082	0.041	3.919	0.048
	[Q1 = 1]	0.113	0.169	0.445	0.505	−0.066	0.193	0.115	0.734
	[Q1 = 2]	0.115	0.175	0.434	0.510	0.443	0.201	4.869	0.027
	[Q1 = 3]	0	−	−	−	0	−	−	−
	[Q10 = 1]	0.488	0.210	5.380	0.020	−0.929	0.256	13.164	0.000
	[Q10 = 2]	0.503	0.400	1.587	0.208	−0.188	0.431	0.191	0.662
	[Q10 = 3]	−0.205	0.453	0.205	0.651	0.561	0.466	1.449	0.229
	[Q10 = 4]	0.763	0.244	9.793	0.002	−0.636	0.283	5.052	0.025
	[Q10 = 5]	−0.021	0.548	0.002	0.969	−0.592	0.547	1.172	0.279
	[Q10 = 6]	−0.111	0.221	0.254	0.615	−0.839	0.265	9.977	0.002
	[Q10 = 7]	0	−	−	−	0	−	−	−
	[Q11 = 1]	−0.463	0.268	2.996	0.083	0.758	0.333	5.193	0.023
	[Q11 = 2]	−0.771	0.301	6.577	0.010	0.181	0.370	0.239	0.625
	[Q11 = 3]	−0.390	0.251	2.410	0.121	0.332	0.309	1.154	0.283
	[Q11 = 4]	0	−	−	−	0	−	−	−
	[DX3 = 1]	−0.835	0.668	1.562	0.211	0.398	1.157	0.118	0.731
	[DX3 = 2]	0.495	0.673	0.540	0.462	0.159	1.166	0.018	0.892

Table 10.A3 (*cont.*)

BWS outcome	BWS outcome = least (−1)				BWS outcome = most (+1)			
	Est.	S.E.	Wald	Sig	Est.	S.E.	Wald	Sig
[DX3 = 3]	−1.246	0.675	3.410	0.065	−0.292	1.162	0.063	0.801
[DX3 = 4]	−1.120	0.753	2.210	0.137	0.199	1.189	0.028	0.867
[DX3 = 5]	−0.510	0.675	0.571	0.450	−0.059	1.175	0.002	0.960
[DX3 = 6]	0.163	0.678	0.057	0.811	0.419	1.173	0.127	0.721
[DX3 = 7]	−0.417	0.691	0.363	0.547	0.124	1.183	0.011	0.916
[DX3 = 8]	−0.540	0.749	0.520	0.471	0.340	1.268	0.072	0.788
[DX3 = 9]	−0.867	0.677	1.641	0.200	−0.007	1.171	0.000	0.996
[DX3 = 10]	−3.020	1.272	5.634	0.018	0.890	1.272	0.489	0.484
[DX3 = 11]	−0.907	0.701	1.674	0.196	0.523	1.179	0.197	0.658
[DX3 = 12]	−0.946	0.686	1.901	0.168	0.336	1.183	0.081	0.776
[DX3 = 13]	0	–	–	–	0	–	–	–
[DX5 = 1]	0.696	0.299	5.409	0.020	−0.010	0.322	0.001	0.976
[DX5 = 2]	0.268	0.366	0.538	0.463	−0.530	0.388	1.864	0.172
[DX5 = 3]	0	–	–	–	0	–	–	–
[DX7 = 1]	0.707	0.325	4.726	0.030	0.508	0.400	1.614	0.204
[DX7 = 2]	0.926	0.353	6.871	0.009	1.239	0.415	8.920	0.003
[DX7 = 3]	0.307	0.324	0.897	0.344	0.619	0.402	2.378	0.123
[DX7 = 4]	0	–	–	–	0	–	–	–
[DX8 = 1]	0.198	0.476	0.173	0.677	−0.338	0.482	0.493	0.483
[DX8 = 2]	−0.201	0.524	0.148	0.701	0.546	0.541	1.021	0.312
[DX8 = 3]	−0.826	0.521	2.512	0.113	−0.064	0.557	0.013	0.909
[DX8 = 4]	−0.091	0.443	0.042	0.838	−0.380	0.480	0.6026	0.429
[DX8 = 5]	−0.262	0.440	0.355	0.551	0.125	0.478	0.069	0.793
[DX8 = 6]	−0.644	0.437	2.170	0.141	0.599	0.452	1.753	0.185
[DX8 = 7]	−0.410	0.434	0.894	0.344	0.023	0.460	0.003	0.960
[DX8 = 8]	−1.084	0.480	5.099	0.024	−0.426	0.445	0.917	0.338
[DX8 = 9]	0	–	–	–	0	–	–	–
[DX9 = 1]	1.428	0.404	12.514	0.000	−0.007	0.468	0.000	0.987
[DX9 = 2]	1.894	0.347	29.795	0.000	0.508	0.410	1.534	0.215
[DX9 = 3]	1.214	0.317	14.648	0.000	0.814	0.348	5.472	0.019
[DX9 = 4]	−0.470	0.456	1.061	0.303	0.026	0.535	0.002	0.962
[DX9 = 5]	1.177	0.797	2.178	0.140	0.439	0.624	0.494	0.482
[DX9 = 6]	0.136	0.398	0.118	0.732	0.090	0.540	0.028	0.868
[DX9 = 7]	1.057	0.472	5.010	0.025	0.285	0.460	0.383	0.536
[DX9 = 8]	0	–	–	–	0	–	–	–
[DX10 = 1]	−1.712	0.274	39.107	0.000	−0.769	0.309	6.193	0.013
[DX10 = 2]	−1.147	0.346	10.962	0.001	−0.496	0.365	1.842	0.175
[DX10 = 3]	−1.062	0.259	16.872	0.000	−0.880	0.310	8.073	0.004
[DX10 = 4]	−1.251	0.333	14.090	0.000	−1.426	0.419	11.591	0.001
[DX10 = 5]	−1.169	0.396	8.699	0.003	−0.394	0.464	0.721	0.396
[DX10 = 6]	−0.940	0.241	15.176	0.000	0.070	0.269	0.067	0.795

Table 10.A3 (*cont.*)

BWS outcome		BWS outcome = least (−1)				BWS outcome = most (+1)			
		Est.	S.E.	Wald	Sig	Est.	S.E.	Wald	Sig
	[DX10 = 7]	0.605	0.406	2.222	0.136	0.715	0.451	2.508	0.113
	[DX10 = 8]	−2.341	0.491	22.732	0.000	−1.163	0.508	5.253	0.022
	[DX10 = 9]	0	−	−	−	0	−	−	−
	[DX11 = 1]	−0.235	0.280	0.707	0.400	−0.197	0.346	0.323	0.570
	[DX11 = 2]	0	−	−	−	0	−	−	−
	[DX12 = 1]	0.206	0.200	1.060	0.303	−0.374	0.241	2.424	0.119
	[DX12 = 2]	0.487	0.229	4.533	0.033	−0.241	0.261	0.853	0.356
	[DX12 = 3]	0	−	−	−	0	−	−	−
	[DX19 = 0]	−0.705	0.173	16.519	0.000	−0.104	0.213	0.241	0.624
	[DX19 = 1]	−0.141	0.195	0.522	0.470	0.069	0.251	0.075	0.784
	[DX19 = 2]	−0.895	0.265	11.401	0.001	−0.273	0.316	0.746	0.388
	[DX19 = 3]	0.607	0.773	0.616	0.432	−1.924	1.105	3.031	0.082
	[DX19 = 4]	−1.836	0.637	8.308	0.004	−0.167	0.671	0.062	0.803
	[DX19 = 5]	0	−	−	−	0	−	−	−
1	Intercept	−2.073	1.124	3.401	0.065	−0.362	1.068	0.115	0.735
	Q3_1	0.055	0.165	0.110	0.740	−0.187	0.156	1.448	0.229
	Q3_2	−0.163	0.176	0.859	0.354	0.198	0.169	1.374	0.241
	Q3_3	0.221	0.108	4.155	0.042	0.085	0.101	0.707	0.400
	Q3_4	−0.184	0.141	1.707	0.191	−0.064	0.130	0.246	0.620
	Q3_5	0.428	0.167	6.548	0.010	0.649	0.156	17.355	0.000
	Q4	−0.179	0.162	1.212	0.271	−0.400	0.150	7.103	0.008
	Q5	0.291	0.057	25.956	0.000	0.153	0.051	8.854	0.003
	Q6	0.424	0.135	9.824	0.002	0.071	0.126	0.322	0.570
	Q7	−0.214	0.090	5.653	0.017	−0.437	0.086	25.998	0.000
	Q8	0.124	0.118	1.094	0.296	0.132	0.108	1.483	0.223
	Q9	0.030	0.060	0.251	0.617	0.185	0.055	11.094	0.001
	Q12	−0.025	0.119	0.044	0.834	0.346	0.109	10.032	0.002
	Q13	0.035	0.072	0.238	0.626	0.107	0.068	2.470	0.116
	Q14	0.006	0.110	0.003	0.954	0.283	0.102	7.744	0.005
	Q15	0.298	0.171	3.026	0.082	0.456	0.165	7.637	0.006
	DX1	0.402	0.115	12.263	0.000	0.051	0.109	0.218	0.640
	DX2	−0.105	0.035	9.298	0.002	−0.146	0.033	19.794	0.000
	DX6	0.008	0.003	7.234	0.007	−0.001	0.003	0.105	0.746
	DX14	−0.167	0.034	23.799	0.000	−0.002	0.031	0.006	0.937
	DX15	0.086	0.075	1.318	0.251	−0.098	0.071	1.927	0.165
	DX16	0.107	0.032	11.350	0.001	0.011	0.029	0.145	0.703
	DX17	−0.023	0.019	1.487	0.223	−0.017	0.017	0.979	0.323
	DX18	−0.025	0.025	0.991	0.319	−0.008	0.023	0.124	0.725
	[Q1 = 1]	0.391	0.126	9.583	0.002	0.070	0.118	0.348	0.555
	[Q1 = 2]	0.706	0.129	29.854	0.000	0.296	0.119	6.209	0.013
	[Q1 = 3]	0	−	−	−	0	−	−	−

Table 10.A3 (*cont.*)

BWS outcome	BWS outcome = least (−1)				BWS outcome = most (+1)			
	Est.	S.E.	Wald	Sig	Est.	S.E.	Wald	Sig
[Q10 = 1]	0.110	0.170	0.420	0.517	−0.337	0.155	4.721	0.030
[Q10 = 2]	0.226	0.297	0.578	0.447	−0.721	0.303	5.657	0.017
[Q10 = 3]	−0.180	0.344	0.274	0.601	−0.530	0.329	2.588	0.108
[Q10 = 4]	0.287	0.191	2.267	0.132	−0.416	0.177	5.510	0.019
[Q10 = 5]	0.241	0.321	0.562	0.454	0.318	0.323	0.973	0.324
[Q10 = 6]	0.147	0.170	0.752	0.386	−0.304	0.158	3.717	0.054
[Q10 = 7]	0	–	–	–	0	–	–	–
[Q11 = 1]	−0.316	0.208	2.316	0.128	0.334	0.185	3.256	0.071
[Q11 = 2]	−0.787	0.224	12.325	0.000	0.455	0.201	5.100	0.024
[Q11 = 3]	−0.102	0.191	0.287	0.592	0.372	0.168	4.914	0.027
[Q11 = 4]	0	–	–	–	0	–	–	–
[DX3 = 1]	−0.296	0.556	0.284	0.594	−1.023	0.546	3.514	0.061
[DX3 = 2]	−0.308	0.566	0.296	0.586	−1.629	0.556	8.594	0.003
[DX3 = 3]	−0.300	0.554	0.294	0.587	−1.308	0.544	5.784	0.016
[DX3 = 4]	0.341	0.580	0.347	0.556	−1.133	0.570	3.951	0.047
[DX3 = 5]	−0.543	0.567	0.917	0.338	−0.908	0.552	2.711	0.100
[DX3 = 6]	−0.356	0.571	0.389	0.533	−0.499	0.561	0.790	0.374
[DX3 = 7]	−0.033	0.568	0.003	0.954	−0.795	0.559	2.025	0.155
[DX3 = 8]	−0.721	0.627	1.325	0.250	−0.863	0.597	2.089	0.148
[DX3 = 9]	−0.105	0.559	0.035	0.851	−1.014	0.549	3.404	0.065
[DX3 = 10]	1.495	0.681	4.823	0.028	−1.053	0.651	2.614	0.106
[DX3 = 11]	−0.832	0.583	2.033	0.154	−1.438	0.569	6.383	0.012
[DX3 = 12]	−0.244	0.564	0.186	0.666	−0.318	0.554	0.329	0.566
[DX3 = 13]	0	–	–	–	0	–	–	–
[DX5 = 1]	−0.020	0.208	0.009	0.923	−0.432	0.192	5.070	0.024
[DX5 = 2]	−0.089	0.246	0.133	0.716	−0.136	0.228	0.357	0.550
[DX5 = 3]	0	–	–	–	0	–	–	–
[DX7 = 1]	0.515	0.242	4.519	0.034	0.654	0.223	8.572	0.003
[DX7 = 2]	0.971	0.259	14.089	0.000	0.637	0.240	7.041	0.008
[DX7 = 3]	0.889	0.240	13.693	0.000	0.501	0.220	5.179	0.023
[DX7 = 4]	0	–	–	–	0	–	–	–
[DX8 = 1]	−0.231	0.311	0.551	0.458	0.276	0.299	0.852	0.356
[DX8 = 2]	0.785	0.360	4.754	0.029	0.519	0.342	2.306	0.129
[DX8 = 3]	−0.073	0.369	0.040	0.842	−0.049	0.349	0.020	0.888
[DX8 = 4]	−0.310	0.313	0.978	0.323	−0.431	0.297	2.102	0.147
[DX8 = 5]	0.248	0.297	0.698	0.403	0.096	0.286	0.113	0.737
[DX8 = 6]	0.298	0.293	1.039	0.308	0.139	0.284	0.240	0.624
[DX8 = 7]	0.633	0.280	5.119	0.024	0.870	0.271	10.345	0.001
[DX8 = 8]	0.104	0.273	0.144	0.705	−0.129	0.273	0.222	0.637
[DX8 = 9]	0	–	–	–	0	–	–	–
[DX9 = 1]	−0.004	0.282	0.000	0.988	0.203	0.264	0.593	0.441

When the ayes don't have it

Table 10.A3 (*cont.*)

BWS outcome	BWS outcome = least (−1)				BWS outcome = most (+1)			
	Est.	S.E.	Wald	Sig	Est.	S.E.	Wald	Sig
[DX9 = 2]	0.076	0.247	0.094	0.759	−0.037	0.231	0.026	0.872
[DX9 = 3]	0.394	0.212	3.438	0.064	−0.001	0.204	0.000	0.998
[DX9 = 4]	0.659	0.250	6.941	0.008	0.102	0.250	0.166	0.683
[DX9 = 5]	1.241	0.422	8.632	0.003	0.398	0.400	0.990	0.320
[DX9 = 6]	0.002	0.304	0.000	0.994	0.414	0.284	2.121	0.145
[DX9 = 7]	1.776	0.287	38.298	0.000	0.788	0.271	8.435	0.004
[DX9 = 8]	0	–	–	–	0	–	–	–
[DX10 = 1]	−0.705	0.205	11.812	0.001	−0.104	0.191	0.297	0.586
[DX10 = 2]	0.236	0.240	0.968	0.325	−0.389	0.229	2.891	0.089
[DX10 = 3]	−1.160	0.213	29.587	0.000	−0.247	0.189	1.705	0.192
[DX10 = 4]	0.525	0.230	5.221	0.022	−0.074	0.218	0.116	0.733
[DX10 = 5]	0.409	0.267	2.346	0.126	0.145	0.249	0.341	0.559
[DX10 = 6]	−0.038	0.188	0.042	0.838	0.184	0.177	1.088	0.297
[DX10 = 7]	−0.039	0.330	0.014	0.906	−0.408	0.317	1.664	0.197
[DX10 = 8]	−1.345	0.297	20.436	0.000	−0.882	0.271	10.558	0.001
[DX10 = 9]	0	–	–	–	0	–	–	–
[DX11 = 1]	−0.100	0.235	0.180	0.672	−0.703	0.217	10.528	0.001
[DX11 = 2]	0	–	–	–	0	–	–	–
[DX12 = 1]	−0.093	0.149	0.394	0.530	−0.023	0.138	0.028	0.867
[DX12 = 2]	−0.414	0.164	6.390	0.011	0.041	0.153	0.070	0.791
[DX12 = 3]	0	–	–	–	0	–	–	–
[DX19 = 0]	−0.338	0.122	7.611	0.006	−0.520	0.114	20.703	0.000
[DX19 = 1]	−0.341	0.151	5.134	0.023	−0.253	0.138	3.371	0.066
[DX19 = 2]	−0.800	0.212	14.226	0.000	−1.066	0.199	28.635	0.000
[DX19 = 3]	−1.182	0.473	6.247	0.012	−0.542	0.414	1.716	0.190
[DX19 = 4]	0.592	0.430	1.895	0.169	−1.160	0.409	8.056	0.005
[DX19 = 5]	0	–	–	–	0	–	–	–

Chapter 11

BWS profile case application: preferences for treatment in dentistry

Emma McIntosh and Terry N. Flynn

11.1 Introduction

This chapter uses Case 2 (the profile case) best-worst scaling to elicit utilities associated with attributes and levels that might result from the extraction of third molar teeth or conservative management. First reported by McIntosh (2003) in her PhD, it was the first Case 2 study conducted in health in Europe and only the second globally (after that of Szeinbach *et al.*, 1999). We use it in this chapter as an empirical illustration of the simpler methods of analysis introduced in Chapter 3; accordingly, we focus on the summary (sample-level) statistics, including the weighted least squares of the natural logs of the choice frequencies. Chapter 12 develops the approach further in the context of the ICECAP-O instrument (Coast, Peters *et al.*, 2008a).The empirical study reported in this chapter was part of a larger study to assess the cost-effectiveness of alternative implementation strategies for third molar clinical guidelines.[1] For the purposes of this chapter only, the methodological components of the benefit assessment of the economic evaluation are reported as per the original research (McIntosh, 2003; McIntosh and Louviere, 2002); for a more detailed guide on the use of discrete choice methods in health care economic evaluation, see McIntosh *et al.* (2010). The aim of the methodological work was to use Case 2 BWS to identify attributes and levels of third molar management (extraction and conservative management) so that preferences could be elicited and attributes of importance identified and valued.

11.2 Methods

The study was conducted as part of the first author's PhD in 2003. A number of methodological issues and analyses were reported when the data were presented at the Health Economists' Study Group conference (McIntosh and Louviere, 2002). Some of the proposed data analyses, such as those involving the decomposition of attribute weight and scale, have developed since those early days (see Marley, Flynn and Louviere, 2008).

[1] Funding was obtained from the R&D division of the UK National Health Service in May 2000, the title of the project being "Effective practice? A randomised trial of dissemination and implementation strategies for guidelines for the appropriate extraction of third molar teeth" (NHS R&D reference number: R2/64). We thank Jordan J. Louviere for his role in the design of the study.

However, the study remains innovative for multiple reasons, including its comparison with conventional discrete choice experiment estimates. These were relatively simple comparisons, reflecting the state of the art at the time; however, such comparisons remain a key issue on the research frontier, and the understanding gained in this chapter is valuable for the reader in comprehending more recent technical papers.

11.2.1 Study sample

Following the revision of the survey instrument based on the pilot results, the questionnaire was finalized and sent to 400 members of the general public in Scotland (identified through the electoral register); we received 54 completed questionnaires.

11.2.2 Study design

The following outlines the main stages in the third molar BWS study.

Stage 1: establishing the attributes

The attributes were identified from the most recent literature on the management of third molars. The attributes and levels are concerned with both the extraction of third molar teeth and conservative management. This literature includes a report of a working party convened by the Faculty of Dental Surgery (Royal College of Surgeons of England, 1997). Brickley *et al.* (1995) also provided information on the probabilities of complications when the conservative approach to third molar management is taken.

Stage 2: assigning levels to the attributes

Levels for the attributes were presented as a range of probabilities associated with attributes of third molar care. These levels were also discussed in the literature discussed in stage 1.

Stage 3: devising a statistically efficient design

Following stages 1 and 2 above, hypothetical profiles were constructed that represent different combinations of levels of attributes. The number of possible profiles was reduced to a manageable level using an orthogonal main effects plan, thus ensuring no multicollinearity.

Stage 4: presenting profiles and eliciting preferences using the best-worst format

Once the design criteria from stage 3 had been fulfilled, the profiles were embedded in a survey with an introduction and example of how to answer the task questions. A Case 2 BWS task presents each profile from the orthogonal matrix one at a time to the experimental participants, who are asked to identify the *best* (most attractive, salient, desirable, etc.) and the *worst* (least attractive, least desirable, etc.) attribute level in each profile; here, they were also asked to state whether they would "accept" the profile. The BWS questionnaire therefore required two extra decisions to be made about each task compared to a standard discrete choice approach, which asks only for first choice (that is, best) or, as here, whether the profile is acceptable.

11.2.3 Analysis: stacking of (pooling) choice frequencies to facilitate regression

Theoretically, if each subject uses a fixed ranking of the attribute levels and always chooses consistently in accordance with that ranking, then the "most" and "least" choices will graph as mirror images. Experience has shown that, if this relationship between most and least choices holds to a reasonable first approximation, one can combine both sets of choices to obtain a set of utility estimates (see sections 2.5.1 and 2.5.2).

Each attribute is broken down into its individual levels by creating dummy variables for each level (minus one). Once the most and least frequencies are graphed to show that they satisfy the assumption about mirror relations to a reasonable first approximation, the best and worst data are stacked for estimation purposes. Combined (stacked) data lead to an improved set of utility estimates. The choices are combined by stacking the choice frequencies and coding the design matrix such that the attribute dummy variables representing the levels have opposite algebraic signs (1, −1) for most and least choices, respectively. The most and least attractive choices for each attribute level are then summed over all respondents to produce aggregate best and worst choice counts, respectively.

This approach assumes that each attribute level occurs an equal number of times in the design – that is, each level of each attribute is "available" to be chosen an equal number of times. When this is not the case, availability bias occurs. To compensate for this availability bias the choices must be reweighted to account for the fact that some levels are available more (less) often than others, and hence may be chosen more (less) often simply because they are available more (less) often. Finally, any non-responses are eliminated from the analysis.

The dependent variable is the natural log of the count data. The best and worst choice counts are the number of times each level is identified as best and worst, respectively. Essentially, in stacked format, one set of data represents the (aggregate) best choice counts, with the (aggregate) worst choice counts stacked below as a second set of data. The two data sets are combined for analysis purposes, and the opposite signs of the dummy variables essentially act to transform the worst choice counts into best counts. Therefore, the variables required for the regression analysis are as follows:

- *count*: the number of times each level is available to be chosen multiplied by the entire sample size;
- *bwct*: best/worst frequency – that is, the number of times each level of each attribute is identified as best (respectively, worst) for the entire sample divided by *count*; and
- *Lnbwct*: the natural log (Ln) of *bwct*.

The independent variables comprise the individual levels of all the attributes dummy-coded as 1 for "level chosen best" and −1 for "level chosen worst" (one level is omitted to set the reference point and avoid linear dependence). Because the dependent variable *bwct* has in effect rescaled all the attribute *levels* as a function of their best or worst count divided by *count*, this process places them on the same underlying scale (that is, frequency/availability). Hence, if one analyzes the best and worst choice frequencies using a suitable regression method, the resulting regression coefficients reflect estimates of the latent (subjective) quantities associated with each level on a common scale.

Denote as f_{ml} the number of times the lth level of attribute m (X_{ml}) is chosen as the best (or most attractive) feature across all N profiles presented. Then the following must hold for each individual:

$$f_{11} + f_{12} + \ldots + f_{m1} + f_{m2} + \ldots + f_{M1} + f_{M2} + \ldots = N. \qquad (11.1)$$

Equation (11.1) shows that the number of best choices summed over all levels of all attributes equals the number of profiles (that is, if there are eight profiles then we must also have eight best observations). Based on this, the probability P_{ml} that an individual chooses level l of attribute m (X_{ml}) as best is given by the following:

$$P_{ml} = f_{ml}/N. \qquad (11.2)$$

These probabilities provide the theoretical basis for estimating the scale position (part-worth) of each level of each attribute using the regression techniques mentioned above. To estimate the *impact* of an attribute – that is, the probability P_m that a particular attribute m (as opposed to the *level* of that attribute) is best – one sums the quantities in (11.2) across all levels of that attribute:

$$P_m = \sum_{l=1}^{qm} f_{ml}/N = \sum_{l=1}^{qm} P_{ml}. \qquad (11.3)$$

If we assume that more heavily weighted attributes are chosen more often as best, the marginal probabilities estimate the weight, or overall effect, of the mth attribute (to the extent that the assumption is closely satisfied).

11.2.4 Comparator analysis: standard random effects probit model

Section 11.4.1 presents the results of a simple random effects binary probit model using the accept (not accept) responses only and compares those results with those of the Case 2 BWS analysis; we call this the DCE task.

Attributes and levels

Table 11.1 shows the attributes and levels that were identified from recent literature on the outcomes of third molar extraction and conservative management of third molars.

The Case 2 BWS task was preceded by detailed descriptions of the attributes and levels and an example of a choice set in the BWS format, as shown in Figure 11.1.

Table 11.1 *Attributes and levels for third molar DCE*

Attribute	Levels (variable names for regression model)
Days of **severe pain** when painkillers are taken	0, 1,3 (days)
	(sev0, sev1, sev3)
Bouts of **mild dental pain** lasting up to 2 days	Never
	Once a month
	Once a week
	(mil0, mil12, mil52)
Prolonged **bleeding**	0, 2.5%, 5%
	(ble0, ble2.5, ble5)
Sensory **nerve** damage	0, 5%, 10%
	(ner0, ner5, ner10)
Probability of **crowding**	0%, 15%, 30%
	(cro0, cro15, cro30)
Pericoronitis episodes (painful inflammation of the **gum**)	0,2,5
	(epi0,epi2, epi5)
Cost (£)	£0, £5, £15, £20, £25, £30
	(cos0, cos5, cos15, cos20, cos25,cos30)

	Description	Which aspects are the most (M) and least (L) attractive?
Number of days of severe pain & swelling	1 day	
Episodes of mild pain	Once a week	
Chance of prolonged bleeding	5%	
Chance of nerve damage	0%	
Chance of crowding of teeth	15%	
Number of episodes of painful inflammation of the gums	2 episodes	
Total cost to you (£)	£20	

Would you consider this treatment option?

Yes ☐ No ☐

Figure 11.1 Example of a BWS question from the molar study

11.3 Main survey results

The response rate for the survey was 54/400 (14 percent). Although this response rate was low, the data were analyzable and will, hopefully, serve to illustrate the key methodological differences between the Case 2 BWS and DCE methodologies. The following section outlines the results of the BWS analysis. The results for the ease of completion of the

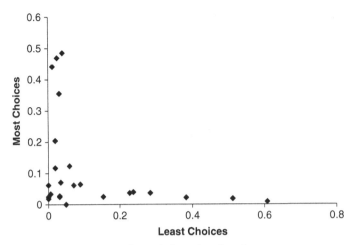

Figure 11.2 Most versus least choices: dental study

BWS questionnaire show that, of the 54 respondents who returned the BWS questionnaire, 78 percent found the questionnaire "moderately to very" easy to complete.

11.3.1 Results of analysis

The observed choice frequencies for most and least choices for each attribute level were obtained and the data stacked for estimation purposes in the manner described earlier. Figure 11.2 shows the extent to which, across attribute levels, the most frequency decreases as the least frequency increases; the inverse relationship is quite poor for the smaller values. This should be kept in mind in interpreting the later results, as the inverse relationship is frequently used as a justification for stacking and recoding the data for estimation purposes.

One feature of this study is that the 6-level attribute (cost) is balanced in the design (that is, each level occurs equally often), but each level only occurs half as often as each level of the 3-level attributes. In other words, each level of cost is available to be chosen only half as often as each level of the other attributes. To compensate for this "availability bias," the choices must be reweighted. This is done either by dividing the choices of all the 3-level attributes by two or by multiplying the choices of the 6-level attribute by two; we did the latter. All non-responses (missing choices for a profile) were eliminated, which were a consistent percentage (approximately 9.5 percent) of the total choices for both most and least choices. Reflecting the small sample size, the utilities associated with each attribute level were obtained using WLS regression (work is ongoing in this area in order to develop techniques for analyzing these data to account for random effects and to incorporate error theories). A more sophisticated and exact method for estimating individual-level parameters is given by Frischknecht *et al.* (2013).

11.3.2 Individual attribute results

The individual level utility estimates were obtained from the WLS estimation (SPSS); they are shown in Figures 11.3 to 11.8 and the corresponding tables. Following on from where *Lnbwct* was defined as the natural log of *bwct* (the number of times each level of each attribute was identified as best (respectively, worst), divided by *count*), the WLS regression estimated the following model (variables names as shown in Table 11.1, α = constant):

$$Lnbwct = \alpha + sev0 + sev1 + sev3 + mil0 + mil12 + mil52 + ble0 + ble2.5 + ble5$$

$$+ ner0 + ner5 + ner10 + cro0 + cro15 + cro30 + epi0 + epi2$$

$$+ epi5 + cost0 + cost5 + cost15 + cost20 + cost25 + cost30$$

The WLS regression used *Lnbwct* as the dependent variable (with *count* as the weighting variable), as discussed by Louviere and Woodworth (1983). The *count* variable was computed by multiplying the total possible number of levels for each attribute arising in the questionnaire by the sample size (54), giving a *count* of 324 (this count was adjusted to account for any missing variables).

11.3.3 BWS utility values

The majority of the individual utility values from the BWS experiment are significant predictors of choice. Figures 11.3 to 11.8 show that the relationship between most attribute levels and their associated utilities were approximately linear. Utility values for each attribute level are provided for each attribute and are directly compared on the common utility scale shown in Figure 11.9; we discuss these results in more detail later. The first observation is that the utility values have face validity, in that no pain and swelling, no

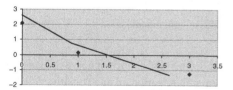

Attribute Level	Utility value	Sig.	WTP
0 Days	2.104	0.000	
1 Day	0.163	0.633	
3 Days	−1.247	0.000	£15.96

Figure 11.3 BWS utility value results: severe pain and swelling (0 days, 1 day, 3 days)

Attribute Level	Utility value	Sig.	WTP
0 Episodes	0.909	0.001	
Monthly	0.068	0.874	
Weekly	−0.368	0.613	£6.08

Figure 11.4 BWS utility value results: episodes of mild pain (never, weekly, monthly)

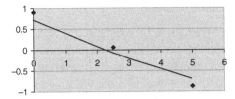

Attribute Level	Utility value	Sig.	WTP
0 %	0.908	0.028	
2.5%	0.051	0.998	
5%	−0.864	0.629	£8.44

Figure 11.5 BWS utility value results: chance of bleeding (%)

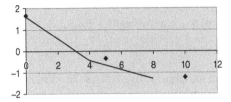

Attribute Level	Utility value	Sig.	WTP
0 %	1.646	0.000	
15%	−0.367	0.206	
30%	−1.218	0.000	£13.64

Figure 11.6 BWS utility value results: chance of nerve damage (%)

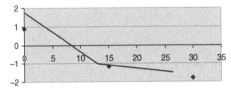

Attribute Level	Utility value	Sig.	WTP
0 %	0.891	0.001	
15%	−1.186	0.002	
30%	−1.8	0.000	£12.81

Figure 11.7 BWS utility value results: chance of crowding (%)

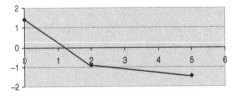

Attribute Level	Utility value	Sig.	WTP
0	1.427	0.000	
2	0.908	0.142	
5	−1.465	0.000	£13.77

Figure 11.8 BWS utility value results: number of episodes of gum inflammation

episodes of mild pain, a 0 percent chance of bleeding, a 0 percent chance of nerve damage, a 0 percent chance of crowding and no episodes of gum inflammation all have positive utility values as compared to the worst levels of each attribute.

Utility values for progressively worse levels give rise to progressively more negative utility values, implying that the worse a level becomes, the less likely respondents are to choose it as best.

Estimating utility values for every level of every attribute as a function of the total underlying count (that is, the same denominator) places individual levels on the same scale, as shown in Figure 11.9. In addition, we know from theory that, under reasonable assumptions, the Case 2 BWs utility values are on a common difference scale (Chapter 5). This is not the case for data from a Case 3 BWS or a traditional best-only (choice among profiles)

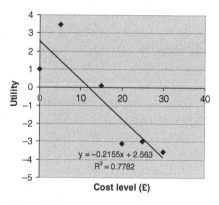

Cost Level Utility values		
Attribute *Level*	**Utility** *Value*	**Sig.**
£0	1.018	0.000
£5	3.454	0.445
£15	0.107	0.000
£20	−3.118	0.061
£25	−2.982	0.073
£30	−3.572	0.034

[Utility = 2.563 − 0.2155x]

Figure 11.9 BWS cost results

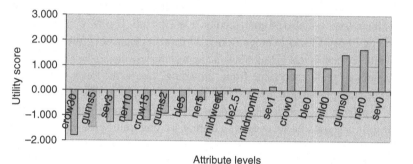

Figure 11.10 BWS common utility scale

DCE. The key advantage of a common utility scale is the ability to place each of the attribute levels in a single preference ordering distinct from an aggregate "attribute preference bundle." The common scale shows a pattern of utility weights that seems to adhere to consistent choice behavior, namely the most preferred attribute level is "No days pain and swelling" and the least preferred attribute level is "30% chance of crowding." This common utility scale ranges from −1.8 to 2.1 – approximately four utility units. This scale could be recalibrated to produce information for a dental health utility scale, but we do not discuss how to do this here.

11.4 Estimating willingness to pay using the BWS data

When cost is included as an attribute in a BWS study it possible to calculate willingness to pay (WTP). Specifically, the first stage is to plot a graph of the cost results, as shown in Figure 11.9.

As can be seen, the cost levels are linear to a close first approximation; hence, one can simply regress the attribute-level utility estimates against the actual price levels (£, 2002 UK sterling) to obtain the appropriate unit of measurement to calculate compensating variation. Specifically, using the utility function estimated in Figure 11.9 ($Y = -0.2155x + 2.56$), differences in any attribute-level utility values can be easily calculated both within and between attributes (as, for Case 2 BWS, all attributes and attribute-level utilities are on a common scale). The implied WTP differences for the lowest- and highest-valued level of each attribute are shown in the small tables adjoining Figures 11.3 to 11.8. We obtained these results by first subtracting the lowest utility from the highest utility for each attribute, and then calculating the willingness to pay by dividing the utility difference (from least to most) by the cost coefficient from the regression. The WTP values for shifts from the least attractive level to the most attractive level are provided alongside each attribute (Figure 11.3 to 11.8). For example, a reduction in the number of days suffering pain and swelling of three days is valued most highly, at £15.96 (Figure 11.3). This is closely followed by a value of £13.77 for a reduction in the number of episodes of inflamed gums from 5 to 0 (Figure 11.8). The WTP values for each attribute *level* can also be compared on a WTP scale. The WTP results show that people are willing to pay £13.64 to move from a 30 percent chance of crowding to a 0 percent chance. While the cost levels in this study are approximately linear, the BWS results reveal that the majority of preference value from "crowding" lies in the lower two levels, namely a reduction from 15 percent to 0 percent, £9.89, with the marginal value of a reduction in crowding from 30 percent to 15 percent being only £2.92. From a policy perspective, this reveals that major efforts should be focused on reducing the chance of crowding from 15 percent to 0 percent.

Such individual-level WTP insights from data rarely have been derived from choice models in health applications to date. The advantages of such detailed information in cost–benefit analysis (CBA) studies are many (McIntosh *et al.*, 2010). Identifying the individual welfare values as well as their position on the underlying scale provides a CBA with enormous flexibility in terms of identifying possible patterns of resource allocation.

11.4.1 Comparator analysis: random effects probit model results

The results from a simple binary random effects probit model fit to the accept (not accept) data (that is, ignoring the best/worst information) are shown in Table 11.2; the repeated measures nature of the data has been taken into account in the reported standard errors. Five of the seven attributes are significant predictors of choice of third molar care, with "Gums" and "Cost" being significant only at the 10 percent level. Greene (2003) quotes a Hosmer–Lemeshow chi-squared value of 50 as being a "large value," and hence an inappropriate model fit; the Hosmer–Lemeshow value of 66.11 therefore suggests an inappropriate fit for the binary probit model, which, when combined with a lack of statistical significance, implies the model is not optimal. However, while not ideal, we will use the results of this section to compare the BWS approach with the results from the DCE approach.

Table 11.2 *Random effects probit results*

Attributes	Unit	Coefficients	Std err	P
Severe	Days	−0.1218002	0.0278	0.000
Mild	Episodes (per year)	0.00035004	0.003	0.9
Bleed	% chance	0.0065184	0.0286	0.8
Nerve	% chance	−0.440501	0.00943	0.000
Crowd	% chance	−0.018479	0.00394	0.000
Gums	Number of episodes	−0.033989	0.0201	0.09
Cost	£	−0.006649	0.003809	0.08

Notes: N = 54. Log likelihood function: −537.93. Restricted log likelihood: −663.20. Chi-squared: 250.52. McFadden's R^2: 0.18. Hesmer–Lemeshow chi-squared: 66.11.

In order to facilitate ease of comparison between the two approaches, Table 11.3 presents the Case 2 BWS results alongside those of the random effects binary choice model. The most obvious difference is that the BWS model provides utility weights on a common utility scale for each attribute and each attribute level. As outlined earlier, for the BWS model, the weight for each attribute simply reflects the overall impact of that attribute $(Pm = \sum_{l=1}^{qm} f_{ml}/N)$, while the individual scale values identify the impact of the individual levels as well as their position on the common scale. On the other hand, the binary probit model provides only relative utility weights for each attribute and, because of the confounding of weight and scale in such experiments, these utility weights are not directly comparable unless transformed by a common numeraire such as cost.

If the BWS attribute weights are compared to the probit utility "weights" in terms of their impact on overall utility, the results are potentially misleading, yet they reveal the key difference between BWS attribute weights and binary probit utility weights. This simple comparison is shown in Figure 11.11. The BWS weights reveal the overall impact of each attribute scaled by a common numeraire, namely total frequency count. However, the probit weights are not scaled by any common numeraire, hence each unit reflects its own individual scale as a function of the unit of measurement (for example, days, %, £); as a result, their comparison with each other is akin to comparing apples and oranges.

11.5 Discussion

The results in this chapter have shown the following for Case 2 best-worst scaling.

- BWS utility estimates differ from standard binary probit utility estimates.
- BWS utility estimates are on a common utility scale, unlike standard probit utility estimates.
- BWS estimates of individual levels of attributes are on a common utility scale.

Table 11.3 *Comparison of BWS utility weights and probit utility weights*

Attribute	Best attribute scaling		Random effects probit
		Parameter estimate	Parameter estimate
Attribute level	Weight*	(scale value)	(arbitrary utility value)
Severe	**0.283**		−0.1218
0		2.104	/
1		0.163	/
3		−1.247	/
Mild	**0.0969**		0.00035
Never		0.909	/
Monthly		0.068	/
Weekly		−0.368	/
Bleed	**0.09**		0.00652
0%		0.908	/
2.50%		0.051	/
5%		−0.864	/
Nerve	**0.238**		−0.4405
0%		1.646	/
5%		−0.367	/
10%		−1.218	/
Crowd	**0.107**		−0.0185
0%		0.891	/
15%		−1.186	/
30%		−1.8	/
Gums	**0.154**		−0.034
0		1.427	/
2		0.908	/
5		−1.465	/
Cost	**0.0285**		−0.0066
£0		1.018	/
£5		3.454	/
£15		0.107	/
£20		−3.118	/
£25		−2.982	/
£30		−3.572	/

Note:* $Pm = \sum_{l=1}^{qm} f_{ml}/N$

There are clear differences in the results of the two analyses, and further research is needed to understand the extent to which they can be put down to different task formats (best/worst attribute levels versus accept/not profiles); limitations of the data (a small sample); or the wrong model of the "accept" decision. Regarding the latter, various individuals may have

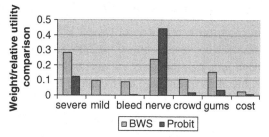

Figure 11.11 Comparison of BWS weights and binary probit utility "weights"

used a deterministic decision rule, such as always using one attribute for best choices and another for worst choices; rather than using the assumed additive rule. Taking account of the limitations of these data, we hope this chapter has shown the potential for Case 2 BWS as a way to provide deeper insights to preferences derived from choice modeling.

11.5.1 Model assumptions

The Case 2 BWS methodology used in this chapter relies on the satisfaction of a number of assumptions. One key assumption is that "most attractive" and "least attractive" choices graph as mirror images. If this is not the case, then more complex approaches need to be used, involving the best and worst choices as separate data (see Chapter 6 for recent work on this approach). Alternatively, information on the "choices" for each profile as a whole could be used to estimate a discrete choice model using a closed-ended (for example, purchase, no-purchase) approach similar to the version used in the random effects probit model in section 11.4.1.

11.5.2 Limitations of the data in this study

The response rate for the main survey was 14 percent. This small sample (54 people) cannot be regarded as representative of the general population. The Case 2 BWS format requires a lengthy survey on account of profiles being presented individually, as opposed to (say) the pairing of profiles in a DCE (and subsequent halving of the number of choice sets). There also was a relatively large number of attributes in the survey, and many contained risk probabilities that may have been cognitively complex for many. Consequently, the data in this chapter were used solely for the purposes of illustrating differences between the Case 2 BWS approach and the standard binary choice model estimation approach, not to draw any third molar management policy conclusions. The Case 2 BWS approach differs from a standard Case 3 BWS (and a DCE) approach, in which choice sets are presented in pairs (or multiples), since it requires the individual assessment of profiles. Such individual assessment requires more questions and increases task complexity. Future work should explore the extent to which this added complexity influences the results.

11.5.3 Potential for the Case 2 BWS approach in health economics

One aim of this chapter was to provide an empirical comparison of Case 2 BWS with a standard DCE method. While the original research on the use of the Case 2 BWS approach in health economics stemmed from the search for a non-monetary measure of benefit, the study also generated WTP values. We hope that the exposition of the technique has shown its potential for both the non-monetary and the monetary measurement of health states in economic evaluation. Indeed, since this study was completed, there has been a significant rise in the number of published Case 1 and Case 2 BWS studies in the literature (Al-Janabi, Coast and Flynn, 2008; Coast *et al.*, 2006; Coast, Peters *et al.*, 2008; Coast, Flynn, Natarajan *et al.*, 2008) as well as methodological work (Flynn *et al.*, 2007; Marley, Flynn and Louviere, 2008).

In addition to the potential benefits of BWS discussed above there are several more general advantages of using the (Case 2) BWS approach. First, while the method can be used as a stand-alone technique, the interpretation of results from other conjoint techniques is also greatly complemented and enhanced by BWS results. In this empirical study, the response functions for each attribute were generally linear; however, it may be the case in other studies that the Case 2 BWS approach identifies non-linear response functions, thus providing information about appropriate specifications of the variable relationships. For example, Case 2 BWS studies may reveal a preference for (say) the lowest price level, showing that price has little additional impact at higher levels. This advantage can be carried over to the valuation of health states, such that it is possible to imagine patients having non-linear preferences for levels of particular health states.

Now imagine that we want to construct a health utility index akin to the utility weights of the EQ-5D health questionnaire tariff obtained using the time trade-off measuring and valuing health (MVH) study for the EuroQol Group (Dolan *et al.*, 1995; 1996). To do so, we need to be able to place health states on a cardinal utility scale. By identifying generic health states such as those used by the MVH study (that is, mobility, self-care, usual activities, pain/discomfort and anxiety/depression), we can imagine using the Case 2 BWS approach to place configurations of these attributes on a common utility scale in exactly the same way as with the dental attributes in this empirical chapter. One advantage of such an approach to the estimation of utilities is the underlying statistical design properties of the methodology (that is, orthogonality), as well as a theoretical basis in random utility theory. Chapter 12 explores such an approach in the context of the ICECAP-O instrument.

11.6 Future work

In light of the above discussion and the limitations of the data used in this study, it is hoped that it can be seen that there is huge scope for further application of this technique in benefit assessment in health economics. While the analysis here was carried out using a simple WLS approach, ongoing work is developing the MNL model with a theory of errors for the analysis of such data.

Although the Case 2 BWS application in this chapter focused on using best-worst scaling to derive non-monetary measures of benefit, there is also potential for applying it in a welfare economic framework to elicit monetary benefit measures. Including an "opt-out" option gives experimental participants a chance to decline to participate, providing welfare estimates consistent with demand theory. It would be useful for future research to explore the added benefit of using a Case 2 BWS approach to derive monetary values for use in CBA applications in health care. Alternatively, one can estimate a model specified in WTP units – that is, one specified by ratios of coefficients to the cost attribute (so-called estimation in WTP space). This latter approach has not been used with Case 2 BWS previously, so it would be worth exploring in future BWS research.

11.7 Conclusions

This chapter discussed one of the earliest empirical applications of the Case 2 BWS measurement and scaling model in health economics. We do not suggest that Case 2 BWS is a substitute for traditional DCEs; rather, the Case 2 approach should be viewed as a *complement* to DCEs that can provide newer and deeper insights to assist the interpretation of results, and/or as a stand-alone technique for part-worth estimation. As discussed in Chapter 6, Case 2 BWS provides new and additional information about utilities that enhances the interpretation of traditional and choice-based models.

Chapter 12

BWS profile case application: preferences for quality of life in Australia

Terry N. Flynn and Elisabeth Huynh

12.1 Introduction

This chapter uses Case 2 best-worst scaling – the profile case – to elicit the scores that Australians associate with aspects of the ICECAP-O quality-of-life (well-being) instrument. It expands upon the methods used in a smaller study to achieve similar aims for the ICECAP-A instrument in the United Kingdom (Flynn *et al.*, 2015). In particular, it demonstrates how latent class analyses can be used to identify distinct clusters of individuals with different preferences in their Case 2 answers. It is written for non-health economists, and therefore includes details of the "non-welfarist" paradigm that many work within.

Health care agencies in a number of advanced industrialized countries other than the United States do not fund interventions according to the patient's willingness to pay. Instead of this traditional economics "welfarist" approach, an "extra-welfarist" (or "non-welfarist") approach is used that assigns a value to every possible health state based on some average of the population's preferences (Brouwer *et al.*, 2008). In order to elicit these population-based preferences *à priori*, the set of "all possible health states" must be circumscribed in some way. This is done via the use of a standardized health (or health-related quality-of-life) instrument. The most common health instrument, the EQ-5D (Dolan *et al.*, 1995; Kind *et al.*, 1998), has five attributes, each with three possible attribute levels (response categories). In DCE parlance, this makes it a 3^5 instrument in 243 possible unique health states.

Once the set of health states has been standardized, a stated preference valuation exercise is conducted to elicit the population's preferences. The aim is to produce an "off-the-shelf" set of values – the "tariff" – summarizing the preferences of the relevant (typically country-specific whole-adult) population. Traditionally valuation exercises used numerical tasks (Arnesen and Trommald, 2005; Richardson, 1994) but in recent years discrete-choice-based tasks rooted in a random utility theory framework have increasingly been used (Flynn, 2010a; Thurstone, 1927). These have included discrete choice experiments, ranking tasks and BWS studies (Coast, Flynn, Natarajan *et al.*, 2008; Ryan *et al.*, 2006; Salomon, 2003). The paradigm used to conceptualize the tariff is described elsewhere but suffice to say that it must be possible to make statements such as "relative to full health, the health state characterized by moderate depression, but otherwise good health, might have a value of 74 percent while that of extreme pain might have a value of 60 percent."

12.1.1 *The distinction between measurement and valuation*

Once policy-makers have their off-the-shelf tariff, they then make a distinction between the measurement and valuation of health. Patients *measure* (judge) their health in a trial or survey (Kind *et al.*, 1998) by ticking boxes to indicate how impaired (for example, depressed, in pain, lacking in mobility) they are using the same standardized health instrument used in the population-based valuation exercise. Thus, for the EQ-5D, they simply tick one of the three possible response categories for each of the five health attributes (dimensions). So, while these (five) tick box answers measure (describe – qualitatively, for certain very subjective attributes such as pain) a health state, the population's *value* associated with that health state is used to summarize how good/bad the state is. In this way, statements are possible such as "on average, treating this patient's depression using a particular anti-depressant is associated with an improvement of 10 percent", while "treating this other patient with hip or knee disease with a total joint replacement is associated with an improvement of 15 percent." In this way, apples and oranges can (in theory) be meaningfully compared: all these scores are on a common latent health scale anchored between zero (death) and one (full health).[1]

12.1.2 *The move away from health towards well-being*

The distinction between measurement and valuation, despite appearing slightly convoluted to the welfarist economist or non-economist, is relatively uncontroversial in western Europe, Canada and Australasia. However, in practice the focus on patient health has proved increasingly problematic. Population values associated with older people (Coast, Flynn, Sutton *et al.*, 2008), children (Ratcliffe *et al.*, 2011) and carer (Al-Janabi, Coast and Flynn, 2008) health states have proved difficult to elicit and/or justify. Better integration of health and social care for key groups such as older people may be hampered by attempts by one government agency to shift responsibilities to another (for example, the classic problem of "bed blocking" in hospitals, when older people have no social care support available on discharge). One solution proposed in the literature is to maintain the measurement valuation paradigm but simply to change the maximand, from health to well-being defined more broadly (Grewal *et al.*, 2006). If all agencies are being judged by the same yardstick, then non-performers or those attempting to game the system become obvious.

The maximand described here is an early extra-welfarist one based on the economics Nobel-Prize-winning work of Amartya Sen on the capabilities approach (see Sen, 1982, for details). Sen's hypothesis was that critical importance attaches to key "functionings" of life and the individual's (cap)ability to achieve the desired levels of these. Functionings (in the developed world) might be higher-order aspects of life, such as being independent and having high-quality social relationships. These would be the attributes in a DCE/BWS framework, but the capability aspect would be captured in the levels by phrasing them in

---

[1] There are issues in anchoring a conventional RUT scale to that used in health that are not dealt with here; see Flynn, Louviere, Marley *et al.* (2008).

terms of the individual's ability to achieve the desired amount. In this way, the "natural loner" is accommodated: he/she might objectively have only one friend in life but subjectively place him-/herself in the top response category (level) of the relationships attribute as being able to have all the high-quality relationships he/she wants. Crucially, while good health may be important, it is its ability to enable the individual to achieve the key capabilities in life that make it valuable, and it might not be the only route towards achieving them (Grewal *et al.*, 2006). Thus, a capabilities-based outcome instrument might not look like a health instrument.

12.1.3 The ICECAP instruments and background to this chapter

From 2001 to 2009 the first author's work on BWS was part of a wider UK Medical Research Council project to develop and value (provide scoring – a tariff – for) a new extra-welfarist well-being instrument, one specifically for older people. The program – Investigating Choice Experiments for the Preferences of Older People (ICEPOP) (Coast, Flynn, Sutton *et al.*, 2008) – first developed the ICEpop CAPabilities instrument for older people (ICECAP-O). Since 2009 ICECAP-A (for adults of any age) (Al-Janabi, Flynn and Coast, 2012) and ICECAP-SCM (the "supportive care measure" for care at the end of life) (Sutton and Coast, 2014) have been developed from qualitative research (Coast *et al.*, 2012). All these instruments have, or are in the process of developing, UK general population tariffs that enable them to be used to value health, social and other relevant forms of care.

During the development of ICECAP-A (around the time the first author moved to Australia, in 2009) the greater potential for BWS to value goods and services (and, indeed, capability states) became clear. In particular, its ability to provide highly disaggregated results gave the Australian research team opportunities to investigate numerous methodological and empirical issues in the valuation of well-being. The results of this research are presented here.

Thus, the Australian study had two main aims: (1) to produce population average tariffs for the ICECAP-O instrument; and (2) to investigate heterogeneity in preferences for well-being (via latent class analyses) and ascertain the extent to which any differences were related to current well-being. In other words, the aims were to answer questions such as "Is there really an average Australian?" and "Do Australians experiencing impairments such as loneliness or lack of independence wish to improve on those or compensate elsewhere in life?"

12.2 Methods

The estimation of a population average tariff using discrete choice tasks necessitates proper adjustment for both mean and variance heterogeneity (Flynn *et al.*, 2010). Any failure to account for the latter would run the risk of respondents exhibiting large variance components being under-represented, thus increasing the likelihood of heterogeneity being misclassified (mean as variance or vice versa) and biasing the estimates. The calculation of accurate population estimates requires good knowledge of sources of heterogeneity, and the sampling criteria should be adjusted to reflect this, with appropriate reweighting then conducted at the analysis stage.

The only subgroup results available in 2009 were for ICECAP-O among British older people. Individuals' own quality of life appeared to affect the size of the variance component: lower scores were associated with lower scale factors (higher variances). If this is true more generally, then respondents in impaired ICECAP-O states should be over-sampled in order to protect against misclassification and misestimation of heterogeneity effects. This study aimed to do this for ICECAP-O. Thus, it is important to note that quota sampling to ensure that the sample was representative of the wider Australian population was *deliberately avoided*: current evidence suggests quota sampling would not be appropriate for ICECAP-O – even if one wishes to estimate a population-average tariff.

12.2.1 Survey samples

A study of 6,000 members (in total) of the Pureprofile panel was funded by a University of Technology, Sydney, Partnership Grant (with Pureprofile as the industry partner).[2] The main study was restricted to 5,000, so as to allow up to 1,000 respondents for the piloting of two instruments, the original ICECAP-O and ICECAP-A, which had recently been finalized by members of the UK research team. Two valuation exercises were conducted, one for each ICECAP instrument, with a sample size of approximately 2,500 for each.

Only the ICECAP-O results are reported. This is because of a serious problem identified with the wording of ICECAP-A among around one-third of (primarily younger) native English-speaking Australians. One of the pilots found that the capability (utility) score associated with the third (second from top) level was substantially higher than that associated with the fourth (top) level for at least one attribute. Although initially dismissed as a coding error or design effect,[3] further analysis, together with anecdotal evidence from Australian, US,[4] Canadian and New Zealand native English speakers, suggested that the qualifier "quite a lot" is considered to be more than "a lot" by non-trivial numbers of younger people and was responsible for this finding. Since ICECAP-A was developed and tested among British English speakers and since that particular form of wording was never used in the original ICECAP-O, the problem had not arisen beforehand. Given the timescale of the project, it was not feasible to obtain agreement and test alternative "non-British English" forms of wording for ICECAP-A. Ad hoc changes to the wording of the valuation

---

[2] Ethical approval: since respondents were anonymous, ethics approval was covered by institutional survey approval from the University of Technology, Sydney, where the study was conducted before the authors changed affiliation.

[3] Co-occurrences in an OMEP are not equalized, and so, unless the sample size is large, highly valued intermediate levels can have high estimated capabilities unless they compete with a particularly attractive top level on other attributes or there are sufficiently large counts overall to offset this tendency.

[4] See www.macmillandictionaryblog.com/the-trickiest-word-in-american.

task for ICECAP-A were instead used, with only mixed success. Therefore, no further reporting of the ICECAP-A results is provided.

12.2.2 Survey designs

A 2 × 2 factorial design was utilized, randomizing respondents to:

- see/not see a page with one-/two-sentence explanations of each attribute ("descriptor"), reflecting the conceptual attributes as described by Grewal *et al.* (2006); and
- one of two equivalent orthogonal main effects plans.

The ICECAP-O study arm also utilized quota-based sampling to increase the recruitment of respondents who themselves were in poor quality-of-life states. These individuals tend to be relatively under-represented in general population surveys, which increases the probability that any differences in their preferences remain undetected. Results from a 2009 study of several thousand Australian members of the Pureprofile panel were used to identify:

- which of the 1,024 ICECAP-O states are typically represented in the general population; and
- what the approximate distribution of people is across these states.

In addition to this, a number of states were identified that were likely to be informative in testing whether specific impairments were associated with differences in preferences and/or scales. In particular, states characterized by a large impairment (for instance, being at level one) in only one attribute were informative: these are useful in determining if the effect of an impairment on preferences is attribute-specific. A total of 435 ICECAP-O states were identified by the above criteria, with around half of these being present (that is, having at least one member of the Australian general population experiencing it) in the 2009 survey.

Table 12.1 contains the OMEP, while OMEP 2 is its foldover. As recommended by Flynn (2010b), these minimize the number of profiles (states) in which the best and/or worst choice is "artificially easy," defined as having only one attribute at the top or bottom level. This, in turn, reduces the vulnerability to variance heterogeneity. It was achieved by checking all possible coding schemes in Excel, outputting the number of profiles in which best or worst choice was likely to be "easy" (defined as only one attribute taking the highest or lowest level present in that profile) or "hard" (defined as more than three attributes all taking the same coding level, with no other attributes taking a more extreme coding level). This avoided profiles in which one attribute was at its top level and the other four were at the bottom level; such a profile has an excessively easy "best" choice and an excessively difficult "worst" choice.

It should be noted that it was impossible to eliminate easy choices entirely, but the optimal design found only five (out of 32) choices that might be considered easier than the rest. In particular, there were two best and three worst such choices in OMEP 1 (and the reverse in OMEP 2).

Table 12.1 *OMEP design*

Choice set	Attachment	Security	Role	Enjoyment	Control
1	2	2	3	2	3
2	2	3	4	3	4
3	2	4	1	4	1
4	2	1	2	1	2
5	3	2	4	4	2
6	3	3	3	1	1
7	3	4	2	2	4
8	3	1	1	3	3
9	4	2	1	1	4
10	4	3	2	4	3
11	4	4	3	3	2
12	4	1	4	2	1
13	1	2	2	3	1
14	1	3	1	2	2
15	1	4	4	1	3
16	1	1	3	4	4

The study consisted of five stages.

(1) A life satisfaction question (to match that used in the Deakin University survey, a Likert-type scale survey of the type used in many countries). This was presented first, so as to minimize any "artificial standardization" of respondents' responses resulting from having seen the five ICECAP-O attributes. Such standardization has not been carried out generally in other life satisfaction surveys.

(2) See/not see the descriptors for ICECAP-O.

(3) ICECAP-O as an outcome instrument (the five tick box questions) to elicit the individual's own quality of life. This was used as a screening question: once the quota for a particular "cell" (quality-of-life state) was full, additional respondents indicating that they were experiencing that state were screened out, thanked for participating and partially rewarded.

(4) The best-worst scaling case 2 (profile case) study in 20 states. The OMEP was supplemented with an additional four profiles. These were not intended for use in principal analyses; they were intended either as a test of the model or as additional choice sets to better distinguish levels three and four of enjoyment. That attribute is the one for which respondents in the United Kingdom appeared not to discriminate between levels three and four, and it can also be penalized in OMEP 1, since level four appears with highly attractive attribute levels more often than level three does.

(5) Finally, there were additional questions included for comparison with UK data that had previously been collected and analyzed; these questions were on health, attitude and social empowerment.

12.2.3 Analysis

Analysis took the following form.

(1) Descriptive (non-model-based) tables containing best-worst (maxdiff) and marginal (summed) best (respectively, worst) choice frequencies.
(2) Investigation of the best-minus-worst scores (the "scores"), including clustering analyses.
(3) Scale-adjusted latent class MNL-based regression models. These used the statistics in (2) as predictors of class to help stabilize solutions, given the issues identified in model stability.

12.3 Results: main Australian survey

12.3.1 Non-model-based estimates

Table 12.2 shows the choice proportions for best-worst pairs for ICECAP-O. The relative frequency with which a given pair was chosen as best-worst is given by the row/column combination. Taking averages to the best (respectively, worst) margins makes clear the relationship between the maxdiff and marginal frequencies (though it should be noted that these are non-model-based estimates and are not the maxdiff and marginal model estimates assuming the processes discussed in Chapter 5).

The results make it clear that it is attachment and control that have the strongest effects on capability. The top two levels for attachment are valued as best more than any other (as in the overall MNL results from the UK study of older people), while the bottom level of control is strongly disliked in terms of worst, unlike the UK study, in which the bottom level of attachment is disliked even more. Security appears to have a larger effect than the remaining two attributes, and therefore, compared to the UK results, may have a stronger effect overall.

12.3.2 Best-minus-worst scores

The best-minus-worst scores (the "scores") were discussed in the theory chapters as a means of both interrogating and summarizing the data. As with Flynn *et al.* (2015), functions of the scores were used to do so here. In particular, squaring and summing the (normalized) scores for an attribute were conducted to produce what was called the empirical sum of squares, or empirical scale parameter (ESP), since it provided an empirical measure of choice consistency.[5] For respondents who understood the task, this statistic typically takes a value between zero (indicating it was never picked) and around 3.125 (a pattern of $-1, -0.75, +0.75, +1$ for the four levels); scores of more than this indicate that

---

[5] Subsequent discussions between Flynn and Marley have led to the conclusion that ESPs are a confound of preferences and variances, not a pure measure of scale.

Table 12.2 *Choice proportions for best-worst pairs for ICECAP-O and marginal best (respectively, worst)*

	level	Attachment 1	2	3	4	Security 1	2	3	4	Role 1	2	3	4	Enjoyment 1	2	3	4	Control 1	2	3	4	MEAN BEST
Attachment	1					0.021	0.019	0.018	0.014	0.017	0.012	0.009	0.01	0.02	0.015	0.016	0.01	0.031	0.025	0.018	0.016	0.017
	2					0.094	0.046	0.029	0.02	0.043	0.03	0.01	0.015	0.118	0.027	0.02	0.018	0.069	0.035	0.021	0.03	0.039
	3					0.211	0.11	0.07	0.044	0.265	0.156	0.059	0.016	0.27	0.146	0.021	0.026	0.37	0.255	0.087	0.026	0.133
	4					0.24	0.26	0.115	0.034	0.274	0.235	0.038	0.017	0.274	0.234	0.031	0.024	0.386	0.272	0.07	0.038	0.159
Security	1	0.012	0.008	0.005	0.004					0.015	0.014	0.014	0.011	0.02	0.016	0.016	0.02	0.016	0.01	0.007	0.012	0.013
	2	0.03	0.019	0.006	0.007					0.016	0.011	0.015	0.012	0.026	0.022	0.019	0.017	0.034	0.014	0.012	0.011	0.017
	3	0.216	0.045	0.007	0.01					0.086	0.038	0.01	0.013	0.087	0.032	0.022	0.017	0.066	0.045	0.019	0.023	0.046
	4	0.252	0.116	0.024	0.007					0.098	0.046	0.057	0.009	0.082	0.163	0.016	0.025	0.228	0.168	0.075	0.015	0.086
Role	1	0.021	0.008	0.005	0.008	0.013	0.009	0.008	0.012					0.012	0.004	0.008	0.006	0.01	0.01	0.006	0.006	0.009
	2	0.07	0.038	0.008	0.008	0.08	0.02	0.016	0.014					0.07	0.008	0.005	0.007	0.028	0.016	0.01	0.008	0.025
	3	0.316	0.118	0.012	0.008	0.067	0.062	0.019	0.016					0.075	0.07	0.01	0.009	0.138	0.038	0.027	0.009	0.062
	4	0.236	0.181	0.006	0.01	0.057	0.094	0.024	0.023					0.074	0.043	0.008	0.006	0.122	0.112	0.016	0.014	0.064
Enjoyment	1	0.014	0.008	0.005	0.005	0.014	0.013	0.01	0.007	0.005	0.006	0.005	0.008					0.012	0.006	0.003	0.005	0.008
	2	0.104	0.011	0.009	0.008	0.03	0.021	0.012	0.012	0.022	0.009	0.006	0.008					0.025	0.012	0.006	0.003	0.019
	3	0.336	0.102	0.007	0.007	0.119	0.038	0.05	0.011	0.058	0.032	0.01	0.007					0.24	0.074	0.012	0.011	0.07
	4	0.255	0.128	0.014	0.005	0.074	0.104	0.026	0.027	0.074	0.078	0.031	0.007					0.171	0.087	0.048	0.012	0.071
Control	1	0.014	0.009	0.004	0.005	0.008	0.003	0.004	0.006	0.004	0.003	0.002	0.003	0.008	0.003	0.003	0.004					0.005
	2	0.102	0.026	0.009	0.01	0.056	0.014	0.008	0.009	0.021	0.008	0.006	0.006	0.056	0.012	0.006	0.008					0.022
	3	0.287	0.116	0.016	0.011	0.104	0.082	0.019	0.017	0.132	0.028	0.019	0.008	0.125	0.051	0.01	0.012					0.065
	4	0.248	0.168	0.012	0.011	0.106	0.056	0.045	0.017	0.08	0.081	0.01	0.01	0.114	0.132	0.008	0.011					0.069
MEAN WORST		0.157	0.069	0.009	0.008	0.101	0.076	0.039	0.021	0.076	0.049	0.019	0.010	0.093	0.064	0.015	0.015	0.122	0.074	0.027	0.015	

Note: Values represent the number of times that a best (row) and worst (column) pair was picked divided by the number of times that pair was available. Higher values are heavily shaded, smaller values have lighter shading.

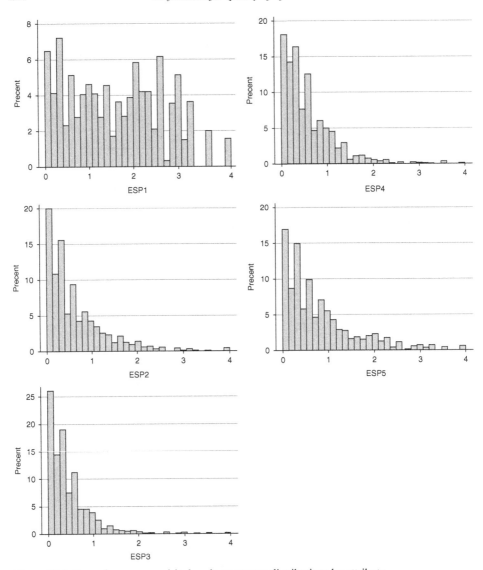

Figure 12.1 Sum of squares empirical scale parameter distributions by attribute

the respondent was ignoring levels and picking the attribute as best/worst no matter what. Figure 12.1 gives the histograms for the five attributes separately.

Attachment is the only attribute not to exhibit a strongly positively skewed distribution; its more even distribution indicates that it is the most valued attribute overall. Specifically, far more respondents have scored in the higher range (that is, between 2 and 4), indicating they are more concerned and/or certain about this attribute in comparison to the others.

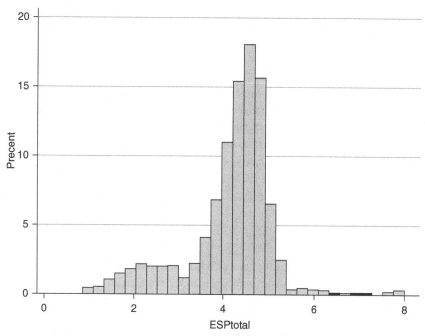

Figure 12.2 Total sum of squares empirical scale parameter distribution

Summing across all five attributes produces Figure 12.2. This (total ESP) is a potential measure of scale across the sample.

This total ESP appears to be (at least) trimodal, with modes around 2, 4.5 and almost 8. When we look at the relationship between the individual respondent's BW score and his/her total ESP score, we can classify them into specific groups.

- Central modal group. The respondents whose total ESP values lie in the main mode have well-defined preferences for at least two attributes. It should be noted that answering the survey deterministically with consistent strong preferences for three attributes produces a total ESP of approximately 4.5.
- Lower modal group. This smaller mode is made up of different types of people: (1) respondents who did not have a clear/strong preference for any attribute; (2) respondents who had a clear preference for only one attribute, but no secondary preference; or (3) respondents who did not answer the task in a very logical/intuitive manner.
- Top tail group. The respondents who lie in the upper distribution (that is, around 6 and above) all appear to have illogical (but in many cases consistent) preferences. Furthermore, we can assume that respondents who scored an 8 tried to "game" the system; they can achieve this score only by picking one particular attribute as best in every single profile, and picking a different attribute as worst in every single profile, no matter what level is presented. Given the design, it is impossible to achieve this score any

other way: picking a given attribute as best whenever it appears at level four automatically rules out any other attribute as being able to be picked as best whenever it appears at level four.

Good designs and a knowledge of common psychological processes allowed these considerable insights into the choice data to be drawn, without the use of complex statistical models. Indeed, given the confounding of means and variances on the latent scale, decisions as to which decomposition of preference and scale is most likely require such knowledge. It will be shown later that proceeding straight to latent class analyses, even those that claim to separate preference and scale heterogeneity, is unwise: solutions from Latent GOLD Choice 4.5 + Syntax were vulnerable to particular choice patterns. The inferences above were used to inform some clustering analyses, in order to provide an initial picture of heterogeneity in the data.

Cluster models

The cluster analysis was conducted using Latent GOLD 4.5. It involves classifying similar objects (that is, respondents) into clusters when it is unknown a priori how many clusters there will be and how their parameters are formed. This analysis technique uses a probabilistic clustering approach, meaning that each respondent and his/her response to each choice set are assumed to belong to each cluster with a probability that can (though usually will not) equal one or zero. Therefore, there are probabilities associated with each point and cluster.

We initially only used the five attribute-specific ESP variables in the analysis, to cluster respondents according to attributes. The aim was to keep increasing the number of clusters until one was identified that contained respondents of type (1) in the lower modal group described above: respondents who had no strong preferences for any attribute and were likely a "small scale" cluster. With replication, we were not able to find a stable model or identify a cluster of low-scale-factor respondents that we had previously observed when looking at the data individually (that is, those who were found in the lower modal group).

Therefore the analyses were repeated, with two additions being made to the model:

(1) the total ESP for each respondent was included as a covariate (predictor of cluster) in the model; and
(2) a known class indicator (consisting of the upper modal group) was included: respondents with an ESP of 6 or more were assigned to a known class (and nobody else was allowed to be assigned to this); having an ESP above this value meant that the respondent almost certainly ignored levels and focused on two or three attributes as a time-saving exercise.

The second factor prevented the data of people who fundamentally misunderstood the task (or who gamed the system) influencing the solution, while adding the first factor caused the type (1) lower modal group respondents to be identified much more quickly: as the fifth class, rather than the ninth when it was omitted. A further check involved increasing the

Table 12.3 *Bayes information criteria for different seeds*

	10 sets		50 sets	
Model	BIC (seed = 0)	BIC (seed = random)	BIC (seed = 0)	BIC (seed = random)
2-cluster	24783.19	24783.19	24783.19	24783.19
3-cluster	22527.01	22527.01	22527.01	22527.01
4-cluster	20933.37	20933.37	20933.37	20933.37
5-cluster	19555.61	19555.61	19555.61	19555.61
6-cluster	18980.28	18969.65	18969.65	18969.65
7-cluster	18579.21	18551.04	18544.21	18560.52

Notes: Only provided results up to a 7-cluster model, as we were only looking to find the most stable model rather than the one with the lowest BIC.

Table 12.4 *Four- versus five-cluster membership*

		ICECAP-O					
		5-cluster model					
Cluster		1	2	3	4	5	Total
4-cluster model	1	674	203	0	0	0	877
	2	60	500	423	4	0	987
	3	51	40	184	317	0	592
	4	0	0	0	0	44	44
Total		785	743	607	321	44	2500

starting number of sets of initial parameter estimates from 10 to 50. This reduces the likelihood of obtaining a local, rather than global, maximum in the likelihood function. Instability for larger number of sets indicates a fundamentally unstable solution. Table 12.3 presents the BICs for the estimated models, according to the different seeds (starting points in the model iteration) and number of sets used.

Increasing the number of starting sets improves the stability beyond the five-cluster solution, but only to the six-cluster solution. Cross-tabulating the various solutions (see Tables 12.4 and 12.5) provides an indication of where each additional cluster comes from: does the "new" cluster come from a simple split of an existing cluster (probably a meaningful solution), or does it come from a reorganization of existing clusters (might or might not be a meaningful solution).

Using the BIC and judgments about the stability of solutions, we found a five-cluster model to be optimal. Using different seeds and repetition, the five-cluster model gave stable (and replicable) results each time with significant and meaningful parameters.

Table 12.5 *Five- versus six-cluster membership*

		ICECAP-O						
		6-cluster model						
Cluster		1	2	3	4	5	6	Total
	1	374	2	404	5	0	0	785
	2	117	531	94	0	1	0	743
5-cluster model	3	23	23	37	523	1	0	607
	4	0	0	0	1	320	0	321
	5	0	0	0	0	0	44	44
Total		514	556	535	529	322	44	2500

As previously noted, to ensure that the models produce more stable solutions and capture a global solution, the number of starting value sets was increased from the default of 10 to 50. The BIC was stable for the six-cluster model in the ICECAP-O sample. Plotting the ESPs against own capability responses (tick box answers to ICECAP-O as an outcome instrument) was useful in gaining an understanding of how heterogeneity might be related to impairment (see Table 12.6), with larger numbers indicating stronger preference and/or greater consistency.

From Table 12.6 we note the following.

• Attachment: as people's own level of attachment increases, so generally does their focus on the "Attachment" attribute.
• Security: as people's own worries about the future decrease, their focus on the "Security" attribute also generally decreases.
• Role: the more people feel less valued, the more they focus on control.
• Control: as people become more independent, they are less concerned about the future.

Table 12.7 gives results in terms of key sociodemographic and attitudinal variables. From Table 12.7 we note the following.

• Health: as the level of health declines, focus on the "Control" attribute increases.
• Influence: as people feel less able to influence the decisions in their local area, they become more focused on security.
• Trust: as people's trust within the community decreases, focus on security and control increases.
• Age: as Table 12.8 also demonstrates, generally, as people become older, they tend to focus more on being independent (at least up until the last age category, where it then slightly declines).

Table 12.6 *Own capability against ESP by attribute*

	Mean of ESP				
	Attachment	Security	Role	Enjoyment	Control
Own attachment					
Cannot have any	1.463	0.605	0.383	0.618	0.997
A little	1.424	0.692	0.497	0.591	0.899
A lot	1.628	0.688	0.476	0.628	0.731
All	1.823	0.600	0.461	0.550	0.792
Own security					
With a lot	1.521	0.814	0.440	0.523	0.808
With some	1.656	0.662	0.447	0.601	0.835
With only a little	1.682	0.558	0.496	0.656	0.805
Without any	1.546	0.580	0.520	0.554	0.816
Own role					
Unable to do any	1.201	0.682	0.509	0.516	0.949
In a few	1.659	0.690	0.452	0.624	0.787
In many	1.644	0.659	0.470	0.583	0.825
All	1.676	0.554	0.492	0.588	0.795
Own enjoyment					
Cannot have any	1.281	0.693	0.432	0.607	0.998
A little	1.586	0.706	0.472	0.573	0.800
A lot	1.714	0.624	0.468	0.605	0.810
All	1.637	0.580	0.490	0.610	0.783
Own control					
Unable to do any	1.423	0.698	0.457	0.473	0.882
A few things	1.631	0.708	0.469	0.613	0.658
Many things	1.688	0.660	0.483	0.610	0.754
Completely	1.560	0.600	0.457	0.581	1.009

12.3.3 *Main solutions using the choice data*

These results of an investigation using the "scores" provided a preliminary indication of preference and scale heterogeneity. It was wanted to use this characterization of heterogeneity to help identify stable solutions from scale-adjusted latent class analyses conducted on the choice data. However, there remained concerns that the class 4 (the "low scale" class in Table 12.4) was too heterogeneous: it did not entirely consist of type (1) or (2) mentioned above. Therefore, alternative SALC models were investigated, after deleting cluster five – the n = 44 "gamers of the system" – in every case:

(1) a model in which the total ESP was a covariate for (predictor of) scale class;
(2) a model in which the five attribute-specific ESPs were covariates for preference class; and
(3) a model in which the total ESP was a covariate for (predictor of) scale class and the five attribute-specific ESPs were covariates for preference class.

Table 12.7 *ICECAP-O sociodemographic variables*

				Mean of ESP		
		Attachment	Security	Role	Enjoyment	Control
Health						
	Good	1.671	0.615	0.486	0.631	0.779
	Fairly good	1.593	0.677	0.461	0.580	0.829
	Not good	1.528	0.717	0.449	0.521	0.894
Influence						
	Strongly agree	1.390	0.556	0.463	0.416	0.902
	Tend to agree	1.566	0.627	0.521	0.580	0.773
	Neither	1.594	0.616	0.469	0.591	0.853
	Tend to disagree	1.710	0.701	0.466	0.608	0.779
	Strongly disagree	1.618	0.732	0.411	0.633	0.837
Trust						
	Strongly agree	1.638	0.588	0.524	0.485	0.831
	Tend to agree	1.676	0.619	0.489	0.603	0.797
	Neither	1.628	0.681	0.466	0.592	0.790
	Tend to disagree	1.548	0.699	0.440	0.624	0.885
	Strongly disagree	1.319	0.735	0.363	0.616	0.910
Age						
	Under 18	1.546	0.500	0.476	0.639	0.590
	18–24	1.678	0.620	0.389	0.636	0.604
	25–34	1.689	0.623	0.462	0.606	0.670
	35–44	1.732	0.635	0.473	0.629	0.771
	45–54	1.579	0.710	0.498	0.574	0.878
	55–64	1.461	0.694	0.464	0.559	1.035
	65–74	1.385	0.685	0.552	0.505	1.165
	75+	1.678	0.478	0.458	0.530	0.958

Table 12.8 *ICECAP-O ESP by age and relationship status*

		Mean of ESP				
Age	Relationship status	Attachment	Security	Role	Enjoyment	Control
	Never married	1.637	0.598	0.408	0.626	0.663
<34 years	Widowed/divorced/separated	1.322	0.588	0.594	0.498	0.667
	Married	1.749	0.642	0.478	0.604	0.534
	Never married	1.579	0.589	0.491	0.667	0.915
35–54 years	Widowed/divorced/separated	1.414	0.703	0.447	0.555	1.037
	Married	1.730	0.653	0.497	0.595	0.693
	Never married	0.990	0.611	0.552	0.651	1.280
55+ years	Widowed/divorced/separated	1.208	0.708	0.445	0.516	1.234
	Married	1.606	0.659	0.507	0.522	0.969

The desire was to test the relative ability of the two measures (overall ESP and attribute-specific ESP) to provide a good SALC solution. In particular, the total ESP might misclassify some "primary preference only" people as "low scale class," whilst the attribute-specific ESPs might be less useful without the total ESP at identifying genuinely low-scale respondents. Thus, models (1) and (2) test each of these, with model (3) including them both. Table 12.9 presents summary model statistics, in each case presenting solutions for:

- one through five preference classes (LC); and
- one through three scale classes (SC).

These regressions (SALC analyses) were therefore estimated for each of the three models. In the interests of parsimony, results are not shown (though they are available from the authors). However, the third model, using all score information, performed best; in

Table 12.9 *BIC and McFadden R^2 valuation results*

SALC model		ICECAP-O	
		BIC(LL)	R^2
Model 1	2SC 1LC	161972.37	0.29
	2SC 2LC	158274.65	0.33
	2SC3LC	156652.31	0.35
	2SC 4LC	155412.42	0.35
	2SC 5LC	154629.35	0.36
	3SC 1LC	161556.42	0.29
	3SC 2LC	157955.78	0.33
	3SC 3LC	156311.76	0.35
	3SC 4LC	155275.09	0.35
	3SC 5LC	154540.97	0.36
Model 2	1SC 2LC	163029.1	0.28
	1SC 3LC	157135.03	0.32
	1SC 4LC	154606.6	0.33
	1SC 5LC	153218.37	0.34
	2SC 2LC	157347.46	0.32
	2SC 3LC	154621.15	0.34
	2SC 4LC	153179.48	0.35
	2SC 5LC	151763.16	0.36
	3SC 2LC	157241.32	0.32
	3SC 3LC	154518.16	0.34
	3SC 4LC	152998.94	0.35
	3SC 5LC	151707.78	0.36
Model 3	2SC 2LC	156185.21	0.32
	2SC 3LC	153449.05	0.34

Table 12.9 (*cont.*)

| | ICECAP-O | |
SALC model	BIC(LL)	R²
2SC 4LC	151898.37	0.35
2SC 5LC	150516.19	0.36
3SC 1LC	161556.41	0.29
3SC 2LC	155882.06	0.32
3SC 3LC	153142.48	0.34
3SC 4LC	151504.87	0.35
3SC 5LC	150189.71	0.36

particular, the total ESP was required in order that many people with a strong primary preference were correctly classified (rather than simply classed as a large-scale version of a "no strong preference" type). In terms of individual preference and scale class solutions, the three-scale class 5 preference class solution was misleading, even though it was optimal using the BIC; when moving to five (from four) classes, the preference class structure changed markedly in ways that were unrealistic given the other analyses (the ESP analyses in particular, which suggested the number of classes to be relatively small). Thus, the model 3 four-preference-class (4LC), two-scale-class (2SC) solution was chosen as the final model.

The tariffs (rescaled values) for each of the four classes are given in Table 12.10. They were calculated from applying a linear transformation to the 20-attribute-level estimates from Latent GOLD. This transformation simply subtracts one-fifth of the score of the state 11111 from each estimate (to ensure that state 11111 – the "utility" associated with summing the five relevant bottom levels – is anchored at zero), then divides by the utility of state 44444 (to ensure that 44444 – the "utility" associated with summing the five relevant top levels – takes value one). In the remainder of the chapter, we refer to the four classes (types) by their names in the second row of Table 12.10 – that is, 1 (security), etc.

This table makes clear the four types of Australian: they differ little in their preferences for role and are mainly differentiated in terms of attachment, control and enjoyment. Respondents were assigned to their "modal class" – in other words, the class (type) that best described them.

It is desirable to be able to score respondents who did not participate in the best-worst valuation exercise. This requires information that allows the researcher to decide the type (class) to which he/she is most likely to belong. To obtain such information, a number of one-, two- and three-way cross-tabulations were run against class to identify any associations with sociodemographic or other variables. The following associations were found.

Table 12.10 *ICECAP-O preference classes*

	Class (type) of Australian				
	1 (security)	2 (control)	3 (enjoy+ attach)	4 (attachment)	Population
Attachment					
Cannot have any	−0.022	0.009	−0.048	−0.078	−0.039
A little	0.08	0.085	0.068	0.062	0.073
A lot	0.19	0.174	0.206	0.242	0.207
All	0.217	0.194	0.252	0.307	0.249
Security					
With a lot	−0.024	0.024	0.034	0.031	0.017
With some	0.076	0.082	0.089	0.08	0.081
With only a little	0.147	0.127	0.117	0.118	0.127
Without any	0.254	0.191	0.178	0.174	0.197
Role					
Unable to do any	0.02	0.023	0.022	0.018	0.020
In a few	0.098	0.096	0.085	0.085	0.091
In many	0.158	0.155	0.158	0.159	0.158
All	0.182	0.182	0.186	0.184	0.183
Enjoyment					
Cannot have any	0.017	0.016	−0.015	0.028	0.014
A little	0.084	0.082	0.069	0.081	0.080
A lot	0.17	0.169	0.198	0.156	0.171
All	0.182	0.187	0.219	0.166	0.185
Control					
Unable to do any	0.009	−0.072	0.007	0.001	−0.013
A few things	0.084	0.057	0.078	0.073	0.073
Many things	0.146	0.175	0.141	0.144	0.151
Completely	0.166	0.246	0.165	0.169	0.185
Number of respondents	573 (23%)	522 (21%)	518 (21%)	843 (34%)	2456

- Women tend to focus more on attachment and control, while men focus more on enjoyment and security.
- Older respondents tend to focus more on control, less on enjoyment and slightly less on attachment; respondents close to, or in retirement, tend to focus far less on security (worries about the future).
- Respondents who have never been married tend to focus far less on security and attachment, but more on maintaining control and enjoyment.
- Single-person households are a particularly extreme form of this, being characterized by a strong focus on control.
- Respondents with children focus slightly more on security than those without children.

- Widowed and divorced/separated respondents focus heavily on control, particularly if they are over 55 years of age.
- Among those respondents who are married, men tend to focus more on security and enjoyment, while women tend to focus more on control and attachment.
- Poorer respondents tend to focus more on control and far less on enjoyment and attachment.
- Respondents who own their homes outright focus less on security than renters and those with mortgages.
- Unemployed respondents focus more on security.
- Those respondents who are employed full-time focus less on control and more on enjoyment than part-time and unemployed respondents.
- Residents of Sydney focus a little more on security and enjoyment than other Australians, while residents of Brisbane focus less on independence than other Australians.
- Respondents who feel unable to trust people locally focus more on security and independence and less on attachment than others.
- Respondents who feel that a fear of crime affects their life focus more on security and less on enjoyment.
- Poorer health and poorer sleep are both associated with greater focus on control and security and less focus on enjoyment.

Few of these associations were strong enough to cause a person's "type" to change, depending on the value of the sociodemographic variable. For example, while the percentage of women who could be characterized as type 4 in Table 12.10 (valuing attachment only) was higher than that of men (36 percent versus 32 percent), type 4 was still the most common type of person among both sexes. There were few variables that showed a different pattern of types. Age-by-relationship status was one of the strongest exceptions to this rule: unmarried over-55s were predominantly type 2 (valuing control) while widowed/divorced under-35s were predominantly type 1 (valuing security). This information is the type that a funding agency or survey company would appreciate, since it shows the degree to which "there is no average Australian in terms of ICECAP-O preferences." They have the option of applying scores – different "tariffs," or values – that are specific to a respondent's own age group and relationship status, rather than the same tariff representing the values of the mythical "representative Australian."

Age and relationship status were therefore chosen as the preliminary variables to provide different sets of "scores" to Pureprofile for use in the future classification of individuals. Three age groups (under 35, 35 to 54, 55 and over) and three relationship statuses (never married, widowed/divorced, married) mean $3 \times 3 = 9$ different sets of scores. Thus, Pureprofile can apply relevant scores to (value) the five classification ("self-measurement" tick box) answers to the quality-of-life instrument from any future respondent in the panel, provided their age and relationship status are known. It should be noted that there remains unexplained variation in the preferences (individual values/scoring) of respondents. For example, the existence of a "typical 55+-year-old Australian divorcee" is still only partly

Table 12.11 *ICECAP-O preference classes*

Age	Relationship status	Latent class				
		1	2	3	4	Total
≤34 years	Never married	0.24	0.14	0.28	**0.34**	581
	Widowed/divorced/separated	**0.38**	0.18	0.15	0.3	40
	Married	0.24	0.12	0.25	**0.39**	233
	Total	0.25	0.14	0.26	**0.35**	854
35–54 years	Never married	0.17	0.27	0.26	**0.31**	215
	Widowed/divorced/separated	0.26	**0.29**	0.16	0.29	214
	Married	0.25	0.16	0.21	**0.38**	637
	Total	0.24	0.21	0.21	**0.35**	1066
55+ years	Never married	0.14	**0.44**	0.22	0.19	36
	Widowed/divorced/separated	0.21	**0.46**	0.09	0.24	156
	Married	0.21	0.27	0.15	**0.37**	344
	Total	0.21	**0.34**	0.14	0.32	536

true, and future work should seek to build on these results in better identifying types of Australian.

Table 12.11 provides the percentage contribution of each of the four types in Table 12.10 to the various groups of Australians defined by age and relationship status. Figures in bold represent the largest contribution of a class to that subgroup.

When referring back to Table 12.10 for the interpretation of the classes, it can be seen that, among the under-35s, type 4 (strongly valuing attachment) predominates, except among those who are widowed/divorced/separated, for whom type 1 (security) is more important. Those aged 35 to 54 also tend to value attachment, although there are shifts away from type 3 (valuing enjoyment as well) towards type 2 (valuing control). Indeed, widowed/divorced/separated respondents are best characterized by type 2. Those aged 55 and over are predominantly type 2, valuing control, except for married respondents, who continue to value attachment only.

Increasing age is therefore associated with small shifts away from valuing attachment and enjoyment when the respondent is married. Those who were never married tend to value control, and the effect becomes more pronounced with age. The direction of causality is unknown here: do naturally independent people avoid marriage, or does failure to find a partner to marry lead to a stronger desire for independence at the expense of relationships? Finally, widowhood/divorce/separation tends to be associated with a strong preference for independence, although if this happens in early adulthood it is security that the individual most values.

These contributions of the four classes to each subgroup of Australians were used to weight the tariffs for the four types, to give the results shown in Table 12.12. Thus, the numbers in Table 12.10 were multiplied by those in Table 12.11 to obtain the correct

Preferences for quality of life in Australia

Table 12.12 *Australian subgroups defined by age and relationship status*

	<35 years old			35–54 years old			55+ years old		
	NM	W/D	M	NM	W/D	M	NM	W/D	M
Attachment									
Cannot have any	−0.044	−0.037	−0.047	−0.038	−0.033	−0.043	−0.025	−0.024	−0.038
A little	0.071	0.074	0.071	0.073	0.075	0.072	0.076	0.077	0.073
A lot	0.21	0.205	0.213	0.206	0.203	0.211	0.197	0.197	0.207
All	0.254	0.245	0.259	0.247	0.241	0.255	0.232	0.232	0.249
Security									
With a lot	0.017	0.009	0.018	0.02	0.015	0.016	0.021	0.016	0.018
With some	0.082	0.08	0.082	0.082	0.081	0.081	0.082	0.081	0.081
With only a little	0.126	0.13	0.126	0.125	0.128	0.126	0.126	0.128	0.126
Without any	0.197	0.208	0.196	0.193	0.201	0.198	0.194	0.199	0.196
Role									
Unable to do any	0.02	0.02	0.02	0.021	0.021	0.02	0.021	0.021	0.02
In a few	0.09	0.092	0.09	0.09	0.092	0.09	0.092	0.093	0.091
In many	0.158	0.158	0.158	0.158	0.157	0.158	0.157	0.157	0.158
All	0.183	0.183	0.183	0.183	0.183	0.183	0.183	0.183	0.183
Enjoyment									
Cannot have any	0.012	0.016	0.014	0.012	0.015	0.015	0.012	0.017	0.016
A little	0.079	0.08	0.079	0.079	0.08	0.079	0.079	0.081	0.08
A lot	0.173	0.17	0.172	0.173	0.17	0.171	0.173	0.169	0.169
All	0.188	0.184	0.186	0.188	0.185	0.185	0.189	0.184	0.183
Control									
Unable to do any	−0.006	−0.008	−0.004	−0.016	−0.018	−0.008	−0.029	−0.03	−0.017
A few things	0.075	0.075	0.075	0.072	0.072	0.074	0.068	0.068	0.072
Many things	0.148	0.15	0.147	0.152	0.153	0.149	0.157	0.158	0.153
Completely	0.178	0.181	0.176	0.188	0.19	0.18	0.202	0.203	0.189

Notes: NM= never married; W/D = widowed/divorced; M = married.

weighted average scores (values) for each subgroup. The fact that no subgroup of Australians is characterized by greater than 50 percent of one of the four types means that the differences between the four types are far less apparent when the weights are used.

12.4 Discussion and conclusions

These results provide valuable insights into the preferences of subgroups of the Australian general population. Such insights are valuable not just for their own sake but in allowing future valuation exercises to correctly sample and reweight results so as to ensure unbiased population average results.

Many of the results are unsurprising: low levels of social empowerment are associated with worries about the future, as is a lack of independence. Increased age is associated with a switch towards a preference for independence and away from relationships. Poor health is associated with a switch towards a focus on independence and worries about the future and away from relationships and enjoyment. Extreme worry about the future is a particularly insidious impairment, since people experiencing it cannot easily be compensated via other attributes; they focus all the more on the effect that attribute has on their capability. This may provide additional evidence as to the large impact that poor mental and psychological health is having upon modern society and the difficulties there appear to be in alleviating it.

However, what is surprising is the apparent lack of heterogeneity in the final subgroup tariffs: age and relationships status are only moderately associated with differences in the ICECAP-O tariff in Australia. Indeed, in the absence of a sensitivity analysis to show what difference in estimated change in well-being these might produce, it is arguable whether researchers should move away at all from the existing practice of using a population-average tariff. If it cannot be demonstrated that subgroup tariffs have real effects upon the decisions taken by policy-makers, then a single tariff can, in fact, be seen as a strength of ICECAP-O: it means that there are indeed some common fundamental values in an industrialized, mainly Anglo-Saxon country and that the ICECAP-O tariff picks these up well. It may also indicate that no further changes in the attributes for younger adults are needed in Australia, particularly in conjunction with the finding that over 200 ICECAP-O states are found in the general population – hardly an indication that the instrument is failing to pick up key aspects of life.

There are limitations to the study. ICECAP-O may be inappropriate for younger adults, though we would suggest that the data show that, if it is wrong, it is not very wrong. If we were conducting a follow-up study, we would rotate the coding in order to eliminate any possibility of the "co-occurrence problem," so that a strongly valued level three of an attribute competes with a sufficiently large number of other strongly valued levels so as to extremely precisely put its value into context.

The potential for the Case 2 BWS estimates to diverge from their DCE/Case 3 counter-parts cannot be ruled out. Flynn, Peters and Coast (2013) found that differences from the (pairwise) DCE responses – requiring individuals to choose between the profile (state) on offer and their own – were found in over 20 percent of respondents in a reanalysis of the original UK ICECAP-O Case 2 valuation data, and the fact that that study was not powered for the DCE should raise concerns still further. It has been argued by the first author and by Coast that, normatively, this is not a pertinent issue. As an index of lack of capability, the tariff based on the Case 2 estimates is entirely appropriate, being essentially a common scale that places all impairments on it (Flynn, 2010b; Flynn *et al.*, 2007). Provided society wishes (first) to eradicate instances of the worst unmet need, the ICECAP-O tariff provides the benchmark against which progress can be judged.

However, it can also be argued that the Case 2 estimates have erroneously aggregated across context effects that are key to policy-making. Suppose (building on certain results here) that the importance of boosting attachment among lonely people falls when they are offered interventions that improve their independence and enjoyment. The relative importance of the attributes varies by context, defined by how impaired they are *on that and other attributes*. Such changes might be normatively good or bad – the latter if they represent adaptation or response shift effects. It is this type of phenomenon that Flynn, Peters and Coast (2013) also attempted to quantify, and that might provide answers as to whether a case 3 multi-profile task is more appropriate than a case 2 profile task. Unlike the UK study, no such task was conducted here, making further investigation impossible. However, the ICECAP-SCM valuation exercise currently being analyzed contains both case 2 and (pairwise) DCE tasks, and should shed further light on the issue, at least in the end-of-life care context.

Finally, the representativeness (defined more broadly) of online panels is an issue. The Pureprofile panel is known to be representative[6] of the wider population on all key socio-economic variables of relevance to major surveys (including the Australian Bureau of Statistics census). However, it is unknown if it is so on a number of attitudinal variables: a person who has no time to participate in a conventional interviewer-administered official survey but who answers Pureprofile surveys on a smartphone is probably time-poor, with other impairments that such aspects of modern life may bring. Summary analyses and the "eyeballing" of Pureprofile, South Australian (SA) Health Omnibus Survey and Bristol City Council (UK) data suggest that the SA data may be quite different from the other two, despite the broad representativeness (in terms of census data) of all the data sets. The SA data are the best in terms of response rate (being interviewer-collected with multiple callbacks), yet the other two data sets appear to include non-trivial numbers of people who feel significantly disconnected from society. Such disconnection magnifies the effect of poor health on capability to an enormous degree, meaning either that online data sets contain an adverse selection of people or, if not, that the modest main effects of poor health on well-being that are seen in some data sets so far are missing huge additional interaction effects.

The large study reported here that followed good sampling practice to minimize and correct for heteroskedasticity means that the tariffs reported here may be applied to the tick box answers of members of the Australian general population in future surveys/trials. In light of Canadian data (not reported here), it is not unreasonable to conclude that the population-average values associated with ICECAP-O impairments are similar across industrialized Anglo-Saxon countries, with what variation there is primarily occurring within the population as a function of age, relationship status and, in some cases, ICECAP-O experience itself. The latter finding suggests that experience is associated with differences in preferences, but work elsewhere suggests that this is not an endorsement of the experienced utility approach. Thus, researchers can be confident that, were ICECAP-O to be included alongside health-specific instruments (such as EQ-5D or EQ-5D-5L) in trials and surveys, the tariff they use is robust – and that, finally, apples and oranges may be compared robustly in the well-being context.

---

[6] With only minor, quantifiable, differences, such as the proportion of retired people.

Applications: Case 3

Chapter 13

The stability of aggregate-level preferences in longitudinal discrete choice experiments

Towhidul Islam and Jordan J. Louviere

13.1 Introduction

The purpose of this chapter is to investigate the temporal stability of Case 3 best-worst scaling – that is, discrete choice experiments. Temporal stability matters, because, if the individuals who participate in DCEs significantly alter their preferences for the same choice options over time, it suggests that some time-dependent or event-associated process underlies the changes or that the participants do not or cannot produce reliable or accurate choices. We studied temporal stability by conducting four waves of DCEs for three product categories (toothpaste, laundry detergent and delivered pizzas).[1] The survey was administered to a random sample of members of the Pureprofile online panel in Australia; the screening criterion was the purchase or use of the product to which they were assigned in the previous three to six months. The design of the DCEs was identical for each of the three products, the only differences being the particular set of attributes that pertained to each product. To anticipate our results, we find very strong aggregate preference stability across all three products.

Case 3 BWS focuses on discrete choice experiments in which the experimental task is (at a minimum) to identify the "best" and "worst" options in each choice set. DCEs were pioneered by Louviere and Woodworth (1983), and are widely used to model sample-, segment- and/or market-level preferences and choices in marketing and other fields. After almost 30 years of applications and many academic research papers on DCEs, surprisingly few papers have investigated the stability of DCE choices over time. Indeed, most external (real-market) prediction tests in marketing and other fields involved relatively short time lags between DCEs and market observations (though see McFadden and Reid, 1975), with some other tests of "back-casting" to prior observations such as scanner panel choices (for example, Swait and Andrews, 2003). So, despite academic and commercial interest in whether DCE choices are stable over repeated administration in panel or cross-sectional samples, there is little work on this topic.

When DCEs are used to forecast the likely uptake or choices of new products and/or technologies, there are time lags between DCE data collection and market introduction.

[1] This research was supported by the Social Science and Humanities Research Council of Canada (SSHRC: Standard Grant no.430060).

Likewise, there are lags (typically shorter) between DCEs and introductions of product variants and/or changes in marketing, management or public policy manifest as changes in market offerings. Thus, unless choices observed in DCEs are stable, it is likely that the longer the time delay between DCEs (or other collection of choice information) and market implementation, the less likely estimated models will forecast accurately (for example, Kivetz, Netzer and Srinivasan, 2004). Moreover, without longitudinal DCE choice data, one cannot study choice dynamics, and there is ample evidence that choices can and do change over time in response to changes in products, competition and economic and other circumstances (for example, Erdem and Keane, 1996).

Moving beyond an obvious need to accurately model and forecast choices of new product introductions and policy interventions, research on DCE choices is incomplete, to the extent that it does not capture true, underlying preference and/or choice processes. However, the majority of published papers using DCEs to study choice behavior exhibit little interest in understanding such processes; instead, the authors seem more interested in fitting state-of-the-art and/or new extensions to existing statistical choice models. Thus, as noted by Louviere and Meyer (2008) and Louviere, Street *et al.* (2008), few published papers on choice modeling have tried to integrate findings from psychological and behavioral studies of preferences and choices. Indeed, many papers in judgment and decision-making and consumer behavior focus on such issues, with many reports of preference instability, including claims that humans "construct" preferences and/or learn as they encounter new product information and/or interact with others and markets (for example, Payne, Bettman and Schkade, 1999). Thus, the stability of choices and associated choice model parameters over time in repeated DCEs matters both academically and managerially.

To anticipate our approach and findings, we investigated choice stability associated with the same panel of consumers participating in four waves of DCEs for three different, well-known consumer products observed six months apart in March 2010, September 2010, March 2011 and September 2011. We found evidence for highly stable choices and model parameters for well-known products.

13.2 Literature review

We begin by reviewing three streams of research that directly bear on preferences over time: (1) work that assumes/claims preferences are temporally stable; (2) work that posits preferences are not stable but, instead, are "constructed"; and (3) work that posits preferences have two components, one inherently stable, and another constructed. We now discuss these three streams.

13.2.1 Preferences are stable

A key underlying assumption in much of economics associated with the rational choice theory approach is that consumers are rational and have well-defined preferences that do not depend on particular description of options or on specific methods used to elicit the preferences. As noted by McFadden (1999), economists vary in the degree to which they believe that well-defined preferences exist, with a common assumption being that "each individual has stable and coherent preferences" (Rabin, 1998: 11) and "people know their preferences" and have the ability and competence to evaluate options and maximize value (Freeman, 1993: 7). It is also assumed that an individual facing the same choice at different points in time will express the same preference (Friedman, 1962; Becker, 1976).

Alston and Chalfant (1991) and de Palma, Myers and Papageorgiou (1994) (among others) provided a different view of preference/choice stability associated with misspeci-fication of the underlying behavioral process. Similarly, recent work by Salisbury and Feinberg (2010a) and Fiebig *et al.* (2010) suggests that preference/choice instability can be (and is) associated with differences in the consistency with which individuals in DCEs make choices. The latter work is consistent with the de Palma, Myers and Papageorgiou (1994) view of mistakes in choice and work in psychology dating back to Thurstone's (1927) original formulation of random-utility-based choice models.

Some behavioral researchers think preferences can be stable. For example, Fournier (1998) suggested that consumers have long-term, lasting attachments to particular brands, and Fischhoff, Slovic and Lichtenstein (1980) suggested that individuals likely have stable preferences for issues that are familiar, simple and directly experienced. Other non-DCE preference elicitation method researchers also find support for temporal preference (for example, Llewellyn-Thomas, Sutherland and Thiel, 1993; O'Connor *et al.*, 1987; Tsevat *et al.*, 1993; Schwappach and Strasmann, 2006).

San Miguel, Ryan and Scott (2002) and Salkeld *et al.* (2005) had previously investigated the temporal stability of DCE preferences. San Miguel, Ryan and Scott (2002) replicated a DCE two months apart to elicit patient preferences for out-of-hours health care for children. The second DCE sample consisted of two groups: (1) one that experienced the service after the first survey; and (2) a control group that had not experienced the service after the first DCE. They showed that preferences did not change with service experiences. Salkeld *et al.* (2005) replicated two DCEs two weeks apart to test preference stability in the surgical management of colorectal cancer, finding agreement in the two DCEs. However, a more detailed analysis indicated that less well educated people exhibited more preference instability.

13.2.2 Preferences are (mainly) constructed

Bettman (1979) proposed that consumers do not make decisions consistent with rational choice theory, and Bettman, Luce and Payne (1998) posited that consumers often do not have well-defined preferences but, rather, construct them using a variety of strategies contingent on task demands. Payne, Bettman and Schkade (1999) went further, suggesting that preferences are mainly constructed at the time of a decision, implying that situational/ constructive components should be larger than stable components. Tversky (1996: 17) also noted that "people do not maximize a precomputed preference order, but construct their choices in light of the available options." This prior work suggests that preferences are constructed and respond differently to monetary incentives, information framing, decision task complexity, and so on. This perspective suggests that preferences are shaped by interactions of cognitive ability in information processing with properties of decision tasks (for example, Payne, Bettman and Johnson, 1992; Slovic, 1995).

As noted earlier, de Palma, Myers and Papageorgiou (1994) suggested that, even if consumers have identical preferences, they can differ in their ability to choose. In turn, this implies that consumers with less ability to choose should make more mistakes as decision task complexity increases. This view is consistent with Salisbury and Feinberg (2010a) and Fiebig *et al.* (2010), who explicitly recognized the role of choice consistency (that is, error variability) in choice. More generally, the more attributes that are used to describe options in DCEs (all else equal), the greater the task complexity (for example, Lussier and Olshavsky, 1979; Miller, 1956). Thus, we need to better understand the role of choice consistency in DCEs to determine if "preference construction" and its associated drivers impact systematic (mean) or error (random) components of preferences or both. In turn, this should allow one to determine if "constructed preferences" are an artifact or a failure to properly control for and/or incorporate choice consistency.

13.2.3 Preferences are both stable and constructed

Simonson (2008) proposed that construction can influence preferences, but that individuals also have inherently stable preference components less susceptible to transient conditions. For example, he suggested that individuals often have pre-existing preferences for specific features unrelated to contexts that can influence receptiveness or tendency to dis/like objects incorporating such features. Simonson (2008) further suggested that preference construction research was largely confined to local decisions less relevant to more enduring preferences. This view is consistent with that of Bettman and Zins (1977), who examined consumers' verbal protocols while shopping for groceries and found evidence for preference stability. More specifically, they found that shoppers' coded protocols suggested that more than 20 percent of choices seemed constructed, but more than 40 percent were stable, and another 35 percent seemed to use rules (such as "Buy the cheapest") that could lead to seemingly stable preferences (see also Amir and Levav, 2008).

Thus, the issue of preference/choice stability over time in DCEs is important and under-researched, and, from a choice modeling standpoint, most work on temporal preference stability has used revealed preference data. This chapter focuses on this gap by investigating preference/choice stability over time in longitudinal DCEs.

13.3 Longitudinal DCEs for familiar products

We designed DCEs for three well-established and familiar products (laundry detergents, toothpastes and delivered pizzas) and administered them as part of a larger survey to a panel of consumers recruited from a large web panel provider. Participants were screened based on (1) having purchased in the category in the past three months and (2) a willingness to participate in four successive survey waves over two years. Each wave was approximately six months apart, and each had an initial sample of 600 consumers. We dealt with attrition following wave 1 by randomly sampling from the same web panel sampling frame and "topping up" the sample. We found remarkable stability of aggregate preferences/choices for all wave–top-up combinations (16), but we discuss only the results to the four major waves.

We used the BIBD design approach proposed by Louviere, Street *et al*. (2008) to design the DCEs: we designed a set of product profiles (attribute-level combinations, product descriptions), and then used a balanced incomplete block design to assign the profiles to choice sets. Specifically, we designed 16 profiles (choice options) using an orthogonal main effects plan sampled from a $4^3 \times 2^6$ factorial. We then used a BIBD to assign the 16 profiles to 20 choice sets that each have four options. Attributes and levels for each product category are listed in Appendix 13.A (Tables 13.A1 to 13.A3). Screenshots of task instructions and the choice task are in Appendix 13.B for the toothpaste DCE. Laundry detergent and pizza instructions and task layout were identical. Actual brand names were used but are disguised in the screenshot. We now discuss the results of the study.

13.4 Research results

13.4.1 Choice proportions by BIBD profiles

Table 13.1 shows choice proportions for each of the 16 profiles for the four waves, clearly indicating the temporal stability of profile choices. Choice proportions for each of the 16 product profiles (all three products pooled together) for waves are shown in Figure 13.1.

We used a non-parametric Friedman's analysis of variance (ANOVA) test to examine choice stability among the four waves for the 16 profiles (see Table 13.1). The advantage of this test is that it is robust under non-normality assumptions and for small samples of profiles. *Friedman's ANOVA* (Friedman, 1937) is a non-parametric test that can be used to test the claim that samples are drawn from dependent populations with the same distribution. Friedman's ANOVA investigates the score differences between treatments of blocks. It can be used to answer the question of whether the samples come from the same population. Friedman's ANOVA measures whether the location of the distribution changed over time. The only assumptions required to implement the Friedman's ANOVA test are that the data come from a simple random sample and that they can be ranked. We did a Friedman test for each product and for the pooled products, with the results shown in Table 13.2. The null hypothesis is that each ranking of random variables within a longitudinal wave is equally likely – that is, each wave has identical effects. We retained the null hypothesis in all four tests, clearly supporting the stability of product profile preferences for well-known and understood products and attributes.

Table 13.1 *Proportions of choices (most preferred) by BIBD profiles*

Profile	Pizza				Detergent				Toothpaste			
	W1	W2	W3	W4	W1	W2	W3	W4	W1	W2	W3	W4
1	0.31	0.26	0.30	0.30	0.47	0.53	0.52	0.52	0.36	0.38	0.39	0.36
2	0.50	0.45	0.44	0.42	0.48	0.45	0.44	0.42	0.22	0.21	0.21	0.22
3	0.24	0.23	0.22	0.20	0.09	0.11	0.09	0.09	0.03	0.02	0.02	0.03
4	0.03	0.04	0.06	0.05	0.04	0.08	0.06	0.06	0.02	0.02	0.02	0.03
5	0.28	0.28	0.29	0.28	0.47	0.51	0.49	0.50	0.48	0.49	0.48	0.48
6	0.12	0.14	0.13	0.13	0.30	0.29	0.33	0.33	0.11	0.10	0.11	0.12
7	0.49	0.44	0.46	0.47	0.21	0.18	0.18	0.20	0.45	0.42	0.41	0.39
8	0.16	0.14	0.12	0.11	0.19	0.17	0.13	0.14	0.11	0.11	0.11	0.12
9	0.39	0.44	0.43	0.45	0.39	0.36	0.40	0.42	0.28	0.26	0.27	0.28
10	0.32	0.31	0.32	0.31	0.16	0.18	0.18	0.16	0.21	0.22	0.22	0.23
11	0.08	0.09	0.09	0.09	0.34	0.33	0.34	0.33	0.23	0.24	0.22	0.24
12	0.12	0.12	0.12	0.15	0.10	0.09	0.13	0.13	0.07	0.08	0.07	0.07
13	0.48	0.51	0.55	0.51	0.16	0.16	0.15	0.16	0.27	0.26	0.31	0.29
14	0.16	0.17	0.16	0.17	0.19	0.18	0.18	0.15	0.60	0.62	0.62	0.59
15	0.09	0.11	0.08	0.10	0.14	0.15	0.15	0.16	0.20	0.21	0.22	0.23
16	0.25	0.25	0.23	0.27	0.26	0.24	0.23	0.23	0.37	0.36	0.31	0.32

Note: W = wave.

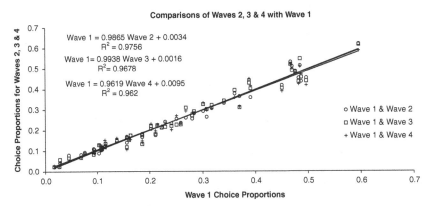

Figure 13.1 Scatter plots of choice proportions for 16 profiles (detergent, toothpaste and pizza)

13.4.2 *Stability of relative importance of product attributes over time*

The relative importance of product attributes is measured by (1) calculating the range of the estimated parameters for each level of each attribute (maximum estimate – minimum estimate), and then (2) dividing each attribute range by the total range of all nine attributes. These calculations for the three product categories are shown in Table 13.3 and Figure 13.2 (all three products pooled). We also estimated a *generalized multinomial logit model* (G-MNL: for

Table 13.2 *Friedman test results*

Test		Pizza	Detergent	Toothpaste	Pooled model (all three products)
Friedman	N (profiles)	16	16	16	48
	Chi-sq.	0.279	0.450	2.642	1.616
	Df	3	3	3	3
	Asymp. sig.	0.964	0.930	0.450	0.656

Table 13.3 *Product attribute relative importance (%) and ranking over time*

Product	Product attributes	Relative importance (%)				Ranks			
		W1	W2	W3	W4	W1	W2	W3	W4
Detergent	Price	29.41	33.62	35.01	35.26	1	1	1	1
	Size	26.14	29.75	31.12	33.51	2	2	2	2
	Brand	11.33	6.18	9.13	9.38	3	4	3	3
	Cold water wash	10.33	9.62	8.25	8.10	4	3	4	4
	Fragrance	6.83	5.03	3.47	4.65	5	6	7	5
	Color care and removes stains	6.16	6.10	3.40	3.07	6	5	8	6
	Eco-friendly	4.91	3.54	3.48	2.95	7	7	5	7
	Fabric softener	3.71	3.03	3.47	2.30	8	9	6	8
	Form	1.17	3.13	2.67	0.79	9	8	9	9
Toothpaste	Brand	29.75	28.93	28.83	27.12	1	1	1	1
	Price	21.62	22.20	23.80	23.51	2	2	2	2
	Strengthens teeth and enamel	10.41	9.73	10.16	10.15	3	3	3	4
	Removes stains and whitens	9.56	9.30	8.26	7.27	4	5	6	6
	Fluoride protection	9.24	8.42	8.27	10.78	5	6	5	3
	Freshens breath	8.78	9.54	9.85	8.36	6	4	4	5
	Size	6.97	7.51	6.38	6.46	7	7	7	7
	Container	3.22	4.27	4.06	5.50	8	8	8	8
	Flavor	0.44	0.10	0.39	0.86	9	9	9	9
Pizza	Price	27.98	28.52	33.30	27.10	1	1	1	1
	Number of toppings	14.79	18.59	18.89	19.88	2	2	2	2
	Free delivery	13.85	13.57	11.11	12.29	3	3	4	3
	Free drink	10.26	10.53	7.39	5.66	4	4	5	8
	Free dessert	9.61	7.05	7.05	9.18	5	7	6	5
	Free salad	9.43	7.52	5.75	6.60	6	5	7	7
	Delivery time	6.58	6.74	12.07	7.44	7	8	3	6
	Brand	6.46	7.19	3.78	10.67	8	6	8	4
	Type of crust	1.03	0.29	0.65	1.19	9	9	9	9

Notes: W = wave; product attributes are listed by rank order of first wave of data.

Table 13.4 *Friedman test results*

Test		Pizza	Detergent	Toothpaste	Pooled model (all three products)
Friedman	N (nos. of attributes)	9	9	9	27
	Chi-sq.	3.533	0.600	0.733	2.956
	Df	3	3	3	3
	Asymp. sig.	0.316	0.896	0.865	0.399

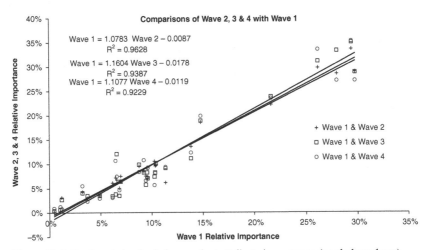

Figure 13.2 Scatter plots of relative product attribute importance (pooled products)

details, see Fiebig *et al.*, 2010) for each product to account for unobserved individual differences and variance heterogeneity, but to save space we do not present these results.

Table 13.3 reveals that relative importance and rank order are stable for the most important product features. For all three categories the rank orders are the same for the first three most important attributes, which represent 60 to 75 percent of attribute impacts across categories. There are some shifts in relative importance measures for less important features, but they play a lesser role in choices. We used the Friedman test to test differences in choice stability for the nine product attributes (see Table 13.3) across waves, as shown in Table 13.4.

The null hypothesis was that each ranking of the random variables within a longitudinal wave is equally likely – that is, that the waves have identical effects. We retained the null hypothesis for all four tests, supporting our hypothesis of preference stability for the relative importance of product attributes over time for cases when products are well known and attributes well understood.

13.4.3 *Stability of model predictions over time*

We estimated conditional logit models (McFadden, 1974) and mixed logit models (McFadden and Train, 2000) from the DCE choice data of each product in each wave (3 products × 4 waves). We used each model to predict the observed aggregate choice

(a)

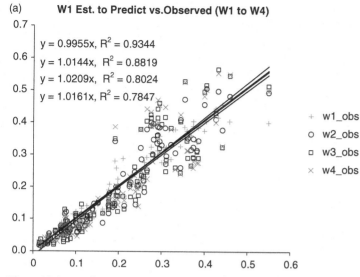

W1 Est. to Predict vs.Observed (W1 to W4)

$y = 0.9955x$, $R^2 = 0.9344$
$y = 1.0144x$, $R^2 = 0.8819$
$y = 1.0209x$, $R^2 = 0.8024$
$y = 1.0161x$, $R^2 = 0.7847$

+ w1_obs
o w2_obs
□ w3_obs
× w4_obs

Figure 13.3a Predictions using wave 1 estimates

(b)

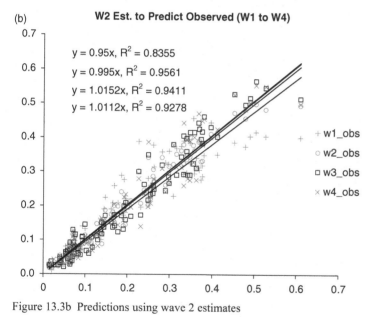

W2 Est. to Predict Observed (W1 to W4)

$y = 0.95x$, $R^2 = 0.8355$
$y = 0.995x$, $R^2 = 0.9561$
$y = 1.0152x$, $R^2 = 0.9411$
$y = 1.0112x$, $R^2 = 0.9278$

+ w1_obs
o w2_obs
□ w3_obs
× w4_obs

Figure 13.3b Predictions using wave 2 estimates

proportions for each choice alternative in each choice set, both including and excluding the choice of none (20 sets × 4 or 5 alternatives per set). The results were very similar for all predictions, showing high stability and excellent fits to the data for each product in each wave, regardless of which model or model type made the predictions. To save space we show only the graphs for pizza using conditional logit models to make predictions, in Figures 13.3a to 13.3d. All other graphs of observed versus predicted choices were similar.

(c)

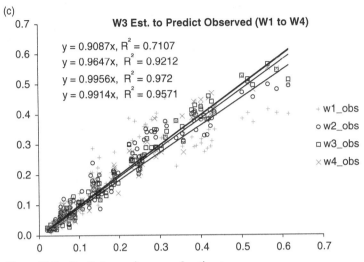

Figure 13.3c Predictions using wave 3 estimates

(d)

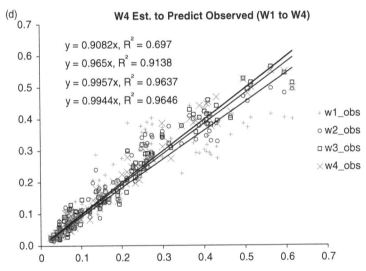

Figure 13.3d Predictions using wave 4 estimates

13.5 Discussion and conclusions

The question of whether consumer preferences are inherent or constructed has long been debated in several literatures. In particular, whether or not preferences are stable poses important issues for applied research in many fields. Current models that purport to capture consumer preferences should be able to predict their evolution over time, whether the research is academic or applied. This chapter focused on the stability (internal and external) of consumer preferences for three familiar consumer products in DCEs, commonly used to study choices in several disciplines. We found that preferences were stable for each of the familiar products. Specifically, the results for product choice proportions and relative attribute importance did not significantly differ across four waves of a panel DCE study for toothpaste, laundry detergent and delivered pizzas. Choice models estimated from the DCEs showed high prediction stability and excellent fits to the data for each product and wave (regardless of type of statistical choice model). In turn, this suggests that for well-known products not subject to external shocks, such as sharp price increases or innovation disruptions, aggregate sample preferences are likely to be stable and can be studied with DCEs. We also showed we can predict aggregate sample observed choices for each wave using model estimates from any wave. However, we did not study the stability of individual choices – a focus of ongoing research.

Appendix 13.A

Table 13.A1 *Toothpaste attributes and their levels*

								Toothpaste					

1	2	3	4	5	6	7	8	9
	Price				Strengthens	Removes		
	per			Freshens	teeth and	stains and		Fluoride
Brand	100g	Size	Container	breath	enamel	whitens	Flavor	protection
Colgate	$1.90	110g	Tube	No	No	No	Mild	No
Macleans	$2.60	130g	Pump	Yes	Yes	Yes	Mint	Yes
Oral-B	$3.30	150g						
Homebrand	$4.00	170g						

Table 13.A2 *Pizza attributes and their levels*

				Large pizza (12")				
		Delivery time	Nos. of	Free	Type of	Free	Free	Free
Brand	Price	(mins.)	toppings	delivery	crust	dessert	drink	salad
Pizza Hut	$12	10	1	No	Regular	No	No	No
Domino's	$14	20	3	Yes	Thin	Yes	Yes	Yes
Eagle Boys	$16	30						
Pizza Haven	$18	40						

Table 13.A3 *Detergent attributes and their levels*

					Laundry detergent			
Brand	Price 100g (or 100 ml)	Size (nos. of washes)	Form	Cold water wash	Eco-friendly	Fabric softener	Color care and removes stains	Fragrance
Radiant	$0.40	0.5kg/litre (10 washes)	Powder	No	No	Not added	No	No
Omo	$0.60	1.0kg/litre (20 washes)	Liquid	Yes	Yes	Added	Yes	Yes
Cold Power	$0.80	1.5kg/litre (30 washes)						
Dynamo	$1.00	2.0kg/litre (40 washes)						

Appendix 13.B Screenshots for toothpaste DCE

In this section of the survey, we will show you **20** sets of **4** toothpaste products that you can choose.

The 4 toothpaste products are described by the features that you reported on in previous questions. What we want you to do is simple: for each of the 20 sets of 4 products, please tell us

1) Which of the four toothpastes would you prefer the **most**?
2) Which of the four toothpastes would you prefer the **least**?
3) Would you actually purchase your most preferred toothpaste if it was available?

Please click on " >> " to continue.

<<	>>

<u>Set 1</u>

Features	Toothpaste A	Toothpaste B	Toothpaste C	Toothpaste D
Brand	Brand A	Brand B	Brand C	Brand D
Price per 100g	$2.80	$2.00	$4.40	$2.80
Size	150g	150g	130g	130g
Container	Pump	Tube	Tube	Tube
Freshens Breath	✓		✓	
Strengthen Enamel	✓	✓		✓
Whitens Teeth		✓		✓
Flavour	Mint	Mint	Mint	Mild
Has Fluoride	✓		✓	✓

Which of the four toothpastes would you prefer the **most**?

  ○ Toothpaste A   ○ Toothpaste B   ○ Toothpaste C   ○ Toothpaste D

Which of the four toothpastes would you prefer the **least**?

  ○ Toothpaste A   ○ Toothpaste B   ○ Toothpaste C   ○ Toothpaste D

Would you actually purchase your most preferred toothpaste if it was available?

  ○ Yes
  ○ No

Chapter 14

Case 3 best-worst analysis using delivered pizza and toothpaste examples

Bart D. Frischknecht and Jordan J. Louviere

14.1 Introduction

The purpose of this chapter is to illustrate how to use Case 3 BW data to understand preference differences between groups and between individuals in a similar way to what we would do with data from a traditional DCE that collected only first-choice (best) responses. Traditionally, collecting best and worst choices has been thought of as a data augmentation process (for example, see Louviere, Street *et al.*, 2008). This view is consistent when best and worst choices are inversely related because, by observing both best and worst choices for a particular choice set, one gets more information about order, which is what matters in choices.

Consider the potential advantages of collecting Case 3 BW data:

(1) more data per respondent from each choice task, thus providing greater precision for model estimates; and
(2) using simple BW measures instead of (or in place of) more sophisticated choice models as a way to estimate preferences.

When the inverse relationship between best and worst choices does not hold, choice models that combine data from best and worst choices generally make poorer predictions of best or worst choices than models that rely, respectively, on either best or worst choices alone. When and if this occurs, the advantage of case 3 BW data is different:

(3) one can gain additional insights into individual decision processes by comparing differences between best and worst choices.

This chapter focuses on illustrating how to use a balanced incomplete block design and simple BW measures introduced in earlier chapters (and formally in Chapter 5) to (1) test assumptions about the substitutability of best and worst data, (2) show how to cluster the data based on BW count data (BW scores) and (3) estimate aggregate- and individual-level models. We illustrate how to apply these ideas about case 3 BW data at each level of aggregation, using two data sets from online choice experiments involving delivered pizzas and toothpaste.

To anticipate our results, we find considerable evidence for differences between best and worst choices in both data sets. Specifically, the evidence includes deviation from inverse proportionality between best and worst choice counts; lack of improvement in the standard errors (that is, the precision of the parameter estimates) for many parameters for models that use both best and worst choices compared to the same models estimated using only the best choices; and better predictions of best and worst choices, respectively, from models estimated using only best choices or only worst choices compared with models estimated using both best and worst choices. These differences are maintained at an aggregate, segment and individual level; and may be associated with different preferences in making best or worst choices.

14.2 Data set description

We study delivered pizzas similar to the example in section 4.2.1, but, instead of four 4-level attributes and two 2-level attributes, the example has three 4-level attributes and six 2-level attributes, as shown in Table 14.1. Toothpaste data attributes and levels are shown in Table 14.2.

Sixteen pizza (or toothpaste) profiles were developed using an orthogonal main effects plan, as shown in Table 14.3. These 16 profiles were assigned to choice sets using a BIBD, as shown in Table 14.4. Each alternative occurs five times and co-occurs with each other

Table 14.1 *Attributes and levels for delivered pizza example*

Attribute	Level 0	Level 1	Level 2	Level 3
Brand	Pizza Hut	Dominos	Eagle Boys	Pizza Haven
Price	$12	$14	$16	$18
Delivery time	10 mins.	20 mins.	30 mins.	40 mins.
Toppings	1	3		
Free delivery	No	Yes		
Crust type	Regular	Thin		
Free dessert	No	Yes		
Free drink	No	Yes		
Free salad	No	Yes		

Table 14.2 *Attributes and levels for toothpaste example*

Attribute	Level 0	Level 1	Level 2	Level 3
Brand	Colgate	Macleans	Oral-B	Homebrand
Price	$2.00	$2.80	$3.60	$4.40
Size	110 g	130 g	150 g	170 g
Container	Tube	Pump		
Breath	No	Yes		
Strengthens	No	Yes		
Whitens	No	Yes		
Flavor	Mild	Mint		
Fluoride	No	Yes		

Table 14.3 *Sixteen profiles for delivered pizza example*

Profile	Brand	Price	Delivery time	Toppings	Free delivery	Crust type	Free dessert	Free drink	Free salad
1	Pizza Haven	$12	40 mins.	1 topping	Yes	Regular	Yes	No	Yes
2	Pizza Haven	$14	30 mins.	3 toppings	Yes	Thin	No	Yes	Yes
3	Pizza Haven	$16	20 mins.	3 toppings	No	Regular	Yes	Yes	No
4	Pizza Haven	$18	10 mins.	1 topping	No	Thin	No	No	No
5	Eagle Boys	$12	30 mins.	1 topping	No	Thin	Yes	Yes	No
6	Eagle Boys	$14	40 mins.	3 toppings	No	Regular	No	No	No
7	Eagle Boys	$16	10 mins.	3 toppings	Yes	Thin	Yes	No	Yes
8	Eagle Boys	$18	20 mins.	1 topping	Yes	Regular	No	Yes	Yes
9	Dominos	$12	20 mins.	3 toppings	Yes	Thin	No	No	No
10	Dominos	$14	10 mins.	1 topping	Yes	Regular	Yes	Yes	No
11	Dominos	$16	40 mins.	1 topping	No	Thin	No	Yes	Yes
12	Dominos	$18	30 mins.	3 toppings	No	Regular	Yes	No	Yes
13	Pizza Hut	$12	10 mins.	3 toppings	No	Regular	No	Yes	Yes
14	Pizza Hut	$14	20 mins.	1 topping	No	Thin	Yes	No	Yes
15	Pizza Hut	$16	30 mins.	1 topping	Yes	Regular	No	No	No
16	Pizza Hut	$18	40 mins.	3 toppings	Yes	Thin	Yes	Yes	No

Table 14.4 *BIBD for 20 choice sets, four options per set*

Set	Four options in each set			
1	2	5	8	14
2	1	5	6	7
3	5	9	12	16
4	4	5	11	15
5	3	5	10	13
6	1	2	3	4
7	2	6	9	11
8	2	7	13	16
9	2	10	12	15
10	1	8	9	10
11	6	8	13	15
12	4	7	8	12
13	3	8	11	16
14	1	14	15	16
15	3	6	12	14
16	7	10	11	14
17	4	9	13	14
18	1	11	12	13
19	4	6	10	16
20	3	7	9	15

alternative once. The toothpaste design follows the same pattern as the pizza design, with toothpaste attribute levels replacing pizza attribute levels.

Respondents were asked to select their most and least preferred profile from the four profiles in each set; then were asked if they actually would buy their most preferred option (profile). A screenshot of one choice set (choice scenario) with the choice questions is given in Figure 14.1. This chapter focuses exclusively on the most and least preferred choices, and ignores the purchase intention question. Respondents were recruited from an Australian commercial web panel, with 503 complete responses collected.

14.3 Best-worst measures

As with Case 1 and Case 2 BW applications, several aggregate and individual measures can be computed using most preferred and least preferred choice counts. In particular, we have profile-level information similar to Case 1, and we have attribute-level information similar to Case 2. We describe and discuss examples of both types of measures at the aggregate, segment and individual levels, and discuss the apparent differences between best and worst choices in the pizza and toothpaste examples.

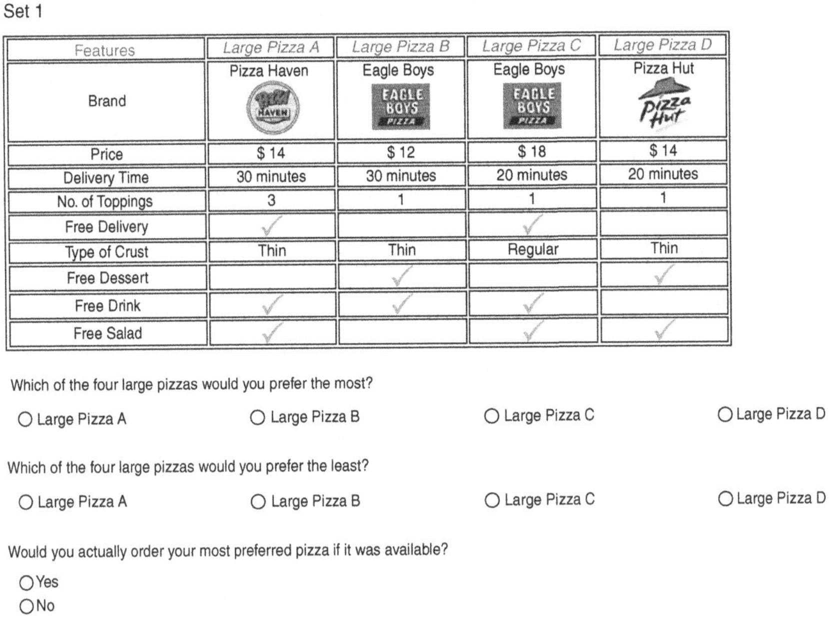

Set 1

Features	Large Pizza A	Large Pizza B	Large Pizza C	Large Pizza D
Brand	Pizza Haven	Eagle Boys	Eagle Boys	Pizza Hut
Price	$ 14	$ 12	$ 18	$ 14
Delivery Time	30 minutes	30 minutes	20 minutes	20 minutes
No. of Toppings	3	1	1	1
Free Delivery	✓		✓	
Type of Crust	Thin	Thin	Regular	Thin
Free Dessert		✓		✓
Free Drink	✓	✓	✓	
Free Salad	✓		✓	✓

Which of the four large pizzas would you prefer the most?

○ Large Pizza A   ○ Large Pizza B   ○ Large Pizza C   ○ Large Pizza D

Which of the four large pizzas would you prefer the least?

○ Large Pizza A   ○ Large Pizza B   ○ Large Pizza C   ○ Large Pizza D

Would you actually order your most preferred pizza if it was available?

○ Yes
○ No

Figure 14.1 Screenshot of a choice task for the pizza data

14.3.1 Measures using profiles

One simple measure that provides an estimate of the preferences (choices) of each profile in the DCE is to count the number of times each profile is chosen as most preferred and the number of times each profile is chosen as least preferred. The measure of interest is the BW score, which is the difference between the number of times a profile is chosen as most or least preferred. These three measures can be computed for the entire sample (the aggregate level), for subsamples (the segment level) or for each respondent (the individual level). Profiles then can be ranked from most to least preferred using any of the three measures.

Each respondent completed the same DCE, with the BIBD ensuring that each profile appeared five times. At the individual level, BW scores (differences) range between –5 and 5. At the segment and aggregate level, the ranges scale by the number of respondents in each.

The pattern of profile BW scores for each individual provides good candidate data for clustering the individuals. In other words, similar respondents can be grouped according to their similarity in BW scores, using, for example, k-means clustering or archetypal analysis.

14.3.2 Measures using attribute levels

Three simple attribute measures for attributes and levels are counts of the number of times each attribute level is chosen as most preferred and least preferred, and calculating the difference in the number of times an attribute level is chosen most or least preferred. These three measures, adjusted for frequency of appearance, can be computed for the entire sample (the aggregate level), for subsamples (the segment level) or for each respondent (the individual level). Attribute levels can be ranked from most to least preferred using any of the three measures.

Each respondent completed the same DCE in which each profile appeared five times. The profiles were designed based on a 16-profile OMEP, which means that the 4-level attributes appear in four profiles and the 2-level attributes appear in eight profiles. We must take into account (that is, control for) the fact that the 2-level attributes appear in the survey twice as frequently as the 4-level attributes and thus are twice as likely to be chosen.

The attribute-level counts can be normalized to account for availability by taking the product of the attribute-level count and the ratio of the number of attribute levels for a particular attribute and the largest number of attribute levels for any attribute. For example, crust type is a 2-level attribute. The counts for crust type levels should be normalized by taking the product of the attribute-level counts and 1/2 – that is, 2 levels/4 levels.

The pattern of attribute-level BW scores (differences) for each individual is an alternative data candidate for clustering compared to profile count differences. Similar respondents can be grouped according to their similarity in BW differences using, for example, k-means clustering or archetypal analysis.

We expect best counts to be proportional to the inverse of worst counts if best choices and worst choices reflect the same underlying decision rules. It follows that best counts should also be proportional to the square root of the ratio of best counts over worst counts, and the BW scores (differences) should be proportional to the natural logarithm of the square root of the ratio of best counts over worst counts. Informal graphical tests can be used to check for the potential compliance (up to a scaling constant) of the proportionality of best and worst data. These proportionality checks require that all attribute levels be chosen as best and chosen as worst at least one time each, as the checks involve ratios of best and worst counts. This requirement is likely to be satisfied at the aggregate level but is unlikely to be satisfied at the individual level, making it difficult to assess the substitutability of best and worst data for individuals.

14.3.3 BW measures for pizza data

Table 14.5 shows the pizza profiles ordered by BW scores (differences). The three-topping level appears in the top four profiles and the one-topping level appears in the bottom four profiles. Low price, free delivery and short delivery time commonly appear among top-ranked profiles, but not exclusively, and no brand clearly dominates.

Table 14.6 shows the ranking of attribute levels by how many times (normalized) they were chosen best or chosen worst and the normalized BW scores. Price, number of

Table 14.5 *Pizza profiles ordered according to BW differences*

Profile	BW diff.	Brand	Price	Delivery time	Toppings	Free delivery	Crust type	Free dessert	Free drink	Free salad
13	1003	Pizza Hut	$12	10 mins.	3 toppings	No	Regular	No	Yes	Yes
7	872	Eagle Boys	$16	10 mins.	3 toppings	Yes	Thin	Yes	No	Yes
2	797	Pizza Haven	$14	30 mins.	3 toppings	Yes	Thin	No	Yes	Yes
9	750	Dominos	$12	20 mins.	3 toppings	Yes	Thin	No	No	No
10	589	Dominos	$14	10 mins.	1 topping	Yes	Regular	Yes	Yes	No
1	270	Pizza Haven	$12	40 mins.	1 topping	Yes	Regular	Yes	No	Yes
5	194	Eagle Boys	$12	30 mins.	1 topping	No	Thin	Yes	Yes	No
3	118	Pizza Haven	$16	20 mins.	3 toppings	No	Regular	Yes	Yes	No
14	−52	Pizza Hut	$14	20 mins.	1 topping	No	Thin	Yes	No	Yes
16	−161	Pizza Hut	$18	40 mins.	3 toppings	Yes	Thin	Yes	Yes	No
12	−366	Dominos	$18	30 mins.	3 toppings	No	Regular	Yes	No	Yes
6	−505	Eagle Boys	$14	40 mins.	3 toppings	No	Regular	No	No	No
8	−571	Eagle Boys	$18	20 mins.	1 topping	Yes	Regular	No	Yes	Yes
15	−675	Pizza Hut	$16	30 mins.	1 topping	Yes	Regular	No	No	No
11	−808	Dominos	$16	40 mins.	1 topping	No	Thin	No	Yes	Yes
4	−1455	Pizza Haven	$18	10 mins.	1 topping	No	Thin	No	No	No

Table 14.6 *Attribute levels ranked according to normalized best counts, worst counts and BW differences for the pizza example*

Best		Worst		BW diff.	
Price – $12	3760	Price – $12	1543	Price – $12	2217
Deliv. time – 10 mins.	3399	Price – $14	1795	Toppings – 3	1254
Toppings – 3	3232	Free dessert – yes	1960	Deliv. time – 10 mins.	1009
Free deliv. – yes	3012	Toppings – 3	1978	Free deliv. – yes	935.5
Free drink – yes	2811.5	Free deliv. – yes	2076.5	Price – $14	829
Free salad – yes	2768.5	Deliv. time – 20 mins.	2105	Free dessert – yes	732
Crust type – thin	2708	Free salad – yes	2196	Free drink – yes	580.5
Free dessert – yes	2692	Free drink – yes	2231	Free salad – yes	572.5
Price – $14	2624	Brand – Dominos	2339	Deliv. time – 20 mins.	245
Brand – Pizza Hut	2535	Deliv. time – 10 mins	2390	Brand – Dominos	165
Brand – Pizza Haven	2532	Crust type – regular	2390.5	Brand – Pizza Hut	115
Brand – Dominos	2504	Brand – Pizza Hut	2420	Crust type – thin	68.5
Brand – Eagle Boys	2489	Deliv. time – 30 mins.	2424	Brand – Eagle Boys	−10
Deliv. time – 30 mins.	2374	Brand – Eagle Boys	2499	Deliv. time – 30 mins.	−50
Deliv. time – 20 mins.	2350	Crust type – thin	2639.5	Crust type – regular	−68.5
Free dessert – no	2338	Price – $16	2734	Brand – Pizza Haven	−270
Crust type – regular	2322	Free drink – no	2799	Price – $16	−493
Free salad – no	2261.5	Brand – Pizza Haven	2802	Free salad – no	−572.5
Price – $16	2241	Free salad – no	2834	Free drink – no	−580.5
Free drink – no	2218.5	Free deliv. – no	2953.5	Free dessert – no	−732
Free deliv. – no	2018	Toppings – 1	3052	Free deliv. – no	−935.5
Deliv. time – 40 mins.	1937	Free dessert – no	3070	Deliv. time – 40 mins.	−1204
Toppings – 1	1798	Deliv. time – 40 mins.	3141	Toppings – 1	−1254
Price – $18	1435	Price – $18	3988	Price – $18	−2553

toppings, delivery time and free delivery each matter for best choices. While these attributes also matter for worst choices, there are some order differences that suggest that most bad is not the same as least good and vice versa. For example, the price of $14 escapes being chosen worst many more times than it would merit considering how many times it was chosen best. No free dessert appears to be a trigger for worst choices even though it is not considered so poorly by the best choice counts.

Differences in best and worst counts can be seen graphically in Figure 14.2. Instead of being perfectly proportional, the two low price levels, free dessert and a delivery time of 20 minutes have many fewer worst choices than would be expected based on the number of best choices. This indicates that profiles with these attributes are unlikely to be considered the worst profiles in a set. In contrast, a delivery time of 10 minutes appears to be a highly desirable attribute level when picking best profiles, but it is not considered when making worst choices.

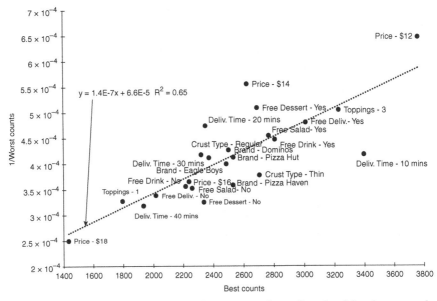

Figure 14.2 Best counts plotted against 1/worst counts by attribute level for pizza example

14.3.4 BW measures for toothpaste data

The toothpaste data can be analyzed in the same way as the pizza data. Table 14.7 shows the toothpaste profiles ordered according to BW scores. This reveals a stronger brand ordering than with pizza, but less price sensitivity. Strengthening, whitening and fluoride appear to be the preferred attribute levels.

Table 14.8 shows the ranking of attribute levels by how many times (normalized) they were chosen best or chosen worst, as well as the normalized BW scores. Price, brand, strengthening and whitening are important for best choices; they also are important for worst choices, but there are some order differences that suggest that most bad is not the same as least good and vice versa. For example, the Macleans brand is almost never chosen worst even though it is below average in being chosen best. Homebrand has markedly more worst choices than the highest price level, but this is reversed for best choices.

Differences in best and worst counts can be seen graphically in Figure 14.3. They are more extreme for toothpaste than for pizza. Instead of being perfectly proportional, the Colgate brand, the lowest price level and the Macleans brand have many fewer worse choices than would be expected based on the number of best choices. This suggests that profiles with these attributes are unlikely to be considered to be the worst profiles in a set. In contrast, the Homebrand brand is a target for worst choices compared to its order for best choices.

Table 14.7 *Toothpaste profiles ordered according to BW differences*

Profile	BW diff.	Brand	Price	Size	Container	Breath	Strengthens	Whitens	Flavor	Fluoride
14	1374	Colgate	$2.80	130g	Tube	No	Yes	Yes	Mild	Yes
5	1047	Oral-B	$2.00	150g	Tube	No	Yes	Yes	Mint	No
7	690	Oral-B	$3.60	110g	Pump	Yes	Yes	Yes	Mild	Yes
9	545	Macleans	$2.00	130g	Pump	Yes	Yes	No	Mild	No
16	397	Colgate	$4.40	170g	Pump	Yes	Yes	Yes	Mint	No
10	319	Macleans	$2.80	110g	Tube	Yes	No	Yes	Mint	No
11	266	Macleans	$3.60	170g	Tube	No	Yes	No	Mint	Yes
13	218	Colgate	$2.00	110g	Pump	No	No	No	Mint	Yes
1	121	Homebrand	$2.00	170g	Tube	Yes	No	Yes	Mild	Yes
15	69	Colgate	$3.60	150g	Tube	Yes	No	No	Mild	No
2	-311	Homebrand	$2.80	150g	Pump	Yes	Yes	No	Mint	Yes
8	-443	Oral-B	$4.40	130g	Tube	Yes	No	No	Mint	Yes
6	-533	Oral-B	$2.80	170g	Pump	No	No	No	Mild	No
12	-647	Macleans	$4.40	150g	Pump	No	No	Yes	Mild	Yes
3	-1386	Homebrand	$3.60	130g	Pump	No	No	Yes	Mint	No
4	-1726	Homebrand	$4.40	110g	Tube	No	Yes	No	Mild	No

Table 14.8 *Attribute levels ranked according to normalized best counts, worst counts and BW differences for the toothpaste example*

Best		Worst		BW diff.	
Price – $2.00	3515	Brand – Colgate	1409	Brand – Colgate	2058
Brand – Colgate	3467	Price – $2.00	1584	Price – $2.00	1931
Strengthens – yes	3272	Brand – Macleans	1599	Strengthens – yes	1141
Whitens – yes	3172.5	Price – $2.80	2064	Whitens – yes	957.5
Brand – Oral-B	2940	Breath – yes	2092	Price – $2.80	849
Price – $2.80	2913	Strengthens – yes	2131	Brand – Oral-B	761
Fluoride – yes	2872	Brand – Oral-B	2179	Breath – yes	693.5
Container – tube	2855.5	Whitens – yes	2215	Fluoride – yes	634
Breath – yes	2785.5	Fluoride – yes	2238	Container – tube	513.5
Size – 170g	2669	Container – tube	2342	Brand – Macleans	483
Flavor – mild	2619.5	Size – 150g	2368	Size – 170g	251
Size – 130g	2550	Flavor – mint	2387	Size – 150g	158
Size – 150g	2526	Size – 170g	2418	Size – 130g	90
Flavor – mint	2440.5	Size – 130g	2460	Flavor – mint	53.5
Size – 110g	2375	Price – $3.60	2644	Flavor – mild	−53.5
Price – $3.60	2283	Flavor – mild	2673	Price – $3.60	−361
Breath – no	2274.5	Container – pump	2718	Size – 110g	−499
Container – pump	2204.5	Fluoride – no	2822	Container – pump	−513.5
Fluoride – no	2188	Whitens – no	2845	Fluoride – no	−634
Brand – Macleans	2082	Size – 110g	2874	Breath – no	−693.5
Whitens – no	1887.5	Strengthens – no	2929	Whitens – no	−957.5
Strengthens – no	1788	Breath – no	2968	Strengthens – no	−1141
Brand – Homebrand	1631	Price – $4.40	3828	Price – $4.40	−2419
Price – $4.40	1409	Brand – Homebrand	4933	Brand – Homebrand	−3302

14.4 Preference heterogeneity in BW data

One explanation for the differences between best and worst choices in Figure 14.2 and Figure 14.3 is that the aggregate counts mask underlying preference heterogeneity. If one takes the heterogeneity into account, the process differences may be resolved. Consequently, the next section explores preference heterogeneity in the pizza and toothpaste examples.

14.4.1 Clustering the pizza data on the basis of chosen profiles

Each respondent completed the same DCE, so each had an opportunity to choose all the pizza profiles as either best or worst a total of five times. The vector of 16 profile BW scores can be used to classify respondents using k-means clustering, archetypal analysis or other taxonomic (classification) techniques. Here we use k-means clustering.

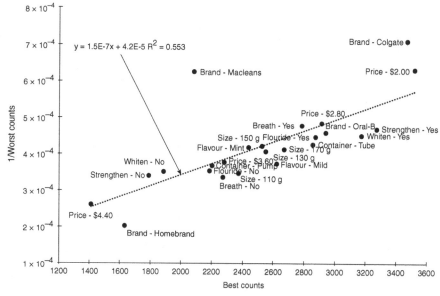

Figure 14.3 Best counts plotted against 1/worst counts by attribute level for toothpaste example

We tested two to five clusters; the distance measure used for clustering was the L1-norm, or city block distance, and the centroid of each cluster is the component-wise median of the cluster members. We chose a two-cluster solution based on the largest average silhouette measure $S_i = (b_i - a_i) / \max(a_i, b_i)$, for i respondents, where a_i is the average distance from the ith point to the other points in the same cluster as i, and b_i is the minimum average distance from the ith point to points in a different cluster, minimized over clusters.

Figure 14.4 shows differences between best and worst attribute counts for each cluster. Rather than consolidating differences between best and worst choices, the cluster results indicate larger differences between best and worst choices for each cluster. One cluster seems to make choices largely on the basis of price, while price plays a differential role for best choices and worst choices. The second cluster seems to trade off the number of toppings, delivery time, low price and free delivery when making best choices; however, the priority for these levels differs substantially for worst choices. Specifically, the two lowest price levels and free dessert are overweighted as deselection criteria in worst choices relative to their use as selection criteria in best choices, resulting in only the slowest delivery time appearing to be a factor in making worst choices with respect to delivery time.

14.4.2 Clustering the toothpaste data on the basis of chosen attribute levels

An alternative way to cluster the data is to use BW scores for attribute-level counts rather than BW scores for profile choices. Here we cluster on toothpaste attribute-level counts. As in the previous clustering example, the vector of 24 attribute-level BW scores can be used to

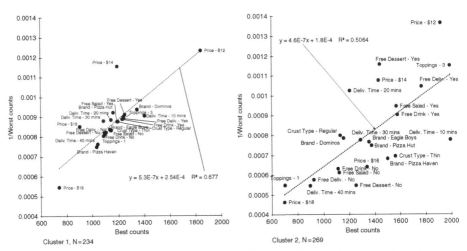

Figure 14.4 Best and worst choice attribute counts for a two-cluster solution based on pizza profile BW differences

classify respondents using k-means clustering, archetypal analysis or other classification techniques. Here, again, we use k-means clustering.

We tested clusters of two to 13 in which the distance measure used for clustering was the L_1-norm, or city block, distance and the centroid of each cluster is the component-wise median of the cluster members. We chose a three-cluster solution based on the largest average silhouette measure S_i.

Figure 14.5 shows differences between best and worst attribute counts for each cluster. As with pizza, the cluster solution identifies groups who make choices differently, rather than consolidating differences between best and worst choices. Specifically, individuals in cluster 1 seems to make best and worst choices exclusively on brand, with these choices being more extreme for worst choices than best choices. Individuals in cluster 2 are the least price sensitive and trade off toothpaste benefits. However, while the Macleans brand is almost never chosen as a best choice, it is almost never chosen as a worst choice either. Cluster 2 also exhibits the weakest preferences, as it has the smallest slope for the best-fit linear regression. Individuals in cluster 3 seem to make best and worst choices almost exclusively on price, and, as we saw with pizza, the lowest two prices are overweighted in importance in worst choices compared to best choices.

14.5 Model comparisons

One can compare formal choice models with respect to parameter values and predictions as well as comparing them with simple measures based on profile or attribute counts. To do this, we estimate aggregate multinomial logit models and hierarchical Bayes mixed logit models using data from best choices, worst choices and both best and worst choices.

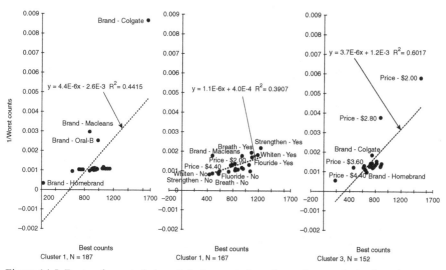

Figure 14.5 Best and worst choice attribute counts for a three-cluster solution based on toothpaste attribute BW differences

14.5.1 Best and worst model parameter values

If best and worst choices are made using the same decision process, we expect the precision of parameter estimates to increase when models are fit using BW data rather than best or worst choices alone, because there is more statistical information. Table 14.9 contains parameter estimates, standard errors and t-statistics for homogeneous multinomial logit models estimated from best, worst and BW data. We estimated the worst choice models using the negative of the utility specification for the best choice models. We estimated the BW model by expanding the data set to include the original choice sets with the best choice as the dependent variable and then the remaining three alternatives from each choice set, not chosen as best, negatively coded as new choice sets with the worst choice as the dependent variable. The estimation procedure for the BW model implies a sequential best then worst choice. Note that this set of models is not exhaustive. Several other models could be specified using the best and worst data.

The t-statistics for the BW model in Table 14.9 can be compared to the t-statistics of the single choice models (either best or worst). Eight of the 15 t-statistics for the BW model are underlined, indicating they are larger than the corresponding t-statistics for the best choice model and the worst choice model. Rather than improve parameter precision, the precision is worse for the BW model for seven of 15 parameters. The parameter for regular crust type is negative and significant in the best model, positive and significant in the worst model and therefore, unsurprisingly, not significant in the BW model. Price parameters are approximately linear for the best model, but for the worst model the two lowest prices have similar utility and act as something of a price threshold relative to the other two price levels.

Table 14.9 *Parameter estimates, standard errors and t-statistics for the homogeneous multinomial logit based on best choices, worst choices or best then worst choices*

	Best			Worst			BW differences		
	Param. est.	Std err.	t-stat.	Param. est.	Std err.	t-stat.	Param. est.	Std err.	t-stat.
Brand – Pizza Hut	−0.0149	0.0226	0.66	0.0245	0.0219	1.12	0.0375	0.0148	2.53
Brand – Dominos	0.0417	0.0221	1.89	0.1033	0.0232	4.45	0.051	0.0149	3.42
Brand – Eagle Boys	0.0053	0.0221	0.24	−0.0162	0.0215	0.75	0.003	0.0149	0.20
Price – $12	0.7046	0.0201	35.05	0.4838	0.0237	20.41	0.5593	0.0155	36.08
Price – $14	0.1407	0.0226	6.23	0.3622	0.0235	15.41	0.2094	0.0148	14.15
Price – $16	−0.218	0.0237	9.20	−0.0994	0.0217	4.58	−0.1103	0.0147	7.50
Deliv. time – 10 mins.	0.3212	0.0237	13.55	0.2677	0.0247	10.84	0.239	0.0153	15.62
Deliv. time – 20 mins.	0.0012	0.0227	0.05	0.1186	0.0223	5.32	0.0642	0.0147	4.37
Deliv. time – 30 mins.	−0.0666	0.0233	2.86	0.017	0.0218	0.78	0.0053	0.0149	0.36
No. toppings – 1	−0.4008	0.0137	29.26	−0.2574	0.0131	19.65	−0.3169	0.0088	36.01
Free deliv. – no	−0.3009	0.0135	22.29	−0.2287	0.0133	17.20	−0.2451	0.0089	27.54
Crust type – regular	−0.0516	0.0133	3.88	0.0379	0.013	2.92	−0.0082	0.0086	0.95
Free dessert – no	−0.1867	0.0133	14.04	−0.2427	0.0127	19.11	−0.1804	0.0086	20.98
Free drink – no	−0.1716	0.0133	12.90	−0.1859	0.0135	13.77	−0.1516	0.0087	17.43
Free salad – no	−0.1446	0.0134	10.79	−0.1336	0.0128	10.44	−0.1468	0.0086	17.07

Collectively, these results further indicate that the best and worst data should be considered separately rather than in a joint model.

We repeat the same comparison using a mixed logit (MXL) model. Table 14.10 contains parameter estimates, standard errors and t-statistics for mean parameter estimates from best, worst and BW data. The means are sufficient to show the same trends as the homogeneous multinomial logit model. We omit the standard deviation estimates for brevity.

More parameters have larger t-statistics in the BW model compared to the best and worst choice models in the multinomial logit case in Table 14.9, but one notable exception is the lowest price parameter, which is the largest-magnitude parameter in the model.

The mean parameters from Table 14.9 and 14.10 are shown graphically in Figure 14.6. The best and worst choice model parameters are proportional, but exhibit deviations similar to the best and 1/worst counts in Figure 14.2. In addition, the slope of the best-fit linear regression line for both the MNL and MXL models is less than unity, indicating that the magnitude of the parameters (or "scale") of the worst model is smaller than the best model.

The MNL and MXL models for toothpaste exhibit similar trends to those described for pizza. The conclusions from the model parameter analysis are that, even accounting for scale differences between best and worst data, the model parameter values differ for best choices and worst choices.

14.5.2 *Best and worst model predictions*

Perhaps the most conclusive test for similarities and differences between best, worst and BW choice models is to evaluate their predictive abilities. In this chapter we compare model prediction using the estimation data, although a more robust measure would be to compare the predictive performance of each model to an outside sample of individuals and choice tasks. We compare the predictive accuracy of each of the six models (MNL-best, MNL-worst, MNL-BW, MXL-best, MXL-worst, MXL-BW) for predicting best and worst choices.

We adopt the root likelihood as a scoring function to measure predictive accuracy. A scoring function is a measure of model prediction performance that relates the probabilistic model predictions to the events that actually occur. Such a measure is preferred to common approaches such as hit rate or aggregate mean squared error because it takes into account the probabilistic nature of the choice model, and it not only rewards accurate predictions but also penalizes poor predictions. The root likelihood for best choices RLH_B is defined as the normalized likelihood

$$RLH_B = \left\{ \prod_{i=1}^{N} \prod_{s=1}^{S} \prod_{j=1}^{J} \pi_{isj}(\hat{\beta}_i)^{y_{isj}} \right\}^{\frac{1}{M}},$$

where

Table 14.10 *Parameter estimates, standard errors and t-statistics for the mixed logit based on best choices, worst choices or best then worst choices*

	Best			Worst			BW differences		
	Param. est.	Std err.	t-stat.	Param. est.	Std err.	t-stat.	Param. est.	Std err.	t-stat.
Brand – Pizza Hut	−0.0462	0.0837	0.55	0.0125	0.0699	0.18	0.0722	0.0586	1.23
Brand – Dominos	0.1574	0.0761	2.07	0.0898	0.0626	1.43	0.1323	0.0442	2.99
Brand – Eagle Boys	0.143	0.0766	1.87	0.0294	0.0622	0.47	0.0119	0.0475	0.25
Price – $12	1.5104	0.0734	20.58	1.0658	0.0666	16.00	1.2223	0.0605	20.20
Price – $14	0.4688	0.0606	7.74	0.7017	0.0647	10.85	0.4502	0.0353	12.75
Price – $16	−0.4074	0.0797	5.11	−0.2332	0.0464	5.03	−0.2441	0.0299	8.16
Deliv. time – 10 mins.	0.5224	0.0761	6.86	0.4735	0.0629	7.53	0.4409	0.0389	11.33
Deliv. time – 20 mins.	0.1806	0.0486	3.72	0.0828	0.058	1.43	0.1464	0.028	5.23
Deliv. time – 30 mins.	−0.1552	0.0622	2.50	0.1021	0.047	2.17	0.0114	0.0294	0.39
No. toppings – 1	−0.9258	0.0612	15.13	−0.5915	0.0394	15.01	−0.6801	0.0381	17.85
Free deliv. – no	−0.6453	0.0478	13.50	−0.5196	0.0386	13.46	−0.5267	0.0323	16.31
Crust type – regular	−0.0335	0.048	0.70	0.0593	0.0375	1.58	0.0004	0.0269	0.01
Free dessert – no	−0.4321	0.0378	11.43	−0.4705	0.0359	13.11	−0.3547	0.0262	13.54
Free drink – no	−0.4459	0.0388	11.49	−0.4178	0.0363	11.51	−0.3324	0.026	12.78
Free salad – no	−0.3424	0.0391	8.76	−0.3071	0.0349	8.80	−0.3071	0.0228	13.47

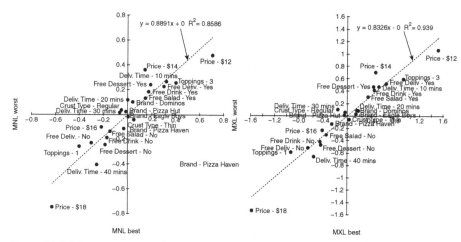

Figure 14.6 Mean parameter estimates for best choice and worst choice models for homogeneous multinomial logit model and mixed logit model

$$\pi_{isj}(\hat{\beta}_i) = \frac{e^{\hat{\beta}_i \mathbf{x}_{sj}}}{\Sigma_{k=1}^{J} e^{\hat{\beta}_i \mathbf{x}_{sk}}}$$

is the predicted probability of alternative j in choice set s for individual i as a function of $\hat{\beta}_i$, the parameter estimates for individual i, and $\mathbf{x}$, the attributes of the alternatives $j = 1, \ldots, J$ in choice set s ($y_{isj} = 1$ if individual i chooses alternative j as best in choice set s and $y_{isj} = 0$ otherwise) and M is the total number of choice sets observed in the prediction pool. When each individual is observed to make choices for the same number of choice sets J, then $M = NJ$, where N is the total number of individuals. The root likelihood is a transformation of the likelihood function that normalizes the likelihood value based on the number of choice tasks, and can be interpreted as the geometric mean of the model-predicted choice probabilities for the observed chosen alternatives.

We change the root likelihood slightly when predicting worst choices. Here we use the negative of all model parameters in order to calculate the probability of being chosen worst π'_{isj} rather than the probability of being chosen best π_{isj}, where $\pi'_{isj} = \pi_{isj}(-\hat{\beta}_i)$, such that

$$RLH_W = \left\{ \prod_{i=1}^{N} \prod_{s=1}^{S} \prod_{j=1}^{J} \pi_{isj}(-\hat{\beta}_i)^{z_{isj}} \right\}^{\frac{1}{M}},$$

and where $z_{isj} = 1$ if individual i chooses alternative j as worst in choice set s and $z_{isj} = 0$ otherwise.

Table 14.11 gives the *RLH* values for each model for both best and worst choice predictions for both the pizza and the toothpaste data. The best choice models best predict best choices, the worst choice models best predict worst choices, and the BW models are

Table 14.11 *Root likelihood values for homogeneous multinomial logit and mixed logit choice models estimated from best choice, worst choice or best and worst choice data, each predicting either best choices or worst choices*

	Pizza		Toothpaste	
	Predict best choices, RLH_B	Predict worst choices, RLH_W	Predict best choices, RLH_B	Predict worst choice, RLH_W
MNL-best	0.306	0.298	0.321	0.319
MNL-worst	0.296	0.305	0.288	0.344
MNL-BW	0.303	0.303	0.314	0.338
MXL-best	0.647	0.323	0.725	0.348
MXL-worst	0.347	0.613	0.337	0.715
MXL-BW	0.569	0.564	0.640	0.663

relatively poor at predicting either best or worst choices. Again, despite the additional information, the BW models fail to improve prediction for either best or worst choices relative to the models based on the single choices. This provides further evidence that best and worst choices are being made by different choice processes.

14.6 Conclusions

This chapter demonstrated the analysis of Case 3 BW data for two examples: delivered pizza and toothpaste. We focused on showing (1) how BW measures from choice counts can be used to understand product preferences for a group of consumers, (2) how BW count measures can be used to segment consumers by similarities in preference and (3) how BW count measures can be used at the aggregate segment levels to identify differences between best choice preferences and worst choice preferences.

Best and worst preferences have substantial differences for the two examples we discussed. Therefore, the benefit of collecting and using the best and worst choices as a data augmentation process for a first-choice or best-choice model is not realized in these examples. We showed this not only with the count measures but also with traditional aggregate- and individual-level choice models. Thus, in this case, the benefit of collecting both best and worst choice data lies in the additional insights into the consumer decision processes that come from comparing differences between best and worst choices. For example, the least popular attribute levels from the worst choice data may indicate consideration thresholds, while the most popular attribute levels from the best choice data may indicate selection criteria.

Chapter 15

Using alternative-specific DCE designs and best and worst choices to model choices

Jordan J. Louviere

15.1 Introduction

The purpose of this chapter is to show how to combine an alternative-specific DCE design with a BW choice task. Secondary aims are (1) to show how to add informative choice sets to DCE tasks to gain insights and information about individual differences and (2) to show how to analyze and report choice totals from this type of DCE task to gain additional insights.

Most private sector organizations need to understand pricing and the likely impacts of differences in and/or changes to prices of their own product/service prices and/or the likely impacts of competitor price changes. Similarly, many public sector organizations need to understand and anticipate the consequences of various pricing policies, such as offering incentives to uptake solar appliances, tolls on bridges and highways, usage fees for parks, and so on. As a result, there are numerous potential choice model pricing applications in both sectors. This chapter illustrates one such application, namely modeling the choices of a relevant sample of individuals faced with different airlines and fares for a holiday trip.

I study the flight choices of a sample of 214 individuals randomly sampled from the Pureprofile online panel in Australia who (1) reside in the Sydney metropolitan area, (2) have flown to northern New South Wales (NSW) for a weekend or longer holiday in the past three years or (3) anticipate doing so in the next three years. At the time of the study there were five potential airline choices for such flights within NSW: Jetstar, Qantas, Rex, Tiger and Virgin. Fares for such flights ranged approximately between A\$89 and A\$239 at various times during the three years prior to the study. Differences between flights within NSW are not large, as most flights are no more than an hour. Airlines flying within NSW try to claim significant differences in services, and, to the extent that such differences exist, I would expect to see them manifest in differential choices of particular airlines.

Thus, one can model and quantify preferences for airlines and fares by designing an alternative-specific discrete choice experiment (ASDCE). Typically, an ASDCE is appropriate when individuals in the market of interest will choose specific offers, such as brands, transport modes, holiday destinations, etc. Without going into details, the vast majority of ASDCEs can be designed using the L^{MA} approach developed by Louviere and Woodworth (1983) and discussed in detail by Louviere, Hensher and Swait (2000). L^{MA} represents M alternatives, each with A attributes that have L levels. Strictly speaking, therefore, one would rarely "see" an ASDCE that exactly matches the L^{MA} specification. Instead, the "name" refers to a class of statistical experiments that are used to make choice sets describing M choice alternatives. The alternatives can have the same or different As (attributes), and the number of levels for each attribute (Ls) can differ.

In the present case, the ASDCE for this problem is very simple: each airline is a choice option (M = 5), with four levels (L = 4) of price (A = 1) nested under each option. The smallest ASCDE design is a particular type of sample from the 4^5 factorial (Louviere and Woodworth, 1983; Louviere, Hensher and Swait, 2000) called an orthogonal main effects plan. OMEPs for the 4^5 factorial can be found in sources such as the SAS design catalogue (http://support.sas.com/techsup/technote/ts723.html). One suitable OMEP produces 16 choice sets that have the property that one can estimate (1) the utility of each airline, (2) separate (alternative-specific) fare effects for each airline (and test if the effects are generic or alternative-specific) and (3) the separate cross-effects of each airline's fares on the choices of other airlines. As discussed by Louviere, Hensher and Swait (2000), significant cross-effects violate the IIA property associated with the independent and identically distributed extreme value type 1 error assumption by implying switching into or out of an option more or less than predicted by the conditional logit model.

I added two choice sets to the OMEP to get (1) a test of airline choice differences and (2) an estimate of the lower and upper bounds of demand in this ASDCE. One set had all airlines offering flights at the lowest fare, and the second set had all offering flights at the highest fare. Later I show that these two sets provide impressive insights not available from the 16 choice sets in the OMEP. Figure 15.1 shows that survey participants were asked to indicate their most and least likely airline choice, and if they actually would choose all, some or none of the options. The answers to these questions allow us to develop a semi-order (partial ranking) of the choice options, including the "None" option. Each participant completed all 18 choice sets (OMEP + two extra). I use these choices to estimate models that represent preference homogeneity, unobservable (latent) preference heterogeneity and observable heterogeneity (that is, associated with covariate measures obtained in other parts of the online survey).

15.2 Analysis and results

15.2.1 Calculating, visualizing and using choice counts (means, proportions)

Table 15.1 gives the mean DCE choice proportions for 16 and 18 choice sets: (1) fare levels; (2) airline and none of the options; and (3) combined airline and fare levels (alternative-specific means). Choice proportions for 18 sets are more extreme than for 16 sets, but both choice set means are highly related (slope = 1.08, R^2 = 0.98). Figure 15.2 graphs sample means against fare levels; graphs for each airline are similar, suggesting generic fare effects (not shown to save space). I tested generic versus alternative-specific fare effects, and found no statistical difference in model fit (omitted to save space). I now further analyze the

The next **18** screens display airfares offered by 5 airlines for you to evaluate and choose among. We want you to evaluate **18 scenarios** that describe **5 airline** offerings for return airfares from Sydney to Gold Coast. For each scenario, please assume that you are booking a ticket to travel from Sydney to Gold Coast for a weekend or longer holiday. We want you to answer 3 questions about each scenario:

1. Which offering would you be *most likely* to choose.

2. Which offering would you be *least likely* to choose, and

3. Whether would you choose *all of them, none at them, or some at them but not others*

There are no right or wrong answers, we are simply interested in how you compare and choose among the offerings.

Please click on " >> " to continue.

| << | >> |

Scenario 1 of 18:

Airlines	Jetstar	Qantas	Rex	Tiger	Virgin
	Jet★	QANTAS	reX.	tiger	Virgin
Returen airfares Sydney - Gol Coast	$89	$189	$189	$89	$139

I would be **most likely** to choose (tick one):
○ Jetstar   ○ Qantas   ○ Rex   ○ Tiger   Virgin

I would be **least likely** to choose (tick one):
○ Jetstar   ○ Qantas   ○ Rex   ○ Tiger   Virgin

Considering all 5 options above, I actually would choose (tick one):
○ all of them
○ none of them
○ some of them but not others

| << | >> |

0%   25%   50%   75%   100%

Figure 15.1 DCE task instructions and example task (choice set)

ASDCE data, in which I refer to quantities labelled "Most2" and "Least2." "Most2" represents the most likely choice when "None" is an option (rejecting all airline offers, or "Not flying"); "Least2" represents the least likely choice when "None" is an option.

One also can visualize ASDCE choice data by calculating choice proportions for each option in each choice set (Table 15.2a). The two extreme sets are in the top left of the table. Table 15.2b sorts choice proportions from highest to lowest using the "Most2" measure (with "None" omitted); proportions greater than 0.5 are lightly shaded at the top of the table; choice proportions less than or equal to 0.05 are more heavily shaded at the bottom of the table. Table 15.2b indicates agreement about the top and the bottom and disagreement in the middle, potentially implying that differences in individuals may be choice consistency differences. I examine this possibility later.

A third way to visualize sample choice results is to calculate them for 0, 1, 2, 3, 4 and 5 (total possible) choices of each airline and fare level (Table 15.3). Table 15.3 shows that the number of times an option is chosen depends on the airline and fare level; choices increase

Table 15.1 *Choice proportions (means) from the DCE*

Fare	16 sets Most2	18 sets Most2
Sample means for fare		
A$89	0.450	0.520
A$139	0.160	0.160
A$189	0.060	0.060
A$239	0.030	0.010
Sample means for airline		
Jetstar	0.180	0.200
Qantas	0.360	0.330
Rex	0.100	0.110
Tiger	0.030	0.030
Virgin	0.230	0.240
None	0.100	0.080
Means specific to Jetstar		
A$89	0.470	0.580
A$139	0.200	0.200
A$189	0.030	0.030
A$239	0.010	0.000
Means specific to Qantas		
A$89	0.820	0.850
A$139	0.290	0.290
A$189	0.170	0.170
A$239	0.090	0.030
Means specific to Rex		
A$89	0.290	0.360
A$139	0.080	0.080
A$189	0.010	0.010
A$239	0.010	0.000
Means specific to Tiger		
A$89	0.080	0.100
A$139	0.020	0.020
A$189	0.010	0.010
A$239	0.000	0.000

Table 15.1 (*cont.*)

	Means specific to Virgin	
A$89	0.600	0.690
A$139	0.190	0.190
A$189	0.060	0.060
A$239	0.040	0.010

Note: Most 2 refers to the choice proportions for most likely choice when "None" is one of the choice options.

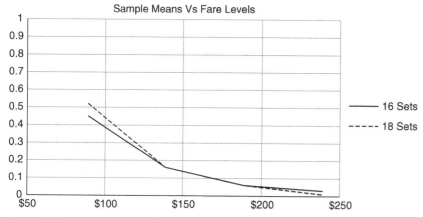

Figure 15.2 Sample aggregate fare graph

(decrease) in 0 choices as the fare increases (decreases), suggesting more consistent choices for extreme levels of fare and airline and less consistency in the middle levels.

The BW task gives a partial ranking for each person in each choice set, so we can estimate individual-level weighted least squares models for each person (Louviere, Street *et al.*, 2008; Louviere, 2013). As noted in Chapter 3, WLS estimates of conditional logit models are first-step estimates of maximum-likelihood solutions. WLS is useful when individual models will not converge using maximum likelihood to fit the (best) choices because of perfect predictors. Another approach is the penalized maximum likelihood proposed and applied by Frischknecht *et al.* (2014). Table 15.4 has descriptive statistics for the 214 individual-level WLS estimates, including alternative-specific main effects and cross-effects; these effects demonstrate violations of the IIA property discussed earlier. Table 15.4 shows minimum and maximum estimates, mean estimates, standard errors, standard deviations, and skewness and kurtosis statistics. The t-statistics understate the true significance because of estimation errors and a failure to take repeated measures into account. Louviere and Woodworth (1983) proposed an approximate correction for the standard errors by dividing them by the square root of the number of choice sets. Even

Table 15.2a *Design matrix with choice proportions*

Choice set	Airlines and fares		Choices with "None"		Choice set	Airlines and fares		Choices with "None"	
	Options	Fare	Most2	Least2		Options	Fare	Most2	Least2
All alts. at A$89	**Jetstar**	**A$89**	**0.03**	**0.07**	10	Jetstar	A$139	0.69	0.04
	Qantas	**A$89**	**0.71**	**0.06**	10	Qantas	A$239	0.05	0.08
	Rex	**A$89**	**0.02**	**0.15**	10	Rex	A$189	0.03	0.05
	Tiger	**A$89**	**0.00**	**0.45**	10	Tiger	A$239	0.00	0.75
	Virgin	**A$89**	**0.24**	**0.00**	10	Virgin	A$239	0.01	0.06
	None		**0.00**	**0.26**	10	None	0	0.21	0.01
All alts. at A$239	**Jetstar**	**A$239**	**0.03**	**0.08**	11	Jetstar	A$239	0.00	0.16
	Qantas	**A$239**	**0.36**	**0.05**	11	Qantas	A$189	0.31	0.04
	Rex	**A$239**	**0.01**	**0.21**	11	Rex	A$139	0.32	0.03
	Tiger	**A$239**	**0.00**	**0.58**	11	Tiger	A$239	0.00	0.75
	Virgin	**A$239**	**0.13**	**0.02**	11	Virgin	A$189	0.10	0.00
	None	**0**	**0.46**	**0.07**	11	None	0	0.26	0.02
1	Jetstar	A$89	0.74	0.04	12	Jetstar	A$239	0.01	0.58
1	Qantas	A$189	0.06	0.15	12	Qantas	A$239	0.03	0.13
1	Rex	A$189	0.00	0.58	12	Rex	A$89	0.51	0.06
1	Tiger	A$89	0.02	0.19	12	Tiger	A$139	0.03	0.20
1	Virgin	A$139	0.14	0.01	12	Virgin	A$139	0.27	0.00
1	None	0	0.03	0.02	12	None	0	0.14	0.02
2	Jetstar	A$189	0.01	0.03	13	Jetstar	A$239	0.00	0.20
2	Qantas	A$139	0.57	0.03	13	Qantas	A$89	0.88	0.02
2	Rex	A$239	0.01	0.29	13	Rex	A$239	0.00	0.51
2	Tiger	A$239	0.00	0.63	13	Tiger	A$89	0.07	0.13
2	Virgin	A$139	0.27	0.00	13	Virgin	A$239	0.02	0.12
2	None	0	0.13	0.01	13	None	0	0.03	0.02
4	Jetstar	A$189	0.05	0.07	14	Jetstar	A$189	0.04	0.07
4	Qantas	A$189	0.27	0.03	14	Qantas	A$239	0.00	0.67
4	Rex	A$89	0.53	0.05	14	Rex	A$139	0.01	0.09
4	Tiger	A$189	0.01	0.29	14	Tiger	A$89	0.08	0.13
4	Virgin	A$239	0.00	0.56	14	Virgin	A$89	0.83	0.01
4	None	0	0.13	0.01	14	None	0	0.04	0.02
6	Jetstar	A$89	0.04	0.05	15	Jetstar	A$239	0.00	0.73
6	Qantas	A$89	0.72	0.01	15	Qantas	A$139	0.12	0.03
6	Rex	A$89	0.01	0.06	15	Rex	A$189	0.01	0.03
6	Tiger	A$239	0.00	0.86	15	Tiger	A$189	0.01	0.18
6	Virgin	A$89	0.21	0.00	15	Virgin	A$89	0.83	0.01
6	None	0	0.01	0.02	15	None	0	0.03	0.02
7	Jetstar	A$89	0.73	0.04	16	Jetstar	A$139	0.02	0.03
7	Qantas	A$139	0.22	0.04	16	Qantas	A$189	0.04	0.03
7	Rex	A$139	0.00	0.06	16	Rex	A$239	0.00	0.78

Table 15.2a *(cont.)*

Choice set	Airlines and fares		Choices with "None"		Choice set	Airlines and fares		Choices with "None"	
	Options	Fare	Most2	Least2		Options	Fare	Most2	Least2
7	Tiger	A$139	0.01	0.21	16	Tiger	A$139	0.01	0.14
7	Virgin	A$239	0.01	0.64	16	Virgin	A$89	0.89	0.00
7	None	0	0.03	0.01	16	None	0	0.03	0.01
8	Jetstar	A$139	0.01	0.03	17	Jetstar	A$189	0.00	0.17
8	Qantas	A$89	0.90	0.02	17	Qantas	A$89	0.90	0.03
8	Rex	A$139	0.00	0.08	17	Rex	A$189	0.00	0.52
8	Tiger	A$189	0.01	0.84	17	Tiger	A$139	0.03	0.17
8	Virgin	A$139	0.06	0.01	17	Virgin	A$189	0.03	0.09
8	None	0	0.02	0.02	17	None	0	0.04	0.01
9	Jetstar	A$89	0.80	0.04	18	Jetstar	A$139	0.06	0.08
9	Qantas	A$239	0.01	0.15	18	Qantas	A$139	0.25	0.04
9	Rex	A$239	0.00	0.62	18	Rex	A$89	0.38	0.06
9	Tiger	A$189	0.00	0.16	18	Tiger	A$89	0.23	0.17
9	Virgin	A$189	0.09	0.01	18	Virgin	A$189	0.02	0.62
9	None	0	0.08	0.02	18	None	0	0.06	0.04

Table 15.2b *Design matrix sorted by choice proportions*

Airline	Fare	Most2	Least2
	Highest choice proportions		
Qantas	A$89	0.900	0.020
Qantas	A$89	0.900	0.030
Virgin	A$89	0.890	0.000
Qantas	A$89	0.880	0.020
Virgin	A$89	0.830	0.010
Virgin	A$89	0.830	0.010
Jetstar	A$89	0.800	0.040
Jetstar	A$89	0.740	0.040
Jetstar	A$89	0.730	0.040
Qantas	A$89	0.720	0.010
Qantas	A$89	0.710	0.060
Jetstar	A$139	0.690	0.040
Qantas	A$139	0.570	0.030
Rex	A$89	0.530	0.050
Rex	A$89	0.510	0.060

Middle choice proportions			
Rex	A$89	0.380	0.060
Qantas	A$239	0.360	0.050
Rex	A$139	0.320	0.030
Qantas	A$189	0.310	0.040
Virgin	A$139	0.270	0.000
Qantas	A$189	0.270	0.030
Virgin	A$139	0.270	0.000
Qantas	A$139	0.250	0.040
Virgin	A$89	0.240	0.000
Tiger	A$89	0.230	0.170
Qantas	A$139	0.220	0.040
Virgin	A$89	0.210	0.000
Virgin	A$139	0.140	0.010
Virgin	A$239	0.130	0.020
Qantas	A$139	0.120	0.030
Virgin	A$189	0.100	0.000
Virgin	A$189	0.090	0.010
Tiger	A$89	0.080	0.130
Tiger	A$89	0.070	0.130
Qantas	A$189	0.060	0.150
Virgin	A$139	0.060	0.010
Jetstar	A$139	0.060	0.080
Lowest choice proportions			
Jetstar	A$189	0.050	0.070
Qantas	A$239	0.050	0.080
Jetstar	A$89	0.040	0.050
Jetstar	A$189	0.040	0.070
Qantas	A$189	0.040	0.030
Jetstar	A$89	0.030	0.070
Jetstar	A$239	0.030	0.080
Rex	A$189	0.030	0.050
Qantas	A$239	0.030	0.130
Tiger	A$139	0.030	0.200
Tiger	A$139	0.030	0.170
Virgin	A$189	0.030	0.090
Rex	A$89	0.020	0.150
Tiger	A$89	0.020	0.190
Virgin	A$239	0.020	0.120
Jetstar	A$139	0.020	0.030
Virgin	A$189	0.020	0.620
Rex	A$239	0.010	0.210

Table 15.2b *(cont.)*

	Lowest choice proportions		
Jetstar	A$189	0.010	0.030
Rex	A$239	0.010	0.290
Tiger	A$189	0.010	0.290
Rex	A$89	0.010	0.060
Tiger	A$139	0.010	0.210
Virgin	A$239	0.010	0.640
Jetstar	A$139	0.010	0.030
Tiger	A$189	0.010	0.840
Qantas	A$239	0.010	0.150
Virgin	A$239	0.010	0.060
Jetstar	A$239	0.010	0.580
Rex	A$139	0.010	0.090
Rex	A$189	0.010	0.030
Tiger	A$189	0.010	0.180
Tiger	A$139	0.010	0.140
Tiger	A$89	0.000	0.450
Tiger	A$239	0.000	0.580
Rex	A$189	0.000	0.580
Tiger	A$239	0.000	0.630
Virgin	A$239	0.000	0.560

without the correction, virtually all model effects are significant. Thus, IIA is systematically violated in these DCE choices.

Figure 15.3 contains histograms of the individual-level estimates; no histogram is consistent with a normal distribution, as is often assumed in random coefficient models such as mixed logit. Most distributions are skewed, consistent with Table 15.4, and there potentially are multiple modes; this suggests that we should identify discrete groups who choose differently.

I begin the examination of individual differences by calculating "Most2" and "Least2" choice totals for each attribute level for each person (not shown). I then use several taxonomic methods to identify discrete structure in these choice totals, such as two-step clustering and archetypal analysis (Cutler and Breiman, 1994). These results suggest that five discrete groups (segments) underlie the choice data; I describe these segments later. We need to test if this finding is reliable statistically; I do this by comparing a simple "one-size-fits-all" aggregate sample conditional logit model with several more complex specifications, including one that interacts cluster membership with the airline and fare effects.

I first estimate a conditional logit model with a generic fare effect from the "Most2" choices (including "None"). The starting log likelihood (LL) for all models is 13674.71 (that is, all parameters = 0). The LL for the generic fare model is 7058.59, a difference of

Table 15.3 *Choice counts by airline and fare levels*

Fare levels	Times chosen	Most totals including "None"					Least totals including "None"				
		Jetstar	Qantas	Rex	Tiger	Virgin	Jetstar	Qantas	Rex	Tiger	Virgin
A$89	0	0	0	0	0	0	0	0	0	0	0
	1	12	6	25	35	8	6	9	31	57	2
	2	48	12	80	38	44	6	4	16	34	0
	3	396	102	198	12	351	3	3	3	21	0
	4	16	76	0	0	36	12	4	8	24	0
	5	25	675	5	0	195	25	10	20	90	5
A$139	0	0	0	0	0	0	0	0	0	0	0
	1	128	80	67	7	63	10	3	24	18	3
	2	36	58	4	10	40	2	10	6	38	0
	3	3	54	0	0	30	3	9	9	9	0
	4	0	56	0	0	24	24	8	16	88	4
	5	0	0	0	0	0	0	0	0	0	0
A$189	0	0	0	0	0	0	0	0	0	0	0
	1	18	38	7	4	31	25	26	73	113	117
	2	4	66	2	4	16	14	4	146	68	32
	3	0	27	0	0	3	6	6	21	42	0
	4	0	12	0	0	4	28	16	12	88	4
	5	0	0	0	0	0	0	0	0	0	0
A$239	0	0	0	0	0	0	0	0	0	0	0
	1	10	68	4	1	24	35	101	19	16	40
	2	0	20	2	2	6	162	54	84	42	172
	3	0	6	0	0	3	78	27	177	96	57
	4	0	0	0	0	0	28	4	88	104	8
	5	0	5	0	0	5	65	45	145	495	20

6616.11 LL points; the pseudo R^2 is 0.512, which is an excellent fit. I next allow airline-specific fare effects, giving a LL of 7054.89. The LL difference with the generic fare model is insufficient to conclude that model two is a significant improvement. Then I compare generic non-linear fare effects with airline-specific non-linear fare effects. The LL for the generic model is 6907.85 and the LL for the airline specific model is 6989.48. The generic non-linear fare effects improve on the generic linear fare effects but do not differ significantly from airline-specific non-linear fare effects. Next I estimate airline-specific linear fare and linear fare cross-effects to capture IIA violations. The LL of this model is 6828.48, which differs significantly from the generic non-linear fare effects model, indicating IIA violations in the choices. A more complex model with non-linear airline-specific fare effects and cross-effects did not converge.

Table 15.4 *Individual-level WLS model estimates and associated statistics*

Effects	Min	Max	Mean	SE	t-stat.	SD	Skew	t-stat.	Kurt.	t-stat.
Jetstar	−0.39	3.28	2.091	0.0369	56.69	0.54	−1.69	−10.11	5.19	15.60
Qantas	0.02	3.47	2.495	0.0391	63.82	0.57	−1.09	−6.55	2.50	7.51
Rex	−0.01	2.80	1.880	0.0288	65.29	0.42	−1.28	−7.68	3.47	10.44
Tiger	−0.27	2.85	1.572	0.0447	35.17	0.65	−1.03	−6.19	0.76	2.29
Virgin	0.00	3.47	2.219	0.0338	65.74	0.49	−0.40	−2.40	1.53	4.60
None	−0.03	3.47	2.097	0.0273	76.79	0.40	−0.21	−1.23	8.48	25.49
FareJetstar	−0.02	0.01	−0.010	0.0004	−27.80	0.01	0.67	3.99	0.04	0.13
FareQantas	−0.02	0.00	−0.011	0.0003	−32.96	0.00	0.49	2.94	0.36	1.09
FareRex	−0.02	0.01	−0.008	0.0004	−19.12	0.01	0.23	1.35	−1.09	−3.29
FareTiger	−0.02	0.01	−0.007	0.0003	−21.87	0.00	0.06	0.37	−0.09	−0.26
FareVirgin	−0.02	0.00	−0.011	0.0003	−32.80	0.00	0.39	2.33	0.21	0.62
FareQonJ	−0.01	0.01	0.002	0.0003	7.47	0.00	−0.54	−3.24	1.33	4.00
FareRonJ	−0.02	0.01	0.002	0.0002	8.27	0.00	−0.71	−4.24	3.94	11.84
FareTonJ	−0.01	0.01	−0.002	0.0003	−8.53	0.00	−0.24	−1.43	0.63	1.88
FareVonJ	−0.01	0.01	0.003	0.0003	13.03	0.00	−1.34	−8.02	2.44	7.35
FareJonQ	−0.01	0.01	0.000	0.0002	−1.65	0.00	−0.39	−2.31	0.01	0.02
FareRonQ	−0.01	0.01	0.000	0.0002	1.35	0.00	−0.24	−1.45	0.58	1.76
FareTonQ	−0.01	0.02	0.001	0.0003	2.23	0.00	−0.18	−1.07	0.97	2.92
FareVonQ	−0.01	0.01	0.001	0.0002	3.13	0.00	−0.24	−1.41	0.17	0.52
FareJonR	−0.01	0.02	0.003	0.0003	8.33	0.00	0.06	0.37	−0.05	−0.15
FareQonR	−0.01	0.01	−0.001	0.0002	−3.58	0.00	−0.05	−0.28	0.35	1.07
FareTonR	−0.01	0.01	0.000	0.0003	−1.64	0.00	−0.41	−2.43	0.53	1.59
FareVonR	−0.01	0.01	0.001	0.0002	4.79	0.00	−0.61	−3.65	0.48	1.46
FareJonT	−0.01	0.01	0.000	0.0003	−0.78	0.00	0.44	2.61	2.28	6.85
FareQonT	−0.01	0.01	0.000	0.0002	0.53	0.00	−0.29	−1.75	0.85	2.55
FareRonT	−0.03	0.01	0.000	0.0003	1.55	0.00	−1.08	−6.45	9.09	27.33
FareVonT	−0.01	0.01	0.000	0.0002	0.26	0.00	−0.13	−0.79	1.63	4.91
FareJonV	−0.01	0.01	0.002	0.0002	7.36	0.00	−0.64	−3.83	1.70	5.11
FareQonV	−0.01	0.01	0.001	0.0002	5.56	0.00	0.04	0.24	0.27	0.82
FareRonV	−0.02	0.01	0.003	0.0003	13.15	0.00	−0.53	−3.17	2.79	8.38
FareTonV	−0.01	0.01	−0.002	0.0003	−7.34	0.00	0.34	2.06	0.21	0.64

Note: "Effects" headings mean, for example, "FareQonJ" = "the effect of Q's (Qantas') fare on J's (Jetstar's) preferences."

Now I consider the five segments identified with two-step clustering. I tried to fit conditional logit models to the "Most2" choices (including "None") for each segment separately, but several models did not converge. I therefore used WLS estimation and the BW choices. The result of interacting each cluster with the options and linear fare effects is shown in Table 15.5.

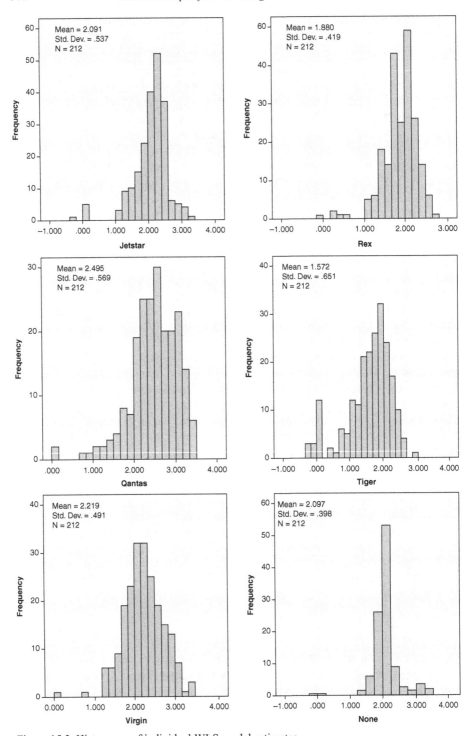

Figure 15.3 Histograms of individual WLS model estimates

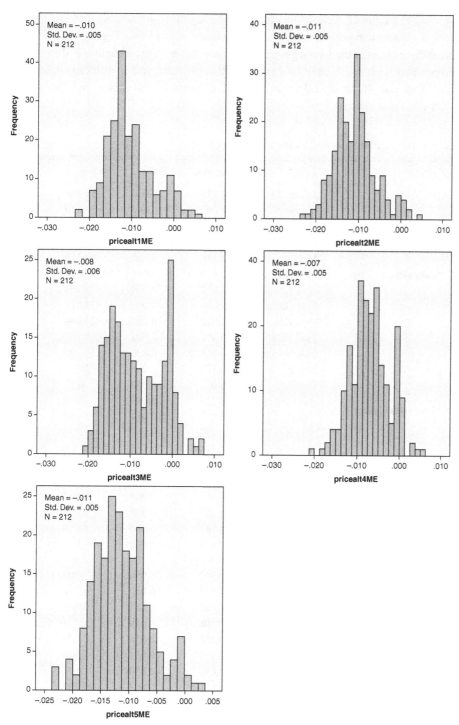

Figure 15.3 (cont.)

The results in Table 15.5 clearly indicate that the segments are reliably different. These differences are now explored in more detail in Figures 15.4a to 15.4c. Figure 15.4a visually compares differences in the five-segment BW differences with the sample BW differences for airlines and fares combined (the next paragraph provides details of these quantities). Figures 15.4b and 15.4c visually compare BW differences for airline and fare levels separately, as I now discuss.

Table 15.5 *WLS estimation results for cluster differences*

Type of effect	Effect	Estimate	Std err.	t-stat	Sig.
	Jetstar	2.273	0.046	48.986	0.000
	Qantas	2.483	0.045	55.110	0.000
	Rex	2.077	0.048	43.676	0.000
	Tiger	1.875	0.048	38.988	0.000
	Virgin	2.238	0.047	47.136	0.000
Main effects	None	2.416	0.045	54.217	0.000
	Fare Jetstar	−0.013	0.000	−29.194	0.000
	Fare Qantas	−0.016	0.000	−39.821	0.000
	Fare Rex	−0.012	0.000	−24.046	0.000
	Fare Tiger	−0.011	0.001	−19.344	0.000
	Fare Virgin	−0.015	0.000	−34.406	0.000
	Jetstar	0.198	0.068	2.908	0.004
	Qantas	−0.023	0.067	−0.35	0.726
Interactions with cluster 1	Rex	0.214	0.069	3.088	0.002
	Tiger	0.235	0.071	3.310	0.001
	Virgin	0.793	0.067	11.793	0.000
	None	−0.318	0.067	−4.739	0.000
	Jetstar	0.046	0.064	0.721	0.471
	Qantas	0.594	0.060	9.812	0.000
Interactions with cluster 2	Rex	0.063	0.065	0.962	0.336
	Tiger	−0.489	0.074	−6.634	0.000
	Virgin	0.147	0.065	2.258	0.024
	None	−0.421	0.063	−6.675	0.000
	Jetstar	0.165	0.058	2.851	0.004
	Qantas	0.397	0.056	7.107	0.000
Interactions with cluster 3	Rex	0.076	0.060	1.276	0.202
	Tiger	0.201	0.060	3.368	0.001
	Virgin	0.108	0.059	1.825	0.068
	None	−0.184	0.056	−3.27	0.001
	Jetstar	0.119	0.061	1.948	0.051
	Qantas	0.091	0.059	1.537	0.124
Interactions with cluster 4	Rex	0.170	0.062	2.732	0.006
	Tiger	−0.027	0.066	−0.415	0.678
	Virgin	0.347	0.062	t5.602	0.000
	None	0.261	0.059	4.453	0.000

Table 15.5 *(cont.)*

Type of effect	Effect	Estimate	Std err.	t-stat	Sig.
	Jetstar	0.000	–	–	–
	Qantas	0.000	–	–	–
Interactions with cluster 5	Rex	0.000	–	–	–
	Tiger	0.000	–	–	–
	Virgin	0.000	–	–	–
	None	0.000	–	–	–
Interactions with cluster 1	Jetstar	0.002	0.001	2.541	0.011
	Qantas	0.006	0.001	8.967	0.000
	Rex	0.003	0.001	3.728	0.000
	Tiger	0.003	0.001	3.582	0.000
	Virgin	0.005	0.001	8.881	0.000
	Jetstar	0.004	0.001	6.452	0.000
	Qantas	0.007	0.001	13.445	0.000
Interactions with cluster 2	Rex	0.004	0.001	6.213	0.000
	Tiger	0.004	0.001	3.962	0.000
	Virgin	0.005	0.001	8.154	0.000
	Jetstar	0.003	0.001	4.506	0.000
	Qantas	0.005	0.000	10.386	0.000
Interactions with cluster 3	Rex	0.003	0.001	4.888	0.000
	Tiger	0.003	0.001	3.814	0.000
	Virgin	0.004	0.001	7.272	0.000
	Jetstar	0.002	0.001	3.172	0.002
	Qantas	0.002	0.001	3.626	0.000
Interactions with cluster 4	Rex	0.003	0.001	4.678	0.000
	Tiger	0.005	0.001	6.411	0.000
	Virgin	0.003	0.001	5.089	0.000
	Jetstar	0.000	–	–	–
	Qantas	0.000	–	–	–
Interactions with cluster 5	Rex	0.000	–	–	–
	Tiger	0.000	–	–	–
	Virgin	0.000	–	–	–

The differences displayed in Figures 15.4a to 15.4c are derived as follows: (1) calculate the best ("Most2") minus worst ("Least2") difference scores ("scores") for the sample as a whole and for each segment; (2) subtract the sample scores from each of the segment scores; and (3) use the subtracted scores in a bar graph to display the differences relative to the sample. The calculations graphed in Figures 15.4a to 15.4c suggest the following segment differences relative to the sample as a whole. Segment 1 chooses Qantas much less and Virgin much more. Segment 2 chooses Qantas much more and Tiger much less.

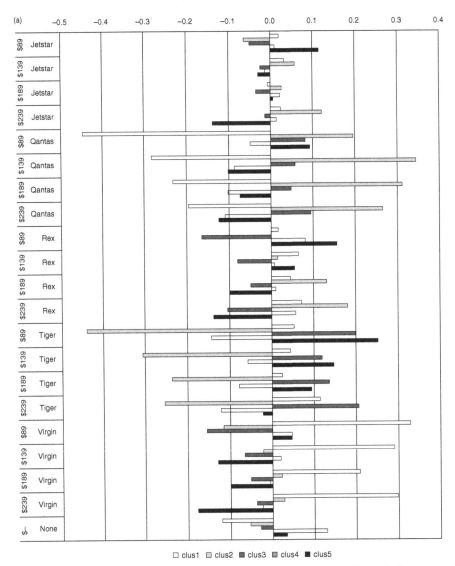

Figure 15.4a Segment BW differences in airline and fare choice proportions relative to sample BW differences

Segment 3 chooses Tiger more and Rex less. Segment 4 chooses the "None" option much more and chooses Tiger less. Segment 5 chooses Virgin less and Tiger more, and is the most price-sensitive segment. This pattern of results suggests that the segment differences are related to choice set formation, by which I mean that the segments differ in terms of which airlines are in or out of the considered choice set. In particular, the analysis suggests that different segments make choices based on different subsets of the five airlines.

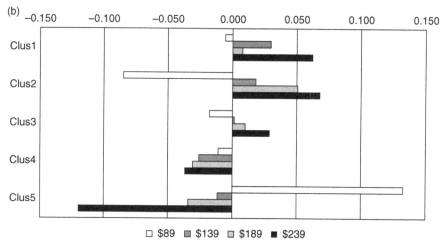

Figure 15.4b Segment BW differences in fare responses relative to sample BW differences

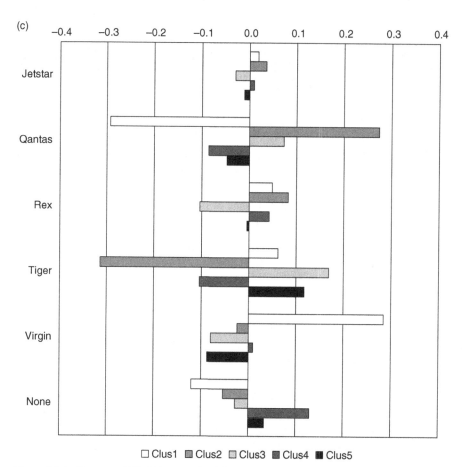

Figure 15.4c Segment BW differences in airline responses relative to sample BW differences

A final and obvious step in the analysis would be to investigate segment differences related to questions asked in the online survey. I do not pursue this here to save space, but note that several covariates are significantly associated with segment membership.

15.3 Discussion and conclusions

This chapter illustrated how to design and implement a best and worst choice task with an alternative-specific DCE (a Case 3 BWS). I explained and illustrated simple calculations from the ASDCE best and worst choices and showed how to use them to produce aggregate- and individual-level results to inform model estimation. Of particular interest was a comparison of generic and alternative (airline) -specific fare effects. A simple graphical comparison of generic (sample aggregate) and airline-specific fare level choice proportions strongly indicates that the fare effects are generic. I tested this hypothesis by estimating and comparing conditional logit specifications from the "Most2" choices, which confirmed that the fare effects were generic; the generic fare effects model fit the data extremely well by choice modeling standards.

I tested whether a conditional logit model was in fact appropriate for the "Most2" choices by fitting a conditional logit model with own (airline) fare and cross-fare effects. These results indicated that a conditional logit model was inappropriate because of violations of the IIA property. I then estimated individual-level conditional logit models by expanding the best and worst choices as partial rankings, as discussed by Louviere, Street *et al.* (2008) and Louviere (2013). I then estimated individual-level conditional logit models that involved both own (airline-specific) and cross-effects (airline i on airline j). I did this to demonstrate that IIA violations cannot be avoided by estimating models allowing hetero- geneous preferences. Many researchers mistakenly think that IIA violations are due to heterogeneous preferences, and that more flexible models such as mixed logit ones avoid the IIA problem. MXL models are individual-level conditional logit models; and my individual-level results clearly showed that many of the fare cross-effects were significant for many individuals. Thus, allowing for individual differences in preferences does not "fix" IIA violations.

Instead, I tried to identify discrete structure in the individual choices, which was suggested by the histograms of individual-level parameter estimates. In other words, it may be that the IIA violations are a result of aggregating over discrete groups (segments) with different choice processes. I identified five distinct segments, and tested if they were reliably different using a WLS approximation to a conditional logit model that included airline and fare effects interacted with the clusters. These results indicated that the five segments were reliably different; indeed, the segments appeared to differ in choice sets, suggesting differences in choice processes, not necessarily differences in preferences per se.

When I tried to estimate conditional logit models by segment that incorporated all airline and fare cross-effects, several of the models would not converge, because of few if any choices of some airline options. I did not pursue more flexible models that allow for IIA violations on account of space limitations, but this would be an obvious next step.

The best-worst choice task provided valuable extra information that allowed me to identify structure and estimate individual-level models. Such Case 3 BWS tasks can be used with almost any alternative-specific DCE to obtain partial ranking information. I did not test whether best choices were the inverse of worst choices because of space limitations, but this also would be an obvious next step. However, more generally, there is no theoretical reason why best choices necessarily should be the inverse of worst choices. Indeed, one might well expect individuals to use best choices as a way to include or accept attribute levels (or attribute-level combinations), while using worst choices as a way to exclude or reject them. So, choice processes for best and worst choices may differ and/or the consistency (error variability) with which individuals make best and worst choices may differ, or both may differ. Future research would benefit from more work directed towards types of choice situations, DCE designs and choice tasks that can lead to such outcomes.

References

Abernathy, A. P., Currow, D. C., Fazekas, B. S., Luszcz, M. A., Wheeler, J. L., and Kuchibhatla, M. (2008). Specialized palliative care services are associated with improved short- and long-term caregiver outcomes. *Support Care Cancer*, 16, 585–97.

Aczél, J., Roberts, F. S., and Rosenbaum, Z. (1986). On scientific laws without dimensional constants. *Journal of Mathematical Analysis and Applications*, 9, 389–416.

Al-Janabi, H., Coast, J., and Flynn, T. N. (2008). What do people value when they provide unpaid care for an older person? A meta-ethnography with interview follow-up. *Social Science and Medicine*, 67, 111–21.

Al-Janabi, H., Flynn, T. N., and Coast, J. (2012). Development of a self-report measure of capability wellbeing for adults: the ICECAP-A. *Quality of Life Research*, 21, 167–76.

Alston, J. M., and Chalfant, J. A. (1991). Unstable models from incorrect forms. *American Journal of Agricultural Economics*, 73, 1171–81.

Amir, O., and Levav, J. (2008). Choice construction versus preference construction: the instability of preferences learned in context. *Journal of Marketing Research*, 45, 145–58.

Amonini, C., Soutar, G. N., Sweeney, J. C., and McColl-Kennedy, J. R. (2007). Positional advantages and related marketing activities: an exploratory study of professional service firms, working paper. Perth: University of Western Australia.

Anderson, D. A., and Wiley, J. B. (1992). Efficient choice set designs for estimating availability cross-effect models. *Marketing Letters*, 3, 357–70.

Anderson, N. H. (1970). Functional measurement and psychophysical judgement. *Psychological Review*, 77, 153–70.

(1982). *Methods of Information Integration Theory*. New York: Academic Press.

Angulo, A. M., Gil, J. M., Gracia, A., and Sanchez, M. (2000). Hedonic prices for Spanish red quality wine. *British Food Journal*, 102, 481–93.

Arnesen, T., and Trommald, M. (2005). Are QALYs based on time trade-off comparable? A systematic review of TTO methodologies. *Health Economics*, 14, 39–53.

Arrow, K. (1963). *Social Choice and Individual Values*, 2nd edn. New Haven, CT: Yale University Press.

Auger, P., Devinney, T. M., and Louviere, J. J. (2007). Using best-worst scaling methodology to investigate consumer ethical beliefs across countries. *Journal of Business Ethics*, 70, 299–326.

Aurifeille, J.-M., Quester, P., Lockshin, L., and Spawton, T. (2002). Global versus international involvement based segmentation: a cross-national exploratory study. *International Marketing Review*, 19, 369–86.

Australian Trade Commission (2007). *Business and Professional Services Capability Overview.* Canberra: Australian Trade Commission.

Baker, D. W., Qaseem, A., Reynolds, P., Garnder, L. A., and Schneider, E. C. (2013). Design and use of performance measures to decrease low-value services and achieve cost-conscious care. *Annals of Internal Medicine,* 158, 55–9.

Banerjee, S. B. (2002). Corporate environmentalism: the construct and its measurement. *Journal of Business Research,* 55, 177–91.

Barney, J. (1991). Firm resources and sustained competitive advantage. *Journal of Management,* 17, 99–120.

Barr, T. F., and McNeilly, K. M. (2003). Marketing: is it still just advertising? The experiences of accounting firms as a guide for other professional service firms. *Journal of Services Marketing,* 17, 713–29.

Batt, P. J., and Dean, A. (2000). Factors influencing the consumer's decision. *Australia and New Zealand Wine Industry Journal,* 15(marketing supp.), 34–41.

Baumgartner, H., and Steenkamp, J.-B. E. M. (2001). Response styles in marketing research: a cross-national investigation. *Journal of Marketing Research,* 38, 143–56.

Beattie, J. M., Flynn, T. N., and Clark, A. M. (2013). Patient preferences for deactivation of implantable cardioverter-defibrillators: a response [letter]. *JAMA Internal Medicine,* 173, 1556–7.

Becker, G. S. (1976). *The Economic Approach to Human Behavior.* University of Chicago Press.

Bednarz, A. (2006). Best-worst scaling and its relationship with multinomial logit, BAS thesis. Adelaide: University of South Australia.

Beggs, S., Cardell, S., and Hausman, J. (1981). Assessing the potential demand for electric cars. *Journal of Econometrics,* 17, 1–19.

Bettman, J. R. (1979). *An Information Processing Theory of Consumer Choice.* Reading, MA: Addison-Wesley.

Bettman, J. R., Luce, M. F., and Payne, J. W. (1998). Constructive consumer choice processes. *Journal of Consumer Research,* 25, 187–217.

Bettman, J. R., and Zins, M. A. (1977). Constructive processes in consumer choice. *Journal of Consumer Research,* 4, 75–85.

Blankson, C., and Kalafatis, S. P. (1999a). Issues and challenges in the positioning of service brands: a review. *Journal of Product and Brand Management,* 8, 106–18.

(1999b). Issues of creative communication tactics and positioning strategies in the UK plastic card services industry. *Journal of Marketing Communications,* 5, 55–70.

(2004). The development and validation of a scale measuring consumer/customer-derived generic typology of positioning strategies. *Journal of Marketing Management,* 20, 5–43.

Brickley, M., Armstrong, R., Shepherd, J., and Kay, E. (1995). The relevance of health state utilities to lower third molar surgery. *International Dental Journal,* 45, 124–8.

Brouwer, W., Culyer, A., van Exel, J., and Rutten, F. F. H. (2008). Welfarism vs. extrawelfarism. *Journal of Health Economics,* 27, 325–38.

Brown, S. D., and Heathcote, A. (2008). The simplest complete model of choice response time: linear ballistic accumulation. *Cognitive Psychology,* 57, 153–78.

Bruwer, J., and Li, E. (2007). Wine-related lifestyle (WRL) market segmentation: demographic and behavioural factors. *Journal of Wine Research,* 18, 19–34.

Bruwer, J., Li, E., and Reid, M. (2002). Segmentation of the Australian wine market using a wine-related lifestyle approach. *Journal of Wine Research,* 13, 217–42.

Burgess, L., Street, D. J., Viney, R., and Louviere, J. J. (2006). Design of choice experiments in health economics. In A. M. Jones (ed.), *The Elgar Companion to Health Economics,* 415–26. Cheltenham: Edward Elgar.

Busemeyer, J. R., and Rieskamp, J. (2014). Psychological research and theories on preferential choice. In S. Hess and A. Daly (eds.), *Handbook of Choice Modelling: The State of the Art and the State of Practice*, 49–72. Cheltenham: Edward Elgar.

Carnegie, D. (1948). *How to Stop Worrying and Start Living*. New York: Simon & Schuster.

Carson, R. T., Louviere, J. J., and Wei, E. (2010). Alternative Australian climate change plans: the public's views. *Energy Policy*, 38, 902–11.

Casini, L., Corsi, A. M., and Goodman, S. (2009). Consumer preferences of wine in Italy: applying best-worst scaling. *International Journal of Wine Business Research*, 21, 64–78.

Chaney, I. M. (2000). External search effort for wine. *International Journal of Wine Marketing*, 12, 5–21.

Cheng, P. Y., and Chiou, W. B. (2010). Rejection or selection: influence of framing in investment decisions. *Psychological Reports*, 106, 247–54.

Cliff, N. (1966). Orthogonal rotation to congruence. *Psychometrika*, 31, 33–42.

Coast, J., Al-Janabi, H., Sutton, E. J., Horrocks, S. A., Vosper, J., Swancutt, D. R., and Flynn, T. N. (2012). Using qualitative methods for attribute development for discrete choice experiments: issues and recommendations. *Health Economics*, 21, 730–41.

Coast, J., Flynn, T. N., Natarajan, L., Sproston, K., Lewis, J., Louviere, J. J., and Peters, T. J. (2008). Valuing the ICECAP capability index for older people. *Social Science and Medicine*, 67, 874–82.

Coast, J., Flynn, T. N., Salisbury, C., Louviere, J. J., and Peters, T. J. (2006). Maximising responses to discrete choice experiments. *Applied Health Economics and Health Policy*, 5, 249–60.

Coast, J., Flynn, T. N., Sutton, E., Al-Janabi, H., Vosper, J., Lavender, S., Louviere, J. J., and Peters, T. J. (2008). Investigating choice experiments for preferences of older people (ICEPOP): evaluative spaces in health economics. *Journal of Health Services Research and Policy*, 13(supp. 3), 31–7.

Coast, J, Peters, T, Natarajan, L, Sproston, K, and Flynn, T. N. (2008). An assessment of the construct validity of the descriptive system for the ICECAP capability measure for older people. *Quality of Life Research*, 17, 967–76.

Coast, J., Salisbury, C., de Berker, D., Noble, A., Horrocks, S., Peters, T. J., and Flynn, T. N. (2006). Preferences for aspects of a dermatology consultation. *British Journal of Dermatology*, 155, 387–92.

Cohen, E. (2009). Applying best-worst scaling to wine marketing. *International Journal of Wine Business Research*, 21, 8–23.

Cohen, E., d'Hauteville, F., and Sirieix, L. (2009). A cross-cultural comparison of choice criteria for wine in restaurants. *International Journal of Wine Business Research*, 21, 50–63.

Cohen, S. (2003). Maximum difference scaling: improved measures of importance and preference for segmentation. In *Proceedings of the Sawtooth Software Conference: April 2003*, 61–74. Sequim, WA: Sawtooth Software.

Cohen, S., and Markowitz, P. (2002). Renewing market segmentation: some new tools to correct old problems. In *ESOMAR 2002 Congress Proceedings*, 595–612. Amsterdam: ESOMAR.

Cohen, S., and Neira, L. (2003). Measuring preference for product benefits across countries: overcoming scale usage bias with maximum difference scaling. Paper presented at ESOMAR Latin America conference, Punta del Este, Uruguay, 5 May.

Cohen, S., and Orme, B. (2004). What's your preference? *Marketing Research*, 16, 32–7.

Coviello, N. E., Brodie, R. J., Danaher, P. J., and Johnston, W. J. (2002). How firms relate to their markets: an empirical examination of contemporary marketing practices. *Journal of Marketing*, 66, 33–46.

Coviello, N. E., Brodie, R. J., and Munro, H. J. (1997). Understanding contemporary marketing: development of a classification scheme. *Journal of Marketing Management*, 13, 501–22.

Craig, C. S., and Douglas, S. P. (2000). *International Marketing Research*. New York: John Wiley.

Crane, F. G. (1993). Professional services marketing in the future: challenges and solutions. *Journal of Professional Services Marketing*, 9, 3–12.

Cutler, A., and Breiman, L. (1994). Archetypal analysis. *Technometrics*, 36, 338–47.

David, H. A. (1988). *The Method of Paired Comparisons*, 2nd edn. London: Hodder Arnold.

Day, B., Bateman, I. J., Carson, R. T., Dupont, D., Louviere, J. J., Morimoto, S., Scarpa, R., and Wang, P. (2012). Ordering effects and choice set awareness in repeat-response stated preference studies. *Journal of Environmental Economics and Management*, 63, 73–91.

Day, G. S., and Wensley, R. (1988). Assessing advantage: a framework for diagnosing competitive superiority. *Journal of Marketing*, 52, 1–20.

De Jong, M. G., Steenkamp, J.-B. E. M., Fox, J.-P., and Baumgartner, H. (2008). Using item response theory to measure extreme response style in marketing research: a global investigation. *Journal of Marketing Research*, 45, 104–15.

De Palma, A., Myers, G. M., and Papageorgiou, Y. Y. (1994). Rational choice under an imperfect ability to choose. *American Economic Review*, 84, 419–40.

Dean, R. (2002). The changing world of the international fine wine market. *Australian and New Zealand Wine Industry Journal*, 17, 84–8.

Diamantopoulos, A., Reynolds, N. L., and Simintiras, A. C. (2006). The impact of response styles on the stability of cross-national comparisons. *Journal of Business Research*, 59, 925–35.

Dibb, S., and Simkin, L. (1993). The strength of branding and positioning in services. *International Journal of Service Industry Management*, 4, 25–35.

Dimitriadou, E., Dolničar, S., and Weingessel, A. (2002). An examination of indexes for determining the number of clusters in binary data sets. *Psychometrika*, 67, 137–59.

Dodson, J. A., Fried, T. R., Van Ness, P. H., Goldstein, N. E., and Lampert, R. (2013). Patient preferences for deactivation of implantable cardioverter-defibrillators. *JAMA Internal Medicine*, 173, 377–9.

Dolan, P., Gudex, C., Kind, P., and Williams, A. (1995). A social tariff for EuroQol: results from a UK general population survey, Discussion Paper no. 138. University of York.
(1996). The time trade-off method: results from a general population study. *Health Economics*, 5, 141–54.

Dolničar, S., and Leisch, F. (2004). Segmenting markets by bagged clustering. *Australasian Marketing Journal*, 12, 51–65.
(2010). Evaluation of structure and reproducibility of cluster solutions using the boot-strap. *Marketing Letters*, 21, 83–101.

Doyle, P., and Wong, V. (1998). Marketing and competitive performance: an empirical study. *European Journal of Marketing*, 32, 514–35.

Dröge, C., and Darmon, R. Y. (1987). Associative positioning strategies through compara-tive advertising: attribute versus overall similarity approaches. *Journal of Marketing Research*, 24, 377–88.

Drolet, A. L., and Morrison, D. G. (2001). Do we really need multiple-term measures in service research? *Journal of Service Research*, 3, 196–204.

Dyachenko, T., Walker Reczek, R., and Allenby, G. M. (2014). Models of sequential evaluation in best-worst choice tasks. *Marketing Science*, 33, 828–48.

Ellis, B., and Mosher, J. S. (1993). Six Ps for four characteristics: a complete positioning strategy for the professional services firm – CPA's. *Journal of Professional Services Marketing*, 9, 129–45.

Erdem, T., and Keane, M. (1996). Decision making under uncertainty: capturing dynamic brand choice processes in turbulent consumer goods markets. *Marketing Science*, 15, 1–20.

Euromonitor International (2008). *The World Market for Wine*. London: Euromonitor International.

Fahy, J., Hooley, G., Cox, T., Beracs, J., Fonfara, K., and Snoj, B. (2000). The development and impact of marketing capabilities in central Europe. *Journal of International Business Studies*, 31, 63–81.

Fiebig, D., Keane, M., Louviere, J., J., and Wasi, N. (2010). The generalized multinomial logit model: accounting for scale and coefficient heterogeneity. *Marketing Science*, 29, 393–421.

Finn, A., and Louviere, J. J. (1992). Determining the appropriate response to evidence of public concern: the case of food safety. *Journal of Public Policy and Marketing*, 11, 12–25.

Fischhoff, B., Slovic, P., and Lichtenstein, S. (1980). Knowing what you want: measuring labile values. In T. S. Wallsten (ed.), *Cognitive Processes in Choice and Decision Behavior*, 117–41. Hillsdale, NJ: Lawrence Erlbaum Associates.

Fishbein, M., and Ajzen, I. (1975). *Belief, Attitude, Intention and Behavior: An Introduction to Theory and Research*. Reading, MA: Addison-Wesley.

Flynn, T. N. (2010a). Using conjoint analysis and choice experiments to estimate QALY values: issues to consider. *Pharmacoeconomics*, 28, 711–22.

Flynn, T. N. (2010b). Valuing citizen and patient preferences in health: recent developments in three types of best-worst scaling. *Expert Review of Pharmacoeconomics and Outcomes Research*, 10, 259–67.

Flynn, T. N., Huynh, E., Peters, T. J., Al-Janabi, H., Clemens, S., Moody, A., and Coast, J. (2015). Scoring the ICECAP-A capability instrument: estimation of a UK general population tariff. *Health Economics*, 24, 258–69.

Flynn, T. N., Louviere, J. J., Marley, A. A. J., Coast, J., and Peters, T. J. (2008). Rescaling quality of life values from discrete choice experiments for use as QALYs: a cautionary tale. *Population Health Metrics*, 6, 1–6.

Flynn, T. N., Louviere, J. J., Peters, T. J., and Coast, J. (2007). Best-worst scaling: what it can do for health care research and how to do it. *Journal of Health Economics*, 26, 171–89.

(2008). Estimating preferences for a dermatology consultation using best-worst scaling: comparison of various methods of analysis. *BMC Medical Research Methodology*, 8: 76.

(2010). Using discrete choice experiments to understand preferences for quality of life: variance scale heterogeneity matters. *Social Science and Medicine*, 70, 1957–65.

Flynn, T. N., and Marley, A. A. J. (2014). Best-worst scaling: theory and methods. In S. Hess and A. Daly (eds.), *Handbook of Choice Modelling: The State of the Art and the State of Practice*, 178–201. Cheltenham: Edward Elgar.

Flynn T. N., Peters T. J., and Coast J. (2013). Quantifying response shift or adaptation effects in quality of life by synthesising best-worst scaling and discrete choice data. *Journal of Choice Modelling*, 6, 34–43.

Fournier, S. (1998). Consumers and their brands: developing relationship theory in consumer research. *Journal of Consumer Research*, 24, 343–53.

Freeman, A. M. (1993). *The Measurement of Environmental and Resource Values*. Washington, DC: Resources for the Future.

Friedman, M. (1937). The use of ranks to avoid the assumption of normality implicit in the analysis of variance. *Journal of the American Statistical Association*, 32, 675–701.

(1962). *Price Theory: A Provisional Text*. Chicago: Aldine.

Frischknecht, B. D., Eckert, C., Geweke, J., and Louviere, J. J. (2014). A simple method for estimating preference parameters for individuals. *International Journal of Research in Marketing*, 31, 35–48.

Ganzach, Y. (1995). Attribute scatter and decision outcome: judgment versus choice. *Organizational Behavior and Human Decision Processes*, 62, 113–22.

Ganzach, Y., and Schul, Y. (1995). The influence of quantity of information and goal framing on decision. *Acta Psychologica*, 89, 23–36.

Giergiczny, M., Chintakayala, P., Dekker, T., and Hess, S. (2013). Testing the consistency (or lack thereof) between choices in best-worst surveys. Paper presented at 3rd "International Choice Modelling" conference, Sydney, 5 July.

Gil, J. M., and Sanchez, M. (1997). Consumer preferences for wine attributes: a conjoint approach. *British Food Journal*, 99, 3–11.

Gill, B., Griffin, B., and Hesketh, B. (2013). Changing expectations concerning life-extending treatment: the relevance of opportunity cost. *Social Science and Medicine*, 85, 66–73.

Gluckman, R. L. (1990). A consumer approach to branded wines. *European Journal of Wine Marketing*, 2, 27–46.

Goodman, S. (2009). An international comparison of retail wine consumer choice. *International Journal of Wine Business Research*, 21, 41–9.

Goodman, S., Lockshin, L., and Cohen, E. (2006). Using the best-worst method to examine market segments and identify different influences on consumer choice. Paper presented at 3rd "International Wine Business and Marketing Research" conference, Montpellier, July 6.

Green, P. E., and Rao, V. R. (1971). Conjoint measurement for quantifying judgmental data. *Journal of Marketing Research*, 8, 355–63.

(1972). *Applied Multidimensional Scaling: A Comparison of Approaches and Algorithms*. New York: Holt, Rinehart & Winston.

Green, P. J. (1984). Iteratively reweighted least squares for maximum likelihood estimation, and some robust and resistant alternatives. *Journal of the Royal Statistical Society B*, 46, 149–92.

Greene, W. H. (2003). *Econometric Analysis*, 5th edn. Upper Saddle River, NJ: Prentice Hall.

Grewal, I., Lewis, J., Flynn, T. N., Brown, J., Bond, J., and Coast, J. (2006). Developing attributes for a generic quality of life measure for older people: preferences or capabilities? *Social Science and Medicine*, 62, 1891–901.

Gupta, A. K., and Govindarajan, V. (1984). Business unit strategy, managerial characteristics and business unit effectiveness at strategy implementation. *Academy of Management Journal*, 27, 25–41.

Gupta, S. (2005). Youden squares and row–column designs. In *Encyclopedia of Biostatistics*, 8. New York: John Wiley.

Hall, J., and Lockshin, L. (2000). Using means–end chains for analysing occasions – not buyers. *Australasian Marketing Journal*, 8, 45–54.

Hawkins, G. E., Marley, A. A. J., Heathcote, A., Flynn, T. N., Louviere, J. J., and Brown, S. D. (2014a). Integrating cognitive process and descriptive models of attitudes and preferences. *Cognitive Science*, 38, 701–35.

(2014b). The best of times and the worst of times are interchangeable. *Decision*, 1, 192–214.

Heady, R. B., and Lucas, J. L. (1997). PERMAP: an interactive program for making perceptual maps. *Behavioral Research Methods, Instruments and Computers*, 29, 450–5.

Heathcote, A., and Love, J. (2012). Linear deterministic accumulator models of simple choice. *Frontiers in Psychology*, 3, 1–19.

Heckman, J. J., and Snyder, J. M. (1997). Linear probability models of the demand for attributes with an empirical application to estimating the preferences of legislators. *RAND Journal of Economics*, 28, S142–S189.

Hensher, D. A., Louviere, J. J., and Swait, J. (1998). Combining sources of preference data. *Journal of Econometrics*, 89, 197–221.

Hensher, D. A., Rose, J. M., and Greene, W. H. (2005). *Applied Choice Analysis: A Primer*. Cambridge University Press.

Herbig, P. A., and Milewicz, J. C. (1993). Marketing signaling in the professional services. *Journal of Professional Services Marketing*, 8, 65–80.

Herche, J., and Engelland, B. (1996). Reversed-polarity items and scale unidimensionality. *Journal of the Academy of Marketing Science*, 24, 366–74.

Hill, C. J., and Neeley, S. E. (1988). Differences in the consumer decision process for professional versus generic services. *Journal of Services Marketing*, 2, 17–23.

Hodge, T. G., Brown, M. H., and Lumpkin, J. R. (1990). The use of market plans and advertising among accounting firms: is this profession a viable candidate for marketing? *Journal of Professional Services Marketing*, 6, 43–52.

Hooley, G., Broderick, A., and Moller, K. (1998). Competitive positioning and the resource-based view of the firm. *Journal of Strategic Marketing*, 6, 97–116.

Hooley, G., and Greenley, G. (2005). The resource underpinnings of competitive positions. *Journal of Strategic Marketing*, 13, 93–116.

Hooley, G., Saunders, J., and Piercy, N. (2004). *Marketing Strategy and Competitive Positioning*. London: Prentice Hall.

Horsky, D., and Rao, M. R. (1984). Estimation of attribute weights from preference comparisons. *Management Science*, 30, 801–22.

Huber, P. J. (1963). Pairwise comparison and ranking: optimum properties of the row sum procedure. *Annals of Mathematical Statistics*, 34, 511–20.

Huber, V. L., Neale, M. A., and Northcraft, G. B. (1987). Decision bias and personnel selection strategies. *Organizational Behavior and Human Decision Processes*, 40, 136–47.

Hume, D. (1889 [1757]). *The Natural History of Religion*. London: A. & H. Bradlaugh Bonner.

Hutchinson, J. W., Zauberman, G., and Meyer, R. (2010). On the interpretation of temporal inflation parameters in stochastic models of judgment and choice. *Marketing Science*, 29, 133–9.

Jacoby, J., and Olson, J. C. (1977). Consumer response to price: an attitudinal, information processing perspective. In Y. Wind and M. Greenberg (eds.), *Moving Ahead with Attitude Research*, 73–86. Chicago: American Marketing Association.

Jenster, P., and Jenster, L. (1993). The European wine industry. *International Journal of Wine Marketing*, 5, 30–74.

Jones, M., Mothersbaugh, D. L., and Beatty, S. E. (2002). Why customers stay: measuring the underlying dimensions of services switching costs and managing their differential strategic outcomes. *Journal of Business Research*, 55, 441–50.

Juliano, L., and Wilcox, K. (2011). Choice, rejection, and elaboration on preference-inconsistent alternatives. *Journal of Consumer Research*, 38, 229–41.

Kahneman, D. (2011). *Thinking, Fast and Slow*. New York: Farrar, Straus & Giroux.

Kalafatis, S. P., Tsogas, M., and Blankson, C. (2000). Positioning strategies in business markets. *Journal of Business and Industrial Marketing*, 15, 416–37.

Kaldjian, L. C., Curtis, A. E., Shinkunas, L. A., and Cannon, K. T. (2009). Goals of care toward the end of life: a structured literature review [review article]. *American Journal of Hospice and Palliative Medicine*, 25, 501–11.

Kass-Bartelmes, B. L., Hughes, R., and Rutherford, M. K. (2003). Advance care planning: preferences for care at the end of life. *Research in Action*, 12.

Keeney, R. C., and Raiffa, H. (1976). *Decisions with Multiple Objectives: Preferences and Value Tradeoffs*. New York: John Wiley.

Khushaba, R. N., Wise, C., Kodagoda, S., Louviere, J. J., Kahn, B. E., and Townsend, C. (2013). Consumer neuroscience: assessing the brain response to marketing stimuli using electroencephalogram (EEG) and eye tracking. *Expert Systems with Applications*, 40, 3803–12.

Kind, P., Dolan, P., Gudex, C., and Williams, A. (1998). Variations in population health status: results from a United Kingdom national questionnaire survey. *British Medical Journal*, 316, 736–41.

Kivetz, R., Netzer, O., and Srinivasan, V. S. (2004). Alternative models for capturing the compromise effect. *Journal of Marketing Research*, 41, 237–57.

Keown, C., and Casey, M. (1995). Purchasing behaviour in the Northern Ireland wine market. *British Food Journal*, 97, 17–20.

Kotler, P., Hayes, T., and Bloom, P. N. (2002). *Marketing Professional Services*. Paramus, NJ: Prentice Hall.

Landon, S., and Smith, C. E. (1998). Quality expectations, reputation and price. *Southern Economic Journal*, 64, 628–47.

Lee, J. A., Soutar, G., and Louviere, J. J. (2007). Measuring values using best-worst scaling: the LOV example. *Psychology and Marketing*, 24, 1043–58.

(2008). The best-worst scaling approach: an alternative to Schwartz's values survey. *Journal of Personality Assessment*, 90, 335–47.

Levin, I. P., Jasper, J. D., and Forbes, W. S. (1998). Choosing versus rejecting options at different stages of decision making. *Journal of Behavioral Decision Making*, 11, 193–210.

Levin, I. P., Prosansky, C. M., Heller, D., and Brunick, B. M. (2001). Prescreening of choice options in "positive" and "negative" decision-making tasks. *Journal of Behavioral Decision Making*, 14, 279–93.

Lipovetsky, S., and Conklin, M. W. (2014). Best-worst scaling in analytical closed-form solution compared with other methods. *Journal of Choice Modelling*, 10, 60–8.

Llewellyn-Thomas, H. A., Sutherland, H. J., and Thiel, E. C. (1993). Do patients' evaluations of a future health state change when they actually enter that state? *Medical Care*, 31, 1002–12.

Lockshin, L., and Cohen, E. (2011). Using product and retail choice attributes for cross-national segmentation. *European Journal of Marketing*, 45, 1236–52.

Lockshin, L., Jarvis, W., d'Hauteville, F., and Perrouty, J. P. (2006). Using simulations from discrete choice experiments to measure consumer sensitivity to brand, region, price, and awards in wine choice. *Food Quality and Preference*, 17, 166–78.

Lockshin, L., Rasmussen, M., and Cleary, F. (2000). The nature and roles of a wine brand. *Australia and New Zealand Wine Industry Journal*, 15, 17–24.

Lockshin, L., Spawton, T., and Macintosh, G. (1997). Using product, brand and purchasing involvement for retail segmentation. *Journal of Retailing and Consumer Services*, 4, 171–83.

Loftus, G. R. (1978). On interpretation of interactions. *Memory and Cognition*, 6, 312–19.

Louviere, J. J. (1988a). *Analyzing Decision Making: Metric Conjoint Analysis*. Newbury Park, CA: Sage.

(1988b). Conjoint analysis modelling of stated preferences: a review of theory, methods, recent developments and external validity. *Journal of Transport Economics and Policy*, 22, 93–119.

(1994). Conjoint analysis. In R. P. Bagozzi (ed.), *Advanced Methods of Marketing Research*, 223–59. Cambridge, MA: Basil Blackwell.

(2001). Choice experiments: an overview of concepts and issues. In J. Bennett and R. Blamey (eds.), *The Choice Modelling Approach to Environmental Valuation*, 13–36. Cheltenham: Edward Elgar.

(2013). Modeling single individuals: the journey from psych lab to the app store. In S. Hess and A. Daly (eds.), *Choice Modelling: The State of the Art and the State of Practice*, 1–48. Cheltenham: Edward Elgar.

Louviere, J. J., Carson, R. T., Burgess, L., Street, D. J., and Marley, A. A. J. (2011). Sequential preference questions: factors influencing completion rates using an online panel, working paper. University of Technology, Sydney.

Louviere, J. J., Hensher, D. A., and Swait, J. (2000). *Stated Choice Methods: Analysis and Application*. Cambridge University Press.

Louviere, J. J., and Lancsar, E. (2009). Discrete choice experiments in health: the good, the bad, the ugly and toward a brighter future. *Health Economics, Policy and Law*, 4, 527–46.

Louviere, J. J., and Meyer, R. J. (2008). Formal choice models of informal choices: what choice modeling research can (and can't) learn from behavioral theory. In N. K. Malhotra (ed.), *Review of Marketing Research*, vol. IV, 3–32. Bingley, UK: Emerald.

Louviere, J. J., and Street, D. J. (2000). Stated preference methods. In D. A. Hensher and K. Button (eds.), *Handbook in Transport*, vol. I, *Transport Modelling*, 131–44. Amsterdam: Pergamon.

Louviere, J. J., Street, D. J., and Burgess, L. (2003). A 20+ years' retrospective on choice experiments. In Y. Wind and P. E. Green (eds.), *Marketing Research and Modeling: Progress and Prospects: A Tribute to Paul E. Green*, 201–14. New York: Kluwer Academic.

Louviere, J. J., Street, D. J., Burgess, L., Wasi, N., Islam, T., and Marley, A. A. J. (2008). Modelling the choices of single individuals by combining efficient choice experiment designs with extra preference information. *Journal of Choice Modelling*, 1, 128–63.

Louviere, J. J., and Swait, J. (2010). Discussion of "Alleviating the constant variance assumption in decision research: theory, measurement, and experimental test" [commentary]. *Marketing Science*, 29, 18–22.

Louviere, J. J., Swait, J., and Anderson, D. (1995). Best-worst conjoint: a new preference elicitation method to simultaneously identify overall attribute importance and attribute level partworths, working paper. Gainesville: University of Florida.

Louviere, J. J., and Woodworth, G. (1983). Design and analysis of simulated consumer choice or allocation experiments: an approach based on aggregate data. *Journal of Marketing Research*, 20, 350–67.

(1990). Best-worst scaling: a model for largest difference judgments, working paper. Edmonton: University of Alberta.

Luce, R. D. (1959). *Individual Choice Behavior: A Theoretical Analysis*. New York: John Wiley.

Luce, R. D., and Suppes, P. (1965). Preference, utility, and subjective probability. In R. D. Luce, R. R. Bush and E. Galanter (eds.), *Handbook of Mathematical Psychology*, vol. III, 249–410. New York: John Wiley.

Luo, X., Rindfleisch, A., and Tse, D. K. (2007). Working with rivals: the impact of competitor alliances on financial performance. *Journal of Marketing Research*, 44, 73–83.

Lussier, D. A., and Olshavsky, R. W. (1979). Task complexity and contingent processing in brand choice. *Journal of Consumer Research*, 6, 154–65.

Lynch, J. G. (1985). Uniqueness issues in the decompositional modeling of multiattribute overall evaluations: an information integration perspective. *Journal of Marketing Research*, 22, 1–19.

MacDonald, E., and Uncles, M. (2007). Consumer savvy: conceptualisation and measurement. *Journal of Marketing Management*, 23, 497–517.

Mack, J. W., Weeks, J. C., Wright, A. A., Block, S. D., and Prigerson, H. G. (2010). End-of-life discussions, goal attainment, and distress at the end of life: predictors and outcomes of receipt of care consistent with preferences. *Journal of Clinical Oncology*, 28, 1203–8.

Magidson, J., and Vermunt, J. K. (2007) Removing the scale factor confound in multinomial logit choice models to obtain better estimates of preference. In *Proceedings of the Sawtooth Software Conference: October 2007*, 139–54. Sequim, WA: Sawtooth Software.

Marley, A. A. J. (1968). Some probabilistic models of simple choice and ranking. *Journal of Mathematical Psychology*, 5, 311–32.

(1989). A random utility family that includes many of the "classical" models and has closed form choice probabilities and choice reaction times. *British Journal of Mathematical and Statistical Psychology*, 42, 13–36.

Marley, A. A. J., and Flynn, T. N. (2015). Best and worst scaling: theory and application. In J. D. Wright (ed), *International Encyclopedia of the Social and Behavioral Sciences*, 2nd edn., vol 2. Oxford: Elsevier Science, pp. 548–52.

Marley, A. A. J., Flynn, T. N., and Louviere, J. J. (2008). Probabilistic models of set-dependent and attribute-level best-worst choice. *Journal of Mathematical Psychology*, 52, 281–96.

Marley, A. A. J., and Islam, T. (2012). Conceptual relations between expanded rank data and models of the unexpanded rank data. *Journal of Choice Modelling*, 5, 38–80.

Marley, A. A. J., and Louviere, J. J. (2005). Some probabilistic models of best, worst, and best-worst choices. *Journal of Mathematical Psychology*, 49, 464–80.

Marley, A. A. J., and Pihlens, D. (2012). Models of best-worst choice and ranking among multiattribute options (profiles). *Journal of Mathematical Psychology*, 56, 24–34.

Marley, A. A. J., and Regenwetter, M. (in press). Choice, preference, and utility: probabilistic and deterministic representations. In W. Batchelder, H. Colonius, E. Dzhafarov and J. Myung (eds.), *New Handbook of Mathematical Psychology*. Cambridge University Press.

McAlexander, J. H., Schouten, J. W., and Scammon, D. L. (1991). Positioning professional services: segmenting the financial services market. *Journal of Professional Services Marketing*, 7, 149–66.

McFadden, D. (1974). Conditional logit analysis of qualitative choice behavior. In P. Zarembka (ed.), *Frontiers in Econometrics*, 105–42. New York: Academic Press.
  (1999). Rationality for economists? *Journal of Risk and Uncertainty*, 19, 73–105.

McFadden, D., and Reid, F. (1975). Aggregate travel demand forecasting from disaggregated behavioral models. *Transportation Research Record: Travel Behavior and Value*, 534, 24–37.

McFadden, D., and Train, K. (2000). Mixed MNL models for discrete response. *Journal of Applied Econometrics*, 15, 447–70.

McFadden, D., Train, K., and Tye, W. (1978). An application of diagnostic tests for the independence from irrelevant alternatives property of the multinomial logit model. *Transportation Research Record: Forecasting Passenger and Freight Travel*, 637, 39–46.

McIntosh, E. (2003). Using discrete choice experiments to value the benefits of health care, PhD thesis. University of Aberdeen.

McIntosh, E., Clarke, P., Frew, E. J., and Louviere, J. J. (2010). *Applied Methods of Cost–Benefit Analysis in Health Care*. Oxford University Press.

McIntosh, E., and Louviere, J. J. (2002). Separating weight and scale value: an exploration of best-attribute scaling in health economics. Paper presented at Health Economists' Study Group, Brunel University London, 6 July.

Miller, G. A. (1956). The magical number seven, plus or minus two: some limits on our capacity for processing information. *Psychological Review*, 63, 81–97.

Mitchell, V. W., and Greatorex, M. (1988). Consumer risk perception in the UK wine market. *European Journal of Marketing*, 22, 5–15.

Monroe, K. B. (1990). *Pricing: Making Profitable Decisions*. New York: McGraw-Hill.

Monroe, K. B., and Krishnan, R. (1985). The effect of price on subjective product evaluations. In J. Jacoby and J. C. Olson (eds.), *Perceived Quality*, 209–23. Lexington, MA: Lexington Books.

Moskowitz, H. R., and Rabino, S. (1994). Sensory segmentation: an organizing principle for international product concept generation. *Journal of Global Marketing*, 8, 73–93.

Mueller, S., Lockshin, L., and Louviere, J. J. (2010). What you see may not be what you get: asking consumers what matters may not reflect what they choose. *Marketing Letters*, 21, 335–50.

Mueller, S., Lockshin, L., Saltman, Y., and Blanford, J. (2010). Message on a bottle: the relative influence of wine back label information on wine choice. *Food Quality and Preference*, 21, 22–32.

Mueller, S., and Rungie, C. (2009). Is there more information in best-worst choice data? Using the attitude heterogeneity structure to identify consumer segments. *International Journal of Wine Business Research*, 21, 24–40.

NIHR (2006). Health technology assessment (HTA) programme. NIHR, www.hta.ac.uk/funding/briefsarchive/06–96.pdf.

O'Connor, A., Boyd, N. F., Warde, P., Stolbach, L., and Till, J. E. (1987). Eliciting preferences for alternative drug therapies in oncology: influence of treatment outcome description, elicitation technique and treatment experience on preferences. *Journal of Chronic Disease*, 40, 811–18.

Orme, B. (2009). Anchored scaling in maxdiff using dual response, research paper. Sequim, WA: Sawtooth Software.

Orth, U., and Malkewitz, K. (2008). Holistic packaging design and consumer brand impression. *Journal of Marketing*, 72, 64–81.

Padgett, D., and Mulvey, M. S. (2007). Differentiation via technology: strategic positioning of services following the introduction of disruptive technology. *Journal of Retailing*, 83, 375–91.

Paine, T. (1776). *Common Sense*. Philadelphia: Robert Bell.

Paulhus, D. L. (1991). Measurement and control of response bias. In J. P. Robinson, P. R. Shaver and L. D. Wright (eds.), *Measures of Personality and Social Psychological Attitudes*, 17–59. San Diego: Academic Press.

Payne, J. W., Bettman, J. R., and Johnson, E. J. (1992). Behavioral decision research: a constructive processing perspective. *Annual Review of Psychology*, 43, 87–131.

Payne, J. W., Bettman, J. R., and Schkade, D. A. (1999). Measuring constructed preferences: towards a building code. *Journal of Risk and Uncertainty*, 19, 243–70.

Perrouty, J.-P., d'Hauteville, F., and Lockshin, L. (2006). The influence of wine attributes on region of origin equity: an analysis of the moderating effect of consumers' perceived expertise. *Agribusiness*, 22, 323–41.

Podsakoff, P. M., MacKenzie, S. B., and Podsakoff, N. P. (2003). Common method biases in behavioral research: a critical review of the literature and recommended remedies. *Journal of Applied Psychology*, 88, 879–903.

Porter, M. E. (1985). *Competitive Advantage: Creating and Sustaining Superior Performance*. New York: Free Press.

(1996). What is strategy? *Harvard Business Review*, 74, 61–78.

Potoglou, D., Burge, P., Flynn, T. N., Netten, A., Malley, J., Forder, J., and Brazier, J. E. (2011). Best-worst scaling vs. discrete choice experiments: an empirical comparison using social care data. *Social Science and Medicine*, 72, 1717–27.

Quester, P., and Smart, J. (1998). The influence of consumption situation and product involvement over consumers' use of product attribute. *Journal of Consumer Marketing*, 15, 220–38.

Rabin, M. (1998). Psychology and economics. *Journal of Economic Literature*, 3, 11–46.

Ratcliffe, J., Couzner, L., Flynn, T. N., Sawyer, M., Stevens, K., Brazier, J., and Burgess, L. (2011). Valuing child health utility 9D health states with a young adolescent sample: a feasibility study to compare best-worst discrete choice experiment, standard gamble and time trade-off methods. *Applied Health Economics and Health Policy*, 9, 15–27.

Reeder, R. R., Brierty, E. G., and Reeder, B. H. (1987). *Industrial Marketing: Analysis, Planning and Control*. Englewood Cliffs, NJ: Prentice Hall.

Richardson, J. (1994). Cost utility analysis: what should be measured? *Social Science and Medicine*, 39, 7–21.

Roberts, K., Varki, S., and Brodie, R. (2003). Measuring the quality of relationships in consumer services: an empirical study. *European Journal of Marketing*, 37, 169–96.

Rose, J. M. (2013). Interpreting discrete choice models based on best-worst data: a matter of framing, ITLS Working Paper no. 13-22. University of Sydney.

Rose, J. M., and Bliemer, M. C. J. (2009). Constructing efficient stated choice experimental designs. *Transport Reviews*, 29, 587–617.

Royal College of Surgeons of England (1997). *Current Clinical Practice and Parameters of Care: The Management of Patients with Third Molar (syn: Wisdom) Teeth.* London: Royal College of Surgeons of England.

Rungie, C. M., Coote, L. V., and Louviere, J. J. (2011). Structural choice modelling: theory and applications to combining choice experiments. *Journal of Choice Modelling*, 4, 1–29.

(2012). Latent variables in discrete choice experiments. *Journal of Choice Modelling*, 5, 145–56.

Ruta, E., Garrod, G., and Scarpa, R. (2008). Valuing animal genetic resources: a choice modelling application to indigenous cattle in Kenya. *Agricultural Economics*, 38, 89–98.

Ryan, M., Netten, A., Skatun, D., and Smith, P. (2006). Using discrete choice experiments to estimate a preference-based measure of outcome: an application to social care for older people. *Journal of Health Economics*, 25, 927–44.

Salciuviene, L., Auruskeviciene, V., and Lydeka, Z. (2005). An assessment of various approaches for cross-cultural consumer research. *Problems and Perspectives in Management*, 3, 147–59.

Salisbury, L. C., and Feinberg, F. M. (2010a). Alleviating the constant stochastic variance assumption in decision research: theory, measurement and experimental test. *Marketing Science*, 29, 1–17.

(2010b). Temporal stochastic inflation in choice-based research. *Marketing Science*, 29, 32–9.

Salkeld, G., Solomon, M., Butrow, P., and Short, L. (2005). Discrete-choice experiment to measure patient preferences for the surgical management of colorectal cancer. *British Journal of Surgery*, 92, 742–7.

Salomon, J. A. (2003). Reconsidering the use of rankings in the valuation of health states: a model for estimating cardinal values from ordinal data. *Population Health Metrics*, 1, 12–14.

San Miguel, F., Ryan, M., and Scott, A. (2002). Are preferences stable? The case of health care. *Journal of Economic Behavior and Organization*, 48, 1–14.

Saxe, R., and Weitz, B. (1982). The SOCO scale: a measure of the customer orientation of salespeople. *Journal of Marketing Research*, 19, 343–51.

Scarpa, R., Notaro, S., Louviere, J. J., and Raffaelli, R. (2011). Exploring scale effects of best/worst rank ordered choice data to estimate benefits of tourism in alpine grazing commons. *American Journal of Agricultural Economics*, 93, 813–28.

Schwappach, D. L. B., and Strasmann, T. J. (2006). Quick and dirty numbers? The reliability of a stated-preference technique for the measurement of preferences for resource allocation. *Journal of Health Economics*, 25, 432–48.

Sen, A. (1982). *Choice, Welfare and Measurement.* Cambridge, MA: Harvard University Press.

Shafir, E. (1993). Choosing versus rejecting: why some options are both better and worse than others. *Memory and Cognition*, 21, 546–56.

Shanteau, J. (1980). The concept of weight in judgment and decision making: a review and some unifying proposals, Center for Research on Judgment and Policy Report no. 228. Colorado: University of Colorado.

Shaw, M., Keeghan, P., and Hall, J. (1999). Consumers judge wine by its label, study shows. *Wine Industry Journal*, 14, 84–7.

Simonson, I. (2008). Will I like a "medium" pillow? Another look at constructed and inherent preferences. *Journal of Consumer Psychology*, 18, 155–69.

Singer, P. A., Martin, D. K., and Kelner, M. (1999). Quality end-of-life care: patients' perspectives. *Journal of the American Medical Association*, 281, 163–8.

Skuras, D., and Vakrou, A. (2002). Consumer's willingness to pay for origin labelled wine: a Greek case study. *British Food Journal*, 104, 898–912.

Slater, S. F., and Narver, J. C. (1994). Market orientation, customer value, and superior performance. *Business Horizons*, 37, 22–8.

Slovic, P. (1995). The construction of preference. *American Psychologist*, 50, 364–71.

Smith, W. R. (1956). Product differentiation and market segmentation as alternative marketing strategies. *Journal of Marketing*, 20, 3–8.

Speed, R. (1998). Choosing between line extensions and second brands: the case of the Australian and New Zealand wine industries. *Journal of Product and Brand Management*, 7, 519–36.

Srinivasan, R., Rangaswamy, A., and Lilien, G. L. (2005). Turning adversity into advantage: does proactive marketing during a recession pay off? *International Journal of Research in Marketing*, 22, 109–25.

Steenkamp, J.-B. E. M., and Baumgartner, H. (1998). Assessing measurement invariance in cross-national consumer research. *Journal of Consumer Research*, 25, 78–107.

Steenkamp, J.-B. E. M., and Ter Hofstede, F. (2002). International market segmentation: issues and perspectives. *International Journal of Research in Marketing*, 19, 185–213.

Steinhauser, K. E., Clipp, E., McNeilly, M., Christakis, N. A., McIntyre, L. M., and Tulsky, J. A. (2000). In search of a good death: observations of patients, families, and providers. *Annals of Internal Medicine*, 132, 825–32.

Street, D. J., and Burgess, L. (2007). *The Construction of Optimal Stated Choice Experiments: Theory and Methods*: Hoboken, NJ: John Wiley.

Street, D. J., Burgess, L., and Louviere, J. J. (2005). Quick and easy choice sets: constructing optimal and nearly optimal stated choice experiments. *International Journal of Research in Marketing*, 22, 459–70.

Street, D. J., Burgess, L., Viney, R., and Louviere, J. J. (2008). Designing discrete choice experiments for health care. In M. Ryan, K. Gerard and M. Amaya-Amaya (eds.), *Using Discrete Choice Experiments to Value Health and Health Care*, 47–72. Dordrecht: Springer.

Street, D. J., and Street, A. P. (1987). *Combinatorics of Experimental Design*. Oxford: Clarendon Press.

SUPPORT investigators (1995). A controlled trial to improve care for seriously ill hospitalized patients: the study to understand prognoses and preferences for outcomes and risks of treatments (SUPPORT). *Journal of the American Medical Association*, 274, 1591–8.

Sutton, E. J., and Coast, J. (2014). Development of a supportive care measure for economic evaluation of end-of-life care using qualitative methods. *Palliative Medicine*, 28, 151–7.

Swait, J. (1994). A structural equation model of latent segmentation and product choice for cross-sectional revealed preference choice data. *Journal of Retailing and Consumer Services*, 1, 77–89.

Swait, J., and Andrews, R. L. (2003). Enriching scanner panel models with choice experiments. *Marketing Science*, 22, 442–60.

Swait, J., and Louviere, J. J. (1993). The role of the scale parameter in the estimation and comparison of multinomial logit models. *Journal of Marketing Research*, 30, 305–14.

Sweeney, J. C., and Soutar, G. N. (2001). Consumer perceived value: the development of a multiple item scale. *Journal of Retailing*, 77, 203–20.

Szeinbach, S. L., Barnes, J. H., McGhan, W. F., Murawski, M. M., and Corey, R. (1999). Using conjoint analysis to evaluate health state preferences. *Drug Information Journal*, 33, 849–58.

Tan, J., and Peng, M. W. (2003). Organizational slack and firm performance during economic transitions: two studies from an emerging economy. *Strategic Management Journal*, 24, 1249–63.

Thompson, K. E., and Vourvachis, A. (1995). Social and attitudinal influences on the intention to drink wine. *International Journal of Wine Marketing*, 7, 35–45.

Thurstone, L. L. (1927). A law of comparative judgment. *Psychological Review*, 34, 273–86.

(1928). Attitudes can be measured. *American Journal of Sociology*, 33, 529–54.

Tsetsos, K., Chater, N., and Usher, M. (2012). Salience driven value integration explains decision biases and preference reversal. *Proceedings of the National Academy of Sciences*, 109, 9659–64.

Tsevat, J., Goldman, L., Soukup, J. R., Lamas, G. A., Connors, K. F., Chapin, C. C., and Lee, T. H. (1993). Stability of time-tradeoff utilities in survivors of myocardial infarction. *Medical Decision Making*, 13, 161–5.

Tustin, M., and Lockshin, L. (2001). Region of origin: does it really count? *Australia and New Zealand Wine Industry Journal*, 16, 139–43.

Tversky, A. (1972). Elimination by aspects: a theory of choice. *Psychological Review*, 79, 281–99.

(1996). Contrasting rational and psychological principles in choice. In R. J. Zeckhauser, R. L. Keeney and J. K. Sebenius (eds.), *Wise Choices: Decisions, Games, and Negotiations*, 5–21. Boston: Harvard Business School Press.

United Nations Conference on Trade and Development (2004). *Trade and Development Aspects of Professional Services and Regulatory Frameworks*. New York: United Nations Conference on Trade and Development.

Van Buiten, M., and Keren, G. (2009). Speakers' choice of frame in binary choice: effects of recommendation mode and option attractiveness. *Judgment and Decision Making*, 4, 51–63.

Verhage, B. J., Yavas, R., and Green, R. T. (1990). Perceived risk: a cross-cultural phenomenon? *International Journal of Research in Marketing*, 7, 297–303.

Vermunt, J. K., and Magidson, J. (2005). *Latent GOLD 4.0: User's Guide*. Belmont, MA: Statistical Innovations.

Wagenmakers, E. J., Kryptos, A. M., Criss, A. H., and Iverson, G. (2012). On the interpretation of removable interactions: a survey of the field 33 years after Loftus. *Memory and Cognition*, 40, 145–60.

Waller, A., Currow, D., and Lecathelinais, C. (2008). Development of the Palliative Care Needs Assessment Tool (PC-NAT) for use by multi-disciplinary health professionals. *Palliative Medicine*, 22, 956–64.

Ward, S., and Lewandowska, A. (2005). Shelter in the storm: marketing strategy as moderated by the hostile environment. *Marketing Intelligence and Planning*, 23, 670–87.

Wetzels, M., de Ruyter, D., and Birgelen, M. V. (1998). Marketing service relationships: the role of commitment. *Journal of Business and Industrial Marketing*, 13, 406–23.

Whitty, J. A., Ratcliffe, J., Chen, G., and Scuffham, P. A. (2014). Australian public preferences for the funding of new health technologies: a comparison of discrete choice and profile case best-worst scaling methods. *Medical Decision Making*, 34, 638–54.

Winkler, J. D., Kanouse, D. E., and Ware, J. E. (1982). Controlling for acquiescence response set in scale development. *Journal of Applied Psychology*, 67, 555–62.

Wong, N., Rindfleisch, A., and Burroughs, J. E. (2003). Do reverse-worded items confound measures in cross-cultural consumer research? The case of the material values scale. *Journal of Consumer Research*, 30, 72–91.

Wyner, G. A. (2006). Truth or consequences. *Marketing Research*, 18, 6–7.

Yavas, R., and Riecken, G. (2001). A comparison of medical professionals with favorable and unfavorable attitudes toward advertising: an empirical study. *Health Marketing Quarterly*, 18, 13–26.

Yellott, J. I. (1977). The relationship between Luce's choice axiom, Thurstone's theory of comparative judgment, and the double exponential distribution. *Journal of Mathematical Psychology*, 15, 109–44.

Zeithaml, V. A. (1988). Consumer perceptions of price, quality and value: a means-end model and synthesis of evidence. *Journal of Marketing*, 52, 2–22.

Subject index

Author index